Timpani and Percussion

THE YALE MUSICAL INSTRUMENT SERIES

Timpani and Percussion

Jeremy Montagu

Yale University Press
New Haven and London

For information about this and other Yale University Press publications, please contact:
U.S. Office: sales.press@yale.edu   yalebooks.com
Europe Office: sales@yaleup.co.uk   www.yaleup.co.uk

ISBN 0–300–09337–3 (hbk)
ISBN 0–300–09500–7 (pbk)

Library of Congress Control Number 2002102864

A catalogue record for this book is available from the British Library

Typeset in Columbus by Northern Phototypesetting Co. Ltd, Bolton, Lancs.
Printed in China through Worldprint

To
Jimmy Blades
master drummer
prince of teachers
in gratitude

Contents

Illustrations

Figures

Acknowledgements

First and foremost to my ever-patient wife who has not only suffered the frequent excuse of 'I'm writing a book' whenever work needed doing round the house or she needed to use the computer but who has read every word and then heard every word read to her, both processes leading to many improvements. Then to my colleagues whose example, throughout my playing career, was the model for many statements below. Foremost my teachers, first Charlie Donaldson and then, and for many years after, whenever I needed help, Jimmy Blades for all he taught me, gave me, or made for me (for he was also a consummate craftsman). Then my friends in the orchestras, principally the Royal Philharmonic and the BBC Symphony, beside whom I stood, played, and often learned, especially Lewis (Titch) Pocock, second only to James Bradshaw as the finest timpanist of my time, Freddy Harmer, master of side drum and xylophone, Harry Eastwood, superb especially on cymbals, and many others with whom it was an honour to play. Without their help and example it would have been impossible to produce a book of this sort, both historical and informed by practical experience.

Then to colleagues in my second, more academic career whose unstinting help makes books like this possible. To those who worked with me when I was secretary of the Ethnomusicology Panel of the Royal Anthropological Institute, Klaus Wachsmann, Father Jones, Nazir Jairazbhoy, Raymond Clausen, Tony Forge, and David Rycroft, and always the encouragement of the Institute's Honorary Secretary, Tony Christie. To those museum curators who set my footsteps on the way, Otto Samson, William Fagg, and his brother Bernard. To Ernst Heins who introduced me to *gamelan*, and to the Cultural Attaché of the Indonesian Embassy who walked into the Bate Collection one day and said, 'Would you like a *gamelan*?'. To my colleagues in the Galpin Society, principally Eric Halfpenny, my predecessor as its honorary secretary and Tony Baines, its editor and my predecessor as curator of the Bate Collection. To those for whom I wrote articles and books, especially John Thomson, the founding editor of *Early Music* who encouraged James Blades and me to write him two books as well as an article on early percussion in his second issue.

For this book, especially to Jonathan Del Mar (son of my principal conducting teacher in my student days, for whom I played many adventurous works as a travelling percussionist-at-need, and to whose knowledge of the orchestra and orchestration I also owe much) for his help on Beethoven, and David Charlton on music in revolutionary (in more than one sense) and imperial France, to Andrew Ashbee on

English Court Records, and to Roy Thomson, Chief Executive of the Leather Conservation Centre, who has been an ever-present help with all queries regarding animal skin. Edmund A. Bowles has been extraordinarily generous in sharing information which will appear in his forthcoming book, *The Timpani: A History in Pictures and Documents* (Hillsdale: Pendragon Press) and I am grateful, too, for innumerable helpful comments. To Peter Ward-Jones of the Bodleian Library and John Wagstaff of the Oxford University Music Faculty Library, neither of whom ever lost patience with my ignorance. To Hélène La Rue, my successor as curator of the Bate Collection for her patience as instruments of mine on loan there travel to and fro between there and home like yo-yos. To all the curators, librarians, and archivists who have been patient and generous in help and in their charges for illustrations. And to many others, all of whom, I hope, are acknowledged in the notes here. To yet others, as I fear there may be, my thanks and my apologies for omission. It is all too easy to forget to note the helpful remark on the telephone or in the bar, and all I can offer in thanks is to pass the help along to those who tackle me.

Jeremy Montagu

Introduction

Percussion is the foundation of many musical ensembles, for rhythm is the rock on which all music is built. Nevertheless, it is extraordinary how little we know of the use of percussion instruments within our own culture until well into the nineteenth century. It is exasperating when we have to say this about Papageno's glockenspiel, and whatever 'Bach' used in the cantata *Schlage doch, gewünschte Stunde*. Did Monteverdi intend timpani to be used in the 'Toccata' to *L'Orfeo* and did they play any part in Shakespeare's tuckets and sennets? Indeed, just what did percussion players do in the Middle Ages and much of the Renaissance?

We have some written sources, of course, but tantalizingly few, all pervaded by the uncertainties of nomenclature. That problem can, perhaps, be best understood by reference to modern jazz parlance, where a musician saying 'Man, I plays my horn' may mean anything from saxophone to grand piano, except the orchestral horn. Equally, in part of the Middle Ages, *cymbala* meant not cymbals but chimes of small bells struck with hammers, one in each hand. To compound our problems, while we have many illustrations of such instruments in manuscripts and stone carvings in churches, we cannot even be certain that they did in fact exist. As our modern medieval ensembles have discovered, it can be very difficult to produce any coherent role for bells in performance, and it is very possible that their portrayal was simply a speculative attempt to illustrate one of the instruments referred to in the Bible. The question of identity is made even more complex because there are illustrations of those instruments that we would call cymbals in the same or contemporary sources.

In modern times we also have to contend with what one might call the personal element. For example, if Stockhausen writes for 'log drums', by which he normally seems to mean Congolese slit drums (ill. 69), and specifies that they are to be tuned to pitches of our equal-tempered scale – pitches which do not exist in the music of the Congo – we can only assume that he has his own slit drums which he has retuned to those pitches or that he has had some specially made. So what is supposed to happen when such a work is performed without his instruments? At the first rehearsal of Roberto Gerhard's Symphony, the composer approached the percussion section with a small Japanese gong, resembling a brass ashtray, and said 'This is what you play at letter Q' (or whatever the point was in the score).[1] Now that Gerhard is no longer with us, what do other orchestras use at that point? Or does the instrument accompany the parts, as the specially-made cowhorn used to go from the Boosey & Hawkes hire library for performances of Britten's Spring Symphony? For that first performance of Gerhard's work, he and Gilbert Webster, then the BBC Symphony's principal percussion player, visited the main percussion hire establishment of those days, the L. W. Hunt Drum Company, selecting the most appropriate Chinese and Korean temple blocks, which are so important a feature of that work – how is that choice to be reproduced?

Such personal idiosyncrasy is an abnegation of responsibility and introduces a generally unrecognized aleatoric element. It makes a specific choice for one performance, and leaves all others to chance. It is as though the composer told one player at one performance to play a certain note, but for all performances thereafter merely indicated in the score that one of the woodwind, which one unspecified, should play a middle C, or that a violinist should play whatever note he felt most inclined to choose. Such an action would be laughed to scorn, but seems to be regarded as natural when writing for percussion.

Percussion instruments can be divided between those sounded by *per*cussion, striking a sonorous object with or against one which will not itself produce sound (though that is a point worth some consideration to which we shall return in chapter 8 when discussing the selection of side drum sticks), and those of *con*cussion, where two, more or less equally, sonorous objects are struck together. Dividing the instruments in another way, that of conventional organological classification, the latter group, the instruments of *con*cussion, are all idiophonic, made of materials so inherently rigid and inflexible that when struck they will produce sounds in and of themselves. The former group, however, those of *per*cussion, may either be idiophonic or have a stretched membrane, which needs to be under tension in order to produce a sound of any musical quality.[2]

It is important to remember that, despite what one may read in most books on instruments, any struck objects, almost without exception, will produce a note of definite pitch. Some idiophones, due to their rigidity and the proper alignment of their molecules, will produce a better-defined pitch than others, of which xylophone bars are a good example, but almost anything struck will produce a pitch that could be hummed by those willing to hear it. Even the best triangle, with its jangle of high overtones which make it almost impossible to identify its pitch, will produce a sound which could clash with the tonality of the music and all percussion players carry more than one triangle to cope with such an eventuality.

Membranophones, or skin drums, depend on a resonant air-body, as well as the stretched skin, to define their pitch more clearly, but even the side drum, whose snares of rattling cords or wires help to disguise any pitch, may need to have its tension adjusted to avoid a disturbing element of pitch in its sound. The general ignorance of this aspect of percussion is due to the failure to listen carefully, and also, regrettably, to the feeling that the sounds of percussion instruments do not really matter much, something that all percussion players would vehemently deny.

Perhaps it is another outcome of that same feeling that while other instrumentalists are specialists, percussion players are expected to be generalists. Not only must they play all the struck instruments, although of course it may be acknowledged that one is more expert on xylophone, another on side drum, and a third on timpani, but they are also expected to play all the effects, whistles, and hooters that the gentlemen and ladies of the woodwind and string sections are too high-minded to play. A cuckoo is required? a motor horn? a swanee whistle? a musical saw? Send for a percussion player. No cellist is expected to bow a saw, no flautist to blow a slide whistle. The percussionists must master all, and as a result will get a good deal more fun out of orchestral life than anyone else!

Inevitably a book of this nature will concentrate mainly on the instruments of our own culture. These chapters are arranged generally chronologically but we have had no hesitation in going outside that framework whenever it may seem appropriate. Because ours is only a small part of the world's musical culture, and because so many percussion instruments from elsewhere are now appearing in the scores of our composers (often, one suspects, on the basis of 'when inspiration fails, toss in some extra percussion'), we have endeavoured to produce a brief but as coherent a picture of world percussion as space permits, in addition to references, where relevant, within other chapters.

There are two deliberate limitations on the material which follows. One is built-in to the general practicalities of book production, and the other is a matter of personal choice. For the first, there is a limit to the amount of illustration possible in a book of this nature, and there are therefore continual references to sources where illustrations may be found; it is hoped that these references will prove more helpful than frustrating, and to aid this, more than one source is often cited. For the second, my own teacher, to whom this book is dedicated, wrote an excellent book on *Percussion Instruments and their History* and there seems little or no point in repeating much of what he wrote; some overlap is of course inevitable and in some areas corrections have had to be made but, in many details, if James Blades has already noted it I have felt no compulsion to repeat it. Equally there are available some very detailed handbooks and lexicons of percussion instruments, listing all those instruments for which any composers might conceivably wish to write, and again it seems unnecessary to repeat all the information therein.[3] It is my hope that there will be found here information of equal utility which is not contained in these other works.

The anatomy of the drum and explanation of terms

Every drum has three essential elements:
- a body, usually called the shell
- a membrane or skin, usually called the head
- and a means of attaching the one to the other in such a way that the head is adequately tensioned to produce the required sound.

Heads may be of any convenient material, from paper and similar thin sheets of vegetable origin, through the skin of almost any animal, reptile, or fish, to thin sheets of metal (a flexible diaphragm behaves in the same way as a membrane). Of these by far the most common is a thinned and prepared animal skin.

Methods of attachment range from glue or wax, through nails and a wide variety of networks and lacings with cords or thongs, to metal screws.

Shells can be of any convenient material of adequate strength and of almost any shape. Within our culture, our concern in this brief chapter, two shapes predominate:

- the closed vessel or bowl (the kettledrum, known orchestrally in Italian as *timpano*, plural *timpani*, in German *Pauken*, in French *timbales*, and in modern English as in Italian)
- the cylindrical tube (side drum, bass drum, tambourine, etc.).

The closed vessel or bowl was called a kettle from analogy with the cooking pot, and this may have been its prehistoric origin: the vessel in which dinner was cooked, covered with the skin in which dinner had lived.

The tube, initially presumably a hollowed segment of tree trunk, has from historical times more often been rolled up from wooden sheet.

The illustrations here show common forms of these patterns with their constituent parts identified by name and described, as a glossary, below.

Fig. 1. Kettledrum, *c.* 1619.

a) the shell, usually of copper sheet

b) the head, usually of calf skin

c) the counter-hoop, usually of iron. The head is lapped round this hoop, without a separate flesh-hoop – see Appendix 2 for this process

d) the tension screws which pull down the counter-hoop over the rim of the shell, so controlling the tension and thus the pitch of the head

e) the lugs into which the tension screws screw

f) the crown or stand, usually of iron, on which the drum rests when in storage; an alternative is three small feet

g) tuning key

h) sticks

i) carrying strap

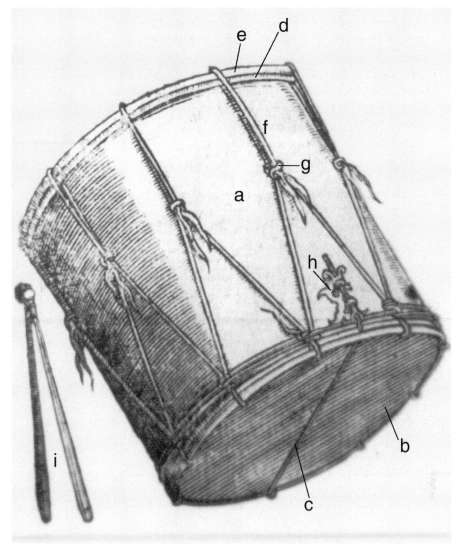

Fig. 2. Side drum.

a) shell, a cylindrical tube usually of wooden sheet but later sometimes of metal, usually brass

b) the snare head; the head on the other end of the shell is called the batter head because it is struck

c) the snares

d) the flesh-hoop, of wood

e) the counter-hoop, also of wood

f) the tension rope, passing round the drum in a continuous series of Vs or Ws, today replaced by metal screw rods

g) the buffs or tug-ears, usually of leather though earlier of cord or cloth ribbon; pulling these down each V draws the ropes together, effectively shortening them, pulling the heads towards each other down the shell to increase their tension

h) the snare strainer, controlling the tension of the snares (strands of gut like cello strings) by a screw

i) the sticks

Some other terms used in this book, grouped as appropriate:

MUSICAL TERMS AND NOTATION

Common chord: notes which in any key sound well together and thus are consonant; they are the keynote and the third and fifth notes of its scale: in the key of C they are CEGC:

Before the middle of the nineteenth century, all trumpet and horn parts were written in C, the player using an instrument with crooks of the right length to play in the required key. In a trumpet fanfare (English: tucket, sennet, touch; French: *touche*; German: *Auszug, Aufzug, Tusch*; Italian: *toccata, sonata*, etc.) the bass parts would consist of the keynote ('tonic') and its fifth ('dominant'), written as C and G:

These notes were transposed to the correct pitch by tuning the drums to the same key as the trumpets.

Overtones: when any note is sounded the 'spectrum' of its sound is made up of overtones whose relative strengths determine the character of the sound. The overtones of a brass instrument are more or less harmonic, consisting of the common chord of the note which is played, reinforcing that note and helping it to sustain, plus other notes in the higher reaches. The overtones of most percussion instruments are inharmonic (i.e. not harmonic), so that the fundamental pitch is not reinforced. This applies particularly to idiophones, though some shaping can help to ameliorate this, as with some xylophone bars and bells.

Octave: a note repeated eight notes higher or lower, thus having the same name. Middle C is conventionally noted as c´, and the C below (the C normally written for timpani) as c and all the notes between that and middle C, such as the timpani's usual d and e, similarly in lower case. The next C down, written on the second leger line below the bass stave (and occasionally written for timpani by some composers over the past century), is shown as C, and all the notes between it and c are written as upper case or capitals, including the timpani's usual A and G.

CLASSIFICATION OF INSTRUMENTS

Idiophone: a technical term in the classification of instruments meaning a material sufficiently rigid, sonorous, and vibrant that it will sound without needing stretched skin, tightened strings, or a column of air. Examples are triangle, cymbals, xylophones, etc. With the last of these, air columns tuned to the pitch of each bar may be used to amplify the sound.

Membranophone: a technical term in the classification of instruments meaning an instrument whose sound is made by a membrane. Most of these are struck, a few are rubbed, also our concern, still fewer are sung (kazoos), not often our worry, though if they were required we would probably find them in the percussion parts.

Concussion: two or more approximately equally sonorous objects struck against each other. Examples are pairs of cymbals or sticks struck together or jingles of metal plates, etc., shaken to rattle against each other.

Percussion: a sonorous object struck with or against a non-sonorous object. Examples are a drum or a triangle struck with a beater, or a stamping tube struck against the ground.

BRASS INSTRUMENTS

Clarino: the uppermost trumpet part and sometimes, by extension, the instrument that played that part.

Crook: a short length of coiled tubing, inserted usually between the mouthpiece and the body of a brass instrument, to alter its length and thus the pitch or key of the harmonic series whose notes it produces.

Principale: a middling trumpet part which played the basic sonata, the principal part, above which the clarino might improvise a decorative melody and below which other players, often including a timpanist, would produce a bass part.

Chapter 1

Speculation and Antiquity

It is the convention when writing a history of percussion instruments to refer to them as man's earliest instruments. This might well be true of the idiophones but it is highly improbable for skin drums, the membranophones, for these are highly developed instruments which require an advanced level of technology. A vessel of some material must either be created or hollowed. A skin must be prepared. and, more important, a means must be found of tensioning it and of keeping it tensioned, for a slack skin produces no sound.

When and how this was achieved we cannot know, but it is unlikely to have been within the first two or three million years of human development and could well be characteristic of the Mesolithic, or even early Neolithic periods, only ten or so thousand years ago. Alexandr Buchner published in several books two earthenware pots of the Neolithic period.[1] These are goblet or hourglass in shape and were found in Bohemia. They have integral projecting lugs, four on one of them about halfway down the body and a dozen or so on the other near the upper rim. The assumption is that these lugs were for attaching and tensioning a drum skin and while there cannot, after four thousand years, be any evidence for such a use, it does seem very likely. It is generally accepted that these were indeed drums.

Idiophones are certainly far more ancient than that, for striking two stones together is as simple an action as clapping two hands and it may be just as likely to produce musical sounds as it would stone tools. We may be allowed to speculate whether music or tools came first. Did man first try to amplify the sounds which kept his steps in time by striking two stones together, until one split, leaving him holding a sharp-edged fragment? Or were two or more men knapping flints, when they started to produce rhythms and counter-rhythms? There is good ethnomusicological evidence for both these hypotheses. There is much evidence that rhythmic movement, even the creation of rhythmic accompaniment to movement, is so basic that it pervades much of the animal kingdom.[2] It is also a commonplace that Beduin grinding coffee in mortars (ill. 72), or people hulling rice, or beating bark-cloth, or smiths hammering metal, fall into rhythms and counter-rhythms with each other. Of course we shall never know which came first, but while the technologists are welcome to claim that it was the tools, any drummer should be proud to claim that music inspired the hand-axe. Certainly we may suggest that concussion instruments, two like objects struck together, whether hands, sticks or stones, could be as early as any, for this is a very natural action. We could even claim that they are the world's oldest instruments still in common use, for concussion sticks are still a feature of children's percussion bands, and are familiar also as the *claves* of Latin-American dance music, and clapping hands are heard worldwide.

But everything more than a very few thousand years before the present day can only be a matter for speculation, with the great advantage that no one can say true or false. A group of mammoth bones found at a palaeolithic site in the Ukraine could be the earliest instruments so far discovered, or they could be the refuse of a hunting party's camp site.[3] No one will ever know for sure. A set of stone slabs in the Musée de l'Homme in Paris may be the earliest known members of the xylophone family or they may be the remains of a fence. These were found in the village of Ndut Lieng Krak in central Vietnam and are dated to the early Mesolithic period.[4] The problem with solid objects is that almost any of them make a noise when they are struck and the fact that they could produce sounds is not evidence that they did. The probability is that both these were instruments, but it remains probability. The technology of interpreting wear marks as evidence of use is in its infancy, despite the work of Graeme Lawson in this area on archaeological and later instruments.[5]

When we reach more recent times, such as the ancient Egyptian or Mesopotamian periods of four or five thousand years ago, we are on much surer ground, for by this time we have both iconography of people playing instruments and the discovery of the remains of developed instruments such as tong cymbals.[6] These are small cymbals, a couple of inches in diameter, fixed to the ends of a pair of arms, of metal or wood, joined at the proximal end. There are examples in a number of museums.[7] How they were used we do not know. It would seem that they were only found singly, and whether there could be any connection between them and those used much later in the European earlier medieval period, from the eighth to the eleventh centuries AD, we do not know. The medieval instruments seem always to have been used in pairs, for all the illustrations show players with one pair of tongs in each hand.[8] The only surviving use is in Turkey, where the *zilli massa* is a triple-branched fork, with six small cymbals, three on each side (ill. 1).

1. Triple-branched pair of surviving tong cymbals, *zilli massa*, Istanbul.

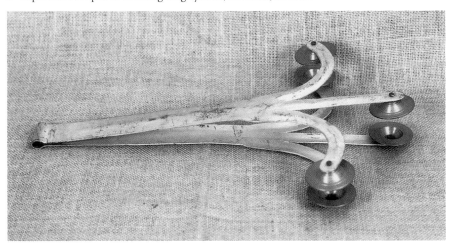

We know no more about hand cymbals, save that they were widely used in both those areas, as well as in ancient Greece and Rome. Many have been found archaeologically, and one of the most popular Egyptian mummies in the British Museum in London has a pair of cymbals lying on his legs.[9] There are also many Greek, Roman, and other carvings and vase paintings showing maenads, members of Bacchic or Dionysiac trains, and others playing cymbals. One rather late Greek use, shown in a statue in the Uffizi in Florence, was a pair of small cymbals in the base of a sandal so that they clinked and clattered as the wearer danced or stamped in time to the music (ill. 2).[10] In more recent times clog dancers in northern England and elsewhere have been known to fit a loose sole or heel to their shoes.

Hand clappers we do know rather more about. Egyptian, Greek and Roman dancers are often shown with a pair of these.[11] Egyptians used them to mark time for a variety of purposes, both for dance and for work. Many Egyptian clappers can be seen in museums, often carved from bone or ivory in the shape of a curved pair of arms, frequently showing the hands as well.[12]

Several drums have survived from ancient Egypt. One in the Cairo Museum is a cylindrical drum, similar to those that players carried horizontally across their chest in wall paintings and carvings. The pattern left on the wood by the criss-cross network of thongs used to brace the heads is still clearly visible.[13] Another is a double-headed frame drum, more or less rectangular in plan, very similar to the Portuguese *adufe* and Moroccan *deff* which (ill. 49) are both still used today.[14] No Greek or Roman drums are known to survive, but many illustrations show them as circular and single-headed; they seem to have been used solely to accompany dancing and singing. Certainly there is no evidence whatsoever for the use of drums to give time to the march in the Roman army, nor for any other military purpose. There are many references to the use of a variety of trumpets and horns, but none at all for military percussion save for the processional dances of the Roman *salii* and Greek *korybantes*. These were both shield dances, the Greeks beating on round shields and the Romans on those shaped as a figure-eight. The use of the shield as a percussion instrument is quite widespread. The Zulu *impis* were famous for it in the nineteenth century and there are many other references. A wooden shield in the Ethnographic Museum in Gothenburg has a long slot parallel with the handle, which would make it useless, even dangerous as a war-shield but improves its sound as an instrument – it produces two pitches when struck.[15]

The Greek and Roman drums were similar in appearance to the later European frame drums such as the tambourine, but we do not know whether they had rattling elements such as the miniature cymbals on our tambourines, or the iron rings fixed to the inner surface of the shell in Central Asia, which we shall encounter in chapter 9, or the snare under the head in North Africa, or that above the head on the medieval timbre. It would seem probable that some such device was used, for the sound of a frame drum, whose tension cannot be adjusted save with the use of heat, is rather dull without it, but this can only remain a supposition.

Round frame drums were used throughout the ancient Near and Middle East, though there is sometimes a doubt, when one sees a female figurine holding such an object flat against the breast, whether it is a dancer or singer with a drum, or an Astarte figure with a full moon.[16] When the figure is holding the object to one side,

2. Copy made for the façade of an English eighteenth-century country house of a Roman copy of a Greek statue of a cymbal player with *scabellum* or foot-cymbals.

and especially when the other hand is flat upon it, it is much more clearly a frame drum. Very large frame drums, fully the size of a modern bass drum, are known from Mesopotamia and were almost certainly cult instruments. Large studs on the sides of the shell secured the heads of bull's hide. Reliefs showing such drums come from Ur and are dated to about 2500–2000 BC, and there is contemporary documentation on clay tablets describing them.[17] Interestingly, despite the size of these drums, whose diameter sometimes equals the full height of the player, and in others equals shoulder to ground, they seem always to have been struck with the flat of the hand, in exactly the same way as the normal small frame drum, even though one would think that this would fail to draw out the full tone.[18] Another drum from much the same area, but about five hundred to a thousand years later, was a huge pot, as large as one of our timpani, with, so far as one can judge from the position of the player's hands, a skin across the top as a kettledrum.[19] This and a pair of small cymbals are being played to accompany a boxing match. Ordinary round frame drums, used with pairs of cymbals, can be seen on many reliefs from Nineveh a thousand or so years later still, and there is no doubt that the frame drum is both the most widespread pattern of drum geographically and that with the longest continuous history.

The giant drums from Ur seem to be unmatched by any others for size. Only in China, so far as we know, were large drums also used in antiquity. These were much deeper, three or four feet, but narrower, a foot or so in diameter, and were double-headed, played by two players, one to each head. They were fixed on top of a pole and mounted on a chariot to transmit commands to an army in battle.[20]

More important than drums in ancient China were bells and stone plaques. These took a number of forms and some were used singly and others in chimes. The stones were most commonly in an L-shape, suspended from the lower left-hand corner of the capital letter, but other shapes existed, especially clouds and fish. Both stone and bell chimes became fundamental instruments of Confucian ritual and were, until very recently, widely used, as they still are in Korea.[21] The bell chimes in Korea seem, today at least, to be bronze bells of a beehive shape, whereas the more important ones in ancient China, the variety known as *yongzhong*, are, when looked at from the front, like a small shovel in shape. The handle, by which the bell is clamped to a frame, is a cylindrical rod and the bell itself, resembling the blade of the shovel, has a narrow oval mouth with pointed ends so that the side view is much narrower than the front view. Both the front and back faces usually carry a number of projecting studs. The bells were arranged in serried rows, each clamped by its handle, on a massive wooden stand.

A large chime could cover a range of several octaves and, like most Chinese bells, was struck with a separate hammer held in the player's hand. The largest chime so far discovered is that which was found in the tomb of Marquis Yi, dating from about 433 BC. This consists of 65 bells, a conflation of several separate chimes covering a range of about six octaves.[22] It is difficult to be certain of the number of pitches in each octave because, as Lothar von Falkenhausen has established, each bell is specially designed and made to produce two different pitches. One sounds when the bell is struck in the centre of the wider face, and the other when struck near the pointed ends. What we do not know is whether these two tones were used as successive pitches or whether they were alternative pitches used when playing in different modes, though the latter seems the more probable.[23] There is also the possibility that players struck both centre and end simultaneously, perhaps producing a chord. Unfortunately, the stone chimes found in the same tomb are too fragile to play, after so long in the earth, and cannot be used as a cross-check. Certainly the capability of each bell to produce two pitches, combined with the fact that Chinese scholars defined the twelve-note equal temperament at much the same date as it was defined in Europe, around AD 1600, must cast doubt on the old assumption that all Chinese music was based on a five-note (pentatonic) scale.[24]

Bells were also used in Mesopotamia and can often be seen attached to horse harness, as indeed they were attached to elephants in India.[25] Some are true bells with an internal clapper, like miniature church bells, and others are pellet bells, which strictly are regarded as rattles rather than bells. Rattles seldom survive from antiquity because most are made from ephemeral materials such as seed-pods and gourds, but they are so widespread today in every culture, in both adult and juvenile contexts, that we can confidently postulate their use everywhere in antiquity also. Both bronze pellet bells and pottery vessel rattles are commonly found archaeologically. Subhi Rashid shows two pages of pottery rattles from Mesopotamia and Joachim Braun from ancient Israel, as could anyone reporting the results of archaeological discovery in almost any other area.[26]

A well-known Egyptian form of rattle was the sistrum, usually either a bronze frame with bars which slid to and fro when the sistrum was shaken, rattling against the sides of the frame, or a more substantial frame, often of pottery or stone in the shape of a temple gateway, with fixed bars and rattling elements which slid to and fro on the bars. As so often with instruments of different forms, one also sees conflations of the two types.[27]

Bells, true or pellet, or rattles of some sort were used in ancient Israel on the hem of the high priest's robe under the name of *pa'amon* 'so that his sound shall be heard when he goeth into the holy place'.[28] Also used there, as in Egypt and Mesopotamia and elsewhere, were cymbals. In the First Epistle to the Corinthians, St Paul refers to a sounding brass, *chalkos ēchōn*, almost certainly a gong, as well as to tinkling cymbals, paraphrasing the Septuagint translation of Psalm 150.[29] There is much evidence to show that the gong was known in ancient Greece, for example at the Zeus cult site at Dodona, and in Crete, where the Curetes used it to drown the cries of the infant Zeus and so prevent his father Chronos from swallowing him as he had all his previous children.[30] There seems little doubt that the tamtam (the flat-faced instrument of indefinite pitch, as distinct from the tuned gong of Indonesia) originated somewhere in Central Asia and diffused thence both towards Europe, as these examples attest, and towards China, where it is said to have come from areas to their west. We have already noted Greek, Roman, Tanzanian, and Zulu use of shield-gongs.

Roman clapper bells are common in museums, but are always very small, no larger than a couple of inches in diameter and in depth (*c.* 5 cm), apart from the handle, and

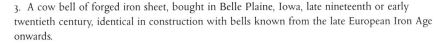

3. A cow bell of forged iron sheet, bought in Belle Plaine, Iowa, late nineteenth or early twentieth century, identical in construction with bells known from the late European Iron Age onwards.

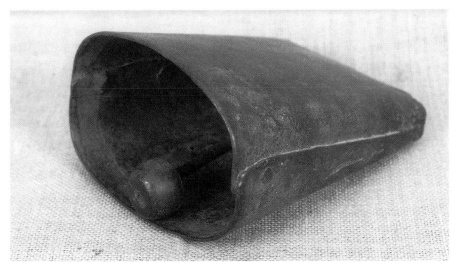

often smaller. The fact that many have a handle suggests that they were used domestically to summon a slave; others may well have been attached to animals or their harness, as in other places which we have mentioned. Clapper bells are open-mouthed, church bells for example, with a clapper, usually fixed internally at the apex of the bell, which can swing and strike the side of the bell, usually near its mouth. External clappers are seen in South-East Asia, but these also are attached to the bell and thus are distinct from the bells which are struck with a separate hammer.

All those bells mentioned so far, like the cymbals, are of cast bronze, but iron clapper bells, formed from folded sheet like modern cowbells, both those which are used on cows, sheep, and goats, and those used by drummers, are also known from the later Iron Age. These bells vary somewhat in detail, in how they are folded, for example with the shoulder points pointing upwards or downwards (downwards seems the most common generally, though in southern France and northern Spain upward points are the rule), and whether round, oval, oblong, or square in section. No one has yet produced a detailed typology, from which one might be able to locate iron bells casually found, and certainly there are not enough bells of this type surviving from antiquity to form any conclusion either about ancient typology or the continuance of patterns in any area in which these bells are used. However, we do know enough to assert that there was a continuous tradition of making and using forged and folded iron bells because at least some such bells have been found from every European period between the Iron Age and the present day. Fivos Anoyanakis provides one of the best and most detailed descriptions, with excellent illustrations, of the manufacture of both forged iron and cast bronze bells in his *Greek Popular Musical Instruments.*[31]

Among early medieval iron bells are the early saints' bells, for example St Patrick's, which is preserved in the National Museum of Ireland in Dublin. The golden shrine in which it was later encased may be elaborate enough, but the bell itself is little different from one which I bought from a farm in the middle of Iowa (ill. 3).

Four centuries later than St Patrick, we have one of the first of our major iconographic sources, the Utrecht Psalter, which was written in France around AD 825, and which shows lyres, kithara, harps, organ, and long trumpets, as well as tong cymbals and something that appears to be an hourglass-shaped drum.[32] Save for the tong cymbals, which are often there as part of the illustrations of Psalm 150, there is very little percussion in other sources before the thirteenth century, but then, from the practical point of view of the aspiring early-music percussion player, there seems not to be any surviving instrumental music earlier than that date in which one might consider using percussion instruments.

Chapter 2

The Middle Ages

There are, basically, four kinds of documentary information from the Middle Ages. One is chronicles, historical writings confined almost exclusively to the doings of courts, church, kings, and armies. Another is account rolls, detailing who was paid for doing what, covering much the same ground but more likely to be factual. Chronicles were often propaganda designed to aggrandize the reputation of the central figure. The third is occasional literary references in verse and song, which are about as reliable as any references in modern-day literature. And the fourth is the constant attempts, still common today, of churchmen to interpret and illuminate the Bible. Until the early years of the previous century, the Bible was, in our culture, the basis of human conduct and life and the root of all knowledge and literature – without the knowledge of and familiarity with the Bible, which could be assumed in all generations previous to our own, any sociological or historical study becomes difficult, for one lacks the knowledge to understand why people behaved in ways that they did. However, this, while vitally important in a history of musical life, is less so for a history of musical instruments. It was unfortunate that the Bible had been written so long ago that all detailed knowledge of such comparatively unimportant objects as musical instruments was already lost by the time that any of the Church Fathers were discussing such matters. When St Jerome produced in AD 405 the standard Latin translation, known today as the Vulgate, he could do little more than guess what instruments were represented by the Greek words of the New Testament and the original Hebrew and the Septuagint Greek of the Old Testament. Similar guesswork was the only resource for the Jewish commentators from the days of the Talmud, from about 30 BC to AD 500, onwards.[1]

After the dissolution of the Roman Empire in the early years of the fifth century, literacy became rare except among the clergy and the only way to teach the Bible to the laity was by narration and by illustration. If one is to illustrate the praise of God, and this is one of the main functions of a church service, it can only be done by portraying choirs of angels doing precisely that with those tools which the psalms denote. If the Bible commands praise with cymbals and other instruments, those instruments must be shown. How trustworthy are the depictions for the musical instruments and practices of their time? We do not know, though it has been suggested that if the illustrators and carvers did not have the instruments, how did they know what the instruments looked like? It probably is fair to say, therefore, that the instruments we see are similar, at least, to those contemporary with the artist, always provided that the depictions have not been restored or otherwise altered since that date.[2]

It is chiefly on the basis of this argument that we accept today that we do have some idea of what the medieval instruments were. We must be more circumspect with the ensembles we see, the groups of instruments playing together, for these 'big bands' are much more likely to be the work of imagination or attempts at biblical reference than are the instruments themselves. We do also have to be particularly cautious when we cannot find among contemporary texts a name that seems to fit an instrument – if it seems never to be mentioned, did it exist?

A medieval renaissance began in the thirteenth century, with much of the culture of the Persian and Arabic Middle and Near East percolating into Europe. This came partly through North Africa and Spain, partly through returning Crusaders, partly perhaps through refugees from Jerusalem and the Near East after that city and the Byzantine dependent territories had been overrun by the all-conquering armies of Islam, and certainly through generally enhanced contact with the Muslim world. It was in that world that much of the learning of the Classical world, which had been lost in Europe after the Fall of Rome, had survived. It should be remembered also that a flourishing indigenous culture of arts and sciences had existed in those eastern areas, especially in Persia and Babylonia, long before there was any great interest in such matters in Northern Europe. Astronomy and arithmetic (to name only two), the latter on the hexadecimal system, much more efficient than anything used in Europe up to very modern times, were far more advanced than anything known in the Classical Greek or Roman worlds. It should be remembered, too, that the universities of the Islamic world are centuries earlier than the European.

It is, perhaps, not surprising that, in the thirteenth century, it began to be realized that much could be learned from such sources. It cannot be coincidence that it is then that quite suddenly we see in the European iconography lutes (Arabic *el 'ūd*), rebecs (Arabic *rebab*), psalteries (also called canon, Arabic *qānūn*), shawms (Arabic *zamr*), trumpets (Spanish *añafil*, Arabic *al nafīr*), nakers (Arabic *naqqāra*), and many other instruments.[3] Nor that these begin to appear in the iconography of the period along with carpets, pottery of distinctive Arabic shape, glass, and many other features of an extra-European civilization. This renaissance was aided by an industrial revolution, which was getting into its full stride at much this period.[4] This made available many materials which had either been unobtainable or rare and expensive, as well as encouraging the rise of an artisan culture. At the same time, as one might expect during a renaissance, there seems to have been a growth of literacy, at least among the upper classes, for there is a sudden increase in the number of illuminated psalters, books of hours, and other religious works. Their illuminations are our source material but one must accept that it was their texts which were important; surely their owners were expected to read the texts, and not use them only to while away the *longueurs* of the service by looking at the pretty pictures.

One of the most comprehensive iconographic sources for instruments is the *Cántigas de Santa María*, a collection of hymns praising the Virgin, compiled by Alfonso X, known as El Sabio, The Wise, King of Castile in Spain. There are three important manuscripts surviving of this collection, one apparently unillustrated and a second with groups of illustrations which show only a few musical instruments.[5] The third, the best-known to us, has a separate illustration for every tenth hymn. Each shows two musicians (occasionally only one), usually each with the same instrument, but sometimes each with a different instrument.[6] This last manuscript, dating from about 1280, shows in its forty miniatures every one of the instruments named above and many others. Spain was not then a homogenous country but one divided between different cultures which for at least some of the time managed to live harmoniously together, and the musicians are drawn from all three major communities, the Castilian, the Maghribi, and the Jewish. While it would be tempting to suggest that the musical and instrumental tastes of each of these three groups are reflected in these illustrations, we have to admit that there is little or no evidence for this.

The importance of this manuscript lies in the fact that there is no evidence for any of these instruments having been known or used in Europe before this period. Even the long trumpet, which is seen in some earlier Spanish iconography, had been then quite a different shape from that in the *Cántigas* and it is the *Cántigas* shape, illustrated at *Cántiga* 320, f. 286, that survives into later periods, not the very wide, often curved form, which had illustrated the music of Nebuchadrezzar's court (Daniel, ch. 3), the Apocalypse, and the End of Days in the earlier manuscripts.[7]

There are at least two percussion instruments known from earlier northern European manuscripts, one a barrel-shaped drum which is found, for example, in a French twelfth-century psalter in St John's College, Cambridge,[8] and the other the pairs of cymbals mounted on tongs which appear in many sources,[9] but neither instrument is seen in the *Cántigas* or anywhere else later than about AD 1200.

The only percussion instruments earlier than the *Cántigas* which do survive, and which indeed are still with us today, are hand-held pairs of cymbals and church bells. The former appear in some Spanish Beatus manuscripts of the eleventh century illustrating Nebuchadrezzar's orchestra in the book of Daniel. This is odd since the list of instruments there does not include cymbals nor, save under the blanket head 'and all sorts of instruments', does it include any percussion instruments.[10] However, cymbals, either hand-held or on tongs, do seem to have been with us continuously from around 2100 BC in Ur in Mesopotamia and, of course, perhaps earlier.[11] Bells first appear in larger and fairly modern form in the second half of the tenth century AD.

Cymbals

If we can trust the illuminations in manuscripts, paintings and carvings, all of which are broadly in agreement, the cymbals used in the Middle Ages, from the mid-thirteenth century onwards, were both smaller than those we use today and thicker. The diameter was usually between six and ten inches (fifteen to twenty-five centimetres) and the thickness looks to have been from an eighth to a quarter of an inch (three to six millimetres). The apparent thickness may be due to the difficulties of showing anything thinner, either in lines on a miniature in the margin of a manuscript, or as a carving in wood or stone in the roof or on the wall of a church.[12] However, while no medieval cymbals are known to exist, we do have a reasonable stock in the world's museums of those from earlier times, from Mesopotamia, from ancient Egypt, and from other areas, and these, while often rather smaller in diameter than the medieval cymbals, are all of that sort of thickness.

If the medieval iconography is realistic in this respect it introduces a definite problem in our understanding of the instrument's use. A disc of brass or bronze, the two most likely metals, both copper-based, the former alloyed with calamine (today with zinc), the latter with tin, and thus rather harder and more resonant, would inevitably produce a note of definite pitch if it really was of the thickness we see. The pitch may not be as clear as that of a modern bell tuned to modern standards, but it would be recognizable (both bells and cymbals are special types of plates whose patterns of vibration show radial symmetry).[13] Indeed, modern Chinese cymbals (ill. 58), of very much the diameter and thickness that we can see in the medieval iconography, do produce sounds of somewhat confused definite pitch.

The defined pitch of cymbals earlier than these is recognized in our orchestras today, for the instruments that we call 'antique cymbals' are not only tuned but are available in tuned sets covering the whole chromatic scale.[14] So how and when were medieval cymbals used? Were they played only when their pitch matched the musical context? If so, did players carry a whole stock of cymbals, each pair tuned to a different pitch, or did they stick to one tonality for each performance? Were the two plates of a pair carefully chosen so that the one was sufficiently different in pitch from the other that their combined sound had enough beats or interference to lose its definition?[15] Or did all concerned agree to ignore the pitch of the cymbals whenever it clashed with whatever else was going on? Judging by the normal conspiracy to ignore the pitch of almost all percussion instruments, to which we shall refer frequently in this book, that last suggestion could well be the answer.

Or, to introduce a third and perhaps subversive possibility, are the illustrations purely illusory, illustrating Psalm 150 and other biblical and historical references but bearing no resemblance to the musical practices of the artists' own times? We do not know the answer to any of these questions, and cymbals, like bells, remain a problem area for our modern medieval ensembles. The one argument in favour of the reality of the iconography is as suggested above: if cymbals were not really used, how did the artists know what they looked like in order to draw, paint or carve them?

At the same time, confusion is further compounded because, as we noted above, *cymbala* had, for no apparent reason, come in the earlier Middle Ages to mean sets of tuned bells. *Cymbala* is the term used in the Latin text of the Vulgate and *kymbala* in the Greek of the Septuagint and the New Testament.

Clapper bells

Small bells of cast brass or bronze were hung on animals from remote antiquity, as we have already noted. The knowledge of how to make them seems to have been lost with the Fall of Rome. Certainly the earliest medieval bells to survive are the iron bells made from folded and hammered iron sheet referred to in the previous chapter.[16] It is not until the eighth or ninth century that we have any very reliable evidence for the medieval rediscovery of the technique for casting of bells in bronze, and until the tenth century they seem to have remained quite small. From then on the use of bells of some size in church towers, and perhaps the craft of casting them, was quite widespread.[17] A set of such bells from the Church of the Nativity in Bethlehem, of Latin Kingdom date (eleventh to twelfth centuries), is preserved in the Franciscan Monastery of the Flagellation in Jerusalem.[18]

It is only at the end of the eleventh century that we begin to find any evidence of the musical use of bells. The earliest source illustrated by Tilman Seebass is from a French psalter of that date, a row of seven bells suspended from a beam and struck with a carpenter's hammer.[19] From much that period onwards we also see one or more people carrying, and sometimes clearly swinging, a bell in each hand. Percival Price illustrates several examples of this practice, some of which are part of a religious ceremony and others part of more secular occasions.[20] The former are obviously realistic illustrations of funeral and other church processions, and the latter may also be realistic.

The sets of bells, struck more usually with a pair of hammers, one in each hand, are illustrated in innumerable sources and are much more problematic. The bells vary in shape. Some are almost hemispherical but most are rather narrower, in relation to their height, than modern bells. Their size appears to be comparable with those of the larger of a modern set of handbells. Brass and bronze are of only moderate hardness and striking them with narrow-headed iron carpenters' hammers, such as are invariably shown in the illustrations, would do considerable damage. The medieval hammers had much narrower heads than those normally used by carpenters today.[21]

The number of bells shown in the medieval sources varies from two or three to a dozen or more, and this, especially the smaller number, does not increase one's confidence in the representations. Smits van Waesberghe tended to think that the illustrations were realistic and that the treatises describing their manufacture were practicable.[22] However, there are several inaccuracies in his descriptions, e.g. that the majority of the bells were without clappers, whereas the converse is true, and that they were struck 'with a small wooden bar or hammer', whereas the vast majority are struck with ordinary carpenters' hammers. Hélène La Rue has recently cast considerable doubt on his whole thesis, and she suggests strongly that while bells were used for signalling, in towers, and for other liturgical purposes, their only musical use was probably as carillons in clocks, for which she cites Jean de Gerson's *Canticordum du Pelerin*.[23]

The carillon, especially those played mechanically by barrels rather than by a human player, is rather outside our sphere. There is a very considerable literature on the subject, both as mechanical music (a specialist interest of its own) and as part of the lore of bells (again a specialist interest) and any reader who wishes to pursue the matter further will find it easy to do by searching general bibliographies under 'bell' or 'carillon', starting of course with Price's book already cited and André Lehr's *The Art of the Carillon in the Low Countries*. Meanwhile it seems fair to say that although there is ample iconographic evidence of the musical use of *cymbala* or bell chimes, it is probable that the representations are simply attempts to illustrate the instrumentarium of King David's court, as named in the psalms of which he was the reputed author, rather than reflecting the musical practices contemporary with the artist or sculptor.

Bells have a number of functions, of which playing music was probably the least important before the introduction of tubular bells into the modern symphony orchestra. Even the invention of the carillon in the later Middle Ages is really only an elaboration of a time signal, for the carillon was normally played from church or other towers in the Low Countries at fixed times of day to signal the arrival of those hours. Bells have, and so far as we know always have had, three primary functions: as signal instruments, as apotropaic protection, and simply to make a nice noise.

They signal the time, whether the hours or that it is time for school, dinner, prayer, or any other occasion. They signal a warning, whether fire, flood, or war.[24] They signal the whereabouts of animals, and it is here that the second purpose becomes relevant, for almost any loud noise, but especially that of bells, averts misfortune and the evil eye. Thus the bell protects the animal and the herd and prevents the elves and fairies from souring the milk at the same time as it tells the herder where the animal is. To protect an infant from such sprites is one reason that a baby's first gift may be a bell, often combined with coral, a material which is also held to be effective against the evil eye. It is also a secondary reason for the presence of bells in a church tower, in addition to summoning the congregation to prayer, for evil spirits and ghosts frequent the graveyard which normally surrounds a church, and the bells are a protection against them. Bells, it is claimed too, can divert thunderstorms. There are many villages which possess a particularly sacred bell with the reputation of that ability.

The third purpose is, along with the apotropaic, why horse and mule harness was often decorated with clapper or more often pellet bells, as were carriages and sleighs, and people's costumes. We find this use almost worldwide. Dancers, especially, in all cultures attach bells, whether made of metal or seeds or nut shells, to themselves or their costumes to add a pleasant jingle as they move to the music. So far as the baby's own opinion is concerned, that is the reason why it has its bell, for it is too young to share the superstitions and fears that led to its gift but it does like the noise it makes.

Triangle

The only other non-skin percussion instrument of the Middle Ages seems to have been the instrument which today we call the triangle. In this period, while it was sometimes triangular, it was rather more often trapezoidal in shape with the upper side shorter than the lower. The upper side, or the apex of the triangular pattern, normally had a suspension ring rivetted through it or attached in some other way for the player's thumb. The instrument itself was made of iron or steel and it was struck with a bar of the same metal. Irrespective of whether the shape was triangular or trapezoidal, the frame was often continuous, without the gap in one corner which all triangles have today. This was necessary because the lower bar of the frame carried a number of iron or steel rings which jingled against the bar as the instrument was struck. The sound was therefore quite different from the 'ting' that we hear today, more a continuous susurration. These rings survived on the triangle certainly to the end of the eighteenth century, as we shall see when dealing with the Classical period in chapter 6. Two triangles with such rings, thought to date from the seventeenth or

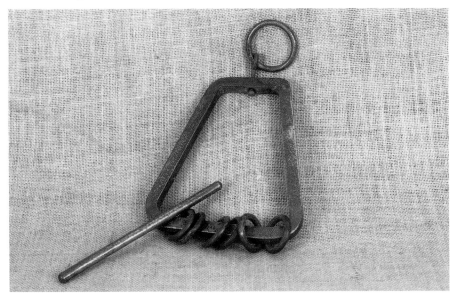

4. Reconstruction of a medieval triangle, made by Mr Swanwick of Lytton Cheney, Dorset, based on a drawing by Merlin and Cellier, Paris, *c.* 1585.

eighteenth century, survive today from the Catajo collection in the Kunsthistorisches Museum in Vienna; one has three and the other has five rings.[25] This evidence, combined with that of illustrations in Mersenne and Praetorius in the seventeenth century, and in many sources reaching back from that period continuously to the Middle Ages, suggests that the early illustrations are realistic and that the triangle not only existed but did have such rings.[26]

It is difficult to trace its use, or even its existence, in written references because there seems to be no word in Middle English which fits it. According to Christopher Page, Jean de Gerson does refer to the Latin word *tripos*, for an instrument which was of moderate size, made of metal and 'beaten on both sides', but there is no real evidence that this was a triangle.[27] Confusion is strengthened by the French manuscript encyclopaedia by Merlin and Cellier, which provides a clear illustration (of which ill. 4 is a modern reconstruction).[28] Like Mersenne, they call the instrument *Cimballe*, a name which was still in use in 1785.[29] As with the cymbals themselves, one can only say, yet again, that if it did not exist, how could they illustrate it?

Also like the cymbals, we have no idea of how or even why it was used. Indeed, if its medieval name really was *cimballe*, it would suffer under the same doubt as applies to cymbals and *cymbala*. It is not really suited as a rhythm instrument; such use is not impossible, for the jingle of the rings is not fully continuous, but the ear quickly tires of its sound if it is used in every bar. With Musica Reservata we have used it in this way in a burden (approximately a refrain, where a group of instruments or singers responds to a verse played or sung by a smaller number), and also in an isorhythmic motet to mark each return of the isorhythm, but the latter was unconvincing and the former without any historical authority.

If it did exist, as seems to be probable, it is possible that its origin lies in a stirrup, for some medieval stirrups were the same trapezoidal shape, and such stirrups made in recent times for 'medieval jousts' not only look like some of the original illustrations but also ring well when struck. However, this can never be more than a hypothesis.

Tabor

The tabor, which with its pipe was the original one-man band, was by far the most important and most widely used percussion instrument of the Middle Ages and it survives to the present day, through continuous use in southern France and northern Spain, and through recent revival elsewhere. It was, and it remains, primarily an instrument for accompanying the dance, but it seems also that it was used for military march music, before the appearance of the side drum and fife in the fifteenth century. In the earliest illustrations, in Spain in the *Cántigas* of about 1280, in Britain carved on the underside of a misericord (a wooden tip-up seat in a church choirstall) in Exeter Cathedral around 1240 (ill. 5), on the walls of Lincoln Cathedral *c.* 1275, Raunds Church *c.* 1275, and Beverley Minster *c.* 1330, it was quite a small instrument, some ten to fourteen inches (twenty-five to thirty-five cm) in diameter (Exeter is rather wider) and quite shallow, certainly shallower than its diameter. Beverley is the deepest (and latest) of those mentioned, the shell being almost twice as deep as that in the Lincoln Angel Choir. Each of these carvings differs in detail and there is no likelihood of any one being copied from any of the others; each was probably carved as a portrayal of an actual instrument.[30]

The tabor seems always to have had a skin or head on each end of a cylindrical body. At Lincoln and in the nave at Beverley (the pipe and tabor in the north aisle is a nineteenth-century reconstruction based, somewhat inaccurately, on that in the nave) it is clear that rope tensioning was used, in exactly the same way as on the military side drum into this century.[31] The heads were lapped or tucked on to a hoop and a rope was passed through the skin immediately above that hoop; the more modern arrangement of pairs of hoops, one a fleshhoop, on which the skin was lapped, and the other, to retain it, a wooden counterhoop with holes through which the rope could be passed, had not yet been devised. The rope travelled to and fro in a V or W pattern from hoop to hoop around the circumference of the drum. Buffs, or rings, of rope or leather were tied over the apex of each V and when these were pulled towards the wider end of the V, the ropes were drawn together and thus tightened, in their turn pulling the hoops down over the shell of the drum and so tightening the skin.[32]

A drumhead of skin cannot produce a sound unless it is under tension and, as all drummers knew to their cost before the days when skin was replaced by plastic, skin is highly hygroscopic. In wet weather it slackens off disastrously, making it almost impossible to play, and when the atmosphere is dry it can become so tight that it may split without even being touched. It was the aim of the military drummers of the nineteenth century so to adjust things that the tensioning rope would shrink enough on a wet day to compensate exactly for the slackening of the heads (for rope is affected by humidity in the opposite way to skin), but it is doubtful whether this was ever really successful. Certainly if a drum is to be usable under all conditions,

5. The earliest known English carving of a pipe and tabor, misericord in Exeter Cathedral, *c.* 1240.

especially out of doors (indoors, the heat from a fire could have been used to tighten the heads), some way of adjusting the tension of the heads is essential.

A constant feature of the tabor was the presence of a snare, a strand normally of gut similar to a thick cello string, running across the struck head. It is unusual for any illustrations, whether drawn or carved, to show the back or underside of the instrument, but when this is visible there is often a snare there also. Whatever the shape or size of the tabor, the batter head (the struck head) was always snared, from its first appearance in the thirteenth century certainly into the eighteenth century.[33] In present-day France and Spain, the snare is only on the lower head (which the modern side-drummer calls the snare head). When this change arose we do not know. Nor do we know whether the nineteenth-century English Morris dance taborer struck his tabor on the snared or the unsnared head; the tabors that survive from that tradition have the snare on only the one head.[34]

The tabor was slung on the shoulder or upper arm in its earliest days, later from the forearm, and it was struck with a single club-shaped wooden beater or stick held in the other hand, while the hand of the arm from which it was slung played a three-hole pipe. Three holes, two for the index and middle fingers and one for the thumb, leaving the ring and little fingers free to grip the pipe between them, suffice for any tunes which stick fairly closely to the diatonic scale. The tube was narrow enough to overblow easily so that the player could use the range from the octave above the fundamental upwards. Thus the melody was played with one hand and the accompanying rhythm with the other.

We know nothing at all of what was played with either hand in this early period. Most surviving dance music of that time is well within the capability of a three-hole pipe, for few tunes exceed the range of a twelfth or so (an octave and a half). From the fact that the player was always called a taborer, rather than a piper, a practice which survives, certainly in the Basque country, into modern times, we can assume that, as one might expect, the rhythmic accompaniment was more important for dance music than the melody. However, there is no information on what that accompaniment consisted of until, in 1588, we get very precise information with very clear explanations. To this we shall return in the next chapter when we discuss the treatise of Jean Tabourot (a significant name) which he published under his nom de plume of Thoinot Arbeau.

As the Middle Ages progressed, the tabor changed somewhat in shape, becoming rather narrower in diameter and deeper from head to head, so that by 1500 or even earlier it was deeper than its diameter and, as can be seen on a misericord in Beverley Minster, it had a buff round the apex of each V, both at the top and at the bottom of the W, giving greater control over the tension.[35]

While what was played on the tabor may be a matter of hypothesis (though it would seem very unlikely that it differed from the styles described so convincingly by Arbeau), there is no doubt whatsoever as to its existence and use. Not only is the iconography voluminous but the records of courts and other establishments are full of references to taborers. 'Taborer' was a common minstrel's sobriquet (the equivalent of the modern surname) and appears incessantly in payment rolls and lists of persons attending events from the beginning of the fourteenth century onwards.[36]

Since some listings in the Rolls seem to be of minstrels and others from the military establishment, it is clear that not only did the instrument fulfil more than one function but that there are likely to have been different sizes. Henry Holland Carter cites a number of examples of such use from chronicles of the period, both of foreign and more local events, and from such quasi-historical texts as the *Recuyell of the histories of Troy*.[37] People must have recognized that the word could mean a large drum, for certainly no contemporary readers would have been very impressed at hearing of Saracens frightening their enemies with tabors, as more than one chronicle relates, by playing the drums shown in the carvings that we have mentioned above.

The problem for us is the lack of iconographic evidence for anything other than the ordinary tabors that we have described. A Serbian fresco dated to 1317 shows the characteristic Turkish drum, which is well-known in that area from later periods and still used there today, and this or something like it may have been what the Saracens had used.[38] A Turkish drum is also shown when the Sultan surrenders to Louis VI in a French mid-fifteenth-century historical manuscript.[39] One source, the less-known *Cántigas* manuscript, does show some large horse-borne drums, but whether those would have been described as tabors we do not know; it is suggested below that they may have been ancestors of the horse-borne timpani.[40] Certainly I have found no illustration of a medieval battle or other military scene from the thirteenth or fourteenth century with any drum significantly larger than those we already know. The earliest I have found so far is Swiss, dating from around 1480, and that is clearly a side drum and will be discussed in the next chapter.[41] As so often, we are left with as much question as answer.

Timbre

Another drum frequently seen in the iconography is the timbre, as it was then known in English, the instrument that today we call the tambourine. This was usually a

single-headed drum with a shallow circular frame, commonly with pairs of miniature
cymbals or jingles let into slots in the side of the frame. There was often also a snare
running across the head, and occasionally there were pellet bells on the frame as well
as the jingles let into it. There is some evidence for the use of a square or rectangular
drum, in addition to the normal round shape, and it seems likely that this type had
two heads, as it does today in Portugal as the *adufe*, and in Morocco (ill. 49). Timbres
of that shape may perhaps then, as they do now, have had the snare and other rattling
elements contained within the body of the drum.

The normal timbre had five pairs of jingles or, as one quite often sees, five double
pairs, two pairs side by side.[42] Why the number five was so universal, and remains so
universal in North Africa and the Middle and Near East today, is unknown. It seems
unlikely that there was any symbolic reason (always the first supposition in any such
matters of number), for it is improbable that any symbolism would cross cultural
borders in this way, and perhaps this is simply the number that was found most
convenient for weight and spacing.[43] The jingles look to have been much heavier than
those used on modern tambourines, certainly wider in diameter and probably thicker.
It may be that, as with ordinary cymbals, we are again misled by the difficulties of
showing something thin and small either in miniatures or in carvings, but since
timbres with large, thick jingles appear also in many larger paintings, where such
difficulties do not apply, it seems safe to accept this as factual. The pairs of jingles
were usually spaced equally round the circumference of the drum (unlike the modern
practice of leaving a gap for the hand to hold the drum).

The instrument was always held in the palm of the hand, held upright with the
hand below the drum, with the fingers on the skin, not held from the side with the
thumb towards the skin, as we play the tambourine in the orchestra today. One must
presume that this was so that the skin could be struck both with the free hand and
with the fingers of the holding hand, exactly as it is today almost universally in the
Arab and eastern world. This would suggest that fairly complex rhythmic patterns
were used with, as today in the east, considerable tonal variety. Players contrast strokes
in the centre of the head with other much sharper sounds on or near the rim, and fill
in with the lighter strokes of the fingers of the holding hand. However, as with all
the other instruments in this chapter, this can only remain a matter of speculation, for
there are no clear descriptions of the instrument's use, nor of its playing technique,
though, interestingly, a number of Carter's references associate it with softness.[44] It is
perhaps also worth mentioning that holding the timbre in the manner described
makes it much more difficult to shake it than when holding it in the modern manner,
suggesting that it was used more as a drum (i.e. an instrument which is struck),
however gently, than as a rattle (an instrument which is shaken), and therefore that its
importance lay in its use as a rhythm instrument.

As ever, the whole use of the instrument is to some extent a matter of speculation,
because, just as the frequent appearance of cymbals (and of bells and triangle) may be
a reference to the *cymbala* of the Bible, so the illustrations of the timbre may refer to
the *tympanum*. This instrument appears, among other places such as the Psalms, in the
book of Exodus when, after the crossing of the Sea, Miriam and her women brought
out their *tympana* and sang and danced in celebration.[45] This use is typical of many of

the biblical mentions of the instrument, to accompany song and dance on joyous occasions, and it was often played by women, as still in the east. Respectable women, before modern times, were seldom seen or described as playing musical instruments, especially in public, but when they are, the commonest instrument is the frame drum, the timbre or tambourine.

Nakers

These are one of the instruments whose name and whose appearance both provide definite evidence of Arabic origin. Both the instrument and the name, *naqqāra*, appear in Arabic and Persian sources, and the instrument is still quite widely in use in those areas. It travelled, with the Moghul invaders, from Persia into India, where the *nagārā* may vary from finger-played instruments of pottery, wood or metal three or four inches in diameter (seven to ten cm) to giant iron cauldrons three feet (a metre) or more across, struck with wooden clubs as part of the ceremonial gate-music of trumpets, shawms and drums of rajahs' palaces. The *nagārā* or *naqqāra* are invariably kettledrums; the word 'kettle' in this context refers always to the cauldron rather than to the modern spouted pot for boiling water. The shell or body is a bowl or vessel, more or less hemispherical in shape, though normally deeper than a strict hemisphere, over the open top of which a skin is stretched. The tension of the skin is usually controlled in the east by a network of cords or more often leather thongs (ill. 54); in Europe most of the iconographic sources that are clear enough to be certain of such details have a similar arrangement.[46] As with other drums, some means of varying the tension has always been desirable, the only exception to this usually being the timbre, whose shallow shell makes any such arrangement of cords difficult, and anyway whose sound is supported by the clatter of the jingles let into the side of the frame. Also, being the most portable of drums and normally with only one head, the timbre can easily be held to the nearest fire and thus use heat to control its tension, or even be rubbed hard by the palm of the hand so that the heat engendered by the friction tightens the skin.

Nakers are normally used in pairs and, in the European Middle Ages, they were almost always suspended in front of the lower body from the player's belt (ill. 6). This arrangement has, from the appearance of the drums, provided a commonly used slang term for the English language, referring to the testicles. This is an interesting sidelight on the longevity of such terms. Nakers fell out of use around 1500, when they were replaced by their larger derivatives, the timpani. They were revived by the present author in the 1950s. Between those dates, nobody using the word colloquially for the testicles can have had any knowledge of their resemblance to that part of the male anatomy, and yet the slang term has been constantly in use. The nakers are occasionally seen placed on the ground in front of the player.[47] In the East the *naqqāra* and the smaller *nagārā* were more often tucked into a fold of the player's robe or, when the player was sitting on the ground, placed on the ground in front of him.

Nakers varied in size in Europe from something like four inches in diameter (ten cm) to something over a foot (thirty cm). The latter is exceptional and one pair of that size is shown in a manuscript being carried on the back of another person, with the

6. Pair of nakers, nave arcade, Beverley Minster, *c.* 1330.

player walking behind, anticipating the occasional processional use of the timpani.[48] Nakers differed from the timpani in two respects: the two drums of the pair were invariably of the same diameter, and there was often, especially from the late fourteenth century onwards, a snare running across the head on each drum.[49] Timpani, on the other hand, differ in diameter. In the Baroque there was an inch or so (there was wide variation) between the two drums of a pair; in modern use about three inches is normal. This is because timpani are most commonly tuned to the tonic and dominant of the music being played, and to get the best results from instruments tuned a fourth or a fifth apart (depending on which note is the lower) a difference in size is essential. This use derives from a musical idiom very different from that current in the Middle Ages. In the thirteenth and fourteenth centuries there was no conception of tonic and dominant harmony in musical use. 'Perfect cadences', a chord on the dominant or fifth leading to a final chord on the tonic or keynote, had yet to be invented, and thus there was no reason for one drum to be tuned higher or lower than the other.

What, then, was the point of using two drums? One feels that it must have been to make two different sounds. What sounds? The only evidence that we have is Jean de

Gerson's *Tractatus de Canticis* where he describes the sound of one drum as *obtusus* and that of the other as *peracutus*.[50] Christopher Page translates these, on the basis of the allegorical usage of such words, as low and high respectively, but it has proved impossible to produce any coherent or logical musical text combining any sensible rhythmic pattern with any two pitches. Either (which is always possible) the pitches of the two drums and the resulting musical clashes were ignored, which would seem to make it unnecessary, even undesirable, to have two pitches, or the plain meaning of the text must have been intended: dull, and clear. Surely this last is the answer: a dull, thick sound contrasting with a bright, ringing sound. There is then a clear differentiation between the two drums without the necessity for the dynamic difference of loud and soft, which anyway does not seem to have been a feature of medieval rhythmic patterning. This would also avoid any pitch confusion with the sound of other instruments, for both drums can be tuned to the *finalis*, the final pitch which was the equivalent of the later concept of the tonic, and produce a drone, a feature appropriate to most monophonic music of this period.

How such a difference of tone quality may have been obtained is, as usual, as much a matter of speculation as whether it existed. One pair of small *naqqārā*, probably from Egypt, in the author's collection has one drum with a small hole in the apex of the bowl, and the other without.[51] This would probably produce such a difference (it cannot be tested because both the heads are broken), and indeed it does help to do so on modern reproductions. More effective, however, is playing technique: a stiffly held beater produces a dull sound, a relaxed grip aids a clear sound; a beater left momentarily in contact with the head produces a dull sound, one springing free produces a clear sound; a stroke towards the centre of the head produces a dull sound, a stroke nearer the rim produces a clear one. And, of course, one has to say that if Page were correct, greater tension on the head of one drum would produce a higher pitch.

How and to what extent were the nakers used? The answer will by now be familiar, even expected: we do not know. There seems to be some evidence from court rolls, chronicles, and elsewhere that the nakerer was more often part of the military than the domestic establishment, though as always there are exceptions to this.[52] There is some bias, in the examples of the word cited by Carter, towards association with trumpets, as there always was with the later timpani, and this again lends emphasis towards a military use.[53] Whether we were correct in our use of the nakers with Musica Reservata in works such as the *Rondeaux* of Adam de la Halle, we cannot say, but I have a suspicion that we were not and that we were seduced, as one can so easily be in the reconstruction of the music of this period, by the attractiveness of an instrument into using it unhistorically.

Other drums

Various other drums and percussion instruments appear in illustrations and carvings, though we have no other English names for them. One is a double-headed drum slung horizontally across the player's chest, much like a military bass drum, of the shape we shall encounter in the eighteenth century as the long drum, deeper from head to head than its diameter. In the carvings it appears to be quite small, but this may be more a matter of available space than reality.[54] There was a drum with a French name, the *bedon*, and this name suggests that it may have been fairly large, for many drum names are onomatopoeic, including the word 'drum' itself as we shall see, and *bedon* suggests a fairly resonant thump with a preliminary tap. Certainly larger drums were known to the armies, for, as we have already said, many chroniclers refer to the large drums of the Saracen armies and their intimidating effect on the Christian forces. It is not improbable that such drums, when captured, may have been turned against their erstwhile owners, but as so often, all can be but speculation.

Other instruments are sometimes seen, among them the *semantrion*, a wooden or iron bar struck instead of a bell in those lands which were under Muslim control and in which the use of church bells was forbidden.[55] Rattles and other such objects also appear, but we have no specific information on their use. Very often seen are people striking anvils with hammers, but this is to illustrate the theorems of Pythagoras and whether people actually experimented in this way we do not know. Even if they did, it was for scientific, not for specifically musical purposes.

Pellet bells

These cannot be considered as separate instruments but they are frequently seen as supplements, either as additions to other instruments such as the timbre, or to the player and dancer and to his or her costume. Their main purpose was to add a pleasing jingle to any movement, especially a rhythmic one, but as with true bells it seems very possible that they also had a magical function. This was certainly a part of their function when they were attached to horse harness and to other animals, including babies, to scare away demons and to protect against the evil eye. Pellet bells consist of spheres, occasionally of pear-shaped vessels, normally of cast brass or bronze, though doubtless sometimes made up of soldered sheet metal. They have a narrowly open mouth, wide enough to permit free vibration but not so wide as to release a pellet of stone or metal. This had been embedded within the wax mould when the bell was cast and thus, when the wax had melted out, remained captive but free to rattle around inside the vessel and, by striking its walls, to produce the sound.

The use of instruments – minstrels and waits

The paucity of information available on what was played on the instruments has already been discussed, but we do know a little more about the players. Minstrels were on the whole professionals. Some would be attached to a prince or a court, and presumably these were of rather higher status, certainly more highly skilled, than those who were peripatetic. Wandering minstrels travelled from one establishment to another, hoping to achieve bed and board, and perhaps some hard cash, by the quality of their performance. Minstrels seem to have been expected to play a fairly wide range of instruments, though it is probable that, as in more recent times, any musician would have been better on some than on others and would therefore have specialized so far as was possible within the customs of the time. The survival of musicians' names as modern surnames does suggest a fair amount of specialization. Just among immediate colleagues and friends I have Harper, Piper, Fiddler, and Horner.

The waits, while also subsumed under the general heading of minstrels, were musicians who were in municipal employment. These, as their name indicates, were initially shawm players (from Maghribi Arabic *ghayta*, the shawm which became in English the wait-pipe and eventually the person who played it). The waits were the town watchmen, perambulating the streets at night and playing at least from time to time to show that they were awake and watching (one wonders how the citizens slept!). Later they became the town bands (in Germany the *Stadtpfeifer*) and their official purpose, as well as to watch, was to play for all civic occasions, festivities and dances of all sorts. With the minstrels, they were the members of the musicians' guilds, the precursors of the modern musicians' unions. One of the reasons for the formation of the guilds was to protect the local members and their livelihood. They made sure that other, 'foreign' or less skilful, people did not play, reserving what musical work was available for their own members, and made it as difficult as possible for newcomers and outsiders to break into the profession. The extent of the power of such guilds would obviously vary from place to place. In a city or major town of any size, they would be powerful; in a smaller town much less so; in a village, where there might only be one or two musicians, non-existent, and perhaps less powerful also at a court, where standards of proficiency and the establishment were differently controlled. They were well organized, at least in Britain. Beverley Minster, in Yorkshire, was the guild church for all minstrels between the rivers Trent and Tweed, the whole north of England, and this is why its many carvings of minstrels and their instruments are so important a source of information.

Court minstrels were regularly paid (often well in arrears, however) and were fed and, for ceremonial occasions, clothed. They were, in effect, salaried with numerous perquisites. The waits, also, would be salaried for their basic function as watchmen, sometimes in kind rather than in cash, but were usually additionally paid as freelances for weddings and most such town-band occasions. How things were managed in villages, whether professionals were hired in from a nearby town, whether the local lord of the manor had any personal establishment of minstrels that he would make available, or whether musically competent locals were paid in cash or kind, is less certain. As the nineteenth-century church bands and brass bands indicate, there has always been a surprisingly large corpus of musically competent people available throughout the towns and countryside, whatever their official occupation might be.

Less certain, also, is the extent to which any of these musicians were percussionists. For weddings and other occasions involving dancing, certainly percussion would have been used, especially pipe and tabor and, judging from many references, timbres. It is difficult for us, today, to conceive of festivities, where music needed to be loud enough to be heard over the general noise of a crowd, which did not use percussion instruments, and here, as we have said above, we have to guess the extent to which the iconography was realistic. There are few scenes showing any number of musicians (as distinct, for example, from just a bagpiper or two) where percussion was not included.

The same applies to groups of soldiers, to jousts, and other forms of tournament, as well as to battles, and here the iconography is confirmed with the frequent references to drum names in the chronicles of the time. Just as today, there was always some employment available for the drummer in the military band. Things in fact change little over centuries: weddings and war are both grist to the drummer's mill.

By the early fifteenth century it would seem that the use of percussion instruments, other than the pipe and tabor and military usage, was diminishing. With the introduction of the *alta* band, over much of Europe, of two shawms and a draw trumpet or later a sackbut, there seems to have grown up a feeling that this ensemble was musically complete in itself, and in the many illustrations showing such an ensemble playing for banquets, dances or other occasions, we seldom if ever see a percussion player accompanying them. However, we do quite often see a pipe and tabor with more heterogenous ensembles, suggesting that while it may not have been used in the rather formal context of the *alta* band, the pipe and tabor still had an important role in the generally mixed ensembles of 'what you will', and to this, as we shall see, Arbeau brings strong approbation.

Nor, curiously, do we see drummers playing with the group of three or more trumpeters which appears with increasing frequency at this time in military and court contexts. Curiously, because there are many references to percussion instruments in the contemporary literature. As early as the mid-fourteenth century there are references to large military drums in German texts. Unfortunately these are seldom explicit, and while there is at least one account of a Swiss army using pipes and drums at the siege of Landshut in 1332, the chronicle illustrating this and showing an undoubted side drum dates from 150 years later, in 1484/5.[56] As always, it is very dangerous to try to identify instruments from written references, for names change and the word that indicated one instrument in one period may indicate a very different one a century later. Hence the constant references in this chapter to the iconography – if we can see and recognize an instrument on a page or a wall, there is a strong probability that the painter or carver had seen that instrument in use and therefore that it existed at that period and that it may have been used in the way and in the context that is shown.

Chapter 3

The Renaissance

Side Drum

The value of war to the drummer became even more apparent with, in the mid-fifteenth century, the arrival of the *Schweitzer-Pfeiffer* with their accompanying side drummers. The Swiss provided, as they still do for the Vatican's Papal Guard, the first mercenary troops of modern Europe. With them, to accompany their march, a new wind instrument and with it a new drum, with a new name and a new playing technique, were introduced.

The new wind instrument, taken over from some source further to the east (it first appears in Europe in late tenth- and early eleventh-century manuscripts from Byzantium) was the transverse flute. Why it had never properly established itself as a normal instrument in Europe at any earlier date, or thereafter until the fifteenth century, is unknown. Until then, it appears only sporadically, for example on a well-known bronze aquamanile (water vessel), which is now in the National Museum in Budapest and which dates from around the twelfth century.[1] This is in the shape of a centaur playing a tambourine with, standing on his back, a little man playing a short transverse flute left-handed. Thereafter it is seen most commonly, but still very sporadically, in some German sources, for example in the *Manessische Handschrift* of the early fourteenth century in Heidelberg.[2]

The military transverse flute, the fife, as the *Pfeif* is known in English, suddenly came into prominence as these new mercenary armies began to march across Europe. The fifer could not provide his own rhythmic accompaniment, as the taborer did, because he needed both hands to play the fife, and therefore he had to be accompanied by a separate drummer. The drum could then be larger than the old tabor and, because a larger drum was heavier, it was better slung at the player's side than from his arm. Hence its later name: the side drum. Since the drummer no longer had to play the pipe with one hand, he could use both hands on the drum. More elaborate rhythms immediately became possible, as did more elaborate playing techniques. It is clear that it was at this period that this elaboration occurred because whereas, in the earlier Middle Ages, drum names had always been based on the sound of separate strokes – tabor, tambour, bedon, and such like terms – suddenly we have the names *trommel*, dromme, drum, and so forth. These names, with their rolled R, are the indications that players had begun to introduce the bouncing strokes that we use today.

We still use onomatopoeic names for these strokes: the flam (a single preliminary note -f-, followed immediately by the main note -lam); the drag (a pair of preliminary notes -dr-, followed by the main note -ag); the ruff (the rolled rrr- the three preliminary notes, and the main note -uff), and so forth.

When teaching side-drum technique, rather than 'drag' I have preferred to use the word 'drum', in contrast with the city name 'Durham' because in this way one can stress the correct accentuation with the emphasis, as it must be, on the '-um' and not on the 'Dur-'; similarly one can use the London borough of 'Fulham' to contrast with 'flam', the accent properly falling on the '-lam' and not on the 'Ful-'. Although we are accustomed to all these terms, and to reproducing their sound, we nevertheless tend to forget that the very name of our instrument is itself onomatopoeic.

The alternative name for the side drum is snare drum. This derives from the snares or rattling strands of gut which are stretched across the lower head. Unlike the tabor, there is no evidence that the side drum ever had snares on the batter head, perhaps because, with two beaters and with these rather more complicated strokes, the sticks might get tangled up in them. The traditional material for snares was plain gut, heavier in the earlier periods than in the nineteenth century when something approximating to a gut violin G was used. The coil of snare at the side of the drum in Rembrandt's *The Night Watch* of 1642 looks to be of gut around a quarter inch thick, much what was used as a double bass EE-string before the days of covered strings (ill. 7). A single strand of that doubled back would probably have sufficed in the fifteenth century.

There have been suggestions that side drums had been used earlier. Some authorities have drawn attention to the *Manessischer Handschrift*, where a drum played with both hands is shown, but it appears to be a large tabor held against the player's chest, rather than anything identifiable as a side drum.[3] It is not until a century and a half later, in the last quarter of the fifteenth century, that we have undoubted evidence of the fifes and the drums, but from then on they appear with growing frequency and ample detail. The earliest sources that I have so far discovered are all, very appropriately, Swiss. The earliest is in a *Berner Chronik*, dated 1470.[4] The second is from the *Amtliche Chronik*, dated to around 1480.[5] The third is a later *Berner Chronik* of 1484/5.[6] It is noteworthy that in all three pictures, the drummer is holding his sticks with the differential grip, exactly as we play the side drum today, something that one never sees with any other type of drum. For further details on this, see Appendix 1.

Sebastian Virdung illustrated the side drum in 1511 and described it disparagingly as invented by the devil and swamping all sweet melodies.[7] A year later the Holy Roman Emperor, Maximilian the Great, dictated to his secretary the specification for his *Triumph*, a graphical representation of his glories in a series of 137 woodcuts by Hans Burgkmair, Albrecht Dürer, and others, giving us a far more favourable impression of the instrument. The *Triumph* is a procession, each woodcut showing a group of marchers or horsemen, or a triumphal chariot carrying a

7. Detail of side-drummer, *The Night Watch*, Rembrandt van Rijn, 1642.

8. (*facing page*) Shawm player and side-drummer, Albrecht Dürer, 1503.

9. Anthony of Dornstätt and other fifers, and side drummers by Hans Burgkmair, *The Triumph of Maximilian the Great, c.* 1515.

number of people. The third scene (ill. 9), preceded only by a herald and by the title of the work, shows

> Anthony the fifer (of Dornstätt) on horseback … [who] 'played my fife for Maximilian, great in strife in many lands on countless journeys in battles fierce and countless tourneys …' with behind him three fifers … on horseback … behind them five drummers abreast in good order on horseback in the act of beating their drums.[8]

The drums are quite large, as deep as a player's forearm and extended hand (a cubit) and only slightly less than a cubit in diameter, with two snares running across the lower head, and, like the old tabor, still with the tension cords passing directly through the skin immediately above the fleshhoop. Their sticks are substantial in diameter, with round beads. Presumably it was already recognized that for the most effective sound, a stick must relate to the drum. Too light a stick will only stir the surface, as it were, even if beaten hard, whereas a stick of the correct weight will draw out the full tone. Too heavy a stick, on the other hand, will stifle the tone. From about a decade earlier than Maximilian, we have a well-known painting by Albrecht Dürer of a shawm player and a side drummer (ill. 8), but here the drum is barely a hand's length in diameter and depth and is played with sticks which, although much slimmer and shorter, as indeed they should be for so small a drum, are much the same shape as Maximilian's.[9]

While such information can never be wholly reliable, it would seem from the illustrations that separate flesh- and counterhoops were not used until the third quarter of the sixteenth century. From that period we have surviving drums such as one in Switzerland dated 1575 and another in Devon which is believed to have belonged to Sir Francis Drake, dating perhaps from 1595.[10] We also have clear illustrations such as that of the Antwerp city drummer, Pierson la Hues, in 1581.[11] The present counterhoops on Drake's drum are known to have been made in 1909, and because all such separable fittings and parts of an instrument must be treated as only possibly but not certainly original, the contemporary illustrations can often be more evidential than the surviving instruments.[12] The absence of separate flesh- and counterhoops on Maximilian's drums might be due to a careless artist (though his artists look to have been extremely careful and the reality of such absence is confirmed by many other illustrations), but the presence of such hoops, in the Antwerp picture and elsewhere, must be positive evidence that by 1581 they did indeed exist.

The Swiss drum of 1575 has an interesting feature, though we cannot tell whether it was original. Instead of the normal arrangement of holes in the counterhoop through which the tension cords pass, eight metal hooks are hooked over the counterhoop, each with an apex of the tension cords looped over its lower end. This would make it very much easier and quicker to rope the drum up than passing the rope through the series of holes in both upper and lower counterhoops. However, there must have been disadvantages in this system, if it were original, because all the other sources either have hoops with holes for the rope, in the manner that has remained normal into modern times, or have ropes passing over the counterhoop and under it, between it and the fleshhoop.

It was in 1588 that Arbeau published the first clear and unequivocal descriptions of what, when, and how military side drummers played. This we owe to a dance manual which was designed to teach any well brought-up young man how to keep his place in polite society. Before turning to social dance, however, Thoinot Arbeau discusses *'la dance guerriere'* and the military instruments which accompany it, and their use. The side drum, he says, which is used by the French measures two and a half feet in depth and the same in diameter.[13] That such enormous drums existed is confirmed not only by his own woodcuts but also by the portrait of the Antwerp drummer referred to above and a number of other illustrations, though no drum so large is known to survive.

The book is written, like many instruction books of its time, as a dialogue between the eager pupil, who asks all the right questions, and the wise instructor. Capriol, the pupil, asks why there are little ties and rings at each apex of the tension cords, top and bottom. Arbeau replies that these are to tension the heads when playing and that they should be slackened off whenever the drum is put away. After the conventional digression into the practices of the ancients and the Bible, Arbeau then goes on to explain that the drum is used to mark the time for the soldiers to march. The rhythm or *battement* used is of eight notes, the first five of which are played:

The first four each with one stroke of a beater alone, and the fifth with two beaters both together, and the other three are kept without being struck.

                  tan tan tan tan tan

During the sound and beating of these five white notes and three rests the soldier takes one step, that is to say, he moves and extends his two legs such that on the first note he places and seats his left foot, and during the three next notes he lifts his right foot, ready to place and seat it on the fifth note, and during the three rests, which are equivalent to three notes, he lifts his left foot ready to begin another step as before.[14]

It is clear that the drummer is expected to play the whole time that the army is marching, because Arbeau and Capriol go on to calculate that he must play two thousand five hundred such *battements* to the league. However, he can relieve the tedium of this by diversifying the pattern of his rhythm. Every note save the fifth, which is always a single note to be struck with both hands together (today called a flam), can be broken into two or four parts. He says that 'during the time of one white, one can beat two blacks or four *crochues*'.[15] The 'white' notes look like our minims (half-notes), the 'blacks' like our crotchets (quarter-notes), and the *crochues* have hooked tails like our quavers (eighth-notes). Arbeau, using onomatopoeic terms just as we do today, calls each single stroke a *Tan* or *Plan* (the *Plan* may also perhaps represent a flam), each double a *Tere*, and each quadruple a *Fre*.

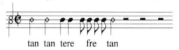
tan tan tere   fre   tan

At a reasonable marching pace, one can divide each *tan* into two distinct notes, as *tere* implies, played hand-to-hand with single strokes, but the only way to divide a *tan* into four is by what we call a five-stroke roll (the fifth stroke being the next *tan*), exactly the sound of *fre* as he names it. Arbeau then writes out for Capriol all the possible permutations of *tan*, *tere*, and *fre* (in fact he misses two), saying that 'among all this diversity set out above, a drummer [literally a drum] will be able to choose those which seem to him to be the most agreeable, and best sounding to the ears'.[16]

Capriol then asks him, 'Why does one put these rests? Why not have eight whites for each step, four for the left foot and four for the right foot?' Arbeau explains that if there were no silent beats the army would fall into confusion because nobody would know on which beat to place the left foot nor which was the first beat of the rhythm. He adds that different armies have different practices and that the Swiss keep silent on the fourth beat as well as on the last three, and that one can even use a triple time rhythm. William Byrd confirms this last point in his keyboard portrayal of a 'battell' in 1591, for his 'Irishe marche' is in triple-time.[17]

As we shall see, this emphasis on using the rhythm, the *battement*, to mark the beginning of every bar and to keep the measures distinct for the marchers, is even more important in dance music, and should inform all performance of early music. In this respect it differs from modern practice, which tends to use either different sounds, such as other percussion instruments, for example the bass drum, to add emphasis to the first beat, or to mark the emphasis by playing more loudly, a concept which Arbeau does not mention at all. This suggests that his player remained at the same dynamic level throughout, understandable on the march but perhaps rather more foreign to modern ideas for dance music.

The use of side drums was not, by Arbeau's time, confined to the Swiss and the French. The instrument had by the first decades of the sixteenth century been adopted by all the armies of Europe. As early as 1491 the English Court had imported two 'Sweches grete tabarers' or Swiss side drummers.[18] Thereafter taberettes appear spasmodically in the court records, sometimes in threes, which strongly suggests that these were side drums rather than tabors, for example at Henry VII's funeral in 1509.[19] From 1513 the new term 'drumslades' appears in the records. Eight are named, all clearly foreigners, either German or Dutch, six of them on 17 April and two more a week later.[20] Thereafter the lists vary in their number from entry to entry, but settle down to half a dozen or so, plus one or two tabrets, who by now are always clearly distinguished. With the drumslades there is always at least one fife and by the middle of the century the establishment coalesces to three drumslades and two fifes.

It is unlikely that Britain was any different from the rest of Europe in maintaining such a group, though these are comparatively rare in the contemporary iconography whereas a single drummer and fifer are illustrated in most countries with increasing frequency from the 1480s onwards. This may be due to the artists' problems. It is easy to show a bevy of trumpet bells pointing skywards above the heads of an army, but much more difficult to show any quantity of fifes and drums, and one may have stood duty for a corps.

Tabor

The tabor appears as frequently as ever, and here again we have detailed evidence of its use from Arbeau. After giving a couple of examples of fife tunes, he goes on to describe the tabor, which is smaller than the side drum, 'about two small feet long and one foot in diameter', and has a snare on each head, whereas the side drum has a double snare on only one head.[21] He describes also the smaller tabor, less than half a foot deep and a small foot in diameter, which is played with the fingers by the Basques and the Béarnais.[22] This has pellet bells and small pieces of brass attached, 'which make an agreeable sound'. It is interesting that he associates this drum with the Basques, for while today the French name for the tambourine is still the *tambour de basque*, the Basques themselves use a tabor with the pipe and claim that this has always been their most important drum.

He then explains how the tabor pipe can function even though it has only three holes.[23] He describes the other wind instruments used by the waits, and says that of course the side drum can also be used with the tabor pipe though it is more useful with the shawms, which make a loud noise. The tabor, on the other hand, can be used not only with the pipe, but also with violins and such like instruments, and it is not so small that it cannot be used with shawms and sackbuts at weddings. This statement, and his *pavane*, which has the music written out in five parts in soprano, alto, tenor, and bass clefs, underlaid with the text in each, with the fifth stave for the tabor, are strong evidence that percussion could be and was used with small ensembles for multipart dance music, both vocal and instrumental, as we suggested that it could be, at the end of the previous chapter.

Describing first the *basse danse*, which has 16 bars in triple time and which, he says, is repeated as often as necessary, Arbeau states categorically that the taborer plays the same rhythm throughout, one white note and four black to each bar or *mesure*, and when later he writes out the music, he writes that rhythm,

again on a separate stave for the tabor, above the melody on each page of the dance.[24] Arbeau underlays the 128 bars of the melody with the movements of the dance: a sixteen-bar A section, repeated, an eight-bar B section, repeated, A again, A′ (which is A slightly varied but the same length), B twice, and A A′, and these are underlaid with the movements of the dance.[25] The tabor rhythm never varies from beginning to end. In his *pavane*, which is in binary rhythm, the taborer again plays incessantly, but this time with one white and two black notes in each measure.

The music is 32 bars long and he gives seven verses of the text, which would imply 224 bars of unvarying tabor rhythm, and perhaps more if one were to allow a bar or two of 'till-ready' for singers to catch their breath between verses.[26]

Capriol asks whether these dances can only be played by the pipe, and Arbeau replies that 'one may play with violins, harpsichords, transverse flutes, recorders, shawms, and all sorts of instruments, and even singing with the voice, but the tabor helps marvellously by its unchanging measures to make the placing of the feet follow the required movements.'[27]

Arbeau fills the rest of the book with many other dances, aligning the melody with the movements of the dancers and detailing their steps, but he gives no further tabor rhythms. His only other mention of percussion instruments is towards the end of the book, during the description of the *morisque*, where he says that the 'cymbale and triangular iron, garnished with rings, makes a pleasant sound to accompany the *vielle*', which could mean the fiddle but is probably the *vielle à roue* or hurdy-gurdy.[28]

The reason for quoting Arbeau at such length is the importance of three particular statements. The first is that it must always be clear which is the first beat of the bar – however much one may diversify the other beats of the march, there must always be the three beats rest. It obviously follows from this that this is why his two dance rhythms have respectively a white and four blacks and a white and two blacks, and never six or four black notes, nor three or two whites. In dance music, just as much as on the march, it must always be clear which is the first beat of the bar. The second applies specifically to the dance music: that the tabor may be, indeed should be used with instruments other than the pipe, both with a single instrument and with small groups, when they are accompanying dancers. This opens the probability that one should, against current ideas in musicology, use a tabor with multi-part Renaissance and early Baroque dance music such as Praetorius's *Terpsichore*, the French dance prints of D'Attaingnant and his contemporaries, the German Hessische dance music and Hassler's and his contemporaries' music, and such works as Adson's *Courtly Masquing Ayres* and Holborne's dance suites. It is at present impossible to ascertain the extent to which other authorities of the period would have agreed with Arbeau in this respect. The third reason, which applies to both military and dance drumming: that there is no place in such music for fancy cross-rhythms or syncopations. What marchers and dancers need is the plain, unvarying rhythm, even if slightly decorated, which helps them to keep their steps. This is, in fact, a universal for every time and place, as any experienced dance-band drummer will know – strict tempo and plain, easily recognized rhythms are what are needed.[29]

Can one project this back into the Middle Ages? It seems probable that one can. It seems especially probable when one considers most other European dance rhythms before the introduction of jazz and ragtime in the early years of the twentieth century. The normal drum pattern for a Viennese waltz is very little different from that which Arbeau described, the only difference being that the beginning of each bar is marked by a different sound rather than by a different length beat. For that matter, while the accumulated effect of a conglomeration of instruments, each with its own individual and unvarying rhythm, may give an impression of rhythmic complexity, most Latin American dance patterns are as simple and as unchanging as Arbeau's. The twentieth-century dance drummer plays steady, repetitive rhythms, just as Arbeau's drummer did, introducing 'twiddly bits' only as the music rounds the corners, when the rhythm is sufficiently obvious. This is true whether one is playing a fox-trot, a Bill Haley-style rock-and-roll, or the most recent house and techno. It is perhaps a pity that many modern early-music drummers have not served a dance-band apprenticeship!

Certainly the tabor was still in general use in Arbeau's time throughout Europe. It appears widely in iconography and literature. We can be certain from sources such as Ashbee and, from the works of many authors and of countless artists that it was as common in high aristocratic and royal circles as it was in towns and countryside. One

10. William Kemp dancing a jig from London to Norwich for a bet, accompanied by Thomas Slye, pipe and tabor, *c.* 1600.

of its most famous appearances is in the *Nine Daies Wonder* of Will Kemp's Morris, the tale of how Shakespeare's clown won a bet by dancing a jigg from London to Norwich. As may be seen in the woodcut which is reproduced in many places (ill. 10), he was accompanied by his taborer Thomas Slye who, we may assume, like Arbeau's side drummer, played non-stop the whole way.[30]

What may well be the earliest tabor to survive was found in the wreck of Henry VIII's war ship, the *Mary Rose*, which sank off Spithead near Portsmouth on 19 July 1545 with the loss of some 700 men under the king's horrified eyes. Only part of the drum has survived, but the dimensions are about a foot (30 cm) in diameter and ten inches or so (25 cm) in depth.[31] There are neither flesh hoops nor counter hoops, though a few fragments of what might have been a flesh hoop are preserved and also the remains of a tanned calfskin case. Three tabor pipes also survived, with two fiddles and the only known still-shawm. Inside one of the pipes was a thin cherry-wood stick and this we presume to have been a tabor beater. Although not shaped like a normal drum stick, it is lively in the hand and a reproduction works extremely well and encourages one to decorate the basic rhythms with some bouncing strokes, similar to the *tere* and *fre* of the side drum.[32] While this goes beyond what Arbeau laid down for tabor rhythms, it is very much what is employed by modern Basque taborers today, as has been demonstrated to me by Sabin Bikandi Belandia, the City Taborer of Bilbao.

As well as Ashbee's many listings and the *Mary Rose*, we have iconographic evidence of the pipe and tabor at Henry's court from a manuscript in which the king himself appears as a musician (playing the harp, to the distress of one of his courtiers who has his hands clapped to his ears) and which shows, on another folio, one of the royal taborers.[33]

Timpani

We begin to get evidence for the timpani in Europe at much the same period as for the side drum. There is no doubt at all that they came into Europe from the east. There are many illustrations, from Turkey to Persia (and thence to India), of pairs of kettledrums mounted on horses, camels, or elephants, and such illustrations even go back as far as the *Cántigas*. The less well known of these thirteenth-century manuscripts, T.I.1, shows the horsemen of the sultan's army at the siege of Tortosa de Ultramar in Syria with four mounted trumpeters and three drummers. The drummer in the foreground – the drums of the others are hidden behind him – has one circular and one hexagonal drum.[34] Whether these are indeed timpani we cannot tell, for they are shown full face, but certainly they are of timpani size. There is no evidence here, or in any other source as yet uncovered, for the use of such large instruments with the Christian armies, either in Spain or elsewhere in Europe, at so early a date. Unfortunately Guerrero, while dealing in great detail with every other aspect of the material culture illustrated in that manuscript of the *Cántigas*, totally ignores all musical instruments.

The earliest European reference so far discovered to large, horse-borne kettledrums, as distinct from the small medieval nakers, is the description of the embassy in 1457 from King Ladislav V of Hungary to Charles VII of France seeking the hand of his daughter in marriage, which included 'drums like great cauldrons carried on horseback such as had never before been seen'.[35] Timpani may have been adopted in France fairly rapidly thereafter, for Edmund Bowles cites an inventory of René of Anjou in 1471 which included 'un grant tabourin en faczon d'un tinballe, couvert de cuir noir'.[36] A covering of leather is not impossible. Roy Thomson suggests that the drum could have been made from 'pieces of another material held together with a shrunken leather outer skin. There are references to the use of leather cannon by the Swedes in the mid-seventeenth century. These were not actually leather but staves of iron bound together with leather which was held on by copper wire. Modern reproductions have been reported to have been made by the Sealed Knot and discharged without blowing themselves up.'[37] It is also possible that the drums were made entirely from leather. Many objects in this period were made of *cuir bouilli*, boiled leather, which was hard and solid enough to be used for jugs, known as blackjacks, bottles, so large that they were known as bombards (presumably referring to cannon rather than shawms!), buckets and containers of all sorts. It is also possible that the 'leather' refers to the drumhead, but then why black? And why *cuir* (leather), rather than a term for parchment or vellum, for tanned leather is not suitable for drumheads?

By the end of the century kettledrums were certainly of metal, for a chronicle of 1492 states categorically that two drums at the court of Maximilian the Great were '*de fin couvre*', of fine copper (or brass – the word often means the same in French), and that they were so big that each held ten cauldrons of water and that they and ten trumpeters played every day before the Emperor's dinner and supper.[38] The Swiss chronicle, which in the mid-1480s seems to be the first iconographic source, shows a pair of kettledrums being played on horseback (ill. 11).[39] One cannot see how the heads were tensioned in this source, but it looks as though it might have been by ropes, as on the side drum and tabor, rather than by the metal bolts and screws that one sees in Maximilian's *Triumph* some decades later.

As with the side drums, the *Triumph* provides some of our best and clearest early iconographic evidence. Maximilian's Imperial Trumpeters included twenty trumpeters and four timpanists.[40] They ride, with the timpanists in the lead, followed by the heralds who precede the Emperor himself. They are quite separate from the fifes and side drums, who are much further ahead in the procession. Thus, certainly in Central Europe, the association of trumpets and timpani as emblems of majesty and state is already firmly established before 1500.

Virdung also associates the timpani (using what became the standard German term, *Heerpaucken* or military kettledrums) with courts, and describes them as being large and made of copper with calfskin heads.[41] He says that they are used with trumpets for fanfares, using the word *tisch* which relates to the later *Tusch*, at princes' tables, and when they march into cities and for signalling in the field (i.e. in battle). He also refers to the terrible row and monstrous rumbling that they make when they are struck with beaters, '*ser laut und helle tummelt*', and says that, like the side drum, they were invented by the devil and ruin any decent music.

It is clear that the English were well behind the Central Europeans in this area. When Anne of Cleves arrived in Calais on her way to marry King Henry VIII, the Earl

11. Rudolf von Habsburg and his trumpeters and kettledrummer, Diebold Schilling, *Spiezer Chronik*, c. 1485.

of Southampton wrote to the king on 13 December 1539: '… here is with my Ladyes Grace, sent by the Duke of Saxony, 13 trompettes, and oon that playes upon two things as drommys, made of a straunge facion … and they bee desiroux to goo over into England to see Your Majestie…'.[42] The king must have given them permission to come, for Edmund Halle in his *Chronicles* describes in his entry for Saturday 3 January 1539/40 the arrival of Anne of Cleve [*sic*] and her train at Blackheath, where the King met her: 'Fyrst her Trompettes went forwarde, whiche were twelve in nomber besyde two kettle Drommes on horsebacke, then followed the Kynges Trompettes…'.[43]

Thus there is no doubt at all that King Henry had heard a Saxon group of trumpets and kettledrums in 1539 old-style, or 1540 as we would term the year, which at that period began on Lady Day, 25 March instead of 1 January. There seem to be no records of what happened to any of Queen Anne's retinue when she was sent away in May 1540, nor when their marriage was annulled on 12 July, though it is recorded that each of the trumpeters, presumably including the drummer, received a reward of £6.13s.4d at some date before 5 May 1540, suggesting, since such reimbursements were usually made well in arrears, that they were sent home straight away.[44] It is quite likely that the Duke of Saxony, who was the husband of Anne's sister, wanted his band back home. Halle's description is unclear, though, for we cannot tell whether there were two kettledrummers, or whether there were two kettledrums played by one player; the reference to the reward suggests that it was one player because the figure in the records is 86*l*.13*s*.4*d*., which converts to an exact figure when divided by thirteen, but not when divided by fourteen. If Southampton got the number wrong, then Halle's twelve trumpeters and one drummer makes sense – thirteen trumpeters would be an unusual number.

Percival Kirby, when he quoted Halle, ignored the word 'her', thus misleading all who followed him by taking this description to refer to Henry's own band, whereas Halle makes it clear that Henry saw these kettledrums in his fourth wife's train.[45] We do know that this gave Henry the idea of acquiring kettledrums of his own, for two years later he wrote to Vienna, seeking his own players. That city was the main *entrepôt* for the import of goods and services from the European provinces of the Turkish Empire.

Writing to Sir Thomas Seymour (the father of his third wife who had died a few years earlier) on 29 August 1542, King Henry said:

> … Further our plesure is, that you shall travaill to conduct and hier there for us, at suche wages as you shall think mete, ten taborynes on horsbak, after the Hungaryons facion, and if it be possible, whatsoever We paye for them, to get oone or twoo of that sorte that can both skilfully make the sayd taborynes and use them; and likewise We wolde you shuld provyde us of ten good dromes, and asmany fifers. … Willing you ernestly to travail that thise taborynes, drummes, and fyfers, or as many of them as you can get, may repayre hither with as good spede as you can convenyently dyvyse….[46]

Note the distinction between the 'taborynes on horsbak after the Hungaryons facion', which from that description must be the kettledrums, and the 'dromes and fifers', which are the side drums. Kirby again misleads us all by truncating Seymour's reply, which was written from Vienna on 12 October, after lifting the siege of Pest five days earlier. Kirby quotes only 'the captaynes that your Heynes would retayne, the dromes and fyffes, the ketyl dromes'.[47] The original letter continues: 'wyche I shall with all my delegent study folow … and have sent a man with delegence to the camp to provyde the dromes and fyffes … I shall inquyre for the ketell dromes that You wolde have provyded, for in the camp thar warre but 2, the on was with the Hongeryns, and the other with the Generall….'[48] The 'captaynes' are mercenaries which the king wants to hire, and there is further correspondence about their costs, including two trumpets and four drums and fifes, but there is no further mention of kettledrums.[49]

It seems very unlikely that Henry VIII obtained his 'ketyl dromes'. There is no evidence at all for the existence of such instruments, nor any mention of a kettledrummer, in the English Court Records until, in 1660, Charles II was restored to the English throne. On 20 June of that year 'John Barteeske ye Kettle Drummer' is sworn, along with John Maugridge, the drum-major.[50] Bowles illustrates the mounted timpanist and twelve trumpeters in the royal procession through London the day before the coronation, 22 April 1661, and Ashbee records the warrant for the liveries for the sixteen trumpeters and one kettledrummer on 2 March.[51]

From then on, the names of kettledrummers do appear in the English Court Records, often foreign names, and normally listed along with the trumpeters, separately from the Drums and Fifes.[52] There is no such separation in the Tudor records, nor even among the earlier Stuarts. The only drummers recorded are the drumslades, who are clearly the side drummers. Nor are any drummers of any kind ever listed with the trumpeters who attend the monarchs on any of their travels, whereas such listings become frequent after the Restoration. This all suggests that there were no kettledrummers on the royal establishment throughout the Tudor and early Stuart reigns, for if Henry VIII did have kettledrums, who paid them? Who provided them with liveries? Why were painted banners provided for the trumpets, but none for the drums? At present we have to say that we do not know the answers to these questions. Nor do we know why in the great inventories of all his musical instruments, prepared after the king's death, there is not one single trumpet (nor are they recorded in the Jewel House records) nor one single drum of any kind.[53] The one obvious answer is that the king's endeavours were frustrated and that he never did succeed in acquiring kettledrums.

There is one tantalizing reference to the use of kettledrums in his son's reign. In 1552 George Ferrers, who was the Lord of Misrule for Edward VI's Christmas revels that year, reported in a letter that 'I haue prouided one to plaie vppon a kettell drom with his boye and a nother drome with a fyffe whiche must be apparelled like turkes garmentes according to the patornes I send you herwith on St Stephens daie'.[54] So far it has proved impossible to find any other references to this kettledrummer and it reads very much as though he was a casual freelance brought in for the occasion, rather than somebody on the establishment. Why did he have a boy? One obvious possibility is that he was a walking drummer, like others whom we shall meet, and that the boy, who might have been an apprentice drummer, carried his drum or drums on his back, walking ahead of him as he played.[55] Certainly there are no payments listed in Ashbee's *Court Records* to a kettledrummer during Edward's reign, nor are there any in the reigns of his sisters, Mary and Elizabeth.

However, we do have one clear reference in Queen Mary's reign.[56] This is the diary of Henry Machyn, a 'Citizen and Merchant-Taylor of London'. He recounts that in 1554, on

> The xxv day of November dyd pryche at Powlles crosse master Fecknam, den of Powlles, and a godly sermon. The sam day, the wyche was Sonday, at after-non, the Kyngs grace and my lord Fuwater [Fitzwater] and dyvers Spaneards dyd ryd in dyvers colars, the Kyng in red, and som [in] yellow, sum in gren, sum in whyt, sum in bluw, and with targets and canes in ther hand, herlyng of rods on a-nodur, and thrumpets in the sam colars, and drumes mad of ketylles, and banars in the sam colars.[57]

Later that same year, on

> The viij day of Desembere, the wyche was the Conceptyon of owre blessed lady the Vyrgyn, was a goodly prossessyon at the Save [Savoy] be the Spaneards, the

prest carehyng the sacrement ryally be-twyne ys hands, and on deacon carehyng a senser sensyng, and anodur the ale-water [holy-water] stoke, and a nombur of frers and prestes syngyng, [and every] man and woman, and knyghts and gentylmen, bayryng a gren tapur bornyng, and viij trumpeters blohyng; and when they had don plahyng, and then begane the sagbottes plahyng; and when they had don theyr was on that cared ij drumes on ys bake, and on cam after playng....[58]

Both these references, to drums made of kettles, and to a player following a porter who carried a pair of drums on his back, can only refer to timpani. What we cannot tell is whether these players were English or whether, as the context seems to imply, they were part of the train of King Philip of Spain, who although he had married Queen Mary, was never officially acknowledged as King of England.[59] This could explain their presence in what seems to be an official capacity but their absence from any payrolls in the English Court Records. If they were on the Spanish establishment, their salaries would be on their records, and not on the English. It could also explain the absence of any further references in Machyn's diary, once the 'Spaneards' had left. He continues into Elizabeth's reign with many other references to trumpets, both with and without drums, though never specifically kettledrums, and to drums with 'flutt', presumably fife and side drum.

One of these was in 1562, when on

The xx day of June was a gret shutyng [archery] of the compene of the Barbur-surgeantes for a gret soper at ther owne hall for a xxx mess of mett of, for they did make ij godley stremars agaynst that day of ther harmes, the wyche they wher agmentyd by the most valeant kyng at armes master [blank] ad they had vj drumes plahyng and a flutt....[60]

There are indications from several other sources that timpani were used with trumpets during Queen Elizabeth's reign. One is the Hunsdon Tomb in St John the Baptist's Chapel in the north choir aisle of Westminster Abbey, which dates from between 1596, when Henry Carey, first Baron Hunsdon and the queen's first cousin (through Anne Boleyn), died, and 1603, when his son George, who erected the tomb, also died.[61] Each of a pair of timpani carved on the south pylon of the monument is draped with banners so that the kettles themselves are invisible, but the use of such banners, the fact that there are the two of them, the general shape, and above all the typical timpani-shape of the beaters behind them, are all evidence that these are kettledrums and thus that the instruments were known and, perhaps, used in England by this date. Another is William Byrd's 'battell' of *c*.1591, where in several of the movements the virginalist's left hand is pounding away at the tonic and dominant in a clear imitation of kettledrum patterns.[62] How would Byrd have known what these patterns were unless he had heard them in use? A more doubtful reference is Kirby's citation of the frequently quoted description from Hentzner's *Itinerarium* of the dining customs at Queen Elizabeth's court in '1548', presumably a misprint for Hentzner's date of 1598, when 'twelve trumpets and two kettle drums, with fifes, cornetts and side drums, made the hall ring for half an hour together'.[63]

The problem of this is not only that Kirby misquoted the date as 1548 but that it is not what Hentzner wrote. His Latin was: 'XII. Tubicines, & duo Tympanistæ, qui tubis, buccinis, & tympanis magno sonitu per sesqui horam clangebant', and Walpole's translation was 'twelve trumpets and two kettledrums made the hall ring for half an hour together'.[64] So where did Kirby get the 'fifes, cornetts and side drums', misleading us and the many others who have quoted him? He may have been trying to provide a more literal translation than Walpole's. A less elegant, but more exact translation than Walpole's might be 'XII Trumpeters, & two Drummers, who with trumpets (*tubis*), horns (*buccinis*), & drums (*tympanis*) with a great noise for an hour and a half sounded aloud'.[65] Thus 'cornetts' (a horn-type instrument made of wood with fingerholes, which was becoming at this time the leading virtuoso wind instrument) could be a fair translation of *buccinis*. The 'fifes' might be a hint towards a problem which remains with Walpole's translation, in that *tympanum* at this date simply means drum and thus that this alone is not evidence that the drums were specifically timpani or kettledrums. Later in the *Itinerarium* there is a description of 'The Manners of the English' and there we read '… delectantur quoqu[e]; valdè sonitibus, qui ipses aures implent, uti explosionibus tormentorum, tympanis & campanarum boatu, ita ut Londini multi qui se inebriaverint turrem unam aut alteram, exercitij causa, ascendant, & per horas aliquot campanis signum dent', or in Walpole's English, 'They are … vastly fond of great noises that fill the ear, such as the firing of cannon, drums, and the ringing of bells, so that it is common for a number of them, that have got a glass in their heads, to go up into some belfry, and ring the bells for hours together, for the sake of exercise…'.[66] Here it would seem very probable that 'tympanis' does refer to side drums. However, trumpets and timpani do often go together, and therefore…. Quite simply we cannot be sure.

This connection between trumpets and the service of meals is referred to in many other sources; as each new dish appeared, a fanfare of trumpets would ring out. Such fanfares were improvisable on a simple chordal basis, as we shall see in the next chapter and, in Italy, were known as *toccata* and *sonata*. Can we assume therefore that Shakespeare's frequent demands for a tucket or sennet (English for *toccata* and *sonata*), when sounded by trumpets, as is often indicated, included timpani? One would like to think so. Certainly it did so in *Hamlet*, our third immediate source, where the stage direction calls for 'A flourish of trumpets, and ordnance shot off within', which Hamlet explains, 'as he [the king] drains his draughts of Rhenish down. / The kettle-drum and trumpet thus bray out / The triumph of his pledge'.[67] In Germany, where the term *Tusch* was the translation of *toccata* and similarly used for a short flourish of trumpets, it can normally be assumed that timpani were also used, as well as for the more formal *Aufzüge* and *Auszüge*, entrance and exit music usually for three or four trumpets.[68] Because such 'touches' were improvised we have very little evidence of their format other than the descriptions and such stage directions as that already cited. There are sufficient references of this sort to make it certain that they occurred in royal and princely houses throughout Europe north of the Alps continuously from the one that we cited for Maximilian in 1492 into the eighteenth century, but there seems less certainty in the south, a problem which will concern us when we come to discuss Monteverdi's 'Toccata'.

Trumpeters and kettledrummers were normally mounted on horseback on the Continent when out of doors, save at special occasions such as funerals. Both Bowles and Kinsky show different parts of the funeral procession of Charles V, the Holy Roman Emperor, in Brussels in 1568.[69] In both scenes the drums are draped to mute them, and in each there is also a large contingent of walking trumpeters. Kinsky shows a timpanist walking behind a man carrying both drums on his back. Bowles's drummers, each with one drum on his back and another on his front, have their drapes suspended from their shoulders to the far side of each drum, so that they are suspended like tents, rather than lying on the drum head. This, combined with the fact that neither drummer could possibly reach the drum strapped to his back, suggests that they were walking as mute mourners, rather than as players. Bowles also illustrates the coronation procession of James II of England and Scotland in 1685, where again the kettledrummer, sticks high in the air to show that he is playing, walks behind his servant, who is bowed down beneath the weight of a pair of drums.[70]

All these drums were quite small, as one would expect if they were to be carried on a man's back, and those on horseback in the *Berner Chronik* were much the same. In Maximilian's *Triumph* they are also quite small.[71] Here the diameter of the drumhead in the foreground is about four-fifths the length of the middle yards of the trumpets, which would give a very approximate diameter of 22 inches (56 cm). It was then the norm, as it still is in German orchestral life and in the British Household Cavalry, to have the lower drum on the right, and therefore this would be the larger drum of the two, with the smaller measuring some 20 or 21 inches. Edmund Bowles has suggested that one reason for having the lower drum on the right (bass to the left is otherwise an almost universal worldwide convention) is to balance the weight of the sword, which hangs from the player's left side.[72] Many early eighteenth-century drums are around these sizes. In another of Maximilian's productions, the *Weißkunig*, where a woodcut by Hans Burgkmair shows the young king visiting his musicians, there is a much larger kettledrum, clearly an orchestral instrument in contrast with the cavalry ones seen in the *Triumph*.[73] Measured against the trombone lying on top of it, the diameter is some 27½ inches (70 cm), a size familiar to orchestral timpanists today. It has many more tuning rods than the cavalry drum, with eight visible on less than half the circumference. Perhaps this is one of the drums described by J. Aubrion in 1492 which was played for the Emperor's dinner and which contained '*dix chaldrons d'yawe*' as mentioned above.[74]

Arbeau tells us, nearly a century later than Maximilian, that 'the drum of the Persians (which is also used by the Germans who carry it on the saddle bow) is made of a hemisphere of copper closed with a strong parchment, about two and a half feet in diameter, and makes a sound like thunder when this skin is touched with beaters'.[75] A drum thirty inches in diameter seems rather large. The largest normally used today is thirty-two inches, suitable for a low C; thirty inches would give the good low E that Reger requires in the *Mozart Variations*, and the E flat and D that Mahler so often requires. A pair of anything like that size would surely be too heavy for a horse to carry. It is very possible that Arbeau is merely repeating what he has heard, especially since Turkey and its Eastern European empire is much more likely than Persia as the source. A slightly worrying aspect of his description is that it does make one wonder whether 'two and a half feet' is his equivalent of 'fairly big' (as in the numerical sequence 'one, two, three, many'), and thus perhaps casts doubt on his use of that same size for the side drum – we do, though, have the pictures cited above to show that side drums really were around that size.

At least we have little doubt of what timpani were like at this period. They had already reached sizes familiar to later generations, and by 1500 were tuned in the way which remained the norm into the Classical period, with square-topped metal rods passing through rings on a metal hoop and screwing into lugs fixed to the shell of the drum. We can see eight such rods on the drums in Maximilian's *Triumph* and ten on each of Virdung's. A loose key with a square socket was applied to each rod in turn, screwing it in to increase the tension and raise the pitch, or unscrewing it to lower the pitch. We cannot see separate counterhoops and fleshhoops, and it is much more likely that, as on German Baroque and Classical timpani, the skin was lapped directly on to the counterhoop, with slits cut in the skin to allow the rings to pass through.[76]

The beaters were made of wood, or sometimes of ivory, quite thick and, in the earlier days, with integral round heads, sometimes quite large balls. Even in Holbein's *Dance of Death* of c. 1525, the skeleton player is using such sticks, and not a spare pair of thigh-bones.[77] By the latter part of the sixteenth century, the beaters' heads were discs of the same materials rather than balls. Caldwell Titcomb quotes Mallet's description from a century later: 'drumsticks of beechwood or boxwood, each eight to nine inches long and having at one end a small rosette of the size of a silver crown'.[78] Three such beaters, though 39 cm long (over 15 inches) and with discs ('rosettes') 4.5 cm in diameter (1¾ inches), made of ivory with gold *appliqué* decoration on the face of each disc, survive in Vienna from the sixteenth-century Treasure Chamber and are now in the Kunsthistorisches Museum there.[79] Each has a hole towards the butt end of the shaft, which suggests strongly that they were for cavalry use, provided with a thong or cord loop to slip over the player's wrist in case they were dropped, and to aid the flamboyant circlings and waving of the sticks so dear to military drummers to this day and illustrated in so many of the sources already cited here.

We do not have much information on how the drums were used. Of one thing we can be certain. These instruments were not, as yet, considered to be part of the musical establishment. Tabors would be used in dance music; the side drum might accompany the fife dance or the sackbuts and shawms or even the trumpets – Bowles illustrates such a scene at the wedding of Duke Wilhelm V of Bavaria and Princess Renée of Lorraine in Munich in 1568.[80] But trumpets and kettledrums were the instruments of ceremony and state, not of music. This is why they appear far away from the musical establishment in Maximilian's *Triumph*, far from the quiet music and the chapel and the loud music of sackbuts and shawms. This is why there is a pair of timpani sitting unused in an alcove below the musicians' gallery in the Bavarian wedding scene just mentioned. Presumably this is why the inventory of Henry VIII's musical instruments contains neither trumpet nor drum.

Other instruments

There is really very little that we know about other percussion instruments in this period. We see tambourines in some of the Maximilian woodcuts, and several of the triumphal carts of his *Triumph* have pellet bells and/or clapper bells hanging from various points. One of his troupes is a group of Indians with an elephant with a bell round its neck and beside it a drummer who has pellet bells on a wrist strap and also a pellet bell at the point of each V of the tension cords of his drum. Among the jesters there is a trump player; this is not normally thought of as a percussion instrument, but almost certainly if one appeared in a score, it would be a percussionist who would be expected to play it![81] There are no signs of a cymbal player in his procession nor do these appear in Virdung, though Virdung does show bells and a pellet bell as well as a trump and such plebeian instruments as a pot and spoon and a child's clappers.[82] Cymbals appear in many other sources, though more often in contexts which appear to be classicizing, reminiscent of Bacchic frenzies, or foreign scenes such as those showing Turkish musicians.

Agricola, who converted much of Virdung's text into verse and reprinted many of Virdung's illustrations, added some new material, including the xylophone, which already has its normal German name of *Stro fidel* (later *Strohfiedel*), not because it was a fiddle but because it was made by laying bars of wood across two hanks of straw. The range that he shows is F–f$''$, three octaves, diatonic but with B natural as well as B flat so that it could play both soft and hard hexachords.[83] Unfortunately there is nothing about the instrument in the text in either edition of his book. He provides only a picture of a series of bars of diminishing size in a single row, each with its note name written upon it, and beside it a pair of short beaters, quite thick with round knobs.

This must be one of the first musical fruits of the Age of Exploration. Europe was beginning to spread across the globe, for the first time since the height of the Roman Empire, seeking the sources of exotic materials and the opportunities for trade. Initially it was a search for luxuries, spices, silks and other such goods, but an item high on the list was always novelties. One was the xylophone, imported from East Africa, where slats of wood were laid across logs of soft and fibrous materials such as banana stems. These in Europe became bundles of straw, tied into hanks to provide a resilient support against which the bars would not rattle as they might against a bare wooden frame. Agricola's picture is one of the earlier examples. Holbein's *Dance of Death* preceded it by three or four years, with a skeleton beating on a xylophone, held horizontally in front of him by a strap round his neck, exactly as folk-musicians play it in Eastern Europe.[84] This association with a skeleton foreshadows, even in its earliest days, the use that Camille Saint-Saëns was to make of the instrument three and a half centuries later, in 1886.[85]

Other percussion instruments were comparatively rare in northern Europe at this period. Looking through Salmen's *Musikleben im 16. Jahrhundert* is most instructive. The majority of his illustrations are drawn from northern Europe and, leaving aside the military side drum and the occasional pipe or transverse flute and tabor, there is only one illustration that shows any significant use of percussion instruments, and that is a German painting of a Morris dance in Spain.[86] This shows a pair of simple rope-tensioned kettledrums played with hooked beaters and an iron ring struck with a long iron staff.

Southern Europe is rather another matter. If we look, for example, at Raphael's *Saint Cecilia* of about 1513 we can see on the ground at her feet a triangle with at least three rings and its beater, a tambourine with a double row of jingles and pellet bells, a jingle ring (as the tambourine without a skin is usually called today), a pair of small kettledrums, perhaps nakers, and a pair of small thick cymbals.[87] Italian painting of that period shows rather more use of percussion than in northern Europe, but there is still a marked reduction, especially in what might be termed art or domestic music, from the amount seen in the later medieval iconography.[88] In the more public scenes, there is a frequent use of tambourine and jingle ring, and the triangle appears much more often than in the north, sometimes used with a pipe as a tabor substitute. Cymbals also appear, sometimes with the plates vertical as we hold them today and sometimes with the plates held horizontally as was rather more common in the Middle Ages. However, one must always be aware of the dangers of classicization. Enough Greek and Roman reliefs of Bacchic and Dionysian processions with cymbals and *tympana*, the frame drums of the period, were already well known, and of course Renaissance derivatives of such scenes as Della Robbia's carvings on the Florentine Cantoria of children playing such instruments, were always to hand.[89]

The question of survival of instruments from the Middle Ages through the Renaissance into later times is a difficult one. We see so many instruments in the fourteenth and fifteenth centuries and so few in the sixteenth. Some, as we shall see in the next chapter, do appear in the two great encyclopaedias of the seventeenth century but there is little evidence otherwise of their use in any known musical contexts either then or through the first three quarters of the eighteenth century until their sudden reappearance in the military band with the fashion for the *alla turca*. Had they survived only in the Eastern European territories dominated by the Turks? Or were they quietly biding their time (perhaps 'quietly' is not the ideal term!) in the hands of folk musicians and the peasantry? That the latter is at least part of the answer is confirmed by one of the very few books before modern times to show the musical practices of ordinary mortals, as distinct from those of the aristocracy and the heavenly host, Bonanni's *Gabinetto Armonico*. Here we see percussion instruments such as tambourines, triangles, and cymbals still in use by country folk, as well as simple folk instruments such as stones, clappers, and ratchets. He shows others deriving from antiquity and many from exotic peoples and distant lands. To these exotic and European folk instruments we shall return in chapter 9.

Chapter 4

The Early Baroque

The earliest years of the Baroque form a period for which we have no distinct name other than the 'Early Baroque'. It begins in 1600 with Caccini's appointment to the Medici Court and the publication two years later of his *Nuove Musiche*, which made a very definite break with the earlier Renaissance styles. It merges into the main Baroque some fifty to seventy years later, after the middle of the century, in Germany with the end of the Thirty Years War, in France with the appointment of Lully as composer to the French Court and, in England, perhaps with the establishment of the Commonwealth, but certainly with the Restoration of the monarchy a decade later.[1] Within this short but musically crucial period came the appearance of two remarkable encyclopaedias. The earlier, compiled by Michael Praetorius in Germany, and the later, by Père Marin Mersenne in France, both cover the whole art of music, and both not only include large sections describing instruments, but both illustrate almost every instrument of their time.[2]

Praetorius is the more useful to the instrument maker because each of his plates is drawn to scale, with the scale included at the bottom of each plate.[3] Mersenne is the more useful to the instrument historian because he gives much more information about the instruments themselves and their use, frequently with musical examples. Especially important are the additional marginal notes and the information, including music and some extra drawings, on the interpolated pages of his own copy, some, but not all, of which were printed in an appendix and are then more legible than his manuscript.[4] His illustrations are sometimes less successful than Praetorius's because he employed three artists, one of whom was good, one mediocre, and the third very poor. There is nothing comparable with either encyclopaedist, save perhaps for Pierre Trichet, a younger contemporary of Mersenne's and to a great extent derivative from him, until the end of the seventeenth century. Then, not very usefully for percussion but otherwise valuable, we have the Talbot manuscript in England and, nearly a century later, in the latter part of the eighteenth century, we have the *Encyclopédie méthodique* of Diderot and d'Alembert in France.[5] A few later but useful texts, for instance those of Daniel Speer and Johann Ernst Altenburg, will be cited as we proceed.[6]

Unfortunately for our purposes, Praetorius, like Talbot, almost totally ignores the percussion instruments in his text. He describes all the wind and string instruments of his day, referring to each relevant plate as he does so. His only textual references for

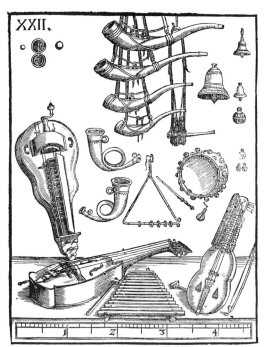

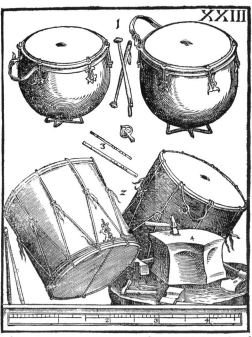

1. Allerley Bawren Lyren. 2. Schlüssel Fiddel. 4. Stroh Fiddel. 4. Jägers hörner. 5. Triangel. 6. Singekugel. 7. Morenpaucklin. 8. Glocken 9. Cimbeln : Schellen.

1. Heerpaucken. 2. Soldaten Trummeln. 3. Schweitzer Pfeifflin 4. Anboß

C iiij

percussion are a mention of the tabor pipe, saying that English people use it with a small drum, and, when he discusses the *Schweizerpfeiff*, that it has a quite different fingering from the ordinary transverse flute and that it is only used by soldiers with their drums. He provides very little text, other than the captions, for his plates XXII and XXIII, which illustrate the percussion instruments (except for the tabor, which is on plate IX with its pipe, among the other flutes), repeating what he had already said about the side drum and the tabor and adding that the large *Heerpauken* are made of copper kettles with calfskins which are hit with beaters. They are used in the establishments of princes and the aristocracy for entrances and exits (*Ein- und Auszüge*) and dances, and in times of war and in the field, and they are like rumbling barrels.[7]

The instruments that he shows are, on his plate XXII (ill. 12), a xylophone, triangle, tambourine, trump, and various bells and jingles. The xylophone has fifteen bars, which suggests a range of two octaves without any chromatic notes.[8] The triangle has the usual rings and is called *Triangel*. The tambourine, called *Morenpaucklin* (small Moorish drum), has pellet bells as well as jingles. The bells and jingles are called '*Cimbeln* : Schellen', meaning small bells, rather than large church bells, and pellet bells. Some of the other casual and folk instruments which Virdung illustrated in 1511 reappear, reproduced from his book, on plates XXXIII and XL.

Plate XXIII (ill. 13) has the more serious percussion instruments, a pair of timpani with beaters and a tuning key, two side drums with a pair of sticks and two fifes of two different sizes, and the anvil and hammers which were obligatory in all such contexts to illustrate Pythagoras's theorems. His side drums but not his timpani (figs 1 and 2 in the Introduction here) have separate fleshhoops and counterhoops, the timpani with iron bolts with square tops, screwing into brackets fixed to the shell. The

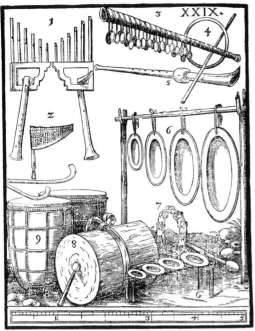

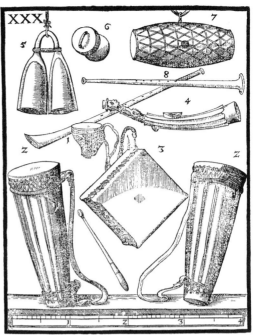

1. 2. Sind Satyri Pfeiffen. 3. Americanisch Horn oder Trommet. 4. Ein Ring so bey den Americanern gleich wie ein Triangel geschlagen wird. 5. Americanische Schalmey. 6. Becken darauff die Americaner/ wie bey uns auff Glocken/ spielen. 7. Ein Ring mit Schellen/ die sie in die höustrwerffen vnd wieder fangen/ etc. 8. 9. Americanische Trummeln. D ij.

1. Ein Türckisch Trümlein oder Päucklein. 2. 3. Moscowitische Trummeln oder Paucken. 4. Indianisch Horn von Helffenbein. 5. Ist von Eisen gemacht/ wird darauff gespielet/ wie bey vns au f der Ristseitrummeln. 6. 7. 8. Indianische Trummeln vnd blasende Instrumenta.

Clockwise from far left

12. *From the top:* Bells, pellet bells, tambourine, trump, triangle, xylophone, and other instruments. Michael Praetorius, 'Theatrum Instrumentorum', *Syntagma Musicum II, De Organographia* (Wolffenbüttel: Elias Holwein, 1619).

13. (1) Kettledrums, beaters, and tuning key, (2) two side drums and sticks, (3) two fifes, (4) anvil and hammers of different weights. Michael Praetorius, 1619.

14. (3) Horn with pendant rattles, (4) iron ring, both allegedly American, (6) gong and *kempuls* and, at the foot of the page, *bonang*, from Java, also allegedly American, (7) jingle ring, (8) and (9) drums, allegedly American, though (9) is *ntumpani* from Ghana. Michael Praetorius, 1619.

15. (1) Small Turkish drum, (2) two views of a drum, probably from the Guinea Coast, allegedly Muscovite, (3) double-headed frame drum, perhaps Moroccan, also allegedly Russian, (5) iron double bell, West African, (6) and (7) Indian drums, (7) a *mrdangam*. Michael Praetorius, 1619.

16. (6) and (7) Jingles and rattles, allegedly and perhaps American, (8), (9), and (10) gourd rattles, also American though allegedly Indian. Michael Praetorius, 1619.

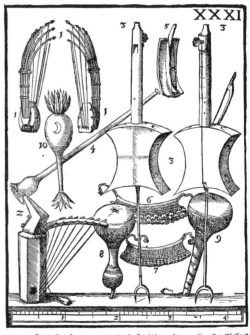

1. 2. Indianische Instrumenta am Klang den Harffen gleich 3. Monocordium ist ein Pfeiff vnd hat eine Säite darneben/ welche mit dem Fiddelbogen gestrichen wird/ den Arabern gebreuchlich. 4. Ein Americanisch Trommet 5. Ein Fischbein darauff zwo Säiten eines Thons. 6. 7. Sind Beinkerder den Americanern an stad der Schellen gebreuchlich : Sind Gewechse von Früchten zusammen gemacht. 8. 9. 10. Indianische Rasseln von Gewechsen/ gleich den Kürbsern.

tuning key is somewhat like a large version of a clock key. This is the first, and I think the only illustration of a timpani tuning key before the days of the T-handle, which rendered such keys redundant, and it deserves to be better known to makers and players of early timpani. The beaters are exactly like those of ivory in the Kunsthistorisches Museum in Vienna, which have already been referred to, and have the loops through the holes in the butt end of the sticks, which Speer recommends.[9] As we said in the previous chapter, these help the player whirl the sticks in the air, without dropping them, in the graceful flourishes beloved by cavalry kettledrummers to this day. The side drums have a snare of a single strand of gut running across the lower head, with a tension screw very similar to those on our late nineteenth-century military drums, save that it is controlled by a wing nut rather than a round nut. The buffs, which are pulled down over the Vs of the tension cords, are ties rather than the plain leather tug-ears, as they were sometimes called, which were used on our drums before players switched to rod tensioning.

Mersenne's pictures are more rudimentary, especially those for his timpani which were patently drawn by someone who had never seen a pair, but his descriptions are detailed and useful. Trichet adds a few points, though mainly he duplicates Mersenne, quite often word for word.[10] Both are quoted below as we discuss each instrument.

It seems also to have been in this period that scholars began to take notice of the musics of other peoples. Mersenne shows and describes a few exotic instruments, a Thai mouthorgan for example, an Indian *vīnā* and a Turkish *saz*, but Praetorius is far more thorough in this respect. He is usually woefully inaccurate in his geographical ascriptions but the illustrations are often so clear and accurate that they must have been drawn from the instruments themselves. Others derive from earlier texts and at least one of the sources for his illustrations is identifiable, which makes the geographical misattribution slightly surprising. His Javanese gamelan (plate XXIX:6) (ill. 14) is taken from *D'Eerste Boeck* of 1597, and is therefore, like the original, somewhat schematic, but he describes it as American.[11] Other percussion instruments on this plate include an iron ring struck with an iron rod 'like our triangle', a jingle ring (a tambourine without a skin), and a pair of large drums struck with curved beaters, which are said to be American but which look not unlike Ghanaian *atumpan*, which are similarly used in pairs. On his plate XXX (ill. 15) the 'Moskowitische Trummeln' is so clear that Klaus Wachsmann was able to equate it with a drum from the original Tradescant Collection in the Ashmolean Museum in Oxford, described in the museum's 1656 catalogue as a drum from *Ginny*.[12] Wachsmann suggested that it was perhaps more likely to have been from East Africa than West. A square double-headed frame drum, such as is still used in Morocco and Portugal, is again said to be Muscovite, and a small kettledrum is said to be Turkish, which it could well be – such drums are used by the Dervishes. A barrel-shaped drum is said to be Indian, again probably true, for it looks much like a *mrdangam*, and the West African iron double bell is accurate in every detail, as is his African pluriarc (attributed to India) on his next plate (ill. 16). This also shows a feathered gourd rattle said to be Indian but almost certainly American Indian, probably from Brazil, some other gourd rattles less easy to identify, and two woven belts with half nutshells pendant from them as jingles, said to be American but equally likely to have been African. These plates of exotica are the first serious survey of non-European instruments (they include, of course, a number of wind and string instruments also) and it is one whose importance has on the whole been neglected by ethnomusicologists.[13]

Timpani

Praetorius's timpani (fig. 1 on p. 4), or *Heerpauken*, measure 1 foot 6¼ inches Brunswick feet and 1 foot 9 inches in diameter (43.4 and 50 cm). They have the usual base of a wrought iron triangular 'crown' as a stand and each has a carrying strap. These stands were mainly for storage; players seldom sat on the floor to play. For performance, the drums were normally either mounted on horseback or placed on a stand of suitable height. The beaters are 1 foot 5 inches long, 40.4 cm compared with 39 cm for those in Vienna, which, when allowing for the thickness of the lines on the woodcut, is pretty well identical. Mersenne says nothing precise about the size of his timpani. He gives no name for them save 'another sort of drums'.[14] He says that their shells are made of brass (*leton*) in the form of a cauldron or hemisphere, that they are around two feet in diameter, that they are carried on the saddle-bow and that they make a loud sound which imitates that of thunder. Trichet is a little more informative. He says that 'the drums which are used nowadays by the Germans are of copper or brass [*de cuivre ou de leton*] and are like a great cauldron two feet wide…'.[15]

Although these authors give us so much information, they still leave many gaps in our knowledge of the use of the timpani. This is all the more frustrating in that this is the period in which the timpani begin to be used in musical, as distinct from purely ceremonial contexts. The change is gradual and, as we shall see, uncertain, but one thing is clear and that is that the timpani came into such use on the trumpet's coat tails. There is little positive evidence for the musical use of timpani with trumpets at this date, but there is none at all for their use without trumpets. The description above of Queen Elizabeth's dinner suggests, if it was with timpani, something more than a routine fanfare – even allowing for the exaggeration natural in a traveller's tale, 'made the hall ring for half an hour together' implies something more than the basic entrance and exit music.

These entrance and exit fanfares were called *Aufzüge* and *Auszüge* in Germany. Every princeling there with any pretension to nobility laid claim to trumpet privileges, the right to have trumpeters in his establishment, and with them there was routinely a timpanist. They played these short fanfares on all sorts of occasions at the court and while, in this early period, we often have only the trumpet parts surviving, it is simple enough for any drummer to improvise a tonic and dominant accompaniment. Normally there were three parts; when there was a fourth trumpet part, it was often confined to the tonic and dominant, clearly a substitute for the timpani. These flourishes are often no more than eight bars long, enough for an entrance or exit. They could be repeated, with some variation, if necessary, and it would be a simple matter to continue in the same vein. Tuition in doing this was a standard part of every trumpeter's training.

Even the paucity of surviving music is little bar to our knowledge, for the trumpet tutors of the period, by Bendinelli and Fantini, and the somewhat later instruction books, such as those by Speer and Altenburg, all give clear instructions as to how such fanfares are to be constructed.[16] One takes a common chord, from middle c′ to the c′′ above, giving it a pleasing shape and attractive rhythm. This was later called the *principale* part, and it becomes the middle one of three. The upper, *clarino*, player improvises something mildly melodic above it, ranging up to g′′ or even the upper c′′′, and the player below produces a simple harmonic combination from the same common chord with an occasional lower g and, for a fourth player, or the kettledrummer, a simpler tonic and dominant pattern on c and g.

We know much more about the status and professional life of drummers in Germany than elsewhere, because there such matters were restricted and formalized, though even there we learn more about their military than their musical functions. In France also, where Allain Mallet is one of our main informants, our knowledge in this respect is greater on the military side.[17] He describes the timpani as large bowls of red copper or bronze with goat-skin heads and tuned with many lugs or brackets (*écrous*) attached to the shell of the drum and the same number of screws (*vissus*) which one tightens and loosens with a key. They are played with boxwood sticks eight or nine inches long with a little rosette at the end which strikes the drumskin and which make a much pleasanter sound than if they were played with side-drum sticks. He then goes on to describe the timpanist (*Timbalier*), who must be a brave man who will gladly risk death in battle, which he can enliven with his timpani. He must have graceful movements with his arms and a true ear, and must take pleasure in entertaining his master with agreeable melodies (*airs agréables*) in battles and triumphs. There is no instrument which can produce a more martial sound than the timpani, especially when they are accompanied by the sound of several trumpets.

In Germany the timpanists were members of the trumpet guild and were both protected and restricted by privilege. Only aristocrats of above a certain status were permitted to employ trumpeters, as were only those cities and regiments which had been accorded the rights to do so. Guild Privileges, the trumpeters' rights, responsibilities, and practices, had first been laid down by the Holy Roman Emperor Ferdinand II in 1623, and were then repeated and confirmed by his successors and by the various Electors and their successors into the latter part of the eighteenth century.[18] However, elements of these had already existed for at least two hundred years, for Altenburg tells us that in 1426 the Emperor Sigismund gave trumpet privileges to the city of Augsburg and Edward Tarr suggests that such practices had been going on for at least a decade before that date.[19]

By the end of the eighteenth century the system was in terminal decline due to the major demographic and social changes of that period. Altenburg wrote his book, partly from nostalgia and partly to reveal what had previously been the guild secrets of the Baroque trumpeters in the hope of preserving at least some of their techniques and skills, in which he was one of the last to be trained, skills which have never been surpassed and which we have still not succeeded in fully reviving today. While the Guild still flourished, employment opportunities were strictly limited, because only members of the Guild were permitted such employment, but once one was established as a Guild member there was little to fear from rivalry. Becoming a member of the Guild was not simple – the easiest method was to be the child of a member. Once in, there was a long period of apprenticeship, for the training that inculcated the skills for playing the most exacting *clarino* parts took some eight years.

Unfortunately Altenburg gives us much less information about the training of drummers than of trumpeters. While not wishing to suggest that a drummer need be any less skilful than a trumpeter, one must admit that the skills needed to perform the timpani parts in Baroque music do not require the same long training as the exacting lip technique and muscular endurance and control required for the trumpet parts. There was also rather less sanction available for use against a drummer who was not a member of the guild. An interloping trumpeter could have his teeth smashed so that he could never play again. Nothing comparable could be done to a drummer other than breaking his arms, which would eventually repair themselves – save amputation, which was probably rather too extreme a course.

Altenburg describes the Fanfare as:

> usable on all days of celebration and state occasions and is usually played on trumpets and kettledrums together. It contains (a) the Intrada or *Intraite* – that is, the introduction to a musical piece which the trumpeters are accustomed to improvising before they play their instruments – [and] (b) Tusch (*Touche*), or flourish – [upon] the word or sign given to the trumpeters that they are to play, when noblemen drink toasts at table. This is the same as the preceding. Properly it is a short free fantasy consisting of nothing but a mixture of arpeggios and runs. Indeed it makes noise enough, but there is neither art nor order in it – that the clarino players like to sustain the high tones c‴, d‴, and e‴ is, to be sure, a good custom.[20]

He makes it clear that kettledrummers were equal members of the Guild from its inception and that they played the bass part in all the processional music that we have mentioned, as well as for the flourish (Altenburg calls it *Touche*, French being more fashionable than the German *Tusch*) which announced any ceremonial consumption of food or drink, and for the general accompaniment of royal and princely meals. We shall leave his descriptions of the beatings and playing techniques until a further chapter, for he is then describing the practices of his own time. The beatings which he gives in 1795 are much more elaborate than those of Speer a century earlier in 1697. This may be due to greater thoroughness, but it may also be that some of Altenburg's techniques had not yet been devised in the seventeenth century. Just as with Thoinot Arbeau's descriptions of tabor playing, back-projection can only be hypothetical, though in this case the customs of the Guild were so rigid, not to say fossilized, that they were unlikely to have varied much over a century or so.

The question is, can one transfer this use of the timpani from books such as Altenburg's and Speer's to the music of other countries at this time? For example, in Italy the two great trumpet tutors referred to above, Bendinelli's manuscript, completed in Verona in about 1614, and Fantini's tutor printed in Frankfurt in 1638, both give full instructions on the art of improvisation. Bendinelli gives examples of a basic text, the *sonata*, which Monteverdi calls *quinta*, and which we referred to earlier as *principale*. Above this the *clarino* improvised his melodic part, and below it the *alto e basso*, the *vulgano*, and the *grosso* improvised harmonic parts, the last in the lowest register, inelegantly known in Germany as *Flattergrob*.

The best written-out example of such a five-part Toccata that we have is Monteverdi's for his opera *L'Orfeo*.[21] The two lowest parts do nothing but sustain tonic and dominant throughout. Did they sustain these as drones, as they are written, or did they break the written semibreves (whole notes) into shorter notes? We do not know. More important to us, we do not know whether those two parts were doubled by a timpani *ostinato*. We can be pretty sure that in Germany they would have been. Altenburg calls such a timpani part, when for lack of kettledrums it is played by a trumpeter, Touqet or *Toccata!*[22] Speer also instructs his timpanists how to play such parts.[23] It seems likely, from what sources we have, that in France and Britain they might well also have been played by a timpanist, but in Mantua, at the ducal court for which *L'Orfeo* was written, we simply do not know. Any timpanist would agree that such an *ostinato* can sound well, for example a crotchet (quarter-note) on the tonic, followed by four semiquavers (sixteenth-notes) on the dominant leading back to a crotchet on the tonic, incessantly repeated. Musicologists, however, tend to be more cautious.

This is all the more frustrating because there is so little certainty about other quasi-orchestral timpani parts until we get beyond the middle of the century. What evidence that we have tends to be one example here and another there. Michael Praetorius was an important composer, especially of church music, as well as an encyclopaedist. Most of his settings are *a cappella* (for unaccompanied voices) and are often complex, written for three or four choirs. Others use one or more instrumental choirs as well as the vocal ones. Only once does it appear that he used timpani. This is in a very elaborate setting of *In Dulci Jubilo* for 12, 16, or 20 parts (one or more of the choirs can be dropped if necessary or if preferred).[24] The first section of the piece is written as three semibreves (whole-notes) to the bar, and the rhythms (still familiar to us today, for it is well-known as a Christmas carol) are semibreve–breve or breve–semibreve, or one dotted breve. While the four 'tubae', as Praetorius calls the trumpets, sometimes move decoratively in minims (half-notes), the bass keeps to the longer notes in the tutti passages where the kettledrums play (Praetorius said at the beginning 'Tutti cum tubis et Tympanis').[25] At the end of the first section a note says 'Intrada auf 8 takt'; no music is given and the players would have improvised those eight bars like any other *Aufzüge*.

The work ends with two bars for the tubae which are very like Monteverdi's Toccata, with the instruction to 'play on like this as another Intrada to end with'.[26] The bass line below this is just a held C. How would a timpanist have handled these long sustained notes? Back-projection from Altenburg and his examples of beatings, as well as common sense, suggests that he would have broken the held notes into rhythmic patterns – there is little else that he could have done. Speer is very specific on precisely how he should play the final cadence, with an extreme elaboration which he calls a *Paucken-Würbel* (timpani roll), a flourish on the two drums very different indeed from anything that we would call a roll, with a *Final-Schläge* ten notes long![27]

Paucken=Würbel

Final Schläge

The resemblance of Praetorius's second Intrada to that of *L'Orfeo* makes it all the more tempting to assume that Monteverdi also used timpani a dozen years earlier, but it is a temptation that it would be wise to resist if only because, even in Speer's and Altenburg's Germany, this is Praetorius's sole use of timpani. Why? Did he try them and not like the sound? Did he find that their players could not read music or, more important, could not count their bars rest (which is a quite possible result of always improvising and of normally only playing short fanfares and flourishes) and so came in at the wrong time? Or were they drunken and dissolute soldiery, despite Altenburg's frequent emphasis on their status as officers, and thus unfit to come into a church again? We do not know and we can only speculate.

We can speculate again why half a century later Heinrich Schütz also used timpani only once, and why he then used only one of them, actually specifying Timpano (as did Sibelius in his *Valse Triste*). Schütz scored his *Herr Gott, dich loben wir* for Clarino 1 and 2, Trombetta 1 and 2, Timpano, Violino o Cornetto 1 and 2, Chorus I and II with trombones on the Altus, Tenor, and Bassus parts, and Bassus Continuus with a trombone only in Chorus II.[28] The *clarino* parts are quite elaborate but the *trombette* and the *timpano* are silent for the first 120 bars or so. The two *trombetta* parts are then fairly standard *principale* parts, with common chord motifs in the lower part of the range, from the third to the eighth harmonics (g to c´´). The *timpano* has, in the score of the Collected Edition, quavers and semiquavers (eighth- and sixteenth-notes), and rolls which, according to the *Revisionsbericht*, were indicated in the original score with ~, a sign like the Spanish *tilde*, above each note.

Analogously with our discussion of Hentzner's *Itinerarium* above, it is always possible that 'Timpano' merely meant drum and that we are dealing here with a side-drum part. Conversely, it is also possible that Schütz assumed that any fool would know enough to use dominant as well as tonic as was appropriate, though his specification of *timpano* both in the singular and in Italian (Latin is *timpanum* or *tympanum*) goes somewhat against this (if the editors of this edition are to be trusted in this regard; they give no indications of original note values or clefs, which tends to make one suspicious). Our lack of contemporary information is, at times, more than merely frustrating!

In England, Kirby mentions two appearances of timpani in masques, one in 1616 in Ben Jonson's *The Golden Age Restored* and the other in Shirley's *The Triumph of Peace* in 1634, and no doubt there were others, but it looks from the scores and the texts as though these are simply stage effects, with trumpeters and drummers cavorting around the scene, often on horseback, no doubt playing, but not as a part of the musical ensemble.[29] There seems to be no trace of these instruments in any of the surviving scores of masque music. It is not until the 1670s, into the next period, that we have a more definite suggestion of their use, in Matthew Locke's *Psyche*, dating from 1675 or perhaps a couple of years earlier.[30] The librettist, Thomas Shadwell, specifies a 'Consort of Martial Music accompanied in the Chorus with Kettle Drums …', and later a Warlike Dance with 'Kettle-Drums beating, and Trumpets Sounding'. Unfortunately, Locke only wrote down the parts for oboe 1 and cornetto, oboe 2 and sackbut 1, tenor oboe and sackbut 2, bassoon and sackbut 3, strings, and organ. It would be easy enough to construct trumpet and timpani parts, and indeed the editor of the modern edition, Michael Tilmouth, has done so, but they can only be speculative. If they existed they would be one of the earliest English examples.[31] At least if drum parts did exist here, they would have been as part of the musical ensemble, as Shadwell indicates.

As we shall see in the next chapter, by this time Lully had begun to use timpani as a matter of course, and it is to him and the fashions that he set that we must look for their general acceptance into the orchestra.

Side drum

Mersenne provides much more information about side drums than for timpani. He also has two pages of text about their *batteries*, plus three pages of music. Praetorius (fig. 2 on p. 5), however, remains uninformative save for the dimensions provided by his scale, his drums being 1 foot 11½ inches Brunswick (55.8 cm) in diameter and about the same in depth. This is much the same size as the drum painted by Bartholomeus van der Helst in his *Banquet of the Civic Guard* of 1648.[32] This drum, and the rather larger one that Rembrandt painted in *The Night Watch* in 1642, have the common feature that the tension cords do not pass through holes in the counterhoop but simply pass over it and under it, between it and the fleshhoop. Rembrandt's counterhoops have a saddle, presumably of metal, on the outer edge of the hoop for each V of the rope to pass over, and a channel cut for each in its inner edge so that they are not pinched between the counterhoop and the fleshhoop and thus can be easily adjusted. Van der Helst's drum has no such provision, though we cannot tell whether this is due to lack of detail in the painting or to a simpler drum; the counterhoop has an overlap secured with three nails rather than a smooth scarf joint, which would support the idea of something less sophisticated. Either of these would seem a much simpler, and possibly earlier, system than the hooks referred to above with the Swiss drum.

A surviving Dutch side drum in the Royal Armouries is almost exactly the same size as that of Praetorius, with a diameter of 1 modern foot 9¹³⁄₁₆ inches (55.4 cm). This was dated at my instigation by dendrochronology, producing a date of 1630–45.[33] The shell was made of two strips of oak joined together so neatly along their long sides to make a single sheet that the joint was invisible to the naked eye and its existence was only realized when the dendrochronology report arrived. The resulting sheet of oak, an eighth of an inch thick, about 1 foot 8 inches wide and about 6 foot 3 inches long, was bent into a cylinder with an overlap formed as a long and very shallow scarf joint securely held with an elaborate pattern of ornamentally-headed nails.[34] There is a circle of these studs round the air hole, which is drilled through the overlap. The nail pattern is not as ornate as on Drake's drum, nor as on Rembrandt's, though the studs are rather pretty rosettes. A snare bed, a channel approximately 3.5 cm wide, was cut at two diametrically opposed points in one end of the shell.[35] It was feeling this snare bed through the skin that proved that the drum was originally a side drum, for it was converted into a bass drum, or long drum, in the early nineteenth century and bears the monogram of King William IV placed so that it would be the right way up with the drum held horizontally across the player's chest. The bed is essential for a snare drum because if gut snares run over the rim of the drum their stiffness makes them stand up in a curve instead of lying against the drumhead. If the rim is carved away to form the bed, making a shallow indentation where the snares cross it, the snare will both curve and lie in contact with the head. There were no traces of any fitting for a snare strainer, as there are on Praetorius's drum, and it is probable that, just as on eighteenth-century English drums, the snare was simply gripped between the fleshhoop and the counterhoop. Rembrandt's drum may also have gripped the snare in this way, for the snares on the side visible to us are knotted in an elaborate cigar-shaped roll, which could be pulled and perhaps further twisted as a crude tensioning device. There is no strainer visible on Van der Helst's drum, either.

Another surviving English drum is a little later. According to Cynthia Gaskell Brown it was bought for the Oxford Volunteer Corps which was raised to fight Monmouth's rebellion in 1685.[36] The drum is now in All Souls College, Oxford, and is painted with the College arms.[37] The drum is made in much the same way as that of the Armouries, from two sheets of wood joined together down their long sides, though less neatly, for the joint between them is clearly visible. The resulting sheet of wood was shorter than was needed for a drum of the size required, and therefore the makers introduced a patch, with the usual wide overlap on one side, which carries the elaborate nail pattern and the air hole, and a rather shorter overlap on the other side, about 3 inches (76.2 mm) long, judging from the positions of the nails. This patch is nailed below the main sheet of wood on each side and it is the only drum that I have ever seen that was made in this way. It is just possible that the patch was inserted to repair war damage received during the Rebellion, but it looks much more as though it was original. The longer overlap is a long, shallow scarf joint as usual, and the thickness in the centre, where the airhole is drilled, is 6mm (about a quarter of an inch). To make it easier to compare the dimensions of the two drums, the measurements are given here in a table. Some of the figures can only be approximate, and conversions from millimetres to inches, or vice versa, are usually to the nearest convenient fraction.

	Armouries		*All Souls*	
	inches	*mm*	*inches*	*mm*
shell diameter	21 13/16	554	21 1/3	543
shell height	19 5/8	495	20 1/2	520
shell thickness	1/8	3.2	3/16	4.2
length of the sheet of wood	74 3/4	1900	63	1600
plus the width of the patch	–	–	3 2/3	92
width of each half of the sheet	–	–	10 & 10 1/2	254 & 267
length of overlap (scarf joint)	6 1/4	160	6 1/2	165
width of the snare bed	*c.* 1 3/8	*c.* 35	*c.* 1 3/8	*c.* 35
counterhoop thickness	3/8 & 5/16	9 & 7.5	3/8	9.2
counterhoop width	1 9/16 & 1 7/16	40 & 37	1 3/8	35
length of overlap (scarf joint)	12 & 11	305 & 280	*c.* 6	*c.* 150
fleshhoop thickness	recent		*c.* 1/2	*c.* 12.5
skin thickness	recent		*c.* 20 thou	0.5
weight of the drum	–	–	10 lb	4.5 kg

The counterhoops on the All Souls drum have a very neat scarf joint, which is almost invisible save for the traces of small nail heads under the paint, and the tension ropes (which are modern) pass through holes in the usual way. The cords are tightened with leather buffs, made of two thicknesses of leather stitched together, folded over the tension cords in the usual way, about 95mm long (3¾ ins), and tied together round the cords by leather, not as they are often tied together today, by strips of surplus drumskin. Six of the original buffs survive, plus four modern replacements. No buffs survive on the Armouries drum (replacements, but in the much wider modern military style, have recently been provided). The counterhoops are fairly roughly made with much longer overlaps than at All Souls, and with slightly different dimensions between the two ends of the drum. The original drummer from All Souls must have been a fairly determined player because the batterhead is split almost right across. Presumably this happened in the field where no replacement was available, because the head is patched underneath (he must have taken it off the drum to patch it). One corner of the head is curled up from where the rest is glued, so its thickness could be measured. It seemed better not to ask whether one could remove the heads from the drum, so the extent and material of the patch are unknown, as are the exact dimensions of the snare bed – judging from the marks on the snarehead there were probably four strands of gut. Again there was no tensioning device; the snare was simply gripped between fleshhoop and counterhoop. The nail or stud pattern is quite elaborate, with four small circles of double rings of nails above and below a large circle of five rings, bordered by two parallel lines of nails on each side and a triple line down the middle dividing each four circles into two pairs.

Mersenne says that a side-drum shell is normally made of oak, as it is on the Armouries drum (because the All Souls drum is painted it was not possible to identify its wood; Drake's is walnut), though brass may be used, and that one could use any wood which can be bent into a circle.[38] The skins, he says, are normally from sheep, and those who say that they should be from donkeys are certainly wrong, as are the fables about using wolfskins.[39] The snare is either two cords, or one doubled, and Trichet tells us that it is of gut and that for the best results it should be thicker than the thickest viola da gamba string, more than two millimetres in diameter.[40] Mallet agrees that the snare, which makes the sound more harmonious, is of gut but he says that the wood is usually chestnut and the heads of calfskin.[41]

Mersenne then describes various methods of notating drum rhythms and signals, and adds to his own copy three manuscript pages of rhythms in normal musical notation, being careful to show the *baton rond*, when one plays hand-to-hand (single strokes with each hand), *baton rompu*, when each stick strikes twice, i.e. two strokes with each hand, and *baton môlé*, a mixture of the two. He also seems to show both hands together, though he does not mention this in so many words, which would equate with our flam. Two samples (*overleaf*) should suffice, first *L'entrée ou la marche simple*, and then *L'assemblée*.

These leave some questions open, for he does not show flams, drags, and rolls as such, though the simultaneous notes may be flams and the single pair of semiquavers (sixteenth notes) might mean a drag in the first example. Repeated pairs of semiquavers and of demisemiquavers (thirty-second notes) in other examples might be

rolls, which were certainly in use by this time. However, the same is true of those signals and marches by Lully and Philidor and written down by the latter at the beginning of the next century, and it is clear that drummers were expected to know what to do.[42] This becomes abundantly clear in Maurice Byrne's lengthy discussion on the English March.[43]

At this period, and for some considerable time earlier, each nation of Europe had its own march, distinct in both rhythm and tempo from those of other nations. This was, apparently, not merely a matter of custom but also so that when a body of men appeared in the distance it could be recognized what nationality they were, from the rhythms that they were playing on the side drum, and thus whether they were friend or foe. We know from the court records that by Charles I's time this tradition was becoming somewhat neglected in England, for in 1632 the King issued a warrant not only saying so but directing that all drummers in the kingdom should henceforth play it 'correctly and as follows'. Unfortunately, what followed was written in the drum notation of the time, a series of Pou, tou, Pou, tou, Poung and similar syllabics such as the following (see p. 66).

Regrettably none of the sources in the seventeenth, eighteenth, and nineteenth centuries which Dr Byrne cites can produce confirmation in recognizable staff notation. Nevertheless, he has collated a number of them and has produced a rhythmic pattern which appears convincing enough, both an earlier duple time version and a later one in triple time.[44] Kastner, while giving the *batteries* of many nations, has only a summary passage on the English, and no English march, and Beethoven's drum introduction for the English forces at the Battle of Vittoria is too different to be a version of it.[45] Byrne cites some early drum tutors of which no copy is known to survive, and perhaps if one of these were to turn up in the future we should then know for certain what was the rhythm of the English March. The importance of its accuracy was sufficient to justify the King sending his warrant the length and breadth of the country and, when it transpired that there was a lack of competent teachers, for John Rudd, who was a drummer in ordinary to the King, to petition that 'he and his deputies may have the teaching of persons desirous to learn truly to beat the English march'.[46] The petition was granted.[47] The March certainly remained in use into the early years of the nineteenth century and we may hope, along with Dr Byrne, that its use and recognition will be revived in our own time.

Side drummers were a part of the infantry regiments, and army life for side drummers is likely to have been much the same in each country: low pay, incessant marching, and hard work carrying and playing the drum on the march. It was also a post of danger, for when the regiment marched into battle they were at as great a risk

The VOLUNTARY *before the* MARCH.

Pou tou pou tou pou R pou tou pou pou tou pou R   Poung

The M A R C H.

Pou   tou   Pou   tou   poung

Pou   tou   Pou   R   poung

R   pou   tou   R   poung

R   R   pou   R   poung

R R pou tou R pou tou pou R tou pou R   poung

R   R   R   R   poung

R R R pou R R pou tou pou R tou pou R poung petang

as the soldiers themselves. Timpanists were also frequently part of the army. Both timpanist and side drummer had a special role, which involved enhanced risks, for as well as being part of the battle array like any other soldiers, either was expected to take part in embassies from their own army to that of the enemy. Any attempt at a parley was conducted with trumpet blowing and kettledrums beating, or if these were unavailable, with fife and side drum, to show that no surprise was intended and to ensure that the herald was recognized as such. Both faced the risk that the enemy might not feel inclined to talk and would repulse the embassy in the most emphatic manner. There are many stories of a herald's head being tossed back as response enough, and it is likely that his musicians shared his fate.

Other instruments

As in previous chapters, we have comparatively little information about other instruments. Mersenne shows the Provençal tabor, a very large and deep drum which is still used in that part of France as the *tambourin*.[48] The name causes confusion because it is almost the same as the German name for the tambourine or *tambour de basque*, whereas the *tambourin* is the *tambour de provence*. As a result, Bizet's use of the *tambourin*, in his incidental music to Daudet's play *L'Arlésienne,* and Milhaud's use in several works such as his *Suite Provençal,* are often misinterpreted by being played on the tambourine, and Rameau's frequent use of the *tambourin* in many of his ballet scores is often ignored. The *tambourin* was later popular at the French court during their pseudo-folk craze immediately before the Revolution. A small one, perhaps made then for one of the princes as a boy, was on display at an exhibition in London in 1973.[49] Mersenne says that the *tambourin* was used with a pair of cymbals, illustrating a pair of plates of comparatively modern pattern, but that seems to be a custom which has died out, if it ever existed. Certainly there is no trace of it in the standard book on the *tambourin*.[50]

Mersenne goes on to the tambourine itself, the *tambour de basque*, which he calls the *tambour de Biscaye*, that being the name of the Basque province of which Bilbao is the capital.[51] He says,

> This has only one skin, which is of parchment like that of the other drums, and has small plates of tin-plate (*fer blanc*) or of brass which are inserted into openings in the shell. These make an agreeable sound in time with the player's movements and his strokes on the skin with his fingers, because there are two plates in each opening and they strike against each other. Some people like to add pellet bells on the rims of these drums to make more sound than just the plates.

Trichet adds the detail that the drum is about one foot across and says that the plates or jingles are of copper (*cuivre*).[52]

Mersenne give much space to bells, for as an acoustician he is fascinated by their sounds and by the acoustic and mathematical problems of their overtones. This, while interesting enough in its own right, is not really relevant to our purposes here, for even the carillon, the method of playing music on bells from a keyboard, is not usually regarded (save briefly, to which we shall return in the next chapter) as a part of the percussion section. More interesting, and well separated from the section on the carillon, is the description of the *Regales de bois*, 'which one also calls *Claquebois, Patoüilles, & Eschelettes*'.[53] His drawing, unfortunately, is not by his best artist. It shows seventeen bars sitting on a frame or box. Below each bar, projecting from the front of the frame, is a lever, one end flat like the handle end of a spoon or fork as the touch for the finger, and the other end a round disk to strike the bar above it. Thus the bars are sounded by a form of keyboard. 'The bars can be made of beech or any wood that one likes, but if they are made of steel, brass, or silver they make a very agreeable sound. They can also be made of stone. Their tuning depends on their size, their hardness, their weight and their dryness. The instrument is used by beginners for learning to play the carillon, and also for practising', and it is one to which we shall return in the next chapter. Because the normal carillon rings out over the whole town from its tower, some form of practice instrument has always been necessary, and André Lehr mentions and illustrates a number, though normally without much detail.[54]

Mersenne describes a twelve-note xylophone, simply twelve bars strung on two cords, each bar separated from its neighbour by a paternoster bead. The bars are struck with a small stick with a ball on the end, and, he says, such instruments are used by the Turks and others. A tutor for an identical instrument was published in Bologna by Giovanni Battista Ariosti in 1686, with a second slightly revised edition by Giuseppe Paradossi, also known as Gioseffo Troili, in 1695.[55] The instrument was called Sistro or Timpano, a good example of the sort of problems we have when confronting written sources, for the sistrum was either the ancient Egyptian rattle described in chapter 1 or, in the nineteenth century, a name for the triangle or, it has been suggested, for the bell tree. Timpano of course we know as the name of an entirely different instrument. The tutor has one short page of very summary instruction followed by seven and a half pages of what James Tyler described as 'hit tunes' of the period. These are not in staff notation but in a numerical system, simply numbering the bars from 1 to 11 (none goes to 12 and only a few to 10 or 11; most stay within the octave) with one extra sign to indicate *Li trilli*. There is no indication of time signature or rhythm, but since these were all popular tunes it was doubtless expected that the player would fall automatically into the correct meter. This is one of the earliest published tutors for any percussion instrument. Similar instruments are described, though without instruction, in other texts of this period, and at least one says that one can play music as well on the xylophone as on any other instrument. Two instruments, each with sixteen bars but otherwise identical to Mersenne's, survive in Florence from the Medici collection, now in the Accademia. They first appear in the 1794 inventory, but may of course be older, as *sistro a stecche*, 'sistrum with sticks' as distinct from the triangles and jingles of pellet bells, which are also called *sistro*.[56]

Both Mersenne and Trichet devote a surprising amount of space to the trump, which they call *trompe, gronde*, or *rebube*, Mersenne giving an excellent drawing of the instrument.[57] Though Mersenne says that it is only used by lackeys and people of low status, he suggests that it is worth study by more respectable folk. He and Trichet are both impressed by the number of notes which so small and so apparently simple an instrument can produce, and at least some of Mersenne's interest appears to be aroused, as a scientist, because he does not understand how the instrument achieves this. Trichet refers to instruments with two or three tongues, and also to the possibilities of an ensemble of trumps of different sizes, thus perhaps foreshadowing the use of the *aura*, which was invented by Heinrich Scheibler sometime before 1816.[58] It has to be confessed that, over 300 years later, there is still debate on how the trump works, and this despite a number of acoustical and other studies and the existence of a specialist periodical devoted to the instrument.[59] A permanent bone of contention is whether the trump is an aerophone, the tongue or feather (the normal English name) acting as a reed on the air-body contained in the player's mouth, in which case it is not our concern, or whether the feather is an idiophone whose overtones, when plucked, are selectively resonated by the variable mouth capacity of the player. Professor Crane and some authorities hold the former view; I and others the latter. The basic mechanics of the instrument are that the frame is held against or between the teeth; techniques vary with players, shapes, and materials which range, worldwide, from idioglottal bamboo, bone, and brass to heteroglottal metals and other materials (ill. 17).[60] The feather or the frame (according to type) is plucked while the player's mouth-shape changes as it would in pronouncing different vowels and the tongue is moved to alter the volume of the mouth. In this way, the overtones of the feather are selected and the instrument can produce not only a harmonic series similar to that of the trumpet (hence its name) but other pitches, making it capable of a considerable melodic range. Its 'orchestral' repertoire is small, though concertos were written for it in the nineteenth century, but it is widely used in folk music and a few composers, such as Charles Ives, have scored it from time to time.

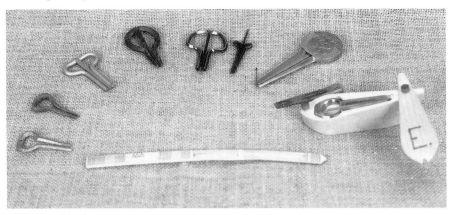

17. Trumps (also known as jews harps or jews trumps): *(left to right)* two medieval English; German by Friedrich Schlütter; Nigerian; Austrian by Karl Schwartz; Indian; Yakut by Revo Chemchoyev; Philippine; Norwegian by Jakob Lavell in its *hus*; and *(foreground)* Mindanao.

Mersenne is also fascinated by the castanets which, he says, are used by the Spaniards to accompany dances such as the sarabande.[61] He stresses that they produce different pitches and that a group of dancers, each with castanets of different sizes, could produce music on them in as many parts as there are dancers. Players can produce '*des cadences, des passages, & des diminutions ou tremblements*', the last so fast that it is impossible to count them. He seems to be using the word 'diminutions' in its normal sense of breaking a slow melody into rapid passage work. Castanets can be made of plum, or beech, or any resonant wood, just like the *regales* described above, and 'they can be tuned to match any other instruments, especially the guitar, with which they are often used. However, they often produce dissonances because people do not understand how to use them properly because of the great differences between their sound and that of string instruments'.

Mersenne is, of course, correct in this respect: very few non-percussionists recognize the pitches of many of the instruments described in this book, and far too often one reads the old dictum that it is only the timpani and the members of the xylophone family that produce sounds of definite pitch. As we have said before, and will probably say again, for it cannot be too often repeated, all percussionists know that every instrument they play produces a definite pitch, even if this is somewhat more difficult to perceive with some than with others, and that they must always stand ready to produce a different specimen of the same instrument if, or very often when, as Mersenne suggests, a dissonance is produced. This applies particularly strongly to the triangle, for the art of making triangles whose pitch was almost impossible to discern, which certainly existed in the nineteenth century as we know from a few surviving instruments, is lost today and one must always carry at least two, and preferably more, to avoid such clashes. A notorious example of the need for this is Liszt's Piano Concerto no.1 in E flat.[62]

Mersenne goes on to the triangle, which he calls *cymbale* and which he equates with the cymbals of the Psalmist 'which were used to give pleasure and for jubilations, as it is said in the last psalm'.... 'It is made of silver, of brass, of all other metals, but normally of steel of which the sound is sharper, more lively, and more dazzling. The beater is usually of the same material, or any other as one wishes, as are the five rings which are hung on the triangle.'[63] He then very briefly mentions the pellet bells which dancers put on their arms, legs, hands, and feet to keep time with their movements. Trichet's cymbals seem to be semicircular bowls, a form which Mersenne also mentions briefly as antique cymbals, repeating the illustration which Praetorius used on his plate XL, one of the three plates which he appeared to add somewhat as an appendix to *De Organographia*. Trichet mainly cites classical authors, rather than describing any modern use, but he does tell us that one must not fall into the error of common people who give the name cymbals to those round jingles which contain an iron ball, meaning pellet bells[64] – even in those days it was necessary to correct the misinformation on terminology and identification disseminated by the ignorant!

Regrettably, we know nothing more of the use of any of these minor instruments at this time. As we have seen, the timpani are beginning to have a musical use as well as a military and ceremonial one. The xylophone seems to have had its own melodic use as an individual instrument. One can only suppose that the tambourine, cymbal, triangle and pellet bells were used by dancers, as Mersenne tells us was true of the castanets, and that these and other instruments enjoyed a vigorous life in those strata of the community which were beneath the notice of the scholars who compiled the treatises, or were thought to be of little interest to their readers.

Chapter 5

The High Baroque

As we enter the High Baroque, with the music of Lully, Purcell, Rameau, Bach, Handel and their contemporaries, we find orchestras increasing not just in size but in the variety and the range of their sonorities. Again we have the work of two encyclopaedists to help us, the first in England and the second in Germany. James Talbot, a Fellow of Trinity College and Regius Professor of Hebrew in the University of Cambridge, was a scholar with enough interest in music to intend a work comparable with Mersenne's. Unfortunately this was never completed and his manuscript survives only as a large bundle of papers in the library of Christ Church in Oxford.[1] There is no date, but various watermarks and cross-references suggest that it is unlikely to have been begun before 1683 and that it was probably put aside and left unfinished on his appointment to Cambridge in 1689.[2]

Talbot borrowed instruments from all the most eminent performers and makers of his day and examined them, taking very detailed measurements and adding brief descriptions, occasionally with such details as fingering charts. Much of his information has appeared in the pages of the *Galpin Society Journal*.[3] Unfortunately he gives very little information on European percussion instruments, though there are some quite interesting details on the gongs and gong chimes of the Philippines, and a fair amount of information on Chinese instruments, with detailed descriptions of their bells.[4] He headed pages for pipe and tabor, tabor, and timbrel, but wrote nothing else on them.[5] He does say: 'Kettle-drum. Body Brass Copper Silver. Copper best. German tuning C. G. English D. A. Tuned by screwing iron higher or lower for lowness or height.'[6] His page headed Cymbal describes the hurdy-gurdy, another example of the problems of terminology, and on his page headed Drum he describes only Chinese instruments.[7] His lack of information on percussion instruments is particularly unfortunate in that he is the only English encyclopaedist and that, especially with the woodwind such as oboe and bassoon, he took note of the contrast between the instruments of the Early Baroque and those of the High Baroque, newly introduced from France.

The second encyclopaedist is Daniel Speer, who wrote, he said, 'a four-leafed musical clover' covering the whole science and art of music.[8] The third leaf of the clover is that on the musical instruments and it consists of brief descriptions with musical examples of how each instrument is used.[9] Of the percussion, he describes only the *Heerpaucken* or timpani, telling us that one kettledrum shell should be smaller than the other and that they are made by the coppersmith. The skins for the heads are not fully tanned and, when fitted to the shells, they should be smeared with brandy and garlic and left in the sun to dry or in front of a small fire, information which was repeated fifty years later by Majer.[10]

While not all authorities would agree with the brandy and garlic recipe (some quite specifically decry it), all would recognize the difference in preparation between tanning, which would produce leather, and the simpler, and much shorter and less smelly, processes which produce parchment or vellum and thus drumskin. The two terms, parchment and vellum, are interchangeable, though some writers try to make distinctions between them, never with the same results. For vellum, skins are washed in running water for twenty-four hours or so and then soaked in lime and water for several days to loosen the hair.[11] The hair is scraped off; the skin is turned over and the parchmenter scrapes off any remaining flesh from the inner surface. The skin is washed again for some days, mainly to remove the lime, and it is then dried while held taut on a frame. The skin is scraped, or skived, first while still wet and then when dry, to reduce it to the desired thickness, with a knife whose blade is shaped in a demilune to avoid sharp corners that might cut the skin.

Tanning, to produce leather, is a much longer and much smellier process. Skins were soaked for anything up to nine months to prepare them for tanning in such liquors as urine or stale beer, or water in which bird droppings or dog dung had been steeped. Tanning itself consisted of further soaking in thick layers of oak bark, a process which could take a further year. Even then the skin was by no means ready for use as leather. The full process, and all the operations, which are of little relevance to our purposes in the history of percussion instruments, save for distinguishing them from the preparation of vellum, are clearly described by Sue Thomas and L. A. Clarkson.[12] Although both leather and vellum start out as the skin of the same animals, the nature and behaviour of the finished materials, like their preparation, are very different, and each is useful for its own various purposes and not for those of the others.

Speer says, further, that the smaller drum is tuned to g and the larger to c, and his musical examples bear this out, with the g drum in the top space of the bass stave, and the c in the second from bottom, as in the example of his *Paucken-Würbel* in the previous chapter, whereas Majer says that the smaller drum is tuned to c and the larger to 'the contra-G at 16 foot a fourth lower'. This suggests, quite strongly, that in the intervening fifty years there was a change of drum sizes in Germany. The only rational explanation for a change from g to the c a fifth lower, and from c down a fourth to G, is that the diameters of the drums had increased by two or three inches. Although we shall consider drum sizes below, so few are securely dated that this musical evidence is better than that of surviving instruments. Majer notes on his illustration that the c drum is played by the right hand and the G by the left, which is the reverse of the normal German custom. Speer also says that the c drum is played by the right hand, but since this is for him the lower drum of the two, this follows normal custom. Speer goes on to say that the kettledrummer must have very supple wrists and hands to produce the roll and that he must be knowledgeable in music to play the notes correctly, to tune the drums properly, and to provide a good bass to the melodies of the trumpets in the *Aufzüge*, and that he must give a good long roll on the final cadence.[13] Unfortunately he does not provide a specific drum part for his two *Aufzüge* for six trumpets, but since the lowest part, entitled *Gröb*, consists only of tonic and dominant and would have been played by the kettledrummer, this is hardly necessary. He gives a four-bar musical example of an ordinary march for timpani.

Marsch oder gemeine Schläg auf der Heerpaucken

As we saw in the previous chapter, he also provides his version of the roll, to which we shall return when we are discussing *Schlagmanieren* below, the way one plays passages. He adds that the drummer should attach the sticks to his wrists with a loop of cord in case he drops them – we have already observed the holes for this purpose in the shafts of the sticks in Vienna and noted the loops passing through similar holes in Praetorius's sticks.

The timpani were the first percussion instruments to be regular members of the orchestra, but we shall henceforth find other instruments appearing, even if only occasionally. Handel, for example, used side drums in the *Music for the Royal Fireworks* and also in *Joshua* (and repeated the same music in *Judas Maccabaeus*), in neither case providing any music for them. In the *Fireworks* he contents himself by saying 'and the side drums' for the third time through 'La Réjouissance' and the final (D major) 'Menuet', and in the two oratorios by writing 'drum warbling' for 'See the Conquering Hero Comes' – as James Blades said, confusing his English 'warble' with his '*Wirbel*', the German word for 'roll'.[14]

Timpani were still indissolubly linked with the trumpets, and as a result could only be used in certain keys, for in this period it was very rare to find trumpets built in any size other than that which would produce the harmonic series of D or, with the use of a short circular crook, of C.[15] Since the Conquering Hero Comes in the key of G, he cannot come with trumpets. It would have been possible to use a timpano in G (the larger drum when playing in C) but, as Blades points out, Handel uses the word Drum instead of 'tymp' (as Handel normally spelt it), which makes it almost certain that it was a side drum, not a timpano, which was required.[16] In the *Fireworks Music* he wrote the plural 'drums'. The scoring for the brass and percussion is for three horn parts, three trumpet parts, and timpani. The brass were specified as three players to a part, nine of each instrument, and presumably the timpani and the side drums were also tripled. Handel specifies that the first time through the 'Réjouissance' and the D major 'Menuet' is for trumpets and timpani, the second time is for horns, presumably without percussion, and the third time is all together, plus the drums.

At least in England, as in France, composers were to some extent free to use timpani whenever they wished to do so and were willing to write in suitable keys. In Germany the old rules of trumpet privilege still held sway and only those composers writing for nobility and cities with such privilege could write for trumpets and kettledrums. It is quite interesting to note the occasions on which Bach could do so. Elsewhere, certainly in Britain where public concerts had begun much earlier than in other parts of Europe, the main restricting factor was that familiar to any concert promoter today: money. An orchestra financed by a prince or wealthy potentate for his own private concerts can include whatever musicians he is willing to pay, and if, as was common in the German cities and courts, there were trumpeters and one or more kettledrummers already employed on the establishment, they would be available for orchestral use whenever required and permitted. With public concerts without the support of such private finance, what controls the size of the orchestra is the number of ticket-buying bodies in the audience and the amount of money thus available for orchestral musicians after overheads, promoters, and soloists have been paid. So even when composers were free to use trumpets and drums, there may have been practical reasons for restraint and this may explain why such use remained comparatively rare throughout the seventeenth and eighteenth centuries.

The timpani

Much music of the middle and late seventeenth century remains as yet unpublished and is only accessible in the libraries or other collections where it has come to rest. As a result it is very difficult to produce broad generalities and it is certainly dangerous to say that any one composer was the first to do anything, for one can never know what may be hidden until another researcher reveals its presence. However, from what music we have, it seems as though Lully was the leader in the introduction of the timpani as regular members of the orchestra, though even in his case it is still difficult to be certain just when and to what extent he used them. The older collected edition of his music is very vague in its indication of which instruments played what, often being little more than a cued piano-conductor score.[17] More seriously, Herbert Schneider's thematic catalogue of Lully's works is inadequate for any proper musicological research, giving no indication of the instrumentation, nor of the original clefs (which can often be helpful to guesswork in this respect), nor of original time signatures.[18]

There is certainly a timpani part, perhaps Lully's first one, in the ballet he wrote for Francesco Cavalli's *Serse: Comédie en Musique*, first performed in the Grande Galerie de Peinture in the Louvre on 22 November 1660.[19] Presumably the timpani were introduced as a special effect, for they appear in only two scenes, one for the sailors playing *trompettes marines* (a tall, narrow string instrument, usually some two metres high, played in natural harmonics and thus producing the same notes as a natural trumpet, and more often known today by its Italian name of *tromba marina*), and the other for the slaves and dancing monkeys.[20] The part for the *Timbales* in the score is for the usual D and A plus the low D below the bass stave; how accurate this is and whether Lully really used three drums is, due to the vagaries of this edition, a matter for conjecture – it would seem inherently improbable.[21] There is a possibility that this passage was not for timpani at all, for as we shall see below, Speer describes a string-substitute for the timpani, which he suggests is particularly useful for playing timpani parts when the trumpet parts are played on a substitute used in churches; he gives no name for this but he is obviously referring to the *Trumscheit* or *Nonnengeige*, as the *tromba marina* was called in Germany. Lully's music is clearly marked 'timbales', however.

There then seems to be a gap, for Lully's next occasion for timpani, in this old edition at least, comes in 1673, on 27 April, with the opera *Cadmus et Hermione*. Since the bass line printed in this edition is fully diatonic, it is impossible to tell which of these notes the *tymballes* played, nor can we see what the timpani writing was like. The next work, *Alceste ou le Triomphe d'Alcide* of 19 January 1674, which has six numbers with timpani, as against only one in *Cadmus et Hermione*, is little better served. For definite information on just what Lully wrote, and when, we can only wait for the new collected edition to progress further.[22] So far only one volume is available, with a choral work, *Exaudiat te Dominus* (LWV 77:15), which includes *tymbales* and trumpets, but which is unfortunately of uncertain date, probably written sometime between 1684 and 1687, and therefore much later than these operas and ballets.[23]

We can, however, form some idea of the possible styles of timpani writing used by Lully and his associates at this period from other music preserved in Versailles and Paris. These include the *Marche de timballes a 2* written for Louis XIV's Carousel of 1685.[24] Although the manuscript was certainly compiled by André Danican Philidor, the royal music librarian and one of the two brothers who first played it, it is possible that, like a number of other works in this manuscript, this march might be by the brothers' father, Jean.[25] It is impossible to be certain, for the score, in André's handwriting, says *Marche de timballes a 2 timballes qui a été faite et batus par philidor au Carousel de Monseig' a Versailles en 1685 par Les 2 philidor Laisné et Cadet*. The upper part is marked *Partie de Philidor cadet* (Jacques Danican Philidor), with timpani tuned to e and g, and the lower *Partie de Philidor laîné* (his elder brother André) with G and c. Thus it is clear that it was the brothers who beat the piece ('*batus*'), but not who made it ('*faite*'), whereas the next piece in the manuscript says very clearly *Marche de timballes faite par philidor Cadet*. It does seem very possible that 'philidor' with neither *laîné* (the elder) nor *cadet* (younger) could be the father, who would require no adjective to distinguish him. Jacques' march is for one player, on c and G, as is Claude Babelon's, who was the royal timpanist, for the *gardes du Roy* which follows it. Lully wrote an elaborate suite for the following year's Carousel, for four trumpets, timpani, and oboe band; the fourth trumpet part is the same as the timpani save that the G is above the C, as is dictated by the harmonic series.[26] The rhythms in these marches are complex, with syncopations as well as rapid articulations, and there are many places where one hand must cross over the other. In one of Babelon's marches there are chords or double stopping, playing on both drums simultaneously. Nothing so elaborate was to appear in the timpani music of other nations until Beethoven's writing in his *Weihe des Hauses* overture and his Eighth and Ninth Symphonies, though as we shall see when discussing playing technique and improvisation, this may not have inhibited other players from introducing equally elaborate passages in performance.

Although the music in this manuscript is, with many other marches and *batteries* with side drum parts, perhaps more evidential for the military use of the instruments than the orchestral, the musicians of the French court were in daily contact with each other. Some were members of the *Violons*, both the small group of musicians of the chamber, which included various other quiet and continuo instruments, and the main string orchestra, the Twenty-Four Violins; others, members of the *Écurie*, belonged to the Oboes, the Trumpets Marine, the Cromornes, or the Bagpipes, and so on. However, these were not watertight compartments. We find the same names, or members of the same families, appearing in the different groups, in addition to which, while the Philidors and others were writing marches for the Carousel and playing as members of the *Écurie*, the *Chapelle*, and the *Chambre*, André Philidor was also, as royal music librarian, copying Lully's opera and ballet scores and writing out his band parts, many of which survive in his beautiful handwriting to this day.[27] Thus it is reasonable to suppose that what they played in one musical genre they, and others, were equally capable of playing in another.

The French styles of music, and the new woodwind instruments which had been developed at the French court to play this music, travelled across Europe, for both, along with French manners, language, dress, and customs, were becoming the height of fashion in all the leading capitals and courts. Purcell in England was able to write for the new oboes and bassoons and to employ French dance forms and musical styles, such as the *chaconne* of which he was one of the greatest exponents. His use of timpani, or rather his lack of use, does raise some questions, to which as yet we have no answers. One of his tasks (one assumes an official task, rather than a voluntary effort) was to write a welcome ode whenever the king came back to London from a trip to the provinces (Newmarket, sixty-five miles north of London and already a centre for horse racing, was a favourite haunt of Charles II) or a somewhat more formal ode for the monarch's birthday, and these odes, as one would expect on a state occasion, normally include parts for a pair of trumpets. Sometimes, curiously, they do not include a timpani part but instead imitate the timpani with their bass line, using tonic and dominant and typical timpani rhythmic patterns.[28]

One wonders why this should be. Was there no timpanist available? As we saw in the previous chapter, they were by this time certainly on the court establishment lists. Could it be that state timpanists had never learned to read music? But if so, why sometimes is there a part for them? Surely there could not be financial restraints, leaving Purcell unable to find a fee or porterage expenses for a timpanist on a state occasion? There are no apparent references in the Court Records which would indicate that a timpanist was not available in 1690 and 1691, but was available in 1694. Seven trumpeters, including the serjeant trumpeter and the kettledrummer John Maugridge, accompanied the King to Holland from 1 January to 13 April, but *Welcome Glorious Morn*, the birthday ode for Queen Mary, was performed on 30 April 1691, by which time they should have been back, and even if they were not, there were at least two other kettledrummers on the royal establishment.[29]

The 1690 ode, *Arise my muse*, which is in the key of D, is scored for flutes (i.e. recorders), oboes, trumpets, strings, and basso continuo and, Peter Holman suggests, 'to which, presumably, was added timpani'.[30] The opening 'Symphony', which Holman describes as 'probably the earliest example of an Italianate trumpet sonata by an Englishman', is for the two trumpets and has a timpani-like bass in C [common] time and in 6/8; the ritornello in 'Sound your instruments' also has a similar bass, with just the obvious timpani notes, D and A. To construct a suitable timpani part would not be difficult; the question is whether, as Holman suggests, one would be justified in doing so, even in so obvious an example as this. Also problematic are some of the earlier odes which have suggestive texts, for example the welcome ode for 1686, *Ye tuneful muses*. This has a chorus 'From the rattling drums and the trumpet's loud shouts' which, although scored only for strings, has trumpet-like upper parts using only the notes of the harmonic series and a bass using only tonic and dominant.[31]

Whether the original performers really did add such instruments is one of the many mysteries which plague musical history, the answer to which was no doubt blindingly obvious at the time, to the extent that nobody bothered to write it down for, as was then normal, the composer was there and in charge of the proceedings. As we have already suggested in connection with Monteverdi's *L'Orfeo*, this is an area where modern performers are often more liberal than musicologists, whose duty is to assess the evidence for every departure from the written notes, and often for the notes themselves. The performer, whose aim is to produce an exciting and convincing performance, is inclined to say 'Of course they did', while the musicologist is more inclined to reply 'But how do you know?' There is no solution, and with every performance a decision has to be made, one which inevitably will fail to please at least one, and often both parties.

When assessing the evidence for the use of timpani and other more exotic instruments one has also to bear in mind the economics of publishing and the practicalities of the market. To take just one example, much of Purcell's theatrical music, the incidental music to plays, survives only in a posthumous publication.[32] This was for string instruments only, presumably judged by his widow and the publisher to be a better-selling format than any more varied combination of instruments. Any purchaser could make whatever elaborations of orchestration he wished in those days long before any considerations of copyright or musicological 'authenticity' arose. It would be rash to take any of the music in this publication as evidence for the original instrumentation, so that we are today ignorant of the original orchestration of much of Purcell's dramatic music.

He used timpani comparatively rarely, even in those of his theatrical works for which original scores do survive, and this was true of his contemporaries also. While one or two trumpets appear in *The Prophetess or The History of Dioclesian* (1690), *King Arthur* (1691), *The Fairy Queen* (1692), *The Libertine* (?1692), *Timon of Athens* (?1694), *Don Quixote* (1694/5), *Bonduca* (1695), and *The Indian Queen* (?1695), it is only in *The Fairy Queen* and *The Indian Queen* that kettledrums appear in the scores, and there only sparingly.[33]

Purcell's near-contemporary Vivaldi seems never to have written for timpani at all, but then much of his music was written for the girls' school by which he was employed and the range of instruments which the young ladies played may have been wide enough without adding such unladylike instruments as kettledrums. It is also possible that the timpani appeared later in Italy than elsewhere.

In Germany and Austria one can find examples of timpani writing scattered through the volumes of the various *Denkmäler der Tonkunst* and *Das Erbe Deutscher Musik*. One example is Schmelzer's *Drei Stücke zum Pferdballet für sechs Trompeten mit Pauken* of 1667, but these are little more than elaborated *Aufzüge*, similar to but more elaborate than those given by Speer.[34] This elaboration of the basic three- or four-trumpet and drum fanfare is clearly an outgrowth from the trumpet-privilege establishments, many of which would show their superiority over the next court or city by increasing the number of their trumpeters. If one has this many trumpets, it is sensible to write for them, and a mounted ballet for the cavalry is a very obvious occasion for the use of trumpets and drums. Biber wrote at least two works of this type with timpani and multiple trumpet parts, Sonata *à* 7, of *c.* 1668, for 6 Tromba and Tamburin (which has the notes c and G and therefore must have meant timpani) and Organo, and Sonata *S Polycarpi à* 9 of 1673 for 8 Tromba, Tympanum (again c and G), Basso continuo, and Violone.[35] The most famous, and perhaps one of the last examples of this style of writing for trumpets and timpani, is the *Concerto a VII Clarini con Tymp* by Altenburg, which he printed as a supplement to his *Versuch* on five fold-out leaves.[36]

A much more normally orchestral work with timpani by Schmelzer is his *Sonata con Arie zu der kaiserlichen Serenada* of 1672, which is written for three trumpets, strings, timpano, but with c and G, and organ.[37] Biber also wrote for more general combinations, but in a rather older style than Schmelzer (much of his music is highly idiosyncratic), for example his *Missa Sti Henrici* of 1701 which is scored for two clarini, three trombe, tympano, again with c and G, and a ripieno of three trombones, strings, voices, and organ.[38] These examples of Tamburin, Tympanum, and timpano show how vague composers were on nomenclature. Biber's Tromba is equally singular, though there are six or eight of them, but other composers happily mix singulars and plurals. It may be that the singular is used for us because there is only one player, but whatever the reason, it does emphasize that one needs always to look at the music.

Except in France, where Charpentier followed Lully with timpani in a number of works, it is not really until the next generation, that of Rameau in France, Bach in Germany, Handel in Italy and England, that the timpani became firmly established as a regular and expected part of the orchestra. Even then, most composers were fairly sparing in their use. One inhibition was the matter of key, to which we have already referred; only when writing in C or D major were timpani and trumpets available.

In England, Handel was well aware that the use of such instruments is effective in inverse proportion to its frequency: the more routine their appearance, the less exciting the result. Thus the first appearance of the timpani in *Messiah* is in the 'Hallelujah Chorus', at the very end of Part 2 of the oratorio, even then only after an initial fourteen-bar rest, and they are heard again only in the penultimate chorus, 'Worthy is the Lamb', and in the final 'Amen' to which it leads. Handel was not alone in this feeling. Rameau, for example, quite often uses them only once, sometimes twice, in the course of one of his stage works and this attitude continued with other composers well into the Classical period.

Timpani – the instruments

This is the period from which we begin to see percussion instruments surviving, though kettledrums are not only rare but almost always very difficult to date. One pair in the Brussels Conservatoire Museum appeared at an exhibition in Paris catalogued as German seventeenth century.[39] They are made of wood and are rope-tensioned, the larger 26 cm in diameter, the smaller 25 cm, the depth of each 19 cm (10¼, 9⅞, and 7½ inches respectively). As Mahillon observed in his Catalogue of the collection, the sizes are more reminiscent of the medieval nakers than of Renaissance or Baroque timpani and he gave no date for them; his text reads as though he suspected that they were

18. Pair of timpani from Schloss Thurnau, Germany, second half of the seventeenth century.

much more recent than the seventeenth century.[40] Schlosser in his Vienna Catalogue preferred to be no more specific for a pair in that collection than '17. bis 18. Jahrhundert' – they look as though they might date from the second half of the seventeenth century.[41] Their diameters are 62 and 57.2 cm, and their depth is 35–36 cm (24½, 22½, and 13¾–14 inches), fairly typical sizes for baroque drums.

A very similar, but much smaller, pair in Cologne is dated to c.1700.[42] The Museum's conservator has kindly measured the drums in more detail than is published in the museum's printed catalogue. The overall diameters are 37 and 38 cm (14½ and 15 inches), shell diameter 34 and 34.3 (13⅓ and 13½), overall height of each 23 (9), of which the kettles measure 17.5 (6⅞) and the iron stands 4 (1½). The diameter of the airhole in the base of each drum measures 1 and 1.2 (⅜ and ½). Over each air hole, projecting up into the interior of the kettle, stands a funnel in the shape of a trumpet bell, that in the smaller drum 7 cm high and 7.5 in diameter (2¾ and 3) and that in the larger 10 high and 12 in diameter (4 and 4¾).[43] We shall return to these funnels below. These detailed dimensions give us a useful distinction between the depth of the drum itself and of the drum plus its stand or feet which were usually fixed to the bottom of the shell to prevent it being damaged when placed on the floor in storage, for copper is a soft metal and easily dented.

A pair that is rather more certainly seventeenth century (ill. 18) was sold at Sotheby's auction rooms in London in 1974.[44] These came, with three side drums, their sticks, and a tambourine, from the Armoury of the Counts von Giech at Schloss Thurnau in Franconia. They belonged almost certainly to the first Count, Christian Carl von Giech, who lived from 1641 to 1695, so they are probably not as early as I suggested in my *World of Medieval & Renaissance Musical Instruments*.[45] Their shells are almost cylindrical with rounded bottoms, not, as is more usual, quasi-hemispherical or -conical shells. Their diameters are 48.9 and 51.4 cm (19¼ and 20¼ inches) and they are 38.6 cm deep (15¼ inches), very different in size from the alleged copies which have been available from a firm reproducing early instruments for over twenty years.

I measured an eighteenth-century pair of timpani in the museum in Poznań many years ago. These were of copper, one with five tuning handles and the other with six. A third drum looked to be of similar date but was made of brass. It had no skin and one could therefore see that it had a metal funnel round the airhole in the base of the drum.[46] During the 1967 Galpin Society tour of museums in Budapest and Prague I measured one pair in Budapest, both of which had the internal funnels.[47] In Prague I was able to measure three pairs and one set of three drums, no. 520. There is little or no evidence for the use of three drums at this period, but these looked as though they belonged together. The pair no. 143 both had the internal funnels and were each the same diameter, whereas pair no. 886 had a funnel only in the smaller drum; the larger showed no trace of there ever having been one – one can usually see traces of solder where one has been lost. The third pair, whose number I failed to record, was very unusual. The shells were lathe-turned from massive blocks of wood. Both had warped slightly so that their circumferences were no longer exactly circular. Each had the internal funnel and these were of pottery instead of the more usual brass.[48] The sizes of these drums are:

	diameter	depth
Poznań pair	58.5 cm (c.23 ins)	–
	55.9 (22)	–
single	58.5 (23)	–
Budapest	60.5 (24)	31 (12¼)
	57.5 (22½)	31 (12¼)
Prague 520	62.0 (24½)	–
	60.5 (24)	–
	52.5 (20¾)	–
Prague 143	54.0 (21¼) both	–
Prague 886	58.5 (23)	–
	55.0 (21⅝)	–
Prague wood	48–50 (19–20)	24 (9½)
	46.5–49 (18¼–19¼)	24 (9½)

These are typical sizes for the period. One reason that the wooden pair is rather smaller than the others may simply be the daunting task of turning them on a lathe. The marked difference in diameter of the smallest drum of the group of three (520) may be an indication that they are not in fact a set; while this would be a normal step in size for the nineteenth century, it is uncommonly wide for the eighteenth.

There are several pairs of early timpani in the Germanisches Nationalmuseum in Nuremberg, and these and their beaters have been catalogued in admirable detail.[49] Their sizes are within the above ranges and therefore do not need to be repeated here. However, this is the only published catalogue known to me which illustrates, in an excellent close-up photograph, an example of the internal funnel around the airhole referred to above. Ill. 19 here illustrates a similar funnel in a drum for which I was asked to provide a new head.

The shapes and sizes of these funnels vary widely from drum to drum, though these can only be exactly determined when a skin is either torn or missing, or when the head is removed for some other reason.[50] Some, like those in Cologne, are the shape of small trumpet bells, others are closer to horn bells, wider and rather flatter in shape, with the flare more exponential than conical.[51] The pottery ones on the wooden drums in Prague are gently flared, rather like flower vases, and are much higher than most in relation to the depth of the drum, coming closer to the heads. The heights of funnels relative to the depth of their drumshell and the distance from the head are other variables which are seldom if ever recorded.

A pair of timpani in the musical instrument collection of the Smithsonian Institution in Washington has funnels which are somewhat like wine goblets, with a cup-shaped opening above a conical shaft.[52] Robert Sheldon was asked to restore these drums, which measured 23 and 22 inches in diameter (58.5 and 56 cm) and reported that when the funnels were reinstalled they 'not only make the drum sound better when struck in the center but also make it possible to use the higher drum in a range where it ought to function in relation to the other drum (a 4th or a 5th higher)'.[53] Dr Sheldon added that 'the higher drum only wants to work in an appropriately higher range when struck near the center of the head'.[54] Various authors have surmised that these funnels amplify or improve the sound, but so far as I know this is the only case where a pair of drums has been tested without and then with them and the result clearly described. Since eighteenth-century drumskins are no longer available, there must still be some slight uncertainty as to the funnels' function, but it seems very probable that these experiments have provided the true answer. One suspects that the drum makers of the period had only a somewhat hazy idea of how these funnels worked, as of acoustics in general, for otherwise there would be much

19. One of a pair of eighteenth-century timpani with an internal funnel round the airhole.

greater uniformity in size, shape, and height (I have never seen two pairs the same in these respects). Any experiments would be very difficult to devise today, for it would require a very considerable number of patterns to confirm both their true purpose, and the best design with which to achieve it.

One confirmation of Dr Sheldon's suggestion is the small difference in the diameters of a pair in this period. As will be seen from the examples above and those in the Nuremberg catalogue cited, there is seldom more than an inch or two between the diameters of each drum of a pair and often less. This is in marked contrast with normal practice from the nineteenth century onwards when what one still thinks of as the D and A drums would show a difference of around three inches (75 mm) in diameter (late nineteenth-century and early twentieth-century standard sizes in Britain were 27½ and 24½ inches, about 70 and 62 cm). And yet tunings were the same in both periods, then and today, a fourth or a fifth apart, centred on d and A and c and G as the most usual pitches, and in the earlier period c and g. It would seem from Dr Sheldon's letter that the funnels helped to achieve this.

As orchestral players, we are taught today to aim carefully to strike the drum in the same place each time, approximately a hand's breadth in from the rim. In military use, kettledrums were part of the trumpet ensemble, and this implies cavalry. When one is riding a horse, and especially when one is flourishing one's sticks in the air with those graceful movements of the arms which were commended by all early writers and shown by many illustrators, so accurate an aim is almost impossible, and this remains true when the drummer has both feet on *terra firma*, as in Weigel's picture (ill. 20) and many other illustrations.[55] So long as one struck the drum somewhere on its head (while avoiding that of the horse!), everyone was happy. The resulting tone quality is not that which one would expect in the symphony orchestra, as anyone who has heard the British Household Cavalry will confirm (their drums do not have such funnels). If these funnels did ensure a good tone quality when the drum is struck in the centre of the head, as Dr Sheldon has shown that they do, it would explain why they were so widely used in Central Europe in the seventeenth and early eighteenth centuries.

Regrettably, at present we do not have sufficient information to know whether the funnels were also used elsewhere. There are still comparatively few museum catalogues which include any detailed information on timpani and it seems to occur to few cataloguers to put a finger through the hole in the base of the shell and feel whether there is a funnel standing round it. The funnels are always a close enough fit to the airhole that they can be felt in this way whenever they are present. When they have been lost or removed, one can often feel the ring of solder which had secured them and which still remains round the hole. Such drums with funnels that I have found elsewhere, for example in St Petersburg and Moscow, looked Germanic in style and I can only say that I have never yet encountered funnels in drums which looked as though they had originated in Britain or France; one wonders why they were not used there.[56] The rarity of reports of the presence or absence of these funnels makes it impossible to attempt any coherent history of their use, but the fact that they were never fitted in the Von Giech drums described above suggests that their provision may have begun at the very end of the seventeenth century, or the beginning of the eighteenth. We have as yet no evidence at all for a closing date.

20. Timpanist. Joh.
Christoph Weigel,
Musicalisches Theatrum,
Nuremberg: Weigel, early
eighteenth century.

   With the exception of the very small pair in Cologne (and of the doubtful pair in
Brussels), all the above drums are the normal instruments of the period. They had to
be of such a size that they could be mounted on horseback or, as in some processions
noted in the previous chapter, on humanback and therefore could not be larger than
a strong horse could carry. However, there was one regiment in every army which,
although it used horses, was not limited to what could be carried on their backs, and
this was the artillery. If guns were to be drawn by a team of horses, then why not also
kettledrums? And so chariots were built, mounting a pair of much larger kettledrums,
with the drummer seated behind them in a commanding position on a raised throne.
   Just when artillery drums were introduced is unknown, but they were certainly in
use in the English armies in Marlborough's campaigns in the Low Countries in the
first decade of the eighteenth century and, as Farmer suggests, they are likely to have
been copied from already-existing Continental trains of artillery.[57] With the drums

21 Double drums, English, mid-eighteenth century (*above*), and single drums by MacConnell, Woolwich, mid-nineteenth century (*below*); the mechanism of the latter is shown in ill. 28.

mounted on a chariot, there was no limit to their weight, though their musical function and the size of available skins imposed some limitations. Certainly they were always considerably larger, and deeper, than normal drums and in English they were known as double drums because they were double the usual size (ill. 21).

Farmer records Handel's use of a pair of these drums, borrowed from the Royal Armouries for special performances, indenting for them to the Master of Ordnance each time he required them. Of the three pairs of drums used for the original performance of the *Music for the Royal Fireworks*, it is thought that one pair was these double drums.[58] Unfortunately there is no contemporary detailed description of them and they perished in the fire at the Tower of London in 1841.[59] All estimates of their size are guesswork, based on measurements of quite modern models and replicas. Tower drums, as Burney calls them, were used at the Handel Commemoration Festival of 1784, but whether these were the same double drums as Handel had used seems uncertain.[60] Burney says that

> the Tower drums ... are those which belonged to the Ordnance stores, and were taken by the duke of Marlborough at the battle of Malplaquet, in 1709. These are hemispherical, or a circle divided; but those of Mr Asbridge are more cylindrical, being much longer, as well as more capacious, than the common kettle-drum; by which he accounts for the superiority of their tone to that of all other drums. These three species of kettle-drums, which may be called tenor, base, and double-base, were an octave below each other.

The 'double-base' drums were specially made on Mr Asbridge's model, and were of copper, 'it being impossible to procure plates of brass, large enough'. There is confusion regarding the medium size because Handel's tower drums are thought to have been part of Marlborough's train of artillery, rather than captives, and anyway the drums now in the Armouries were said to have been captured at Blenheim, not Malplaquet. Certainly the idea of three octaves is improbable and it is possible, as Blades suggests, that the difference between the Tower drums and Asbridge's lay in the 'length', and thus the capacity, rather than the diameter.[61] A surviving pair of double drums in the author's collection measures 27½ and 33 inches (70 and 84 cm) in diameter and 18½ and 21¼ (47 and 54) in depth.[62] They are more cylindrical than hemispherical, and thus similar to Mr Asbridge's. Whether they sound an octave below normal drums of the period is debatable – it is very difficult to distinguish between the much richer tone quality and a lower pitch. Another drum of this type is in the Museum of Theatre, Music, and Cinema in St Petersburg, where it is labelled as a *tulumbaz*, a Russian folk instrument.[63] It may well have been used in this way, but undoubtedly it began life as one of a pair of artillery drums. Unlike my drums, it once had a funnel over the airhole.

Skins in this period were thick. Edmund Bowles suggests that the surface was fairly rough and uneven in thickness, but states that they were normally made by the parchment maker by 'the traditional method [which] corresponded almost exactly with that employed in the production of parchment sheets for medieval manuscripts'.[64] It is a rare medieval manuscript whose leaves are left rough by the parchment maker (it would make writing very difficult and illumination impossible) and, while some leaves in manuscripts do differ in thickness, sometimes quite considerably, even from one edge of the same folio to the other, many do not. Some manuscripts have leaves as even in thickness, from folio to folio, as the pages of any modern book, showing that many parchment makers were highly skilled, as indeed one would expect in a trade whose customers were royalty, bishops, and other people of wealth and status. A military drummer might not have been too concerned about tone quality but been content with a rough and uneven skin which would, as Bowles rightly observes, provide a very dull tone. An orchestral player, on the other hand, would be more likely to pick his heads with as much care as any modern player and to demand a much higher quality. The skin of the smaller of the Von Giech drums described above was torn, and therefore I was able to measure its thickness, which varied from 0.42 to 0.25 mm (0.0165–0.0098 inches), bearing out Edmund Bowles's remarks on the unevenness of many drumskins, but these we know from the Sotheby catalogue came from the Armoury of Schloss Thurnau and were therefore military instruments.[65] The drums are now in a European private collection and, because their purchaser at the sale intended to play them, I fitted skins of similar but much more even thickness.

Skins were then skived by hand (scraped with the special demilune knife described above while stretched on a frame), and it is a mistake to assume that modern machinery can do more accurate work than the experienced craftsman can do by hand and eye.[66] One always tries a number of skins when choosing heads, whether for early or modern drums, and selects what seem to be the most appropriate in thickness and the best for texture and evenness. When doing so, I have found that finger and thumb are a perfectly adequate check for uniformity of thickness, and the general feel to the hand to be a sufficient check for texture, smoothness, and consistency.[67] Thus it would seem unfair to castigate all drummers of this period as producing crude tone and harsh sounds. Some undoubtedly did so; we have enough contemporary remarks to prove it, but some do so today also, and yet other timpanists are as consummate artists as any other musicians. Such accusations against long-dead musicians whom one has never heard seem to be on a par with the condemnation of all Baroque trumpeters simply because some were unable to bend their 11th and 13th partials into tune. It is axiomatic that composers do not write notes which they know are going to be ugly or out of tune in the hope that in two hundred years time someone will invent valves for trumpets and new skins for timpani – if the music could not be played to the composers' satisfaction in their own day, they would not have written it that way. The fact that they did so is in itself evidence that at least some performers could play with grace, musicality, and beauty.

As we saw in Vienna and elsewhere, the sticks were normally plain wooden, or occasionally ivory shafts with discs for their heads. There were three pairs in the Prague museum, two with plain wooden discs, the third with the discs covered with kid leather. Modern performance has shown that, with evenly lapped heads of a good thickness and good quality, wooden discs give a precision of rhythm, a clarity of pitch, and a quality of tone quite impossible to achieve with modern drums, modern heads, and modern felt beaters. The harsh rattling sound demanded by Holst, for example, in 'Mars' from *The Planets*, and by other composers who in modern times ask for wood sticks, comes from the use of wood on modern, thin heads, whether they are made of skin or of plastic.

The change in heads came, as Berlioz was the first major composer to note, in the middle of the first half of the nineteenth century and it followed the general adoption of the splitting machine. Various mechanisms for splitting skins, and thus getting two or even more usable sheets of leather or parchment from a single animal, were invented from around 1780, though not until 1811 was a method devised for controlling the thickness precisely.[68] Further improvements in this technology followed throughout the nineteenth century.[69] Once the thickness could be controlled, these machines could produce much thinner skins than could be skived by hand. We simply do not know when thinner drumskins became available, nor when musicians became dissatisfied with the sound of plain wooden sticks. As we shall see in chapter 7, Berlioz must have heard the sponge-headed sticks at the Paris Opéra in his student days, and he seems to have been the first composer to ask for them, in his *Symphonie fantastique*.[70] We can only assume that from 1815 or so, some timpanists at least had been using thinner skins and that at least one had invented a stick capable of producing a good tone quality from them. As so often, things come fortuitously together, and thin skins with soft-headed drum sticks were ideal for nineteenth-century music, just as thicker skins with wooden-headed sticks were ideal for the music of the Baroque and Classical periods and, as we shall see in the next chapter, in the late eighteenth and early nineteenth centuries allowed Beethoven's drummers to play with ease patterns which today are a constant worry to even the best of us.

What is unknown is the extent to which covered sticks were used in the earlier periods. We do know that drums were draped (*coperto*) to mute or muffle them for funerals, because we have noted examples above.[71] Speer says that the drum heads were covered with a woollen cloth for this purpose.[72] Whether players also used covered sticks to add to the dullness of the sound is unclear. Altenburg says that they did for funerals; this was in 1795, but they may well have done so earlier also.[73] It is possible they may also have been used in orchestral concerts to give a softer sound, for Eisel said in 1738 that cloth or leather covers could be used on the beaters.[74]

Edmund Bowles suggests that covered sticks should be used for all music written between 1750 and 1850, save for fortissimo passages when plain wood is permissible.[75] It is important to stress that this is one player's opinion and one that may possibly be biassed due to difficulties in obtaining skins of adequate quality – I can only say that I (no doubt equally biassed) have had no problems with plain wooden sticks and careful playing, and in fact that my own inclination would be the reverse of Dr Bowles's, to use covered sticks only in fortissimo passages, to ameliorate any consequent harshness of sound.[76] Speer suggests controlling tone and volume by playing near the centre of the head for louder sounds, and near the rim for softer, so producing echo effects.[77] He makes no mention of covering the sticks, nor does he mention the existence of internal funnels, which would help in this process, but perhaps he took those for granted.

Timpani – players and playing technique

As the use of timpani in orchestral music became more and more a matter of course, it is quite apparent that a new breed of timpanists grew up to cope with it. Where some of the earlier music referred to in this chapter is very simple, at least in its written form, often appearing only in *tutti* and *ritornelli* passages, usually no more than any competent *Aufzüge* player could be expected to improvise, as we move into the early eighteenth century, timpani writing became not merely more elaborate but more subtle. In 1733 Bach opened his *Dramma per musica* for the birthday of the Queen of Poland and Electoress of Saxony with a solo for the timpani, an effect repeated the following year when he used this opening movement of *Tönet, ihr Pauken* again for his Christmas Oratorio.[78] Nor is this his only solo passage; there are many throughout his *œuvre*. Much of his writing requires considerable subtlety in its performance and careful phrasing in its execution. The same is true for Handel and other composers. By this time solo passages abound and the marking *piano* or 'soft', and similar indications of precise requirements in other languages, are not infrequent.

The extent to which players added improvised figuration to their music is less well understood. This was undoubtedly the custom in the fanfares and *Aufzüge* to which we have frequently referred, both because sometimes there is no timpani part at all, so that it must be improvised, and because the bass line is often obviously unsuited to timpani, with long, held notes which any drummer, just like any harpsichordist, would automatically break into suitable figuration. Altenburg gives us some information on this, with a number of examples of *Schlagmanieren* or stylish beatings.[79] Unfortunately he leaves it to the teacher to explain just how these 'single-tonguings', 'double- or crafty tonguings', 'dragged tonguings', 'double-cross-beatings', 'rolls', and 'double rolls' should be used.[80] Although on the next page he gives an example of a timpani part for an *Aufzug*, this is very simple and does not include any of these fancier beatings.

The use of the word 'tonguing', while not unexpected in a tradition in which trumpeters and timpanist were trained together, is itself useful. When a trumpeter is single-tonguing, each note is separated by a stroke of the tongue against the back of the teeth while maintaining the air pressure; the closure of the space between the teeth by the tongue and, most important, the tongue's sharp removal from the teeth, as in enunciating the letter 't', gives a clean and incisive beginning to each note. Similarly, the drummer's single-tonguing on the drum gives a clean, clear rhythm. When the trumpeter double-tongues, the tongue is bounced to and fro between the back of the teeth and the roof of the mouth, practised (today) by articulating 't-k-t-k', though in the Renaissance and Baroque less crude consonants were preferred such as 'diddle-liddle' and 'tirra-lirra'.[81] The initial and thenceforth odd-number consonant might go at the same speed as the single-tongued notes, with the even-number bounces effectively doubling the speed.

With the wooden-headed sticks then in use, the drummer could do exactly the same, using the same technique as his non-commissioned colleagues on the side drum.[82] Thus one can assume that the drummer's double-tonguing (see music examples below) was played by using the 'dada-mama' technique and could easily run at double the speed of single-tonguing.

Equally, the *Tragende Zungen*, 'dragged-tonguings' of two notes on each drum, could easily be played in this way, with interesting implications for many of Beethoven's timpani parts. Triple tonguing was also used on the trumpet, using either 't-t-k-t-t-k' or the rather more difficult 't-k-t-k-t-k', according to which the player finds easier or more convenient. Altenburg does not mention this for the kettledrummer; his *triolen* are simply eighth note (quaver) triplets. His *Doppel-Kreuzschläge* are just that: both hands crossing from drum to drum so that both beaters strike each drum, presumably simultaneously. The notes are written as a single note each time with two stems, one up and one down, but it would take careful playing to avoid a very close flam, and in fact this is how Richard Strauss does notate very close flams in the side-drum part in *Der Rosenkavalier*, especially when writing in waltz rhythm.[83]

We have seen Speer's version of a roll in the musical example on p. 60.[84] No drummer in recent times has been heard producing such a figuration, which represents a very different interpretation of the word roll from that which we normally understand. On the other hand, Altenburg's roll or *Wirbel* is also very different from what we would expect. There is still much we do not know.

To what extent were such techniques used in the eighteenth-century orchestra? And to what extent were written parts elaborated in performance by the players? There is at least a little clear evidence for some such use. Mozart provides a much more elaborate timpani part for *Messiah* than Handel does, not only breaking and elaborating long notes at cadences, but also breaking a number of single quavers into semiquavers in general passage work.[85] One presumes that the reason that Mozart had to do this was precisely the same as that which impelled Altenburg to produce his treatise. The great social changes at the end of the eighteenth century meant that people were no longer constrained to follow the same trade as their fathers – no longer was it true that if your father was a baker, almost certainly so were you, and equally so with trumpeters and kettledrummers. In addition, the courts with their corps of trumpeters and drummers were breaking up as Napoleon overran the German states, and also musical styles were changing. There was no longer the demand for the high and exacting trumpet parts which had necessitated so many years of apprenticeship and training; at the same time, there was no longer the willingness to undergo such training and, with the beginnings of the collapse of court patronage, such training was often no longer available. Which of these was chicken, and which egg, is beyond the scope of this book, but the result was that Altenburg, one of the last trumpeters to be trained in this way, against all tradition decided to reveal the secrets of the trumpet guild, an action which, a generation earlier, would have resulted in condign punishment from his colleagues. Equally Mozart, because no kettledrummers were being trained in such improvisations, felt that he needed to write out the parts when he produced his own edition of *Messiah* with 'modern' orchestration so that the drummers of his day would play what Handel's drummers would have done automatically as a result of their training.

There is, of course, the performance-style implication that Mozart expected the drummers of his own period to play what he put before them, neither more nor less, both in his own music and in his Handel arrangements. Was he alone in this respect? As so often, we do not know.

Handel, of course, was not the only composer of his period to write timpani parts, so what about other composers in the Baroque? Purely subjectively one has the feeling that Bach did not expect such elaborations, that when he wanted them he wrote them himself, and this applies to all instruments save for the most obvious cadential trills. Even in the 'Dona nobis pacem' (and of course the identical music of the 'Gratias agimus tibi') of the B minor Mass there seems no need to break the long notes into smaller units, but I emphasize that this is a personal reaction. For me, even the last note can sing in the air without a roll, but this is a specific contradiction to what Speer said. However, there are still questions left to the drummer's good taste, even in the B minor Mass. The timpani part in the 'Sanctus' cannot be played as it is written. A quaver plus four demisemiquavers (eighth-note plus four thirty-seconds) cannot be consonant with the prevailing triplet quavers of that chorus (music example a). Either one plays, in triplets, crotchet and four demisemiquavers (music example b), or quaver and four semiquavers (music example c, see all overleaf). The former (b) is exciting and effective; the latter (c) is what happens in the 3/8 'Pleni sunt coeli' into which the 'Sanctus' runs without a break. Each drummer (unless constrained by the

conductor) has to choose between excitement and what I suspect Bach intended.[86] For other composers, one can only say that it depends on the taste of the player and, inevitably, the permission of the conductor or musical director.

It is undeniable that we use far less ornamentation today than would have been taken as a matter of course in the eighteenth and nineteenth centuries. No violinist today would ornament the adagios as specifically taught by Corelli and Telemann.[87] Nor would any singer or other soloist be permitted today to ornament the *da capo* repeats as extensively as everybody did then. It is thought that modern audiences would not appreciate it, though it is difficult to see on what grounds this conclusion is reached, since they have never been given the opportunity to try. At least one should be aware that gracing, as it was then known, was expected originally, and one should also be aware that to some extent the timpanist was a soloist and would be expected to lead in such matters, something which might not apply to other bass members of the orchestra – his status as an officer lingered on after Altenburg's time and even today, enthroned above the rest of the orchestra, some elements of this status are still with us.

One ever-present form of elaboration was *stile francese* or French style. We noted above the influence of French fashions in all aspects of upper-class culture. This was just as apparent in music, with composers such as Telemann, a far more fashionable and esteemed composer than J. S. Bach in their day, introducing the French *Ouverture*. Even Bach succumbed to fashion and wrote Overtures and French Suites. The two main French musical characteristics in this period were the use of ornaments, especially to fill gaps between non-adjacent notes (everybody ornamented cadences, not just the French) and the use of *notes inégales*, lengthening the first of a pair of notes so that they become slightly unequal. It is arguable that when composers used French for the titles of their works, rather than their own language or the normal Italian, they were indicating their desire for this effect. Hence, for example, Menuet rather than Minuet in Handel's *Fireworks*. Certainly 'swinging it a bit', probably the nearest equivalent in our language, adds a great deal of life to that and other music and lifts it from the stodginess one sometimes hears without the need for the excessive speed which is a common modern recourse.[88]

A substitute for timpani

Daniel Speer describes very briefly, and somewhat obscurely, an instrument designed to substitute for timpani in churches, especially when used as a bass to the *tromba marina* instead of to real trumpets.[89] This is a wooden box just over a metre long and about a foot (30 cm) wide and deep, standing on four legs with a heavy contra-G gut bass string running across the top, with a tailpiece at one end and a tuning screw at the other. The string is divided by a bridge, higher than that of a bass violin [the name used for the violoncello at that period], so that one part of the string is longer than the other. It is tuned with a tuning key to g and c, like the kettledrums, and is played with drumsticks which are wound tightly one hands-breadth from the tip with strong string. This instrument sounds like covered kettledrums.

Speer thus makes it clear that it can produce a tonic and dominant and provide a timpani part, and of course one must wonder, as suggested above, whether this might have been the instrument which Lully used in the *Serse* ballets. I have never encountered another description of such an instrument, but this is not necessarily evidential though it may suggest that the instrument was used only in Germany or even only in 'Würtenbergerland', the state in which Speer's town of Göppingen was located. String substitutes for drums are not rare across the world. Instruments made of bamboo are common throughout Indonesia; the string is usually cut and raised from the cortex of the bamboo itself.[90] In Hungary the *gardon*, an instrument looking like a roughly made cello, is struck with a drum stick and also plucked with sufficient force that the string slaps on the upper surface of the neck, an effect frequently imitated by Bartók in his string quartets. According to Bálint Sárosi, the only drum used in traditional Hungarian music (other than military bands) is the friction drum, and the *gardon* is thus a drum substitute, with the additional advantage that it is tuned to act as a drone.[91] Another drum substitute which produces a drone is the Basque *txuntxun* (there are various names), a rectangular zither with half a dozen or so strings tuned to the tonic and dominant and all struck together with a wooden stick to give a drone of dual pitch. This is used with the pipe as a substitute for the tabor, though today rather more among the French Basques than the Spanish – one of its names is *tambourin de Béarn*, the name of one of the French Basque provinces. It can be seen in a few medieval illustrations and it is clear that the instrument once enjoyed a wider distribution than it does today.[92] Even now its influence is strong enough that the main Basque pipe and tabor periodical is called *Txuntxuneroak*.

Other drums

The tabor was still in use, especially the deep Provençal *tambourin* in France. Rameau scored it in *Hippolyte et Aricie* in 1733, for the 'Rigaudon en tambourin', and it is arguable that it should be used in other dances which are entitled 'Tambourin' – at least this was why I was asked to play it in the production of *La Princesse de Navarre* around 1970. Rameau also scored for side drum in *Zaïs* in 1748 and in *Naïs* in the following year. The available edition of his music, while perhaps somewhat clearer in score than that of Lully, is little more reliable, and again we await better versions.[93] Unfortunately, none of the conductors who are performing such sterling work in the revival of Rameau's music seems willing to publish the scores that are used.[94] The *tambourin*, like any other tabor, would have been widely used as a folk instrument, as it still is today in Provence.

The side drum was of course still in use as a military instrument and the Philidor manuscript cited above is full of *batteries* for side drum and marches with side drum accompaniment. They are interesting for their rhythms but give us no indication of any use of rolls or other typical side drum techniques – no flams, drags, or ruffs, just some occasional demisemiquavers (thirty-second notes) which one would assume to have been played on the bounce.

Bells and their substitutes

Bells are always a problem for percussion players. Real bells are enormously heavy, far too heavy to put on the concert platform, weighing tons rather than pounds. In the Baroque period, Bach was, until recently, thought to have used two of them, Handel wrote some quite extensive melodic parts for them, and Mozart, if we may run on into the period covered by the next chapter while we are on the subject, wrote at least one very elaborate part for them.

The mourning cantata, no. 53, *Schlage doch, gewünschte Stunde*, was once attributed to J. S. Bach.[95] This requires two bells, one written in modern editions as the E a third above middle C and the other as the B a fifth higher.[96] The score says *campanella*, which suggests a small bell, rather than *campana*, but one feels that an 'awaited hour' should strike rather than tinkle; the text does say '*schlage doch*', 'strike please'. One of the Westminster quarter-chime bells which precedes Big Ben, the hour bell, sounds that same E, and that bell weighs 33 hundredweight (1676.5 kg).[97] The B would weigh rather less, but still far more than could be accommodated inside a church, and the mind boggles at the idea of trying to persuade two musically illiterate ringers up the tower of the church to sound their bells at anywhere near the right points in the score. However, the 1990 second edition of Schmieder's catalogue now relegates the work to Anhang II. 23, citing Alfred Dürr's reattribution of the work to Georg Melchior Hoffmann, and adds a note of 'Orgelregister' against the bells.[98]

What sort of bell substitutes might have been built into the organ is unfortunately not specified; Karl Hasse calls it a *Glockenspiel*, which suggests steel bars, and it may well have sounded an octave or two above the specified pitch, as would a normal glockenspiel, though this would seem to ruin the effect suggested by the text.[99] An *Orgelregister* could be some combination of pipes whose sound, in conjunction, might produce some imitation of the sound of a bell. Such an effect was well within the powers of a 1930s cinema organ – whether it was possible for mid-eighteenth-century organ builders must be left to the experts in that field. The only thing that is certain is that the part cannot have been played on real church bells.

Handel wrote for Carillons in the third scene of the first act of his oratorio *Saul*. The part is written for a transposing instrument in G.[100] It is in the treble clef on one stave but with two lines of notes. On its first appearance in a 'Sinfonie pour les Carillons' and in the following chorus 'Welcome, welcome mighty king' it is mostly in parallel octaves, though with occasional four-note chords. The compass covers a range of two and a half octaves, though each line requires only an octave and a half. The writing is mainly diatonic, in running quavers (eighth-notes), with only a very few chromatic notes, occasional B naturals and C, F, and G sharps. It reappears in the next chorus, 'David his ten thousands slew', with rather more confidence: above the parallel octaves there is now figuration in thirds, and the lowest note extends the range a tone lower. In this chorus the scoring is typically full, with two oboes, two trumpets, timpani, three trombones, and strings, which suggests that it must have been quite a powerful instrument to have been audible in such a context. So what was it?

Charles Jennens, Handel's librettist, wrote to his cousin Lord Guernsey on 19 September 1738:

> Mr Handel's head is more full of maggots than ever. I found yesterday in his room a very queer instrument which he calls carillon (Anglice, a bell) and says some call it a Tubalcain, I suppose because it is both in the make and tone like a set of Hammers striking upon anvils. 'Tis played upon with keys like a Harpsichord and with this Cyclopean instrument he designs to make poor Saul stark mad.[101]

This does not, unfortunately, tell us much. It suggests that it had iron or steel bars, and although the term 'cyclopean' suggests that these were large, the facts that, if there were only one player, the keys had to be played in octaves with one hand and in thirds with the other, and that Jennens says that they were like those of an harpsichord, suggest that the bars cannot have been much larger than those of a modern glockenspiel.

Michal's recitative 'Already see the daughters of the land', which follows the Sinfonia in which the carillons first appear, was, in the autograph, originally to be accompanied by carillons, and this short recitative is there fully figured.[102] Since the figuring includes such chordal indications as 8/5/3 (a common chord of third, fifth, and octave), an indication of the harmony so simple that no normal continuo player would require it, it is absolutely clear that the intended player was not a keyboard player. Thus even though Jennens said that it had keys like a harpsichord, Handel cannot have meant the harpsichordist to play it. While the first entry, in the Sinfonia, could have been played on an instrument like a Flemish carillon, with wooden bars struck with the fists as a 'keyboard', the last entry, in the chorus, could not unless there were two players, one playing the octaves of the lower part, the other playing the thirds of the upper part. The earlier four-note chords, like those of Michal's recitative, could have been spread.

The part in *Il Penseroso* (contrasting with *L'Allegro*) of 1740, where it is used in only one aria, is much more complex. It is written there on two staves, treble and bass, mostly with each hand (or just possibly each player) in parallel octaves again. The range is much wider, covering over three octaves. This part survives only in a manuscript in the Fitzwilliam Museum in Cambridge and it does not appear in all editions of the score.[103] The instrument was used also in the 1739 revival of *Trionfo del Tempo*,[104] and in performances of *Acis and Galatea* in the winter of 1739/1740.[105] What happened to the instrument after 1740 is not known, but Handel seems not to have used it again. However, it or perhaps some substitute presumably continued in use, for a certain Mr W. L. describing a new organ stop in 1772 compares the sound to 'the steel bars used for the Carillon in the oratorio of Saul'.[106]

Thus we are still left with very little idea of what it was. The sound resembled that of hammers on anvils; it was a transposing instrument, sounding either a fourth lower or a fifth higher than written; it was loud enough to be heard through a full orchestra and chorus; it could play semiquavers (sixteenth-notes) in running octaves and in broken chords at a normal *allegro* pace; it had keys like a harpsichord but it was not played by an experienced keyboard player, at least not on its first appearance in *Saul*. It seems unlikely that we shall ever know anything more about it, though speculation is fascinating. For example, if, as Jennens states, it sounded like hammers on anvils, it is likely that it was a series of steel bars. The bars must have been quite thick, to sound like anvils, which suggests that the pitch was above rather than below the written notes.[107] It also suggests that the action must have been quite heavy because a light hammer would make little impact on a thick bar, and would not sound like a hammer on an anvil. Perhaps this is why the player was not accustomed to playing keyboard instruments – on the other hand he would have needed a reasonable keyboard technique to be able to play the part. At every turn we meet another puzzle or another contradiction.

Purely as a speculation, it might, in its initial appearance in *Saul*, have been a form of Flemish practice keyboard.[108] These have the normal wooden-bar 'keyboard' of the real carillon, but there are hammers which strike bronze (bell-metal) or steel bars so that the whole instrument requires little more space than an upright piano. It could then have been played by one, or more probably two *carilloneurs*, expert on the instrument but not familiar with harmonizing bass parts and therefore needing the help of the figures for those basic chords which were normally recognised without figures. Still more speculatively, by the following year, perhaps an improved model had appeared, with lighter action, a wider range, and a true keyboard action, so that a more complex part could be written for it, and perhaps played by a harpsichordist. One should bear in mind that there is no evidence for such speculation other than the diverse musical parts written for the instrument and the other considerations cited above.[109]

Unfortunately there is no reference to any such instrument in the Patent Office records, nor has anyone yet produced any other reference to it. Handel was quite enterprising in his orchestration, as we have already seen with timpani and side drums, and he experimented with some otherwise unknown string instruments, including one invented by the leader of his orchestra, and occasionally scored such unusual instruments as a bass transverse flute.[110]

We know little more about the instrument which Mozart used for Papageno in *Die Zauberflöte*, save that it was made of steel, for Mozart calls it, on its first appearance, *strumento di acciajo*. Again it must have had a keyboard, and one that was capable of quite florid writing, for the part in 'Ein Mädchen oder Weibchen' is played three times, each time more elaborately than the time before, and it certainly needs a properly skilled keyboard player. The range is quite small, from the C within the bass stave to the D above the treble, three octaves and one note, and it may not have been fully chromatic – the only notes required are those of the keys of G, C and F major, the 'white' notes plus F sharp and B flat. Whether it had bars or small bells, we do not know. A small instrument with hemispherical cup bells, perhaps laid out like a glass harmonica, each cup set concentrically within the next larger so that only enough of each projected to match the width of each key, would have been perfectly practicable, and would perhaps have sounded better than one with bars. There is an instrument in the Museum of Rosenborg Castle in Denmark, built into a very elegant bureau made for Frederick V, with exactly the range required, though with brass bars, and Mette Müller, who played the music on it, reported that 'the instrument suited the purpose well'.[111]

Others

One rather unusual 'instrument', one that is a special form of bell, appears in Marc-Antoine Charpentier's incidental music for the first production in 1672–3 of Molière's play about an inveterate hypochondriac, *Le Malade Imaginaire*. This, according to Hitchcock's Thematic Catalogue, is an unspecified number of apothecaries' mortars.[112] They seem to have been dropped from the music for the two later productions in 1674 and 1685 for which Charpentier's music survives. A passage from the autograph quoted by Shirley Thompson shows quite rapid reiterations in two interlocking parts, one on c″ and the other on g a twelfth lower, though this seems likely to have been intended to sound an octave higher.[113] These accompany a chorus in praise of the doctor. A traditional mortar is a bronze vessel looking very much like a bell but standing on its apex instead of hanging from it – resting bells, though more bowl-like in shape, are common in Japan and other eastern areas – and many bell-founders had a useful sideline in the production of such mortars.[114] The demand for church bells may be somewhat spasmodic, but there are always more apothecaries coming into the profession and needing mortars. Certainly such a mortar, when well made, will ring like a bell and, in a comedy such as Molière's, make a very satisfactory jangle.

The use of domestic and suchlike paraphernalia for quasi-musical purposes has a long and respectable history. The London apprentices had a well-founded tradition of bringing out the tools of their trade on which to bang and clatter, and there is of course the constantly repeated Shakespearian reference to tongs and bones. Many cultures also had their 'rough music', which is perhaps best known from Italy, as a standard expression of social disapproval of misconduct. It is not often that such 'instruments' appear in the concert orchestra or even the opera, though Wagner's anvils and Johann Strauss's spurs and pop-guns are obvious examples, but the film studios are another matter. Anything which will make a particular sound may be called into play, both for feature films and for advertising material. Even in my own fairly limited experience I can recall being asked for tuned Chinese tea-bowls (with specific pitches unlike Britten's slung mugs for *Noye's Fludde*), sounds that would imitate whales, another to characterize a larcenous spider, and I can remember wandering around the studio hitting everything therein to find something which would effectively represent John the Baptist's head falling to the ground.[115]

Chapter 6

The Classical Period

This is the period, from the 1750s onwards, in which our symphony orchestra became established in its present form. With it, for the two are inextricably linked, came many of the musical forms which today we take for granted, such as the solo concerto, which in this period was changing from its Baroque style, and the overture and the symphony, which initially were more or less interchangeable in name and indistinguishable in form.

The basis of the Baroque orchestra had been a string band, varying in size and constituents, with the occasional addition of such wind instruments as were required. During the second half of the eighteenth century, as composers moved through the Rococo towards the Classical style, the string band stabilized as first and second violins, with a single group of violas, and a foundation of *bassi*, a term covering both violoncello and double bass and usually still a keyboard continuo. To this band were added a pair of oboes, who might often be asked to double on transverse flutes for a central slow movement, usually softer in style than the outer allegros, and a pair of horns. Bassoons played *col basso*, often whether specified in the score or not, probably resting when the oboes did so. Trumpets and timpani were sometimes added, but still only when the key of the music was suitable. In England, some composers wrote for timpani with horns, which could already play in almost any key because by now they were provided with a larger range of interchangeable crooks than were trumpets. This practice seems to have been less common on the Continent, where trumpets and timpani remained, in the early part of the period, almost inseparable.[1]

By the end of the eighteenth century, this linkage between trumpets and drums had weakened. This was partly due to the gradual break-up of the trumpet guilds and to the contemporary social changes, and partly to a growing adventurousness among composers and to a desire for greater freedom in their orchestration. In the middle of the century, when trumpets were still built only in D, the linkage had remained strong. While the addition of a crook between mouthpiece and instrument allowed them to play in C, there was no way to subtract tubing to play in higher keys than D, and when composers wrote in those keys trumpets and usually drums were perforce excluded. Even when the shorter E flat trumpet was introduced in the last decade or so of the eighteenth century, this was only a partial relief.[2] One way out of these restrictions was to write for timpani in the home key and for trumpets in C or D if either key would produce any useful notes. Natural trumpets, without valves or any other artificial aids, could produce the common chord of their own key from the second to the twelfth harmonics:

So for a work in G major, the composer could use trumpets in C for their G and D and, as the music moved to other keys in its progress, some other notes as well, and could happily write for the timpani on G and d.[3]

Haydn could write for C trumpet and F and c timpani in the slow movement of his Symphony 102 in England in 1794, but this seems not to have been possible for Mozart in Austria eleven years earlier in the slow movement of his Linz Symphony, no. 36, which is also in the key of F, for while the horns are in F and the trumpets in C, the drums are in G and c. The most probable reason was the lack then in Austria of a drum big enough for a good low F.

The timpani

Judging from the music that was written for them, it was towards the end of the eighteenth century that the timpani began to increase somewhat in size, especially the larger drum of the pair.[4] When instruments were made specifically for orchestral use they did not need to be small enough to carry on horseback. For the same reason the use of the internal funnel seems to have died out. This growth coincided with the adoption of a longer crook to take the trumpet down to the low B flat, which seems to have come in the 1790s in England and perhaps not until the end of the century on the Continent. This made larger drums necessary because in the key of B flat players would need a good F on the larger drum of the pair and an equally good B flat on the smaller, notes which were available to Haydn from 1792 in London but perhaps not to Beethoven in Vienna until 1807.[5] A drum that had been used for G and A would not be large enough for a good F; tuned down that extra whole tone, the head would be too slack to give a good sound. The same would apply to the smaller drum, and the obvious answer would be to tune the larger drum up a semitone from A to B flat, where it would have a good ringing sound, and bring in a new drum, some two or three inches wider in diameter, for the low F. This would also mean that when, in a slow movement, the key changed to E flat, as it does in Beethoven's Fourth Symphony, the B flat could remain on what has now become a middle-size drum and the upper e flat could go on the old smaller drum, tuned up a semitone from its normal d. It would have been very difficult to play those three notes, low F, B flat, and e flat on the older pair of drums because it would mean taking each from very slack to quite tight, and then back again, taking the large drum up from F to B flat between the first and second movements and down again for the scherzo, and the smaller drum similarly from B flat to e flat and back.

If these three sizes of drum did exist, as it seems certain from the music that they did, the older model pair measuring something around 22 and 24 inches in diameter, and the newer pair measuring around 24 and 27 inches, the question is whether there is any evidence, rather than the surmise above, that anybody used them as a set of three. Did Beethoven's drummer really use three drums when the Fourth Symphony was performed? Perhaps. Jonathan Del Mar pointed out that Beethoven wrote to

Count Oppersdorf in 1808, saying that his 'new symphony [the Fifth] has three trombones but certainly not three timpani'.[6] Why should he have said this unless his drummer had had the sense to bring in a third drum to make his life easier in the Fourth and both Beethoven and the Count had noticed this? There is no evidence to support this hypothesis, but the combination of tone quality and convenience on the one hand and the letter to Count Oppersdorf on the other would seem to encourage such speculation.

Certainly Abt Vogler had already used three drums by 1803, when he wrote a true three-drum part with effective quasi-melodic figuration for them in the overture to his opera *Samori*,

and his pupil Weber added a third drum to the overture to his opera *Peter Schmoll* when he prepared the concert version in 1807, the same year as Beethoven's Fourth. Weber also used three in the overture to *Beherrscher der Geister* in 1811.[7]

Pride of place, though, must go to Mozart's rival, Salieri who wrote for three drums in c, G, and d throughout his opera (strictly a *dramma eroicomico*), *La secchia rapita* in 1772, with true three–drum parts such as the following short example.[8]

Edmund Bowles cites many early nineteenth-century authors bemoaning the lack of a third drum in the orchestra, long after the dates of the above works.[9] As will be apparent from the foregoing, I have a strong suspicion that the lead here came from the drummers, some of whom were more enterprising than others, and that some composers, seeing what was available, took advantage of it. Certainly today any drummer will work out for himself a convenient solution to any problem in the music and there is no reason to suppose that earlier players were any different – independently minded, we always like to go our own way.[10] The remaining puzzle is why any other composer or orchestral director who wanted a third drum, and had the space for it, did not apply a little persuasion to that end. While there are always some players who resist any change, the extra *thaler* or two is often persuasive.

Another major change at this time was the demand for players to retune the drums. In the Baroque period, once the drums were set, that was it, except for the constant need to check for drifting due to changes in ambient temperature and humidity. With the new freedom, it often became necessary to retune between movements. In the orchestral world this may have been no problem, for there was normally little imperative for great haste between the movements. In the opera pit this could be quite another matter. A few bars of recitative, a couple of lines of dialogue, are sometimes all that divide one aria or chorus from another. For this reason, T-handles were introduced to replace the old tuning screws, which had been topped with a square block to which a loose key had to be applied, one by one. According to Edmund Bowles, T-handles were invented by Rolles, a French maker of military instruments, around 1790.[11] An eighteenth-century pair of drums with tuning handles in the

Kunsthistorisches Museum in Vienna looks somewhat older than that, but dating such instruments precisely is always difficult.[12] The intention was not only to avoid the inevitable clank as the key was put to and removed from the block topping each screw, but more importantly to allow the player to use both hands to tune. Turning two handles at a time, one can retune by a tone in three or four *moderato* beats. This allows no time to check the pitch, so that one or two extra bars rest are always much appreciated, but with one's own drums one can be surprisingly accurate. Composers were, as always, happy to take advantage of any new development and began to expect a change of pitch during a movement.

Here again, Salieri seems to have led the way. In his *La Grotta di Trofonio* of 1785 he asks for both drums to be retuned, from c and G flat to d and A.[13] He allows sixteen bars for this, a very short time if a loose key was still the only available tool. This use of a tritone, a semitone more than the more usual fourth, c and G flat instead of c and G, was also a radical step in the use of timpani. His pupil Beethoven used a similar interval in *Fidelio*, but here a semitone less than a fifth, A to e flat. This is far better known but it was not the first, though it is the earliest example that still holds the stage.[14]

Tuning drums a fourth or a fifth apart is no great problem even during the course of a piece of music, for one can always check the pitch of one drum against the other. With a fourth between them, humming the octave of the lower drum into the upper will produce a resonance that shows that the drums are in tune – if there is no response, humming a little flat or a little sharp until the resonance responds will reveal which way the error lies. With a fifth between them, humming the pitch of the upper drum into the lower will achieve the same result. This is why members of the audience sometimes ask us if we are smelling the drums, leading to the answer, among others perhaps less printable, that when perfectly in tune they smell of roses. Changing from d and A to G and d, as in Beethoven's *Missa Solemnis*, between the 'Osanna' and the 'Benedictus', would thus take far less time than the forty slow bars which Beethoven allows, especially since by then T-handles were surely available in Vienna.[15] One needs only to sound the d drum quietly, with a flick of the finger, to remind oneself of its pitch, and then while humming that pitch quietly into the larger drum with one's mouth and ear close to the head, turn the handles until the drum responds evenly to the hummed pitch.[16]

Tuning a tritone, as in Salieri's *Trofonio* and Beethoven's *Fidelio*, is more difficult, as is the somewhat improbable minor sixth, A and f natural, in the scherzo of Beethoven's Seventh Symphony. Octaves, as in the Eighth and Ninth symphonies, are also surprisingly difficult because, with the skin of one drum fairly slack and that of the other very tight, their overtones are not as well in tune as they should be. As a result, what should sound as an octave, with the first overtone of the lower drum adding power in unison with the upper, may not do so.

So far as we know, skin thicknesses were still much as they had been and, as a result, some of Beethoven's characteristic passages were very much easier to play then than they are now. With wooden-headed sticks one can employ the various bouncing strokes characteristic of side-drum technique and controlled double strokes are easy.[17] Such notorious passages as the repeated octaves at the end of the finale of the Eighth

Symphony can be played with one hand on each drum. The rhythm can be as precise, and the sound clearer than with the modern elaborate cross-hand technique which is essential with thin skins and felt-headed sticks. This applies to all those passages with pairs of rapid notes on each drum, a favourite practice of Beethoven's. Even if soft leather or cloth were tied over the wooden heads, as James Blades, Edmund Bowles, and other writers have suggested, this technique remains possible, as experiment will show. It is, however, the present author's firm conviction that accusations of harshness of sound from wooden sticks are quite unfounded, provided that both sticks and heads are suitable and well chosen and that the player shows proper musicality and skill.

There is no evidence at all for how other passages were played, whether rolls, for instance, were played hand to hand as we do today or with double beats as on the side drum, and it is probable that players, as always, simply pleased themselves:

or L RxLR L RxL R etc.

When played hand-to-hand, as in the lower handing, the 'x' shows where the left stick crosses over the right. The track of the two sticks is somewhat like a rainbow, the left stick following the upper margin of the bow, the right stick the lower, so that each forms its own arc.

Nancy Benvenga says that when using a side-drum-style roll the sound is stifled because the second stroke stops the vibrations of the first.[18] This would, of course, be true with modern felt sticks as well as with the sponge-headed sticks which came into use in the first quarter of the nineteenth century. It is not true, however, with wooden-headed sticks or even with such sticks with a thin leather cover, any more than it is for the side drum. The drumheads also make a difference; the thinner skins of the nineteenth and twentieth centuries are more adversely affected by double-beating than the thicker heads of this period, for these help to encourage a livelier bounce. It should be unnecessary to add that timpanists never held their sticks as a side drummer does. The two grips are quite different and each can be seen clearly in Weigel's engravings in ill. 20, in the previous chapter, and ill. 22 here.[19]

It is important to stress, though, that there is no written evidence for the use of double beating, using one hand on each drum, in the Beethoven passages referred to, but it was so recently a normal part of the technique of any properly trained timpanist, and so much easier and more natural than the modern cross-handing, that it would be incredible were it not to have been used.

Timpani notation

This sometimes causes problems. While timpani parts today are always written at pitch, both for contemporary music and for modern editions of earlier works, many composers of the Baroque and Classical periods treated the timpani as transposing instruments, writing c for the tonic and G for the dominant, but noting 'in D' or 'D & A' for whatever key or pitches were required at the beginning of the first line. This causes no problems in the keys of C, D, or E, but in the key of G it means that the

22. Military side-drummer, Joh. Christoph Weigel, *Musicalisches Theatrum*, Nuremberg: Weigel, early eighteenth century.

instruments are reversed because the keynote or tonic G must be on the lower drum and the dominant D on the higher. However, the music will have the tonic G written as c in the second space of the bass stave and the dominant D written as bottom-line G. Thus the player must play the low drum when he sees the higher note and vice versa, something that one can get used to but which is distinctly confusing. I for one would prefer to write the part out in the normal modern way if there is time to do so.

Ways of writing rhythms and rolls can be more seriously confusing. So long as rhythms are written out in normal note values there are no problems save those of compatibility, as in the Bach 'Sanctus' discussed in the previous chapter. Equally, so long as rolls are notated with *tr* or some other conventional symbol such as the ~ noted above in Schütz's music, again there is no problem. Where the problems arise, as they begin to in the Classical period, is with abbreviations. A short diagonal line through the stem of a minim or crotchet, or above a semibreve (half, quarter and whole notes respectively), is the conventional abbreviation for quavers (eighth notes). Similarly, two such lines (and one line through the stem of quavers, which already have one tail) indicates semiquavers (sixteenth notes). Neither of these abbreviations is likely to cause any problems in music at slow or moderate speed, but in *allegro* and faster *tempi* the two slashes might indicate a roll. To my mind it should always be possible, in a Haydn symphony, for example, where one often finds this notation, to keep such passages rhythmic, especially while using wooden sticks and if necessary a controlled double-beating. It could be argued, though, that wherever the number of slashes indicates a note value shorter than that prevailing for other instruments in the movement, they do mean a roll: if the fastest notes in other parts are quavers, then two slashes in the timpani part could be a roll. As so often, we have to use our best judgement and our own preferences.

But three slashes can indeed cause problems. While that did become accepted notation for a roll in the later nineteenth century, in much of Schubert's and Beethoven's music it becomes far more difficult to assess. For instance, in the slow movement of Schubert's Unfinished Symphony, rhythm seems the more effective realization, and this applies to many other passages in his music also. For example, in bar 50 of the slow movement of the Unfinished a roll might be intended, for the mark is *pianissimo* and *diminuendo*, but from bar 96 onwards other members of the orchestra are playing demisemiquaver (thirty-second note) passage-work, scales and arpeggios, so obviously we should also. My own feeling is that we should do so throughout, save in the final bar. The first movement of Beethoven's Ninth is a real problem. At bar 17 we have *tr* ⌇⌇⌇⌇ marked, so clearly this is a roll. To shoot ahead, from bar 387 we have crotchets with three slashes, *pianissimo* with a steady *crescendo* to *forte* at bar 401, at which point we have a group of four demisemiquavers leading to a quaver. Difficult as it may be to articulate demisemis clearly when *pianissimo*, it is not logical to play a roll and end with rhythm for the same note values. Between these examples, from bar 301 we have the famous passage with the single demisemiquaver A at the end of the bar.

Obviously this must be rhythm. But, because all the wind instruments also have the final demisemi as a separate note on the end of a note held through the rest of the bar, there are few conductors who can be relied on to give this strictly in time. So what does the poor drummer do? Play fifteen Ds and an A, as Beethoven wrote and not worry about anyone else? Go on playing as many Ds as may be necessary to fill up the time the conductor holds on? Or play a roll and stick the A on the end of it? And in that case there is likely to be muttering from the cellos and basses who have been faithfully playing steady demisemiquavers on each crotchet beat. One thing is certain: if the final A is not exactly in time with the wind, the drummer is in trouble. Just to keep one's wrists supple, the demisemi Ds go on for another twenty-eight bars after the last A. As always, any realization must depend on the taste and musicality of the player, as well perhaps as on the speed which the conductor adopts and the instruments, the beaters, and the acoustic of the hall.

A problem that arises more often in the middle or later nineteenth century, but which it may be sensible to mention here while we are discussing the matter, is the presence and more particularly the absence of ties. Where a roll is carried across several bars, linked with a tie from bar to bar, clearly one smooth roll is intended. Where, however, either there are three slashes or a *tr* in each bar, and no ties, does one play one smooth roll or does one mark each bar line with a slight accent suggestive of a renewed attack? Dvořák was a particular offender in this respect, writing a separate *tr* over each of a number of consecutive bars.[20] It is generally assumed that one smooth roll is required, but it is only an assumption.

Composers can be very careless in this and other details, often due to haste. Schubert provides another example of this: when he wrote an accent it was often as a slashing horizontal V instead of the short > to which we are accustomed, and this has frequently been misinterpreted in modern editions as the sign for a *diminuendo*. It is very unlikely that he expected some of his final chords to fade away – far more probable that he expected them to start with a good thump and then sustain.

Timpani parts

Many works from this period have already been mentioned and the standard Classical period repertoire is well enough known that little more needs to be said. Edmund Bowles's forthcoming book on the history of the timpani will be a mine of information in this respect, especially the section 'Representative Milestones in the Music for Timpani' which he was kind enough to send me in advance.[21]

Haydn is in some ways the most satisfying to play of the 'big four' composers of this period, for he was himself a competent timpani player and his writing is always pointed and effective. He gives us many good moments, including effective solos as in the roll which gives Symphony 103 its name and in the *crescendo* semiquavers that follow the trumpet's interjection in the second movement of the Military Symphony. He asks for muted drums in Symphony 102, but this is a subject better discussed in the next chapter because it is so common a feature in French operas.[22]

Although his writing for timpani is seldom as graceful and as grateful as Haydn's, Mozart provided us with one of our few solo roles, in his *Serenata Notturno*, K. 239. This is an unusual work, a late *concerto grosso* for two violins, viola, bass, and timpani, with a *ripieno* of string orchestra.[23] There are also two *divertimenti* for flute, five trumpets and four timpani, the second of which (K. 188) was written by Mozart, presumably in emulation of the first (K. 187), of which he and his father had made a copy but which had been written partly by Joseph Starzer and partly by Gluck.[24] They are, of course, pieces written for special occasions, like the Philidor marches and Biber and Schmeltzer works mentioned earlier, and quite distinct from orchestral and operatic works.

Beethoven is always exciting to play, and sometimes hair-raising (for example, the 'Minuet' of the First Symphony, which goes at *scherzo* speed). His parts vary in complexity, one of the most elaborate being the overture *Weihe des Hauses*. There seems no particular reason why Beethoven should have written a more elaborate timpani part there than in any other overture, but he did. He also provided us with another solo role, though it is very seldom heard. The year after writing the Violin Concerto he transcribed the solo part for piano and provided his own cadenza to the first movement in the form of a duet for piano and timpani. This version of the work is hardly ever played, but Max Rostal, and perhaps some other violinists, have arranged the piano part of that cadenza for violin and retained the timpani part. In some respects Schubert, who was untrammelled by the deafness which afflicted Beethoven, wrote more effectively for the timpani, as he certainly did for trombone. His timpani parts are always a delight to play, even if they are not always as concordant with the harmonic context as they should be.

Military percussion

The second half of the eighteenth century saw an increase in the size and sonority of the military band. Where the fife and side drum had sufficed, something with greater panache was now required. New wind instruments had been developed, oboes, clarinets, horns, and bassoons, which together became the standard wind octet and sextet under the name of *Harmonie Musik*. This ensemble was used both as a military band, with an increase in the number and type of percussion instruments to match, and for the entertainments similar to those for which our own military bands still play on civic band stands and for private parties. Many composers wrote serenades and divertimenti for these ensembles and, just as for military bands today, all the popular theatrical works had their best tunes arranged for *Harmonie* in suites or *potpourris*. Unfortunately, these arrangements and serenades seem never to have included percussion; this was reserved for the marches for the band and for the *alla turca*, the Turkish Music, used either to signify the fashionably exotic or to suggest the military, as Haydn did in his Military Symphony, no. 100, and Beethoven in his Ninth.

The side drum remained as important as ever, and was still used by itself or with the fifes as an accompaniment to the march when the band was absent. With the increase of noise on the battlefield, with musketry and artillery now the norm, there was less use for it as a signal instrument, though every European war office published manuals of signals for side drum well into the nineteenth century. Kastner prints the Hanoverian drum signals for 1821, an undated Bavarian set, the Austrian signals for 1846 and the Prussian ones for the same date, the French for 1831 and for earlier periods back into the seventeenth century.[25] He also gives trumpet signals for these and other nations, many of which, similar to *Auszüge* and *Aufzüge*, are for three or four trumpets with a bottom line which is clearly also for timpani, using only tonic and dominant.

The side drum itself was getting smaller with time, as it had done since the Renaissance. Arbeau's two and a half feet had shrunk by the mid-seventeenth century to the sizes we gave above for the Armouries and All Souls. The Hanoverian drum was somewhat smaller again, as was the Napoleonic – many examples of the last can be seen in the museum in the Invalides in Paris. Their snares had multiplied, and two strands back and forth to make four seems to have been usual. The thickness would have been that of a cello A or less.

Turkish percussion

The most impressive innovation of the eighteenth-century military band was a set of instruments adapted from those used by the Turkish armies which still dominated much of Eastern Europe. The principal members of this ensemble were the bass drum, cymbals, and triangle, and the most eye-catching was the Turkish Crescent or Jingling Johnnie, a pole surmounted by a flattened brass cone, somewhat in the shape of a Chinese hat (hence the French name, *chapeau chinois*) with pellet bells or small clapper bells suspended from its rim (hence the German *Schellenbaum*), and usually a crescent moon above that (hence Turkish crescent), again often with bells. The whole thing rattled and jingled (hence jingling johnnie) as it was struck on the ground at each step. This was one instrument which did not make its way into the orchestra, though Berlioz scored for it in the *Symphonie funèbre et triomphale*. It was used comparatively seldom in Britain, where the drum major was more inclined to retain his staff. With this he could (and still does) signal, twirl it in the air, throw it up and catch it again, and remain the cynosure of all eyes as he leads the procession.[26]

Many composers in the latter part of the eighteenth century used the bass drum, cymbals, and triangle to add an exotic effect to their non-military music, and the *alla turca* became very popular. Michael Haydn's incidental music to Voltaire's *Zaïre* and Mozart's Singspiel *Die Entführung aus dem Serail* are only two of the more obvious examples. So popular did such exoticism become that piano manufacturers built these effects into their pianos, though for lack of space the bass drum was normally replaced by a hammer thumping the underside of the soundboard. The cymbal was not always a real cymbal – a metal plate would, when struck with a metal beater, produce something like the right sound. These Turkish effects were operated by a pedal, and presumably any 'authentic' performance of Mozart's *Rondo alla turca* should be played in this way and with these effects, and so probably should Schubert's *Marche militaire*.

In the band and in the orchestra, all three instruments were very different from those that we use today. The bass drum, which had derived from the Turkish *davul*, was much smaller than modern instruments, not more than two feet in diameter, and usually less. It was deeper from head to head than its diameter, being anything up to three feet deep, which is why in Britain it was called the long drum (ill. 23). It was played somewhat after the Turkish manner, where a solid wooden beater is used on one head and a light stick on the other or on the shell.[27] In the European armies the light stick was replaced with a switch (German *Rute*), like a miniature besom, or witch's broom, made of birch twigs.[28] This is why in all reputable editions of such music, some of the bass drum notes have their stems upwards, some have the stems downwards, and some have stems in both directions. The notes on the strong beats of the bar were played with the solid beater, and those filling-in on the weaker beats were played with the switch. Where stems go both up and down, both beaters were used simultaneously. Thus the later eighteenth- and early nineteenth-century bass-drum sound in a bar of typical 4/4 time military percussion was thump-chack-chack-chack, entirely different from the modern unremitting boom-boom-boom-boom which, with its overhanging resonance, is essentially unrhythmic but which plagues our performances of Mozart and Haydn.

23. Long drum, Edin[bu]r[gh] Royal Highl[an]d Vol[untee]r Reg[imen]t, *c.* 1800.

The cymbals were smaller and thicker than those used today, though larger and thinner than the medieval instruments. The sound was more of a clang than the modern clash and it was much shorter in duration. The modern sound has changed radically over the last fifty years, with the move of the major manufacturer from Istanbul to Boston, but even the late nineteenth- and early twentieth-century Turkish instruments had a much fuller, louder, and longer-lasting sound than those of the eighteenth century. Thus modern, or even fairly modern, cymbals can badly overbalance the eighteenth-century ensemble.

The triangle was essentially the same as that used in the Middle Ages, as we can see from the two examples preserved in Vienna which we have already mentioned.[29] These retain the continuous frame of the earlier instrument, and each carries steel rings, one with three rings, the other with five. Thus the reiterated ting-ting-ting-ting of the modern symphony orchestra, sounding like an impatient customer at the shop counter, is again totally different from the continuous susurration of the eighteenth century.

When did the triangle lose its rings? It is impossible to be sure. Certainly they had gone by 1855 when Liszt wrote his E flat Piano Concerto, where the writing, from bar 78 in the second movement onwards, is entirely in the modern manner. It seems very probable that they had gone by 1825 when Beethoven wrote his Ninth Symphony. Both that work and Haydn's Military Symphony, no. 100 in G, include these percussion instruments as a simulacrum of the military band, rather than to introduce any exotic Turkish atmosphere. Whereas Haydn's writing for the triangle in 1794 is the same as his brother's in 1777 and Mozart's in 1782, Beethoven's is quite different, and while one cannot prove anything, the difference seems to be due to the use of a different instrument, rather than to a different compositional style.

In the military band the players of these instruments were often dressed in uniforms as exotic as the instruments themselves, with turbans and other pseudo-Turkish dress, and there was a fashion to employ the tallest Africans that could be found – just as Othello, the Moor of Venice, has often been played in black-face, so in the popular imagination there was no distinction between sub-Saharan Africa and Turkey.[30] Both were foreign and exotic and, as this was still the period of black slavery in Europe and America, Africans were easily available whereas genuine Turks were not. Whether these players were also used in the orchestra, or whether conventional musicians also learned to play the instruments, we do not know.

Tenor drum

A new drum, the tenor drum, was introduced around the end of the eighteenth century. Its first form in England was that of a small kettledrum (ill. 24), and one of its first appearances is in an illustration showing the Changing of the Guard at St James's Palace around 1790.[31] The guard is led by the drum major with his staff,

24. Tenor drum, English, late eighteenth century. The head, now very battered, may be original.

followed by the new-fashioned wind band, with trumpet, oboes, horn, bassoon, and serpent, followed by a boy playing the new kettle tenor drum, then three Africans wearing turbans and playing the Turkish music of cymbals, long drum, and tambourine, followed by a squad of old-fashioned but still commonly used fifes and side drums, and finally the colours and the guard itself. Within a few decades the tenor drum became a cylindrical instrument, a larger version of the side drum without snares. In Germany it was usually snared and there is confusion between it and the large side drum, the *Rührtrommel* (American field drum, French *caisse roulante*). Terminology in this area is sufficiently confused that players, meeting a foreign drum name in a score, either guess, rely on tradition, or use whatever is most convenient and nearest to hand.

In the modern military band, especially the Highland Scots pipe band, the tenor drummers seem to spend more time with their sticks in the air than on the drums. Both bass drummer and tenor drummer are showmen, but since the sound of the bass drum is essential for the band's march rhythm and to signal changes when performing the intricate patterns of countermarching and the moves from one piece of music to another, the bass drummer does have to play as well as to show his virtuosity. Doubtless the tenor drummer plays also, but to the admiring eye his flourishes seem more important than his notes.

There was little uniformity between one band and another, for as yet, with the exception of France under the Republic and then Napoleon, where there was a laid-down establishment of numbers and instruments, the bands were provided by the officers of each regiment rather than by the war office or its equivalents.[32] In Britain, if the Colonel was wealthy enough he might shoulder the financial burden alone, for in those days the regiment was often his personal property – he had recruited it and he maintained it, as it were lending it to the War Office for use. If he was not sufficiently wealthy, or if the regiment was already an old-established one to which he and the other officers had been appointed, all the officers would club together to pay for bandmaster, instruments, and uniforms. The most that the government would usually do was to lay down the maximum number of soldiers that the band might include. All the same, there was a fairly general consensus on what instruments were suited to a band and, so far as the percussion section is concerned, while the instruments may have altered in shape and sound, all those that were used in the eighteenth century are still with us today.

Of all the military music of this period, what one might call the apotheosis is the symphony that Beethoven wrote in 1813 to celebrate one of the major battles of the Peninsula Campaign, *Wellingtons Sieg oder die Schlacht bei Vittoria*, op. 91.

This was written originally for a precursor of the record player or gramophone, Mälzel's Panharmonicon, a giant barrel organ with most orchestral instruments built in.[33] Arthur Ord-Hume's illustration, from a contemporary engraving, shows a pair of timpani, side drum, long drum, and a number of somewhat improbable brass-instrument bells. Alexandr Buchner's photograph, taken before the instrument was destroyed during World War II, shows one of the timpani, a side drum, a pair of cymbals, a triangle (without rings!), and parts of a number of clarinets and transverse flutes. If it included a clarinet for each note in that instrument's range, plus a similar number of flutes, and doubtless oboes and bassoons as well, rather than the more normal imitative organ pipes, it must have been a formidable instrument indeed. Although Beethoven composed his symphony for this machine, he also wrote out a score and parts for orchestra, the form in which, as the Battle Symphony, it is frequently played today.

It begins with two marches, one for the English and one for the French, each preceded by an 'Entrada', as Beethoven calls it, first for side drums and then for trumpets. Beethoven specifies that on each side of the platform there must be two suitable military drums, for the drums must provide an Entrada for each march, 'only note that the Entradas must not be too long'.[34] The marches are played by military bands of piccolo, clarinets, bassoons, horns, and trumpets, with triangle, cymbals, and bass drum for the English, and the same plus larger flutes and oboes for the French. The British march is *Rule, Britannia* and the French *Malbrough s'en va-t-en guerre* – the Duke of Marlborough was an English general but the song was a French folk song. The same music is still used for an English drinking song, *For he's a jolly good fellow*, so that the whole thing is somewhat confusing for English audiences, suggesting that both the armies were British. When each army is assembled, trumpet calls from each side of the platform signal 'let battle commence', with ratchets providing the musketry and extra large bass drums the cannon.

Beethoven is very specific. In his instructions for performance he says that the two large drums for the cannon must not be large Turkish drums but must be of the largest size:

Here they were five Viennese shoes square [does this perhaps mean five Viennese feet in diameter?] such as are used in the theatre for thunderbolts; the ordinary Turkish drums [long drums in English] are only heard in the orchestra. The cannon must be separate from the orchestra, each on their own side, one for the English and the other for the French army, as far apart as the hall allows without the audience being able to see them, so long as the director will be able to give them the beat. Whoever plays the cannon must be a good musician, and here in Vienna they were played by assistant *Kapellmeister*.[35] The machines called ratchets [*Ratsche*] which provide the small-arms fire are those often used in the theatre for thunder-cracks or platoon-fire, and they must also be on each side, like the cannon, and close to them.

The ratchets are notated simply as trills, the English on one line of the score and the French on another. The cannon are marked as black or white zeros above the score, black for the English and white for the French. The side drums, in the Entradas, are given a rhythm with four dots over some crotchets (quarter notes), presumably indicating that those crotchets should be broken into five-stroke rolls. However, when the English drums start to dominate with the 'Sturm-Marsch', Beethoven writes ruffs, three grace-notes before a pair of crotchets. Timpani are not heard until the second part, the 'Sieges-Symphonie', in which *God save the King* eventually defeats all comers.

Ratchets had long been available, for they were a standard watchman's instrument. They were even more familiar in all those parts of Europe that had adhered to the

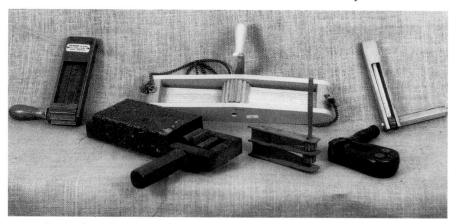

25. Ratchets: *Left to right:* orchestral by Hawkes & Son, London; English World War II ARP gas warning; English nineteenth-century child's toy; London police or watchman's *c.* 1800; American *gregger* for Purim by Simon Franks; and *(at the back)* Easter ratchet from Prague.

Roman Church, as Austria certainly had done, because they were used in Roman Catholic churches during Holy Week when the bells are silent (the traditional explanation is that the bells go to Rome to be blessed, though of course they do not actually leave the church). While children run in the streets with small hand-ratchets of much the sizes that we use today in the theatre pit or the football field (ill. 25), very much bigger ones, as substantial as small tables or on wheels like a wheelbarrow, often with several tongues each a couple of feet long and a cog with very large teeth, are used by the sexton and others in authority, and they can make a very considerable racket.[36]

Modern performances of the Battle Symphony often replace Beethoven's large bass drums and ratchets 'with Cannon and Mortar Effects', as the advertisements proclaim. These are either generated electronically, sometimes by recording real artillery and musket fire, or alternatively, when the local fire regulations permit, with fireworks. None of these sound anything like as convincing as the effects that Beethoven specified – as so often, real instruments sound better than imitations even when the instruments are themselves imitating something. As a piece of music, it really is the worst thing that Beethoven ever wrote, but as an example of the theatrical percussive elements entering the orchestra, it is a fascinating historical document.

Other instruments

So far as modern repertoire is concerned, Beethoven's Battle stands alone, but in its own time and place it might well have been influenced by the work of a composer who was unknown to the modern world until R. M. Longyear described his 'percussion enterprises'.[37] Ferdinand Kauer seems to have been the first composer since the Philidor brothers to write melodically for timpani, scoring for six drums.[38] He wrote also for xylophone, using instead of the usual German term *Strohfiedel*, another German name for it, *Hölzernes Gelächter* (wooden clatter). He used it in a number of works, sometimes with quite tricky writing including chordal passages in thirds, sixths, and fifths.[39] He anticipated Berlioz's scoring in the slow movement of the *Symphonie fantastique* by writing soft rolls for bass drum to suggest distant thunder. In his oratorio *Die Sündfluth* of 1807, which recounts the story of Noah and his Flood, the Deluge itself is depicted by full orchestra and chorus plus a wind machine, two different sorts of rain machine, a *Wetterpauke*, literally a weather-kettledrum, perhaps one of those machines that rotate barrels full of boulders or cannon balls, a lightning machine, and a ratchet.[40]

To what extent Kauer's Noah's Flood in 1807 might have influenced Beethoven's Battle in 1813, we can only speculate. Longyear could find no contemporary Viennese references to 'his orchestration or his writing for percussion'.[41] And yet if this music was performed at the Leopoldstadt Theatre and other works were played in the Josefstadt Theatre, where Kauer was music director, and elsewhere in Vienna, it is hard to believe that Beethoven had never heard of him. Vienna was not so large a city, nor were its musical circles so wide that one musician could be unaware of the work of another. Unless other researchers follow Longyear's example and discover further 'enterprises' we must assume that Kauer was unique and without successors, but nevertheless, the use of percussion instruments in non-military contexts was becoming more widespread and was already prevalent in other musical centres.

Here the conventional terms 'Classical' and 'Romantic' can become seriously misleading. 'Classical', usually meaning Haydn, Mozart, Beethoven, and Schubert, with less-known contemporaries, is taken to cover the last third of the eighteenth century and the first quarter of the nineteenth. 'Romantic', meaning Weber, Rossini, and their successors down to Wagner, Verdi, Mahler, and Puccini, is taken to cover the nineteenth century. But Weber was already eleven years old when Schubert was born and he died a year before Beethoven did. Cherubini was ten when Beethoven was born, and Spontini was born four years after Beethoven. The music of all three nevertheless belongs in the next period, and it is to them that we look for the beginnings of the general acceptance of percussion instruments in the orchestra.

Chapter 7

The Romantic Period

It was in the nineteenth century, with the rise of romanticism and scene-painting in music, that the timpani acquired a wider role as colourists and that the other percussion instruments, with which we are so familiar today, began to come into the orchestra as normal instruments, rather than as special effects. As we have seen, and as with many other instruments, the pathway into the orchestra for most of the percussion began with the military band, though a few may have first appeared in the opera pit. A common route was from the band into the theatre and thence to the concert platform. While the concert orchestra is staid and conventional in its nature and prefers to wait until instruments have acquired a veneer of respectability in other fields before accepting them, both army and stage are constantly striving for new effects to dazzle and amaze the spectators and the audience. The equivalent routes in our time are the jazz and dance bands and then through the film and television studios to the symphony orchestra. Where once it was important that one regimental band was more dazzling than the next, and thus attracted more recruits, and one opera more amazing than another, and so sold more tickets, now a new aural excitement can sell more soap-powder, cram more people into a cinema, or boost an album up the charts. Today such new sounds can migrate to the concert hall almost overnight, but two hundred years ago it had taken half the eighteenth century before composers began to think of percussion instruments, other than timpani, as sounds rather than signals.

Before the early nineteenth century, bass drum and cymbals had been exclusively for military or oriental effect, and the sound of a side drum only presaged the arrival of soldiers, as in Mozart's *Le Nozze di Figaro* and *Così fan Tutte* and in Beethoven's incidental music for Goethe's *Egmont*. Now side drum, bass drum, and cymbals came into such prominence at the hands of one early nineteenth-century opera composer that he became known as Tamburossini, from a conflation of the Italian word for drum, *tamburo*, and his name. A trawl through the volumes so far issued in the collected edition of his works suggests that the only opera in which Rossini used the side drum is *La Gazza Ladra*, first performed in 1817. The overture opens with a pair of rolls for two opposed side drums, an effect which has had many an audience on its feet expecting a National Anthem, but although they had so large a role in the overture, the drums reappear only very briefly in the finale of Act 1 and twice in Act 2. It is unlikely that it was this which made so strong an impression as to give him that nickname, so perhaps it was his frequent use of the bass drum, called both *gran cassa*, as it appears in the scores of his collected edition, and *tamburo grande*.

It is notoriously difficult to discover just what Rossini expected from his percussion players. The editors of the Fondazione Rossini Pesaro, who are producing the complete edition of his works, admit to confusion whether *gran cassa* and *piatti* (cymbals) play together all the time or not (we have much the same problem with the French opera composers whom we shall encounter shortly). Very occasionally we see indications for either bass drum or cymbals alone, but normally there is simply the single note, leaving us to guess whether both were used together or not.

In the Fondazione's scores, when they use a single-line stave, there may sometimes be a suggestion of clarity in that occasionally the note either hangs from the line, implying bass drum, or sits on it, perhaps indicating cymbals. Usually, however, the line bisects the note, meaning either both together or that our guess is as good as theirs. Confusion is worse when the indication in the margin is for *gran cassa, piatti, e triangolo*, for then one can only assume that all three play simultaneously. *Triangolo* is sometimes replaced by *sistro*, the writing for which is similar enough to that for the triangle that it is generally assumed that the two are equated.[1]

When Rossini wrote for *gran cassa* and *piatti*, he normally wrote in the modern manner, though in *Il Turco in Italia* in 1814 the *gran cassa* is written with the first beat below the line and the second, third and fourth beats above it. This is unlikely to mean one bass drum stroke followed by three cymbal clashes and probably indicates, appropriately enough for its subject, the Turkish beater plus switch of the old *alla turca* style. In several operas, for example in the overtures to *L'Italiana in Algeri* and *Tancredi*, both in 1813, and in 1817 in *Armida* and *William Tell*, he also wrote for *Banda Turca*. Here we are even further in the dark, because again there is only a single line and nowhere does this edition specify, or even discuss, the instruments which Rossini may have expected to be included in his Turkish Band – perhaps whatever the management could afford and thought would sound well. Curiously, he seems not to have asked for a *banda turca* in *Il Turco in Italia*; perhaps because the Turk was in Italy, the bass drum sufficed. It could be a valid assumption that we are here dealing with two quite different bass drums: one approaching the modern idea of a drum with a wider head but shallower in depth, contrasting with, for the *banda turca* and the Turk in Italy, the older pattern, deeper from head to head than its diameter.

Rossini specified a tamtam in *Armida* and towards the end of *Otello* he provides a five-line stave for *pioggia* (rain), *lampi* (lightnings) *e tuoni* (thunders), but all that appears on that stave is a small double slash through alternate bar lines, without indication of rhythm or dynamic, still less of instrument or sound. Once again there is no editorial discussion, in the introduction to that volume of the collected edition, of what Rossini may have intended. So far as the timpani are concerned, he seems never to have used more than two, writing for them as *Tp in mi* (with e and B on the stave) and similarly tonic and dominant in whatever other key it might be.

According to the editor of the *La Gazza Ladra* volume, an interesting note by François Henri Joseph Castil-Blaze was found on the last page of his 1824 Paris edition of *La pie voleuse*.[2]

The bass drum should be played tastefully so that it always produces a volume proportionate to the numbers of the orchestra and the character of the work. The bass drum does not play here the same role as it does in the military band and it must therefore be attacked with extreme moderation. It is only in Fortissimo that its strokes should be individually perceptible by those sitting in the centre of the stalls. It should produce in the orchestra a sound comparable with that of the tenor drum in the military band.... Sometimes its notes are printed in octaves, in which case one plays the lower notes with the *balle* [presumably the round head of the beater] and the upper with the switch of twigs or else with the *balle* Pianissimo.[3]

Rossini was not the first to write for percussion in the modern style, even if today he is the most famous. He was preceded by several of the composers for the Paris Opéra. Cherubini seems to have been one of the first there to extend the percussion beyond timpani. In his opera *Eliza ou le Voyage aux Glaciers du Mont St Bernard*, published in Paris in 1795, he uses pellet bells and jingles, as one might expect for a mule train, *tambourin*, presumably the deep tabor, with triangle for the Savoyards, a bell to attract the travellers to the monastery before they are benighted in the extreme cold, and a larger bell for the tocsin, as well as thunder effects.

Spontini went much further, calling for triangle, cymbals and bass drum in *La Vestale* in 1807, with a tamtam in one scene[4]. Two years later, in *Fernand Cortez ou la Conquête de México*, as well as adding a tambourine he asked for an *ajacatzily* which, according to Curt Sachs, was a traditional pellet-filled [*kugel-gefüllten*] gourd or clay vessel with a handle.[5] The tamtam appears again, and there are side drums, both with snares and with snares relaxed. The thunder at one point is provided by the timpanist, who has quite an active evening with a part that looks a little tricky in places, with quick and precise rhythms.

David Charlton has provided a history of the introduction of the tamtam, saying that it was first heard in the early days of the French Revolution, at a funeral ceremony for Swiss guards in 1790.[6] Gossec was the first composer to score it, in his *Marche Lugubre*. There was, at this time, no shortage of occasions when a funeral march was required as the Revolution consumed its own leaders. Gossec was followed very quickly by a number of other composers who included it in their operas and in other works in the 1790s and the first decade of the nineteenth century, and the association with funerals was firm enough for the instrument to be scored in similar contexts in operas also. Where and how the particular tamtam that was used came to Paris seems not to be known, but it is clear that there was just this one instrument. Berlioz also says that the tamtam is only used in funereal music or at moments of horror and in dramatic situations.[7]

The treatises

Berlioz's *Traité d'Instrumentation* is the first of two influential treatises on composition of this period, the other being that of Georges Kastner.[8] Kastner also wrote excellent tutors for a number of instruments and his *Méthode de Timbales* is one of the earliest of the many written for that instrument.[9]

In the percussion section of his *Traité* Berlioz, naturally, devotes the most space to the timpani, discussing their range, which he says is limited to one octave, F to f, with the larger drum covering F to B flat and the smaller B flat to f. He points out that the sound of the two lower extremes (the F and B flat) is poor because the skins are too slack, and that the alternative, in that key, of B flat and f is likely to be better because both drums are then at the top of their range and the skins are tight. He does not mention Spontini's use, in *La Vestale*, of high g as a matter of course, and even high a at one point. He inveighs against the custom of writing for the timpani as though they were transposing instruments, pointing out the difficulty of playing backwards, as it were, with the higher note written as the lower and vice versa. He says that the problem of getting good low notes is the difficulty of getting skins wide enough to cover larger drums, and that there would be no problem in making smaller drums for higher notes. One wonders whether English cattle were, at this date, larger-bodied than the French, for it would seem that drums in Britain had no trouble with these pitches, and indeed that the reverse was true, that it was often difficult to get up to f, still more to the high g. Could it be that the well-known affinity for beef in Britain encouraged larger breeds of cattle than on the Continent and thus led to the earlier introduction of larger drums?

Berlioz bewails the lack of the third drum in most orchestras, though he does mention that the Paris Opéra uses three.[10] He says that it would be better to have two players, each with a pair of drums, and better still to have the two pairs of drums with four players, one for each drum. He then cites, as an example of what one can really achieve, the 'Tuba mirum' from his *Grande Messe des Morts* of 1839. This requires two pairs of drums with a player to each drum and a further six pairs, each with one player per pair, ten players on sixteen drums.[11] Nor is this all: there is also a bass drum tuned to B flat, playing rolls with two timpani sticks, another bass drum playing repeated sextuplets with the normal heavy beaters or *tampons*, a tamtam and three cymbals which, like the tamtam, are to be struck with beaters. While this may seem excessive, it is in fact a glorious noise, especially when one is in the middle of it.[12] Equally effective, although not cited in the *Traité*, are the *pianissimo* passages (with *crescendi*) for four players, each on one drum, in the *Symphonie fantastique* at the end of the third movement, and the *pianissimo* passage for eight at the end of the *Grande Messe des Morts*.

What is especially significant here, bearing in mind Berlioz's reputation as a great innovator, is the rigorous adherence to pairs of drums. The preference for two or four players on two pairs of drums over one player, or even three, on three drums is surprising; the advantages of three or more sizes are, as we discussed in the last chapter, so great that it is astonishing that Berlioz seems never to have used them.

He describes three types of timpani beater, those with wooden heads which are best used for loud and violent passages, those with wooden heads covered with skin, which are therefore less loud and which regrettably, he says, are usually the only beaters used in most orchestras. The third are the *baguettes d'éponge*, the sponge-headed sticks, which are the best and the most musical in use and the best in sound. 'They allow the player to produce many nuances in style and they have the advantage that their elasticity helps the timpanist to play *pianissimo*.' He says, too, that composers in the old days used to ask for veiled or covered drums, using a piece of cloth on the head to reduce the sonority, but that the use of *baguettes d'éponge* achieves the same results and is greatly preferable.[13]

One sees this request for *voilées, couvertes,* or *sourdines* (muted) in many French operas from the end of the eighteenth century onwards, and according to Edward Cone, Berlioz wrote *sourdines* in the autograph of his *Symphonie fantastique,* changing it to *baguettes d'éponge* in the printed score.[14] This suggests that such sticks were fairly new when he was writing that work in 1830, or, as Edmund Bowles points out, when he called for *baguettes d'éponge* in *Eight Scenes from Faust* two years earlier, and therefore later in development than is suggested below.[15] It seems unlikely that Berlioz, whose knowledge of the orchestra was already clearly very considerable, would have been unaware of their existence if they were already in common use. Certainly he became a strong advocate for their use, and it was he who introduced such sticks to Germany on his 1842 tour, where they were previously unknown, carrying several pairs with him.[16]

Finally, Berlioz emphasizes that, contrary to the belief of many musicians, the pitch of timpani is as written in the bass clef, in unison with the same notes played by the cellos, and not an octave lower. This belief that the timpani sound at sixteen-foot pitch, an octave lower than written, has been so strong that Percival Kirby went to considerable trouble to prove that the perceived pitch is as written.[17]

Berlioz goes on to discuss the use of bells, illustrating it with Meyerbeer's famous f and c bells in *Les Huguenots.* Curiously, he does not mention any problems in obtaining notes so low. Meyerbeer himself was emphatic that those pitches were essential and that the effect would be lost if they were an octave higher, but he does not say how this is to be achieved. If they were true bells, the c would weigh anything from six to ten tons and the f more than three, and would require cradles and enough height for the ropes to swing them or their clappers, which one would think impossible for any theatre, though perhaps Paris was so equipped. Meyerbeer was also concerned about the clappers for the bells which should, at different points in the last act, be covered in leather to give a distant effect. We do not know what his bell *tampon* was like (if he used a real church bell, the striker would be the usual massive iron clapper), but in the orchestra today on tubular bells (orchestral chimes) we normally use the hammers of coiled rawhide that one can buy from any ironmonger (hardware or tool store). Most of us glue a disc of sole leather to one end of the hammer for precisely the same reason: to produce a softer sound when required.[18]

Under the name of *jeux de timbres* Berlioz describes a bell tree, a set of eight or ten cup-bells mounted concentrically in a pyramid on an iron rod and struck with a small hammer in military bands.[19] He describes the *Glockenspiel* as a keyboard instrument used by Mozart in *The Magic Flute,* and the *harmonica à clavier* as an instrument with glass bars. The last of his instruments of definite pitch are the antique cymbals, describing those in the museum in Pompeii as no bigger than a *piastre,* and saying that he used some rather larger ones in his *Symphonie Roméo et Juliette.* Any bell-founder can make such instruments, he says.

He does not mention the anvils which Halévy used in 1835 in *La Juive,* writing G octaves, the g′ on the second line in the treble clef and the g below. The part is very simple, crotchets in 4/4, rest low high low, rest low high low, and so on. Kastner cites the passage in the Supplement to his *Traité.*[20]

Berlioz is vehement about the use of the bass drum, saying that many composers ruin everything with their continual thump, thump, thump, wiping out the orchestra and exterminating the voices, so that there is no melody, nor harmony, nor pattern, nor expression.[21] As for the economical custom of fixing the cymbal to the bass drum so that one player can manage both, this, Berlioz says, is intolerable for the cymbal loses all tone quality, sounding as though one dropped a sack full of old iron or broken glass, and is only fit to accompany dancing monkeys, jugglers, and those who swallow swords or snakes.[22] He also makes the very telling point, in his appendix on the art of conducting, that using the bass drum on a regular rhythm, such as the first beat of each bar, will almost inevitably slow the orchestra down because the drummer usually plays behind the beat.[23] He does point out how valuable the bass drum can be, when well written, and describes his own use in the *Symphonie fantastique*, with the drum up-ended like a side drum, rolled on by two players (in the fifth movement, 'Songe d'une nuit du sabbat').

The other percussion instruments covered are the cymbals, tamtam, tambourine, and side drum (*tambour*, also called *caisse claire* – some composers contrast these two names). He also mentions the tenor or field drum (*caisse roulante*), which is larger than the side drum, with a wooden shell instead of a brass one, and has no snares, the triangle, an instrument which he says is abused as much as the bass drum, and the *pavillon chinois* or jingling johnnie.

Kastner provides much of the same information, though he gives the range of each drum of a pair of timpani as F to c and B flat to f, so that there is an overlap of a tone.[24] He makes the same remarks about the difficulties of getting skins wide enough for the larger drum to go any lower, and of the ease of making smaller drums so that the range could go higher, even to middle c′, whereas Berlioz stopped at the b flat a tone lower. In the main text he commends Meyerbeer for his use of three drums in *Robert le Diable*. In the supplement he says that the part was originally written for four drums but that when Meyerbeer reflected that no other orchestra had so many he reduced it to three.[25] He stresses the value of having three drums, saying that it would be desirable to add a third drum to the other two so that one could have the tonic, dominant and sub-dominant.[26] Like Berlioz, he expresses a preference, though, for two pairs with two players and he then cites Antonín Rejcha's use of eight drums with four players in the accompaniment to Schiller's ode *Die Harmonie des Sphären* under the name of *L'Harmonie des sphères*, covering a complete chromatic range from G to e flat save for the B natural. The parts consist of nothing but rolls, mostly *piano*, the chords changing all the time, of course.[27] He gives the following as an example of the four timpani parts.

Kastner describes the same three types of timpani beater as Berlioz, saying that 'the first, with wooden heads, are used mainly for short notes, and also are those which are used by military bands. The second, on which the wood is covered with a skin, are much less strident and this is the type most universally used; finally, the third, with heads of sponge (a perfection owed to Mr Schneitzhoeffer), give the most gentle and darkened sounds and therefore those most appreciated, for the less one bangs on the timpani, the more the sound is clear and pure.'[28] Jean-Madeleine Schneitzhoeffer was the timpanist at the Paris Opéra from 1815 to 1823 as well as being a composer.[29] Kastner continues: 'Of these three types [of stick] each presents different qualities, and it is up to the composer to use them appropriately. For example, in a brilliant and noisy context, the wood sticks are preferable, and equally one would choose the sponge sticks in a magical or mysterious situation. It is essential that the composer mark in the timpani part the type of sticks he wishes to be used, though up till now, such instructions have been, in general, totally neglected.'

He goes into considerable detail on the tambourine, describing a number of subtly different ways of playing the instrument, always with the fingers, never by shaking it.[30] Other than that, his coverage is much the same as that of Berlioz, to the extent that one suspects that each was familiar with the work of the other.

Timpani – their mechanization

Once three drums had come into use, the next stage was, naturally, a fourth drum, and here, as Kastner told us, Meyerbeer seems to have been the leader, writing a true four-drum part in *Robert le Diable* in 1831. This so frightened his publisher that the score was bowdlerized and the fourth drum's notes put on the basses, (see music example below), probably quite sensibly if they hoped for further performances in less well-equipped houses with smaller pits.[31]

Edmund Bowles cites several followers, particularly Franz Lachner in his first symphony in 1834.[32] It is noteworthy that eighteen years later, the atmosphere had changed so much that the publisher was willing to include all four pitches in the timpani part of *Le Prophète*.

Writing such as Kauer's and Rejcha's was never to become mainstream, even in our own day, nor were all composers quick to follow Meyerbeer's lead or Berlioz's example, but three drums did eventually become the norm. Which three notes were used would naturally vary from composer to composer and from work to work, but a very common result was that the middle drum had a very awkward role, for its pitch was seldom actually in the middle. It often varied from just above the low drum (a very common tuning is G, A, d, or the equivalent in other keys: sub-dominant, dominant, and tonic) to just below the upper, frequently within the same work. An

26. Timpano without shell, Adolphe Sax, Paris *c.* 1860 (patent 22113 of 30 January 1859).

example is Tchaikovsky's Sixth Symphony, where the middle drum has to cover the range of G to e flat. Both the lower and higher drums have a much smaller range, the lower F sharp to A and the upper only d and e. The obvious solution for us today is to follow Meyerbeer's example and use four drums.[33] This is the commonest sight in our modern symphony orchestra, but it was seldom adopted in the nineteenth century. Even fifty years ago the commonest sight on the concert platform was the set of three drums.

Adolphe Sax, always enterprising and, as usual, going better than anyone else, suggested a series of drums which, because they had no shells, could be placed partly overlapping each other so that half a dozen or so could be accommodated in the space normally occupied by two or three (ill. 26). They could also nestle inside each other for storage. These drums were made with the usual uppermost four to six inches of the shell, to allow for the tuning screws and their lugs, and an iron supporting framework inside. They resemble giant rototoms, though without the screw mechanism. Judging by those in the Musikinstrumentenmuseum in Berlin, the weight was considerable, but there was surprisingly little difference in tone quality and volume between these and normal timpani.[34] As we shall see in the next chapter, Sax's idea has been brought up to date by Marcus de Mowbray, who has provided good scientific evidence to explain why Sax's, and his own drums, sound so much better than one might expect from looking at them. It is clear that Sax, as so often, had the right idea. Sax called his instruments *timbales chromatiques*, but this was because with six of them one could cover half the chromatic scale. De Mowbray's drums (ill. 38) are truly chromatic, with pedal tuning.

Three normal drums, or even four, will not suffice for all eventualities and well before the middle of the century composers, especially French and Italian opera composers, were writing notes for the timpani which clashed with the prevailing harmony. A question which is hotly debated is whether the composer expected his audience to have cloth ears and so would not notice that the drums were a tone or two out of tune, or whether the composer hoped that players would have some device which would allow them to play not the written note but one which would fit the harmony and that they would edit the part accordingly for themselves. Certainly we have frequently remarked above on the general lack of perception of pitch on percussion instruments, and this may have combined with the common difficulty for the untrained ear to recognize accurately the pitch of low notes. Nevertheless, there were many contemporary comments, by the more musically competent critics, on the clashes in harmony caused by writing notes for timpani that no longer fitted the key into which the music had progressed. Equally, there have always been comments by musical analysts, when discussing the works of more careful composers, on places where timpani were used at certain points in the music and then were lacking when the same musical phrases reappeared in a different key.

Two further questions follow: the first, once the technical solution to these problems had been found, to what extent was it applied historically? The second, to what extent should it be applied today? It would seem obvious to bring written notes into the correct harmonic relationships by retuning once this became possible, and it is generally suspected that many timpanists have unobtrusively done so, and it is certainly true that many do so today. But is it equally obvious to write in the missing notes in the music of the more careful composers? And further, if it were thought justified to do so within this period when composers were divided between those who wrote 'wrong' notes and those who left the timpani silent, why should one not do it also in the earlier periods when 'surely the composer would have welcomed it had it been available when he was alive'?

This last recourse could return us to the use of bass drum, trombones, and tuba in, for example, Handel's oratorios, a nineteenth- and early twentieth-century practice now long discarded and derided.[35] But it does raise a serious musicological and ethical problem when considering nineteenth-century composers: why should A be corrected and not B? Only the performer can decide, and in so serious a matter, normally only in conjunction with the conductor, but it is as well for all concerned at least to be aware that the problem exists.

The earliest trace of a quick-tuning device or machine timpani so far discovered is that of Gerhard Cramer, a single handle leading to a massive system of gears, invented in Munich in 1812. No patent has ever been traced, nor do the drums themselves survive, but Edmund Bowles and Nancy Benvenga both include a drawing that is generally thought to be of this system, and Herbert Tobischek includes a detailed description.[36]

A few years later a much longer-lasting device was invented by Johann Stumpff (ill. 27). This worked by screwing the drum further on to or off a threaded central pillar. Drums which work in this way are still to be found in some concert halls and theatre pits and they all suffer from the same disadvantage. Every drum head has a

27. Pair of Stumpff system rotary-tuned timpani.

best playing spot, and if one has to rotate the drum to tune it, that spot moves away from the player. One then has the choice between playing on a less responsive part of the head and reaching across the drum to follow the peregrinations of the preferred area, neither of which is ever attractive. However, drums which work in this way are usually efficient and tuning is so quick and easy that it is sometimes possible to turn the drum with one hand and play with the other.

As with most things, players argue about the 'best playing spot', but many would agree that if the backbone, which is always visible on a calf head, and is always diametric if properly lapped, runs from twelve o'clock to six, they should play at about seven o'clock or perhaps half past. Even with a plastic head, one feels, perhaps only as imagination, that one area responds better than another.

Far more useful are the various systems for tuning with a single handle. Cornelius Ward invented a cable system in 1837 which was widely copied (ill. 21, lower, and ill. 28) and improved by a number of makers.[37] A handle at the side of the drum turns the internal threaded rod along which the two wooden bars travel. These control the tension of a wire cable which passes over pulleys, and hooks over tension points on the fleshhoop (there is no separate counterhoop). There is no other tensioning, so that accurate tuning is very dependent on skilled lapping of the heads. Any inequalities of tension introduced at that stage are there for ever.

Ward's drums, or their offshoots by other makers such as that shown here, were used in the London opera and theatre pits and also by the Household Cavalry where, somewhat modified by Potter, they can be heard to this day. Their only disadvantage for orchestral use is their rather small size, with diameters of 51 and 60 cm (20 and

28. The interior of the larger of a pair of timpani by MacConnell of Woolwich, mid-nineteenth century, based on Cornelius Ward's patent, 7505 of 1837. The lower pair in ill. 21.

24 inches). Ward's patent covered side drums and bass drums as well as timpani, and Blades illustrates an example of the bass drum which survives in Keswick where it was used with the famous Rock Harmonicon.[38] Ward also patented at the same time a much more elaborate rack and pinion mechanical system for timpani, which may have been more efficient than the cable system; whether it was ever built is not known. Far more devices are patented than are ever made, and even of those made there was often no more than the initial prototype. Another single-handle system uses levers and cams to push up an internal ring against the skin, so raising its pitch (ill. 29).[39]

More efficient were systems which, like the Stumpff, had external tensioning rods connecting the counter- or fleshhoops to a central 'crown' in the base, but with a single tuning-handle, by turning which the crown could be pulled down or pushed up, rather than rotating the drum on a screw. One of the earliest pairs of such drums to survive is now exhibited in the Medici collection in the Galleria dell'Accademia in Florence and was purchased for the Tuscan Grand-ducal court in September 1837 (ill. 30).[40] They are small, only 50 and 53 cm in diameter (19½ and 21 inches), and they have a very simple mechanism, unfortunately of unknown origin. The catalogue suggests that the drums may be by Johann Kaspar Einbigler, to whom we shall turn in a moment, but their mechanism bears no resemblance to his.[41] The single tuning-handle ends in a cog-wheel which engages with another cog-wheel in the base of the pedestal (ill. 31). The first cog turns the second and that draws down or pushes up the crown to which the tuning rods are attached, acting on all equally and simultaneously, and so tightening or relaxing the drum-head. The crown is very much lighter than Stumpff's, which was a heavy iron wheel; Einbigler's is thought to have been equally heavy. The essential characteristics which these drums share with Einbigler's are the basic concepts of tension rods going to a central crown or wheel with a single tuning-handle, and brackets holding the drum shell to the pedestal that were bolted to the shell as high up as possible, unlike Stumpff's, leaving the shell free to vibrate and thus to enhance the tone quality considerably.

By far the best-known and most successful single-handle system was invented in Frankfurt by Johann Kaspar Einbigler in 1836.[42] This had three overriding advantages: a) the mechanism was not attached to the drum shell, either internally or externally, so that the shell was suspended in a frame and was free to vibrate and improve the sound; b) the shape of the shell, which became the typical Dresden pattern, was one that was ideal for tone quality, and c) the mechanism was simple, elegant, and efficient (ill. 32). Like the previous drums, the iron frame from which the shell was suspended was incorporated into the pedestal. The tension rods screwed to the counterhoop ran down to a heavy wheel-shaped base plate resting on a pivoted rocking arm or lever. The single tuning-handle passed through a threaded hole in one end of this lever and rested on the pedestal. The other end of the lever moved up or down, according to

29. Detail of the internal mechanism of one of a pair of timpani by Köhler, London, *c.*1885, based on Gautrot's patent.

30. Early machine timpano, pre-1835.

31. (*facing page*) Detail of the mechanism of the timpano in ill. 30.

which way the tuning-handle was turned, and either pulled down the counterhoop, and thus the fleshhoop, over the shell, so raising the pitch, or released its tension, so lowering the pitch. It operated equally on all the tension screws simultaneously, but these could be individually adjusted to compensate for any unevenness of the head or its lap. The only problem with this description is that there are no known drums by Einbigler surviving. The description is taken from later drums which are referred to as Einbigler system. Whether he ever designed an earlier system, similar to the Florentine drums, to be followed by the system we know, seems improbable but, because the two are so similar in essential concepts, it cannot be ruled out. What could well have been a problem with the Florentine drums is the lightness of the 'crown'. All the tension of the drumhead bears on this and it was precisely this element of the mechanism which was made heavier and heavier with each improvement that was to come.

32. Pair of single-handle ('tram handle') timpani, anonymous but Einbigler system.

Kastner quotes a report from the *Gazette musicale*, no. 43, about Einbigler's new drums, with a short passage showing what they were capable of doing (see music example below), suggesting that new inventions such as this became known across Europe reasonably rapidly.[43]

Four of the leading German composers of the day were equally enthusiastic, Mendelssohn, Hiller, Guhr, and Ries signing a note of commendation in the *Allgemeine musikalische Zeitung* in 1836.[44]

Einbigler's mechanism was improved by Ernst Pfundt, the timpanist of the Leipzig Gewandhaus Orchestra, and then considerably modified by the maker Carl Hoffmann, also of Leipzig. The tone quality of these drums was further enhanced because, by making the mechanism and framework heavier and stronger, the kettles could be lighter and therefore had greater freedom to vibrate. It seems not to have been a problem that it takes two or three strong men to move them. German orchestras tend to work in their own halls and, when they do have to work elsewhere, to have fairly large staffs of porters to move the instruments. English orchestras seldom have their own halls and are much more peripatetic, sometimes rehearsing in one or more different places every day. Also, it is more common in Britain, certainly today, for players, rather than the orchestra, to own the instruments, especially in the freelance world, and therefore often themselves to be responsible for moving them. Drums that are not too heavy and that will fit into an estate car will therefore always be popular.

In 1881 Carl Pittrich of Dresden patented a further modification with two major elements. One was a gauge to show the pitch. The other was the use of a pedal to operate the mechanism in addition to the single handle. Thus were created the Dresden pedal timpani which are still widely used, and the usefulness of Pittrich's design was all the greater because these two additions could be fitted to the ordinary Pfundt/Hoffmann drums. Single-handle drums such as those remain useful, as we shall see, for a drummer has only two feet. There have, of course, been many modifications and new developments since the 1880s, but in the vast majority of German and neighbouring area timpani systems, the ancestry and descent, for pedal timpani, from Pittrich's design is clear, as is, for both pedal and single handle drums, the derivation from Einbigler's lever.[45]

A tuning gauge can only be accurate in relation to a basic pitch. A drum is tuned, by hand, to a starting point, let us say G. The pedal or single handle is then used to move to other pitches, and the gauge follows suit, but unless it has been set to G, rather than F or A, as a starting point, it can only mislead. The Köhler drum illustrated above (ill. 29) also has a gauge with a pointer which moves as the single handle is turned, but it is not adjustable and is therefore of little use. One would have to reverse

33. Pair of Pittrich-system pedal timpani by E. Queisser, Dresden, *c*.1900, imported by Sir Henry Wood, when awaiting repair by the L. W. Hunt Drum Co.

the process by turning the handle so that the pointer was at G and then tuning the drum by its ordinary tuning screws to that pitch. Unless temperature and humidity were at a desired level, this could mean having the head inconveniently tight or slack. On Pittrich's gauge the note names could be moved, as on modern pedal timpani, so that although it had to be reset each time the drum was tuned up, it would then be accurate while the tuning mechanism was used, until a change of the basic pitch necessitated resetting. Even then there are so many imponderables, weather, head elasticity, and so on, that it is a rash timpanist who reads a gauge as anything better than to the nearest quartertone. There is, too, often need for three eyes: one for the conductor, one for the music unless it is a straightforward block of rests of the same time signature, and one for the gauge, so that it can be a distraction.

The later models of the Pittrich pedal mechanism had a massive iron ball as a counterbalance, which increased the weight of the drums even further and this is one reason why, although Sir Henry Wood imported a pair into London in 1905 (ill. 33),[46] his example was not followed by other British orchestras. British orchestral practice simply could not countenance the use of anything so statuesque. Not until the use of more modern materials, as strong and rigid but lighter than the massive bars of cast iron, made it possible for each drum to be lifted and carried by the player could such drums be acceptable in Britain. Today there are several players whose appreciation of tone quality is sufficiently nice that they use these lighter versions of the Pittrich drums in preference to the more portable, but tonally inferior, British and American pedal drums.

The extent to which single-handle or pedal drums were adopted is difficult to determine. Some of the complaints mentioned above of the lack of a third drum date from some decades after the earlier of these mechanisms, which would make the third drum sometimes unnecessary, were already available. It has been suggested that evidence for the use of some such device is the increasing tendency of composers to ask for changes of pitch with ever-shorter rests in which to execute them. While this may well be valid, it does not allow for skill and dexterity. Mendelssohn's *Elijah* is often cited as a case in point. This is scored for two drums with many changes, but only two of them are tricky. In 'The fire descends from heaven' there are three quick bars to change from e flat to e, and in 'Thanks be to God' there are six bars to go from A to B. Neither of these is impossible on two hand-tuned drums and performance is quite straightforward with three. It is one of many works which are very much easier to play with machine drums but which are perfectly possible without, either by using an extra drum or simply by deft tuning. Tucking a stick into the palm of each hand with two fingers so that one can turn two T-handles at a time with the thumb and other fingers, one could tune a whole tone in three beats rest, and easily a semitone in three bars, and, with one's own drums, one knows just how much turn to give each pair of handles.

It was really not until quite modern times with, for example, Richard Strauss's *Till Eulenspiegels lustige Streiche*, with the famous five-note pattern,

34. Pair of pedal timpani by Leedy, Indianapolis, pre-1929, the smaller dismounted to show the pedal and dome and the screw in the base of the drum.

d'Indy's Second Symphony, Mahler's Seventh, Carl Nielsen's Fourth, and Bartók's *Music for Strings, Percussion and Celesta* and Violin Concerto with their *glissandi* and other chromaticisms, that pedal drums became essential.

This is another reason why such instruments were seldom used in Britain, though Sir Henry Wood took full advantage of them in his own (or, as he preferred, Klenovsky's) transcription of Bach's D minor Toccata and Fugue. Comparatively few symphonic orchestral players in England used pedal timpani of any sort until the 1960s or so (three or four hand-tuned drums were the norm), even though drummers in light music, and in the theatres and opera houses, had been using them routinely from the 1920s. My own pair of Leedy pedal timpani (ill. 34) came over with Paul Whiteman's orchestra in 1929 and had been sold to a light-orchestra drummer in London because their American owner knew that a new model was about to appear from Indianapolis. Playing mainly symphonically, it was not until 1957 that I found the need for such instruments, by which time that first British owner was retiring.[47]

The first American pedal mechanism was William F. Ludwig's hydraulic system of 1911. This was followed in 1917 with a somewhat more practicable system, with cables to connect the pedal mechanism to the tuning handles, which was developed in conjunction with his brother-in-law, Robert Danly.[48] Then in 1920 came the balanced-action system which is still often used. Both the hydraulic and the cable model used a gland on the pedal gripping a curved post to control the pedal's travel, a method which is still often seen and which works tolerably well provided that it is kept clean and that nothing that might encourage the gland to slip is allowed to contaminate it. The balanced action depended on an extremely powerful spring in a housing above the pedal (James Blades once warned me that the accidental release of the spring could break an arm) with, instead of a pedal which, as on all other systems, travelled up and down, a rocking pedal on which pressing with the toe raised the pitch and pressing with the heel lowered it, the pedal itself remaining balanced on its axle.

Leedy's system, which had been invented by his foreman Cecil Strupe, came apart into three pieces, the pedal, the dome or bowl which fitted on top of the pedal and in which the drum rested, and the drum itself. Three trips sufficed to carry a pair of these drums from the car to the studio, one for the pedals and domes, and one for each of the drums, and it needed only two or three minutes to put them together and tension the heads. Leedy's first model had the height adjustment between the pedal and the base, which meant that one pedal of the pair was usually higher from the floor than the other. The second model, which was copied in Britain under licence by Premier, had the adjustment above the pedal and some other improvements. The pedal was controlled by a comb of teeth which fitted against a stepped quadrant. Some players complained that this series of steps, although they were very small, inhibited precise tuning, one reason for preferring the Ludwig balanced-action, but most players were content – one could always 'touch-up' with the tuning handles.

In the 1960s Ludwig introduced their Dresden model. This had a deeper shell, which improved the tone quality and, they claimed more importantly, had the mechanism outside the drum instead of inside it. The previous patterns, both Ludwig's and Leedy's as well as others, had a crown wheel inside the base of the kettle, connecting by a screw to the top of the pedal mechanism. From this crown a steel rod, or in Ludwig's earlier model a cable, ran to a rocker at the base of each tuning handle. It was generally held (though very difficult to prove) that this internal mechanism interfered with the soundwaves passing to and fro within the kettle. This may be true, though I suspect that the different shapes of the shell and the freedom of the shell itself to vibrate in the German model had much more to do with it. A comparatively shallow rounded bowl, like the Leedy and Ludwig, can never produce as good a sound as the deeper shell with sides which are straight until they reach the bowl at the base of the kettle, like the Dresden, whose sides slope inwards but are almost straight, or the English Hawkes-Cummings, whose sides are vertical. Ludwig called his new model the Dresden pattern partly because the shell shape, though parabolically curved, was reminiscent of the drums emanating from that city, but chiefly because all the control rods were external. Premier produced a similar type of drum in England, and these two models dominate the orchestras in the English-speaking world today.

There have been many other patterns of machine drums in all countries. Bowles describes and illustrates a number of them and Tobischek includes patent drawings of a great many; Benvenga has photographs, some rather obscure, of a number.[49]

Today it is very unusual to see hand-tuned drums with plain T-handles and no further mechanism in a professional orchestra other than an early-music band or a chamber orchestra playing Baroque or Classical music. Ever since the invention of machine timpani there have been some players, especially with German drums where the pedals are side-mounted, who found it easier to use a mixed set of four, with two pedals as the centre pair and a single-handle drum on the outside to right and to left.

Such a choice was partly based on the belief that the inner drums usually had to change pitch more than the outer, and partly on the fact that players had only two feet and that it was easier to use a hand on each of the other two. Side-mounted pedals have the advantage, with two drums, that the feet are side by side, but the disadvantage with four drums that much greater movement is necessary from the middle to the outer drums, drawing the foot back from the pedal and then round the base of the drum, to reach the pedal on the outer drum, and back again. Hence it could be easier to use the tram-handle, as it was called in Britain from its similarity to that used to control a tram, on the outer drums.

Other drums

While the normal bass drum in the early years of the nineteenth century was often still the Turkish or long drum, there were frequent demands for something larger and more the shape we use today. Henry Distin carried this about as far as it could go when he produced his Monster Bass Drum for the Handel Commemoration Festival in 1857.[50] This stood some eight feet high, as may be seen in ill. 35, the head, which was made from the skin of a prize ox, being over seven feet in diameter (nearly two and a half metres). Smaller models of this type of single-headed bass drum, called a gong drum, were widely used in British orchestras because the tone was considered better than that of the normal double-headed drum. It was certainly easier to control, for there was only the one head to damp for short notes. Because it was tensioned by a series of iron bolts, rather than by the ropes which were still normal on the double-headed drum, the tension was easier to control, though it took longer than simply pulling up a number of buffs. For a work such as the Verdi Requiem, where the composer asks for the ropes to be well tensioned for the short and very loud, *secco e molto forte*, whacks in the 'Dies irae' but slackened off for the *ppp* strokes in the 'Mors stupebit', it is less suitable, but this can be, and today usually is, overcome by using two bass drums. While the player is instructed to tighten the ropes again for the return of the 'Dies irae' motif both in that movement and towards the end, nothing further is said about slackening, this being left to the player's good sense.

Boosey, and later Boosey and Hawkes, retained Distin's old workshops in Frederick Mews, Stanhope Place, behind Marble Arch, which can be seen here (ill. 35), but when they moved out around 1960, there was no room for this drum in any other of their premises. It was offered to me for the Horniman Museum, but they also had no space for it, and tragically after a century of occasional use it was broken up.

Despite Berlioz's strictures, the use of one cymbal, fixed to the bass drum shell so that it could be struck with the other cymbal by the same player, was common throughout the nineteenth century and into the twentieth, especially when military bands were playing in concerts. Mahler sometimes requests this as 'military style'.

The military band was considerably enlarged in the early years of the nineteenth century with the advent of the keyed brass instruments such as bass horns, followed by key-bugles and ophicleides, and the percussion used grew commensurately. With the end of the Napoleonic wars, many army bandsmen found themselves back in civilian life and this, combined with growing industrialization, with workers coming

35. Monster bass drum ('gong' drum) by Henry Distin, 1857, played by Ronnie Verrell to Sam Norton *(left)* and Ken Spacey of the Boosey & Hawkes, London, drum department *c.* 1960.

together in large numbers in mines, mills, and factories, led to the creation of many popular bands. Initially these were on military lines but, after the introduction of valved brass instruments, which were both cheaper and easier to play than woodwind, it led in Britain to the brass band movement and to similar bands elsewhere. Percussion here was simple and consisted mainly of bass drum, cymbals, and side drum, with the occasional use of timpani, tambourine, and triangle.

At much the same time, from the mid-century onwards, the military band was stabilized under the War Office and, less subject to the colonel's whim, became established in its modern form. There was still plenty of scope in most armies to the end of the century for drummer boys, children of surprisingly young age, beating the armies on, while on the march and even into battle, with the side drum.

One instrument entered civilian life in a manner which we do not fully comprehend today. The tambourine became a fashionable ladies' instrument and was used quite widely to accompany songs and even as a solo instrument with piano or harp. What was played on it, and with how much dexterity, seems as yet to be unknown, though some of Kastner's examples, for instance his *murmures*, could well be relevant here, for few of these relate to any orchestral parts for the tambourine in the normal repertoire.[51] Though it does not seem to be the most obvious instrument for a virtuoso career, even in amateur circles, this was often achieved. Surviving instruments are not uncommon, often with attached coloured ribands. Their heads are usually decoratively painted and are usually tensioned with iron brackets and small wing nuts.

Tuned percussion

Carnaval des animaux of 1886 was a work in which Camille Saint-Saëns satirized many composers, including himself. The music of his own *Danse macabre*, originally in 3/4, became the rattle of the skeletons in the 4/4 'Fossiles'. We do not know what form of xylophone he used, but it was most probably the four-row instrument (ill. 36) such as had been used by the great Polish virtuoso Gusikow who so impressed Mendelssohn and others in the 1830s.[52] Like all the early xylophones, this had its lowest note nearest to the player's body and its highest furthest away, so that the player reached further and further forward when going from bass to treble, rather than from left to right as on today's instruments. Unlike Agricola's and Mersenne's instruments, with their single row of bars, the three or four rows of bars of these xylophones had, as the Eastern European folk instruments still have today, the most needed accidentals duplicated to right and left.[53] This arrangement, once learned, allows for considerable virtuosity, for many apparently quite tricky passages lie neatly under the hands.

Xylophones of this pattern remained the norm into the early twentieth century. Their bars were usually square in section, giving a hard, dry rattling sound, eminently suitable for the representation of skeletons and fossils, and there were no resonators to add any amplitude to the sound or to help it sustain. Our modern instruments have a quite different ancestry, and quite a different sound, warmer and, thanks to their resonators, perceptibly longer, especially in the bass which is anyway extended an octave or more lower than the instruments that Saint-Saëns knew. In Central America, the slave-owners were more liberal in their treatment of the slaves than in the United States or the Caribbean, where there was a practice of banning any serious use of their own musical instruments. West Africans, carried as slaves to the Hispanic parts of the New World, recreated in Mexico and Guatemala newer and more elaborate versions of the *marimbas* they had known at home.[54]

These differed from the contemporary European instruments in three respects. One is that the series of bars ran from side to side, rather than from front to back, usually with the lowest to the left, though why this should be an almost worldwide universal, I do not know. The second, and more significant, is that each bar had its own resonator. The resonators on these Central American instruments were usually tubular, either round or square in section, rather than the spherical or piriform gourds which were commonest in West Africa, but like those of the African instruments they often had a hole covered with a thin membrane which added a buzz to sweeten the sound. The third, and most important, is that the bars were tuned not only by their length and natural density but by being rectangular rather than square in section, wider than they were thick, and by being thinned into an arch under the centre of each bar.

36. Four-row xylophone, photographed from the side.

The pitch of a free-free bar (a bar that is unattached, or free, at both ends) depends on the density of the material, its length, and its thickness. The width may affect the tone quality somewhat but not the pitch. On each bar the nodal points for the fundamental pitch, the points of minimal vibration, are two-ninths from each end. These are therefore the points at which a bar should rest on its frame – resting at any other points will inhibit its freedom to vibrate in its fundamental mode and thus degrade its tone quality.[55] By hollowing the bar in an arch between these points (it is more convenient for the player to do this on the under side than the upper) the pitch is flattened and, as an additional benefit, the tone quality is greatly enriched. Such flattening is achieved quite quickly and a fifth lower is easily obtained and an octave not impossible. A combination of length and thickness is used to keep the lengths of the series of bars in reasonable bounds for a manageable shape of instrument.[56]

Deagan of Chicago is thought to have been the first to transfer these characteristics, except for the buzzing membrane, to the orchestral instrument, and so to devise both the modern xylophone and the marimba, adopting the layout of the piano as the most convenient for players within our culture, rather than the single line more usual south of the Rio Grande. Although the bars are all the same colour, either that of West Indian rosewood or of some modern synthetic substitute (rosewood is an endangered species), we refer to white notes and black notes in the same way that a pianist does. This resemblance to the piano keyboard can cause problems, for it encourages composers to write parts which, while easily played on keys an inch wide with the ten fingers of two hands, are rather more difficult when there is only one beater in each hand (or even two or three in each hand, as vibraphone and marimba players do), especially while looking at the music and the conductor rather than at the instrument. It has often been necessary to make this plain by asking the composer to play the passage on the piano with one finger of each hand while keeping the eyes shut!

A further complication is that instruments vary in size and range from one maker or model to another, but most players become adept at changing octaves at a musically logical point, just as doublebass players do when playing *basso* parts which go down to CC in octaves with the cello.

As well as writing for xylophone, Saint-Saëns included what we presume to have been a form of glockenspiel (orchestral bells) in the same work, in 'Les Oiseaux'. He called for *harmonica*, a word of somewhat indefinite import.[57] The original harmonica was the musical glasses, and more specifically the instrument invented by Benjamin Franklin while visiting England in 1761. This had concentric glass bowls rotating on a spindle above a water-filled trough so that dampened fingers could rub on the lip of the bowl required.[58] The name, as Berlioz used it in his *Traité*, seems to have been transferred during the course of the nineteenth century to any instrument made of glass, including those whose glass bars or plates were struck with light wooden hammers and which are the ancestors of our modern glockenspiel. It is almost certainly one of these glass-bar instruments, with a range of a twelfth or a couple of octaves, that Saint-Saëns had in mind. Unlike those of the contemporary xylophone, the bars were usually laid out in either one or two rows.

Before the end of the nineteenth century the glass bars were replaced by steel and were sometimes struck by a small and inefficient keyboard. The keyboard glock, as it was known in Britain, was capable of little or no dynamic variation. When played too gently nothing was heard, when played too hard a bar might jump from its seating. Nevertheless, some composers wrote extensive parts for it, one of whom was Paul Dukas in *L'Apprenti sorcier*.

The glockenspiel also became a military instrument, replacing the old jingling johnnie. It is possible that it was this form which induced the change from glass to steel, for steel is a much more practicable material to fix into a lyre-shaped frame at the top of a pole and play on the march. German regiments tied the same horsehair plumes that they had used on the *Schellenbaum* to the arms of the lyre. Parts for the instrument had to be kept simple because the player had only one hand available, the other being used to steady the pole, which was held in a socket fixed to shoulder straps in the same way as the regimental colours and other flags.

The Exotic

Certainly since the Baroque, perhaps even since the Renaissance, composers have been trying to portray foreign peoples and exotic customs in their music. Rameau wrote *Les Indes galantes*, and many other composers wrote similar works. Save for the *alla turca*, most did so with the instruments normally in use (we have already noted Spontini's use of a Mexican rattle), writing music which would sound appropriate in its style, just as Telemann imitated the windmills and Sancho Panza's ass with ordinary instruments in his *Don Quichott*, and Beethoven the 'Peasants' Merrymaking' and the 'Storm' in his Pastoral Symphony.

This approach continued into the nineteenth century, for Dvořák introduced no new instruments for his New World Symphony, nor for his string quartet whose name can no longer be used, nor for that matter did Smetana in his Czech cycle *Má Vlast*. Berlioz had succumbed to the temptation of the exotic in *Carnaval romain*, with the cymbals and tambourine characteristic of southern Italian music, but then Berlioz was usually the first to do something new and exciting.

It was perhaps Tchaikovsky who first deliberately used percussion instruments to portray national characteristics, just as he was the first major composer after Rejcha to use irregular time signatures, with 5/4 for a Russian folk tune in his Sixth Symphony. In *Casse-Noisette* of 1892 we have the 'Danses charactéristiques' with a tambourine for the 'Danse Arabe' (and immediately before it for the Russian 'Trepak'), and a glockenspiel for the 'Danse Chinoise'. In his 1812 Overture he employed cannon and bells, though the bells are notated only as trills on a single-line note, leaving it to the player to decide what to play, and the part for the cannon, marked *ffff*, seems to be partly based on tradition.[59] As with Beethoven's Battle Symphony, 1812 is often played 'with cannon and mortar effects', usually less convincingly than with a good, big bass drum, but some recordings are improved over what we can do in the studio by dubbing in real church bells.

Tchaikovsky was followed by Rimsky-Korsakov with his *Caprice espagnol*, with a full battery of percussion instruments characteristic of Iberia but which since then have simply become standard sounds without local association. The only one of these that retained a specific location until quite recently was the castanets. The moment we heard that exciting rattle, for instance before the rise of the curtain in de Falla's *Tricorne*, we knew where the composer was taking us.

It may be noteworthy that in this period at least, it is the lighter music, save for Tchaikovsky's 1812 and Berlioz's *Carnaval romain*, that employs these effects, for few of the above works can be counted among the composers' more serious *œuvres*. In an even lighter vein we have the pop-guns of Johann Strauss's polka, and other effects in his music such as the spurs in *Die Fledermaus*.

Museums

The late nineteenth century was when many of the great public and private collections of instruments were formed. As a result there grew up a demand for old musical instruments, and wherever there is a demand there will be a supply. Fortunately, perhaps, for us there was comparatively little interest in percussion instruments so that whereas there was a very active market in violins and harpsichords, for instance, which was readily satisfied when original supply fell short of demand, there was less need for such creativity in percussion instruments. Nevertheless, there are at least some drums and other percussion instruments in the catalogues of the most famous of such suppliers, Leopoldo Franciolini.[60] Many of his instruments can still be seen in the world's museums, some recognized as such and others still masquerading as originals, as they did to the collections' founders and creators.

In addition to his productions there were at least two collectors whose main endeavour was to show the forms of all the instruments for each musical period. One of these was Victor-Charles Mahillon, the great curator of the Brussels Conservatoire Museum.[61] The other was Canon Francis W. Galpin, most of whose original collection is now in Boston.[62] Neither had any inhibitions about producing or obtaining a reproduction where no original was available, and Galpin extended this practice when he was helping Mrs Crosby Brown to form her collection which became the nucleus of that of the Metropolitan Museum of Art in New York.[63] Mahillon had the advantage of being able to call on the family firm, the well-known instrument makers, for help in this endeavour.

Doubtless there were other people similarly involved and therefore, while we do not need as yet to be quite so wary as the historians of some other instruments, when we find an instrument that seems improbable for its alleged time and place, we must remember the possibilities of this form of supply and demand. Future generations will also have to reckon with the Early Music Movement. Many reproductions and reconstructions of all periods, as yet mainly pre-1800, are being made today for modern performance with no intention to defraud. One wonders how many curators and collectors in a century or two will distinguish these from originals, especially where a modern maker, as some do, has marked the instrument solely with the name of the maker whose work is being copied.[64]

When considering what earlier instruments looked like, we need also to consider 'improvement'. Few museums are willing to display dirty, battered, and damaged specimens. This is why the counterhoops on Drake's drum were replaced.[65] Sometimes such work is new but designed to suit the age of the instrument, when it can be positively misleading. Sometimes new, modern materials are used and these are thus easily detected.[66] Some of the All Souls side-drum buffs and all those on the Armouries side drum are simply replacements, using modern buffs in the modern pattern. This may mislead the general public over what they looked like originally, but it is no recognition problem for us because modern buffs are quite different from earlier ones. Other work, such as new heads, may be less easily detected.

These are all factors to bear in mind when visiting any museum and when looking at any of their exhibits, especially when studying early material with a view to making reproductions for period performance.

Chapter 8

The Twentieth Century

The end of the nineteenth century and the beginning of the twentieth mark what would seem to be the culmination of the traditional symphony orchestra, the end of a process begun by Haydn and his contemporaries and fuelled by Wagner and such followers as Richard Strauss and Gustav Mahler into what has been variously described as a pantechnicon and a dinosaur. Wagner himself had been surprisingly temperate regarding percussion. He added much to the woodwind and brass, using a second timpanist, already fairly common among other composers, throughout *The Ring*. The most famous passage is probably Siegfried's Funeral March in *Götterdämmerung*, where two timpanists, often in unison, contrast rhythms and rolls with each other.

Other than this and a collection of anvils used without any great musical enterprise elsewhere in the Ring, there is nothing very out of the way in his general percussion writing.

His followers were also temperate in their demands, with occasional exceptions, such as Schönberg's iron chains in *Gurrelieder* and Mahler's hammer blows in the Sixth Symphony.[1] Nor was the hammer alone in the Sixth, for the score includes two pairs of timpani, triangle, side drum, cymbals, bass drum, sometimes struck on the rim, tamtam, glockenspiel, whip [*Rute*], cowbells [*Herdenglocken*] for which no pitch seems to be intended, even though all such bells do have a pitch, and *Tiefes Glockengeläute*, for which Mahler provided a footnote: 'Two or more very deep bells, untuned but each with different sounds, played gently and irregularly in the distance'. What Mahler meant by 'untuned' we cannot tell – bells are inevitably tuned, even more than most other percussion instruments, unless he meant a pair that had been so badly cast or cracked that their pitch wobbled widely enough between different pitches as to be almost indiscernible. It is more likely that he meant that he did not care what pitch they had, leaving it to us to decide how dissonant to be. Apart from such instances as these, it was really a matter of the orchestra growing ever-larger with ever-thicker sonorities. Therefore a rather larger percussion section was kept ever-busier doing much the sort of things they had done before but with a wider range due to composers' demands.

Mahler's low D on timpani in several symphonies requires a thirty- or thirty-two-inch drum and the low C written by some other composers would need a drum thirty-four or thirty-five inches in diameter, almost a yard across. The problem with such a size is that is impossible to make such a kettle deep enough to produce a good tone and match the other drums of the set for height. Delibes's piccolo timpani in *Lakmé*, an octave above the usual instruments, requires nineteen-inch and smaller drums, as does Britten's *Turn of the Screw*, but these are easily made and are only extensions of what was already used. Even Stravinsky's *Le Sacre du printemps* shows only slight changes from what had gone before so far as the instruments themselves are concerned: the tamtam is scraped with a triangle beater and he asks for a *güiro* or *rape*, a scraped gourd. Contrasting with this, there was a very considerable increase over the past in Stravinsky's expectation of competence among players; *Sacre* was still frightening the older generation of percussionists into the 1960s.[2] This was deliberate on Stravinsky's part; the work is supposed to sound on the verge of the possible, especially the opening bassoon solo.

Significant changes in composers' approach were brought about by a combination of the financial crises after the First World War, when it became difficult to fund performances by the giant orchestras, and the general revulsion against such monsters, perhaps because they were reminiscent of the huge armies which had consumed the youth of Europe. As a result, Stravinsky and Kurt Weill started to produce such works as *L'Histoire du soldat* and the *Dreigroschenoper* respectively, which require only one player, with a considerable quantity of instruments and of dexterity. These examples were followed by many others, and led to works nearer our time by composers such as Stockhausen, where even the chamber ensemble has vanished, leaving the percussionist in sole majesty.

Multiple and solo percussion

A major work for percussion alone is Edgard Varèse's *Ionisation*. This has no melodic content at all. Nevertheless, in performance after a good number of rehearsals, some simulacra of melodic and harmonic content became apparent. The scoring is for thirteen players who cover: large Chinese cymbal, very deep bass drum, and muted cowbell (muted by stuffing a cloth into it); gong, high and low tamtams, and muted cowbell; two bongos, tenor drum, a medium and a large bass drum both laid flat; military drum and tenor drum; high siren (which must either be mechanical with an immediate-stop button, not blown by mouth, or replaced with a *théremin*) and lion roar (friction drum); low siren (as above; both could nowadays be replaced by electronic devices), whip, and *güiro*; three Chinese blocks (temple blocks rather than woodblocks), *claves*, and triangle; side drum without snares and a pair of *maracas*; shallow side drum (*tarole*), ordinary side drum, and suspended cymbal; pair of cymbals, sleighbells, and six tubular bells played always as pairs in tritone, minor ninth, and seventh; *güiro*, castanets, and keyboard glockenspiel playing chords similar to those on the bells; tambourine, two anvils, and large tamtam; and finally whip, triangle, sleighbells, and piano which is played by leaning the forearms across the keyboard and playing all the notes between the bottom AAA and the e flat two and a half octaves above, plus chords similar to those of the bells and glockenspiel.[3] As one gets to know it in rehearsal, a logic becomes apparent, but one cannot imagine that anybody could really comprehend it at one hearing.

Ionisation dates from 1931 and it was preceded by at least two important chamber works, Stravinsky's *L'Histoire du soldat* and Walton's *Façade*. Both are for voice plus small chamber ensemble. The vocal parts are speaking rather than singing, quite different from Schönberg's *Sprechgesang*. Stravinsky's is mostly an acting part for three people (the Princess dances but never speaks), with some of the text spoken rhythmically with the music. Walton's is rhythmic throughout, the speaker as though another instrument taking its part in the music. The instrumentation in *L'Histoire* is for violin and double bass, clarinet and bassoon, cornet and tenor/bass trombone, the top and bottom of each orchestral section, plus percussion.[4] Performance of the percussion part is not helped by the fact that the full score and the miniature score disagree on a number of details of which instrument is to be struck with which sort of beater at various moments and that both scores are contradicted by the player's part. Nor does it help that the layout of the percussion part, especially in the last movement, 'Marche Triomphale du Diable', makes it quite unplayable; every player has had to write it out.[5]

There have always been numerous other problems with the percussion parts of this work. Stravinsky asked for two *caisses claires sans timbres* (without snares) and two *tambours*, one *sans timbres* and the other with snares, all of different sizes. The distinctions between these two types of side drum, *caisse claire* and *tambour*, has never been clear outside France (and seldom within that country). Nor does anyone today know what a *baguette à tête en capoc* was in 1918 – capoc (a fibrous vegetable matter not unlike raw cotton which used to be employed for filling marine life-jackets) seems an unpromising material for the head of a drum stick. Nor do Stravinsky's own recordings help in these or other problematic areas, for there are numerous differences between them. Those of us who have been fortunate enough to learn the part under someone who had played it with Stravinsky, as I was with Jimmy Blades, at least have some anecdotal evidence to assist them. Certainly the original printed music is legible and, where necessary, easily transcribed, unlike Stockhausen's *Kontakte* which, as James Holland relates, was impossible to read and impracticable to transcribe.[6] Today, thanks to the new 1987 edition of *L'Histoire*, these problems are solved, provided one is willing to accept a modern player's interpretation of the composer's original thoughts.[7]

Composers seem to delight in making things more difficult than they need be, and even when they do try to help us, they often make it more complicated. Stravinsky tried to play the percussion part of *L'Histoire* himself and tells us in the 'Danse du Diable' to put two of the side drums on the floor, standing on edge very close to each other, and to move the beater rapidly from one to the other. It is said that this was because it was the only way that he could play the rhythm absolutely metronomically, but since this is something that we are all trained to do, this instruction can safely be ignored. At least *L'Histoire* is a delight to play, as is *Façade*.

For both works the player needs to make some sticks and other gadgets, for which see Appendix 3. As James Holland points out, one also has to remember how things have changed since 1922 and where, for example, Walton asks for the side drum to be played 'on the wood' or 'on the rim', it is best to use a woodblock for those notes now that our side drums have metal shells instead of wood, an ordinary rectangular woodblock, not a temple block, a pair of which Walton wrote for specifically.[8]

Façade, dating from 1922, four years after *L'Histoire*, is scored for a slightly jazzier ensemble, flute and piccolo, clarinet and bass clarinet, alto saxophone, trumpet, percussion, violoncello (if necessary split between two players) and reciter (again often shared by two people, one of them memorably on several occasions, the author of the poems, Edith Sitwell herself). While just as demanding in performance, Walton's music has none of the rhythmic complexity of Stravinsky's score, with its continually changing bar lengths, or his own *Portsmouth Point*. Perhaps for this reason much of the music, arranged for orchestra, was effectively used for a ballet. It is that version which was the basis for the concert suites, whereas the suite drawn from *L'Histoire* must be played by the original instruments.

Die Dreigroschenoper or *The Threepenny Opera* is probably Kurt Weill's best-known work. Dating from 1928, it could be called a jazz operetta or, following the analogy of Mozart's *Zauberflöte*, a jazz *Singspiel*. Scored for quite a wide range of instruments, it needs only nine players. The two woodwind players must cover soprano, alto, tenor, and bass saxophones, flute, clarinet, bass clarinet, and bassoon between them, the trombonist also plays double bass, and the banjo player is responsible for cello, guitar, Hawaiian guitar, bandoneon, and mandolin. The percussion parts are laid out in the miniature score as in orchestral works for a full section, but they can all be played by one person provided that pedal bass drum and both pedal and suspended cymbals are used.[9] The only special gadget necessary in quite a big kit is a pair of timpani sticks with knobs on the handles so that they can also be used on a side drum. It needs three timpani, a jazz side drum (shallower than the usual size) as well as an ordinary side drum and a tenor drum, plus woodblock, tomtom, bass drum, cymbals, tamtam, triangle, glockenspiel and two bells in f sharp and g. There is little to distinguish *Dreigroschen* from the night-club bands of its day or other pit orchestras of the first half of the century, but it was a novelty when it was new and even still when it appeared in London in 1956 at the Royal Court Theatre.[10] Since then the requirements of the pit drummer have increased sharply and works such as Leonard Bernstein's *West Side Story* have called for something very different from the Kurt Weill or the older Ivor Novello style of musical.

It may have been the concept of works such as *L'Histoire*, *Façade*, and *Dreigroschen*, the realization that if the parts were sympathetically written they could be played by one person, that led to the greater use of solo percussion by composers such as Berio, Boulez, Stockhausen, and others. Their use coincided with several other changes in compositional style. One, peculiar to percussion, was the introduction of the exotic, the wide range of instruments from other cultures that began to be imported, mainly after the Second World War. Another was dissatisfaction with the older styles of composition, which led to such extremes as the musical Dadaists between the Wars and *musique concrète* after the Second War.[11] Another was the general feeling, fuelled by excesses in the visual arts, that one could get away with anything, combined perhaps with a mischievous desire to see just what one could get away with. Another was an abrogation of responsibility for form, cohesion, and continuity, with the use of a style that became known as aleatoric. Here the composer gave the players the freedom to begin and end wherever they fancied, to play movements in any order, to choose their own tempi and dynamics and therefore play quickly or slowly, loudly or softly, just as the whim took them on that occasion, and sometimes to choose their own instruments. As a result, no two performances would be the same and this outcome of musical 'freedom' was the aim of the composer. Never before had composers so abandoned responsibility for the performance of their works to so extreme a degree.[12]

There was one outcome which had not been a part of the composers' intentions, and this was the great success from the 1950s onwards of the Early Music Movement. The general musical public was totally alienated from contemporary music. Melody had become a dirty word. No music sufficiently tuneful that it might conceivably be whistled had the slightest chance of passing the BBC review panel or any similar body which controlled the funding and opportunities for performance elsewhere in the world. The result was that the apparent simplicity and immediately approachable melodic content of medieval and renaissance music was widely welcomed. Large concert halls saw rows of empty seats for new music while smaller chamber halls were sold out for old music.

The movement had begun a century or so earlier, with the establishment of the Bach Gesellschaft and similar organizations interested in the publication of the works of the earlier composers in editions bearing some resemblance to what had actually been written. Many such organizations provided reasonably clean scores in the collected edition volumes but felt that orchestral scores and parts should conform to the *mores* of 'modern' times with heavy editing full of slurs, bowing indications, added dynamics and other undesirable features. In the 1950s there was a revulsion against this, as well as against the more overtly modern musical styles, and 'authenticity' became the ideal. I was one of the leaders in this and was the first to inveigh against a prevailing practice of striving for correctness in recorders, lutes, viols, and other instruments, while accompanying these with any drum that came to hand, often played with currently fashionable syncopations and other jazz rhythms. Study of medieval iconography led to my recreation of tabors, nakers, and other instruments and to their adoption by many other makers and players.[13]

While the success of the Early Music Movement was clearly beneficial to the state of music in general, the antipathy towards contemporary music was decidedly unhealthy and detrimental. Over the half century since then, this antipathy has been somewhat reduced and percussion solos and percussion ensembles have proliferated. The popularity of, first, the West Indian steel band and more recently the Balinese and Central Javanese *gamelans*, both with strongly melodic styles, may have contributed towards this acceptance of percussion as a solo medium, as perhaps has a fashion for North Indian classical music where the *tablā*, a pair of unequal kettledrums, fill the same role as accompanists as does the piano in our music. Certainly the inclusion in a programme of Stockhausen's *Zyklus*, a work for one percussion player alone who has an almost balletic role, surrounded by innumerable percussion instruments and confronted by a score in a wholly new notation impenetrable by ordinary mortals, no longer empties a hall any more than does Bartók's Sonata for Two Pianos and

Percussion, which involves two percussionists in a comparatively modest array of instruments.[14]

Change

Before we turn to consideration of the individual instruments, we need to realize that this is a period of change in all orchestral instruments. Hardly a single instrument on the concert platform today is as it was in 1950, still less in 1900. Instruments have changed, string materials have changed, the sounds have changed. In our department, not only have the instruments changed but there has been an even greater change in the variety of instruments which have become available, and a change in their use. Whereas in the nineteenth century there had been some imitation of exotic percussion to give a flavouring of local colour, in the twentieth century there came the wholesale adoption of foreign percussion instruments into Western music. Sometimes this was again for the sake of an exotic flavour, but usually it has been simply to make more and different sounds available. This has been helped by the enormous changes in speed of travel and of world trade. Today it is easy for people to travel to far-away places and hear their music at first hand, and to acquire and bring back the instruments. Many of these are now available commercially through the normal dealers in percussion. It has to be said, also, that this change has been partly due to a paucity of inspiration on the part of some composers – when all else fails, to throw in some extra percussion has become a well-worn road as we noted in the Introduction.

A problem which seems to have little exercised modern composers is that many such instruments are tuned and that the scales to which they are tuned bear no resemblance to our own scales. The resulting harmonic clashes have not endeared the works in which such instruments are used to the public, nor have they increased the respect in which the composers are held amongst percussionists. There is often a feeling that if they don't care what sounds come out, why should we? To some extent this problem has been ameliorated by the manufacture of imitation exotica by makers within our own tradition, so that nowadays 'African' or 'Oceanic' slit drums are available tuned to equal temperament, as are sets of gongs. Even so, the propensity of composers such as Messiaen to call for 'medium' or 'high' gongs, when they would never dream of asking for anything so vague as a medium or high note on woodwind or strings, does make percussion players feel that their instruments are undervalued. For that matter, one has less respect for Mahler after playing his low cow bells whose pitch does not matter so long as it's different. Did he ever say this for any instruments other than ours?

The changes to the instruments themselves are all the more evident because many of us have lived through them. It is possible that Georges Kastner and Constant Pierre could have said much the same in the mid- and late-nineteenth century, as might Johann Joachim Quantz in the mid-eighteenth, but unfortunately none of them did so in their books, and none was a professional percussion player.[15] My professional experience of percussion began exactly in the middle of the century.[16] Since that time every one of our instruments has changed, and changed far more, judging from the experience of my older colleagues, than they had since the middle of the previous

37. Side drums: *left to right:* rope-tensioned military or 'guard's' drum by A. F. Matthews, London, early twentieth century; 'The Snapper' by Hawkes, London, single-tensioned, *c.*1920; the '2000' by Premier, Leicester, double-tensioned and with plastic heads, inverted to show the coiled-wire snares and the interior, *c.*1972.

century. Few of the instruments on which I learned would have been strange to a player at the beginning of the century – almost all were out of date and unusable in any professional orchestra by the time I joined the Musicians' Union.

Some of these changes have been due to changes in musical styles. Where around 1900 a few of the more advanced composers expected some rapid tuning changes from timpani, today almost every composer regards them as fully chromatic instruments. Some are due to commercial changes. The cymbal makers Zildjian moved from Istanbul to Massachusetts, and different metals, and a different environment, have led to different cymbals and different sounds. Despite the imprinted claim 'Genuine Turkish' on each instrument, the modern Avedis Zildjian cymbals made in the USA do not sound remotely like the old K. Zildjian cymbals made before 1940 in Istanbul. Nor, one has to say, do some more recent cymbals bearing the K. Zildjian mark.

Some changes are due to different manufacturing styles. Where side drums and bass drums had been tensioned with ropes, metal rods with a screw at one end were developed. These were called 'single-tensioned' (ill. 37) and had the advantage that tensioning became more precise, because it was easier to tighten each point as much or as little as required, and more consistent because metal rods, unlike ropes, do not stretch as humidity changes. These were followed by separate rods screwed from each end, 'double-tensioned', so that the tension of each head could be controlled separately. Single-tensioned side drums were used in the nineteenth century, usually with gut snares. More serious players used snares of wire on silk to give a better sound. These were made like covered fiddle strings, a wire covering close-spun over a silk base. For the drummer in lighter music, a new style of snare was developed, like an open coil spring. These buzzed more than snapped, a difference which made playing easier in music for which sharp, precise rhythms were seldom required.

And some changes, perhaps the most effective so far as sound was concerned, came from the availability of different materials. The use of plastic film instead of animal skin for drumheads has been of far-reaching effect.

Plastic drumheads have the great advantage that they are almost immune to changes in temperature and humidity and as a result they can be used in almost any conditions. A number of makers experimented with them in the 1950s, once Mylar and other polyester films became easily available.[17] They can also be mass-produced in an endless stream, ready-welded to their fleshhoops, with none of the mess, smells, problems of supply and high cost of processing animal skins, and then the need for careful lapping and maintenance The military drummer no longer need fear the wrath of the colonel who knows nothing of musical instruments and who blames the player for his inability to produce a drum roll in the pouring rain. The studio timpanist can work unperturbed beneath the heat of television lights without need for a bucket of water and a sponge to dampen the heads and keep them somewhere near their intended pitch. The orchestral player can leave the instruments on the platform between rehearsal and concert and disregard the depredations of the heating engineer who will flood the hall with cold moist air in the middle of summer and hot dry air in winter. The drummer who suffers a split head can slap on a replacement in minutes and not have to wait twenty-four hours for a newly-lapped calfskin head to dry out.

The disadvantage of plastic is its tonal quality, which is thin and impoverished compared with that of natural animal skin. It does not respond satisfactorily to the same beaters that work well on natural skin and while for the side drummer this may be no more serious than finding a stick of slightly different weight, the timpanists' problem is much more difficult to solve. The listener's ear suggests that while some may have found a solution, many are once again in the same position as Berlioz's contemporaries: making an unpleasant sound because they have failed to come to terms with new drumhead materials. Edmund Bowles points out that plastic has less 'bounce', less natural elasticity, than natural skin, which because it thus requires firmer mallets accounts both for the louder bangs of so many modern timpanists and their lack of ability to execute a fast roll.[18] I would blame both this lack of elasticity and the resulting hard beaters, combined with the inherent poorer tone quality, for the common lack of ability to produce a true roll, a continuous sound, without the awareness of individual impacts; what one hears so often instead today sounds like a machine gun. So far as I can discover, nobody has yet conducted full tests with calf and plastic heads on the same drums, using a full range of beaters on each, to see just how the two materials compare in their overtone spectra, but I think that most of us would agree that plastic wins for convenience and calfskin for tone. As a result, many of the best timpanists today still use calf, or have in the last few years returned to calf, despite its very considerably greater cost and inconvenience than plastic.

We shall return to these and other changes as we discuss each type of instrument in greater detail.

Drum and other beaters

Leaving aside the player's fingers, each type of drum and each other sort of percussion instrument has its own proper style of beater. To take just two examples, the Nigerian and Ghanaian hourglass-shaped talking drums have a crook-shaped beater, whereas the Ghanaian *atumpan* have a beater more sharply angled, shaped like the number 7. Within these styles there is further variation, sometimes regional, sometimes personal to the player. Laurence Picken shows a page full of different patterns of *davul* beater, all used for the same type of drum by different players from different regions of Turkey.[19]

This is true in our own music also. Each type of drum, in each period and musical style, has its own model of beater, while each player will suit him- or herself within that model. Composers seem blithely unaware of this individuality among instruments and their beaters, or at best uncaring. They will ask for the bass drum to be played with timpani sticks, which are far too light for that purpose and will not elicit the full tone, or will ask for timpani sticks on the cymbal, for which they are too soft and too fragile, and other similar inanities. For rolls on a suspended cymbal a solid hard felt ball is much more effective than a normal timpani stick. A timpani stick is especially dangerous for a quiet stroke, when a marginally more gentle attack than intended may result in the disaster of total silence. Players ignore such instructions and use whatever beaters will best fulfil the composer's apparent intent, even sometimes improving on the composer's request, as with Charles Henderson's famous use of half-crowns instead of side-drum sticks.[20]

Timpani

Any older English drummer would class the Hawkes-Cummings model of hand-tuned timpani as tonally superior to any pedal timpani except the deep-shelled German Dresden model with its external mechanism. Regrettably, Parsons of Birmingham was the only British firm willing to fit Leedy-style pedal action to existing timpani. The tonal result was better than that of most pedal timpani, despite the internal mechanism, but the drums were awkward to play because the greater depth of the Hawkes-Cummings shell, compared with the normal pedal-timpani shell, raised the head inconveniently high. As a result, few players have continued to use such drums. Even in Germany the Dresden model has shrunk somewhat in depth, perhaps for precisely that reason, and the tone quality has diminished proportionately.

Timpani share with string instruments the problem that their contained air-body must be something of a chameleon, able to resonate to as wide a range of pitch as possible. The ideal machine drum would not only vary the tension of the head but also its diameter and, more important, the volume and shape of the shell. The movement of the soundwaves within the shell would then be the same at any pitch as would the responding resonance. Such an ideal is, at least at present, physically impossible, though probably easily achieved on a computer as 'virtual reality'. As things are at present we have to compromise. We know that a deeper shell gives a better tone and that that depth must relate to the diameter. We know, too, that the drumheads of a set of timpani must be at the same height (nobody could play on a flight of steps, though Sax advertised his shell-less drums in just such a pattern) and that they must be within the reach of a seated timpanist (nobody can use pedal timpani fluently while standing). The result is that the second drum from the top of a set of hand-tuned drums, the d drum as it were, can be close to the ideal. The f drum, and any special higher drums, can have higher stands or longer legs to compensate for their shallower shells, but the A drum and still more the F drum must be squatter than the ideal, and any specially low drum, such as those for low D or C, will look more like a washtub than a musical instrument.

This problem becomes far worse with pedal timpani because of the height required for the pedal mechanism. Here the Dresden model has an advantage over others because the pedal is at the side and the kettle can come much lower within its frame of mechanism. The disadvantage is that it is more difficult for the feet to move from drum to drum. It means also that if one wishes to have the pedal on the near side of the drum, it must, like the controls of automobiles, be adaptable for different markets. Drummers of Central and Eastern Europe like to have the high drum on the left, whereas most, but by no means all, drummers of Western Europe and the Americas prefer to have it on the right. With the modern mobility of populations, any pair of drums, still worse any set of four, may find a player of the opposing tradition doing something akin to the splits as he repositions the drums to suit himself and then finds the pedals as far away as possible.

38. One of a pair of 'Tour Timps', pedal timpani without shells by Marcus de Mowbray.

Recently considerable doubt has been cast on the effects discussed above, of the air capacity of the shell, by the work of the London drum-maker Marcus de Mowbray. He has developed a modern version of Sax's *timbales chromatiques*, in his 'Tour Timps', light-weight pedal timpani without shells (ill. 38). These share with Sax's drums the convenience of portability, and improve on them with lightness of weight, and are very quickly and easily assembled. More important, laboratory acoustic tests show that they produce a fuller and more resonant sound, with a greater harmonic amplitude and better sustaining power, than timpani with a conventional shell and it is suggested that normal drumshells, by containing and inhibiting the vibration of the air, reduce the freedom of the heads to vibrate. They are clearly an important development and it may be that before long we shall have to reclassify timpani as chromatic frame drums rather than kettledrums! De Mowbray's work on side drums has produced even more astonishing results: a drum without a shell, with only pillars to hold the heads apart and accommodate the tuning lugs, produces a loud and clear tone, with full snare response even though there is nothing but open air between the batter head and the snare head.[21]

The enhanced chromaticism of modern timpani writing is not always as successful as the composers intended. Most pedal timpani today have tuning gauges which, in theory, allow one to see what pitch one has reached when there is no time to try the drum with the finger. However, as we said in the previous chapter, few gauges are accurate to better than a quarter-tone, nor do they allow for any variation due to climatic conditions, when using natural skin, nor for any tendency for the head to hang or slip on the rim, leading to lesser or greater pitch change than the movement of the pedal might indicate. Nor do they allow for those many occasions when one has to watch the conductor through shifting time signatures and glue one's eyes to the music through a minefield of rests of differing lengths and tricky rhythms to play. It is surprising how accurate fast tuning changes can be, without access to gauges, when using one's own drums, but nevertheless one does always listen with interest to the next note to see whether one has guessed right!

Some composers do their utmost to help, and one of the best examples of this is the timpani variation in Benjamin Britten's *Nocturne*. From figure 15, a solo for four drums, from low F sharp to upper e sharp, is relatively straightforward, but from figure 17 onwards it becomes increasingly chromatic and rhythmically increasingly 'hairy', as James Blades for whom it was written always described it. But every change of pitch is made on a drum that one is playing so that one can hear what one is doing, and every move from one drum to the next is to the pitch at which one left it. Never, as in so many other scores, does one have to tune one drum while playing another and simply hope that one has come out within reasonable distance of the intended pitch. Britten's *Nocturne* is an object lesson to all composers in the art of writing for chromatic timpani.

The earlier wooden timpani beaters have already been described as has the possible use of leather covers. We do not know to what extent players may have experimented with such covers, using different varieties, thicknesses, and softnesses of leather or cloth, but it would seem unlikely that early players were any less inclined to experiment than modern ones. It is a fair assumption that almost any material which was available in any period will have been used from time to time and place to place, according to the temperament and ingenuity of the player.

The sponge-headed sticks that Berlioz demanded were made from the natural marine creatures of the Mediterranean, which provide a wide range of hardness and firmness.[22] There seem to have been several ways of making such sticks, for instance by covering a wooden or other core with a layer of sponge, or by compressing a ball of sponge between a collar round the stick and a washer and screw.

Gerassimos Avgerinos, late timpanist of the Berlin Philharmonic, says that flannel was used as early as 1800.[23] Flannel is a woollen cloth of one-to-one weave, with the same number of warp threads as weft, unlike a twill or a tweed, for instance. As a result it will compress equally in any direction. Certainly flannel was used later in the nineteenth and into the twentieth centuries. An innumerable stack of discs was compressed to an inch or so thick between a horn collar and a screwed washer at the end of a malacca stick. If such sticks were available as early as 1800 it is surprising that Berlioz and Kastner did not mention them.

Felt was also common from the mid-nineteenth century, probably as early as the 1830s. Kirby has an excellent photograph of an 'exploded' stick, showing exactly how it was made, with a solid felt disc as a core and a softer felt cover stitched over it.[24]

When I entered the profession many players were still using such sticks, either the felt or the flannel. I was unhappy with the flexible malacca shafts, feeling that they took too much control for themselves, and devised a rigid shaft, initially of thicker garden cane and then in emulation of the timpanist of the Copenhagen Tivoli Gardens, of three-eighth-inch aluminium tubing. The heads were of cork, which seemed to give too hard a tone quality despite the covers of soft felt. This is still the problem with many sticks that are commercially available.

Feeling that James Bradshaw of the Philharmonia produced a more beautiful tone than anyone else, I asked him how he made his sticks. The answer was a balsa wood core, rounded to a cylinder, covered in two layers of split piano damper felt. This is a very soft material and, when half-inch felt (12 mm) is split by hand into four thicknesses, what was the inner surface becomes a very soft outer surface for the beaters. Two thin layers are better than one thicker because the air caught between the loose fibres between the two layers gives a better result. Ill. 39 shows several sizes of stick for different tone qualities (one of each pair) and the inner and outer covers. The rubber knob on the proximal end of the shaft helps one to feel that the stick will not fly from the hand, acts as a counterbalance to the head, and serves as an emergency side-drum beater.[25]

Today, many players are more inclined to buy than to make their sticks, and turned wooden shafts with wood or cork heads covered with felt are available in any drum shop. However, any really careful players will still make their own or have them made to their required patterns. Certainly every professional player will take a case full of different beaters, changing many times in the course of even a single work to produce the ideal tone at every point in its duration. Nor will the same sticks be used at every performance, for different halls with different numbers of people in them, even in different weather, will have a different acoustic and thus require a different sound from the drums.

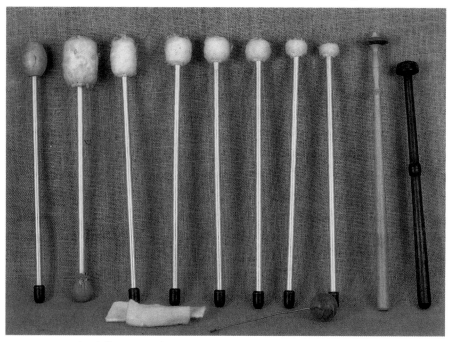

39. Timpani sticks, different sizes for different tone qualities, one from each pair: wooden stick for modern music (*left*), two reproduction wooden sticks for early music, one from Switzerland, the other from Tony Bingham (*right*), with different sizes of normal felt-on-balsa sticks in between, and (*foreground*) the inner and outer layers of felt, and a superball on a wire handle, all, save the two early, my own design and make.

Always, always, always, it is the sound that matters, and this we each achieve in our own manner with our own drums and our own beaters.

Side drum

The main changes here have been those mentioned above, to tensioning and to materials. Plastic heads are now almost universal, as are metal counterhoops. Metal shells are also common and so are the coiled wire snares of the dance-band world, even though these give a buzz rather than the snap which used to characterize the old gut or the wire-on-silk snares. The coiled wire makes the roll easier because the buzz lasts perceptibly longer than the snap of gut and for that reason the wire snares soon came to dominate the orchestral world as well. It is only very rarely today that one hears the precise rhythm of a side drum part without the blurring caused by the use of wire snares. The set of wires comes soldered to a plate at each end so that the tension of each strand is fixed. Ludwig did try to market a drum some years ago on which not only could each snare be individually tensioned, but snares of different materials could be mixed to produce a wide variety of tone quality and response. Excellent though it was, few players were willing to take the trouble.

The popularity of the side drum has increased enormously, for it is at the centre of the drum kit, though mastery of its fundamental techniques has not kept pace with its popularity. Exceptions to this are some specialist circles such as the Basel drummers in Switzerland and the American groups that specialize in rudimental drumming where mastery of the basic techniques and an almost infinite variety of increasingly complex variations on them would put to shame most orchestral side-drummers.[26] The average pop-group drummer is no more a master of the side drum than the leader is of the guitar.

Side-drum beaters are plain wooden sticks, tapering towards one end and then widening again abruptly into a bead. The bead may vary from spherical through oval to acorn in shape. The taper may be gradual in a light stick or more sudden and late in a heavier one. The wood is normally a hardwood and it must be one which will not warp for a bent or twisted side drum-stick would be almost unusable. For this reason, every drummer, when buying a pair of sticks, rolls them along the shop counter, and even the slightest tremor of the bead as it rolls leads to an immediate rejection. Various synthetic materials have been tried, even metal, but most players find that these feel dead in the hands and prefer wood.

Players who are sensible check the pitch of their sticks. When one plays the drum the main sound element is that of the drumhead, resonated by the air between the heads and modified by the buzz or rattle of the snares. However, if one listens carefully, there may be a slight pitch difference perceived between the strokes of the two hands, and this can be caused by sticks which are disparate in pitch. It can also be caused by playing in different areas of the drum head, which is why ideally one should use a small practice pad, to get used to keeping the sticks close together.[27]

The weight of the stick must match the size of the drum and the larger the drum the heavier the sticks should be. Beef wood was used in the eighteenth century (ill. 40 left). Ebony has been used, especially for heavy military beaters in the late nineteenth and early twentieth centuries (ill. 40, next from left). The modern military drum, though still the same shape and size as the earlier, has plastic heads which respond more sharply and quickly than the heavy calf skins previously used, and therefore something more like an orchestral stick is more appropriate. This is certainly true for the Scots drums, used with the Highland pipes, which are always braced very tightly. Japanese oak began to appear as a material in the late 1950s and proved immediately successful for this and orchestral use (ill. 40, third from left), as did many Japanese makes of instrument. Hickory has been a popular wood especially in America, where it is native.

The kit drummer normally uses a lighter stick than the orchestral player because the drum is shallower and is aimed at a different sound. The bead will usually be of nylon rather than wood, for use on the ride and other cymbals, woodblocks, and other hard instruments. Nylon will survive such use longer than wood, which would chip quite easily and could then damage the drumhead (ill. 40, fourth from left).

Wire brushes are a standard part of the dance-band drummer's equipment, partly because they are quieter than sticks, partly because their rhythm is less demandingly precise, and partly because the swish of the brush on the drumhead gives a continuous sound less domineering than a side drum roll. A basic technique for foxtrots and such dances is a circular swish with one hand and a light tap with the other. The only reasonable alternative in such contexts would be incessant *pianissimo* rolls and both the player's wrists and the audience's ears would quickly tire of that.

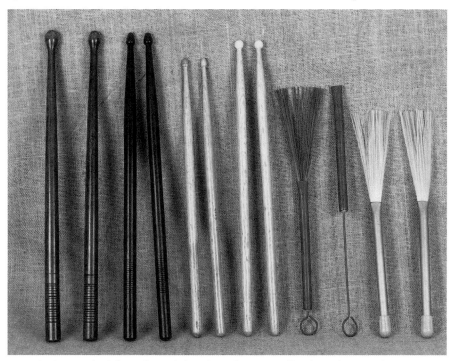

40. Side-drum sticks: *left to right:* English eighteenth century of beef wood, twentieth century military sticks of ebony by Henry Potter, London, orchestral sticks of Japanese oak, kit drummer's sticks with nylon beads, also Japanese, telescopic wire brushes, nylon brushes.

Wire brushes are normally made from innumerable strands of thin steel wire. This has two disadvantages. One is that it leaves a black mark on the drumhead, which is unsightly. The other is that it is easy for one or two wires to become bent and stick up at a sharp angle and catch on the head. This can be discouraged, if not avoided entirely, by using brushes that telescope into their handles to protect them when not in use (ill. 40, right). This, in turn, can cause problems if the brushes are used for rim shots, as they may well be in jazzier numbers, for the handles get dented and then are either difficult or impossible to telescope. One solution was the nylon brush which neither leaves dirty marks nor bends any of its strands, but the sound of the nylon strands was never quite as good as that of wire. It is also essential to have at least one pair of brushes with a solid knob on the handle end. A few composers have demanded the use of brushes and sometimes one has only a beat or two to return to normal sticks. Flipping them over and using the other end is the solution.

The drum kit

Jazz and ragtime bands are always said to have derived from the marching bands which played for funerals in the black communities of the southern states of the USA, specifically in New Orleans. The bands were often equipped with cast-off instruments from the War between the States, including side drums, bass drums, and cymbals, the cymbal usually attached to the bass drum. When such bands became sedentary, whether riding on a cart or sitting in a hall, one drummer became expected to play all the instruments, and it was from this that the drum kit evolved. Initially the side drum was set in such a position, retaining the traditional marching tilt, that the right-hand stick could flip across and strike the bass drum, a technique called double-drumming. Skilled players could produce a side-drum roll while simultaneously playing a rhythm on the bass drum, never allowing this flick of the right-hand stick to interrupt the smoothness of the roll.[28]

Cymbals were more of a problem, one that was not really solved until the bass-drum pedal was invented around the turn of the century. The early pedals had a solid head to strike the bass drum and a metal rod projecting from the side of the bass-drum beater which simultaneously struck the cymbal, which was clamped to the rim of the bass-drum shell. The disadvantage of this was that bass drum and cymbal would always sound together so that the cymbal could not be used on the offbeat or back-beat. The solution was to make a new pedal for the other foot with a hinged pair of wooden jaws held open with a bed spring and a cymbal screwed to the end of each jaw (ill. 41). With this contraption placed on the floor, a foot on the upper jaw could clash the cymbals together; a loop of rope round the hinge of the pedal and the leg of the drummer's stool or chair prevented the pedal from making its way across the stage. These pedals were usually called floor pedals or, from their appearance, snow-shoes, to distinguish them in the transitional period from their successor, the later hi-hat pedal. There was normally also a cymbal attached to the bass drum or on a separate stand so that it could be struck with a drum stick when required; a popular model was the Chinese crash, which had a faster decay than a Turkish cymbal.

Other instruments were gradually added to the kit. Hooters, whistles, washboards, Chinese temple blocks or skulls, and the ordinary rectangular woodblock were popular, and so were the Chinese tomtoms, used either singly contrasting with the

41. Floor-pedal cymbals, the pedal home-made with a bed-spring, perhaps by James Clubb, London.

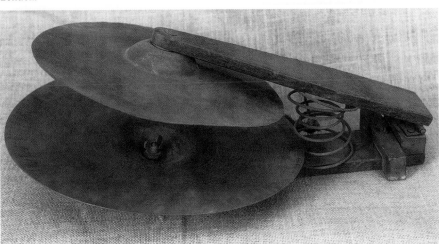

42. Trap tray, set up with Chinese crash cymbal (*left*), snap cymbal (*right*), Chinese temple blocks (*back*), tambourine (*back right*), Chinese woodblock (*centre*), pair of cowbells (*front*), pair of spoons (*front right*), and wash-board (*foreground*).

side drum or in pairs. To facilitate such use of the side drum, a quick release for the snare became commonly used. On the military drum the snare tension had been adjusted with a screw-nut, but to release the snares completely took some time, and screwing them back up again took even longer and was obtrusive because the tension had to be checked by tapping the drum to hear its sound. A lever which would drop the snares and bring them up again to the pre-set tension avoided such delays.

All these accretions developed gradually, but by the 1930s they had become standardized enough that most players used a trap tray, a wooden tray fixed to the bass drum with a series of arms and posts to which many of these traps, as they were known, could be attached (ill. 42). Two higher arms, one on each side, could hold a Chinese cymbal and a sizzle cymbal (a cymbal with holes drilled in it, each filled with a loose rivet to add a sizzling sound) or a snap cymbal (a light-weight cymbal whose vibration could be quickly damped with the hand to give a sharp snap). Four posts along the back would hold a set of skulls, and so forth. Tomtoms were by now being commercially made with screw tension to the upper head so that their pitch and tone quality could be controlled even though the lower head was still nailed. On the old Chinese tomtoms both heads were nailed and were subject to the hazards of climatic variation, though a thick coat of varnish on very thick skins helped to keep them stable (ill. 59). The modern tomtom has screw tension on both heads.

The normal set of tomtoms became a pair fixed one to each side of the bass drum plus a tenor tomtom or floor tom standing on its own feet. The desire to use the cymbal for rhythmic decoration led to the invention of the high-hat or hi-hat, a pair of cymbals on the top of a post, the lower one fixed and the upper pulled down to clash on it by a pedal. This was less effective as a crash pair than the old floor pedal but it had the great advantage that it could be played with a side-drum stick either open or closed; half closed was an additional effect.

The invention of bebop, followed by rock and roll and then by pop, led to further developments and to a very considerable expansion of the basic instruments of the kit. The traps mostly vanished, though several were later reinvented for the revival of traditional jazz, but bass drums, cymbals, and tomtoms multiplied. A pair of bass drums was often seen, leading to the exclusion of the high-hat, for drummers had only two feet, with a great row of tomtoms, up to as many as a dozen, though this was mainly for show bands and as much for ostentation as for use. Flights of cymbals appeared all over the kit on rods and extended stands, again as much for show as for use, though the new styles led to the development of new sonorities and the need for a multiplicity of cymbals. As long as players used the high-hat as a ride or rhythm cymbal its tone could be controlled by choking the upper cymbal against the lower. When the high-hat vanished, a reiterated rhythm on a suspended cymbal led to an undesirable build-up of volume, the same effect as was achieved by a roll on a suspended cymbal in the orchestra. Makers therefore developed the ride cymbal, one that would withstand reiterated strokes without crescendo. Today one can visit a specialist drum shop and buy a variety of cymbals, each with its own tonal characteristics to fulfil a different function. Similarly, different types of plastic drum head are made to produce different sounds on tomtoms, and the rototom, a plastic head on a frame without a shell that screws up and down, altering its pitch just like screw-machine timpani, can be used in sets to produce a complete scale of tomtom pitches.

In addition to all or much of this, any dance-band drummer needs a set of Latin-American instruments for rumbas, congas and other dances from that part of the world (ill. 43). Here the basics are the bongos, timbales, maracas and other rattles such as

43. Instruments of Latin-American dance music: *left to right:* maracas, bongos (*back*), claves (*front*), güiro and scraper.

cabaça, a güiro, a pair of claves and, for the Caribbean, a hoe blade or similar piece of iron, and a pair of conga drums.

The bongos are a pair of small, single-headed drums, usually held between the knees though sometimes on a stand, and always played with the fingers. The heads are thick, often goatskin, and the shells, which are normally wood, should be thick enough to withstand high tension. The timbales (not to be confused with timpani, which are called *timbales* in French) are also single headed but somewhat larger, usually metal-shelled, and with thinner heads. They are usually set on a stand and are played with light sticks; in effect they are a pair of small tomtoms. Maracas are gourd vessel rattles on handles, often today made of wood rather than gourd, or even of plastic, always played in pairs and, like most paired instruments, always with one higher pitched than the other. The cabaça is a larger gourd with a network of seeds or pieces of gourd outside it, played by twisting the instrument rhythmically inside the net. The güiro is a scraped gourd, again often made of wood or plastic today, and the claves are a pair of hardwood rods, ideally rosewood, the same as for xylophone bars, six to eight inches long and about an inch thick. One rests on the fingers and heel of one hand, resting at its nodal points over the cupped palm, and is struck with the other held in the other hand.

It is a characteristic of all the Latin-American percussion instruments that most of them play a steady, constantly repeated *ostinato*. Little in the dance band's life is more boring than playing this music and it is always done with constant smiles, unless one is singing, to disguise this. The drummer, fortunately, is normally responsible for the bongo or timbale parts, which are the most important and which do have a good deal of variation and room for improvisation. The *ostinato* instruments are usually handed round to the rest of the band and the leader. The conga drums are tall, narrow, barrel-shaped drums, again with thick heads at high tension. They play a very elaborate role with considerable pitch variation achieved in much the same way as on the left-hand *tablā* and drums of the *darabukka* family, for which see the next chapter.

Bass drum

Returning to the orchestra and the basic drum kit, the bass drum is an essential instrument for both even if, as Berlioz never tired of pointing out, it was sometimes over-used, as it certainly is in much popular music today, as one can hear from passing cars or through the wall from one's neighbours. At the beginning of the twentieth century, bass drums were either rope-tensioned as in the military band, or had metal rods. They were still often single-headed in Britain and known as gong drums. The rope-tensioned military drums were normally 30 inches in diameter (75 cm) and 15 inches deep; dance-band drums were rod-tensioned and rather smaller, about 24 inches (60 cm) in diameter and wide enough to support a trap tray laid on top of the drum, which would then be at a convenient height for a drummer seated on a stool. The drum stood on the floor with a pair of spurs attached to the rim of the shell to dig into the floor and stop it from wandering away under the impulse of the pedal. When the 22-inch kit bass drum came into fashion in the 1960s or so, it meant a radical redesign of the metalware that attached the tomtoms and other instruments, to keep them within the player's reach, and these ancillary instruments started to appear on top of the bass drum rather than at its sides. The main purpose of the smaller drum was the search for shorter sounds, sharper rhythms, and less boom.

Things went the opposite way in the orchestra, where more sound was desired rather than less. This had been the main purpose of the single-headed bass drum: to avoid the interference of one head with the other. The military bass drum had never really been big enough, either in diameter or depth. While avoiding the extravagance of the great Distin drum, orchestral bass drums are built a good foot wider than the basic military drum and nearly twice the depth. They are usually placed in a stand on wheels for ease of transport and slung so that they can be tipped at an angle from the vertical for ease of playing. The wheels have brakes to prevent the drum from descending accidentally from its normal position on the uppermost rise of the platform.

The eighteenth-century bass-drum beater and switch gave way to a lump of felt, made of a series of felt discs compressed together by the screw that held them to the bamboo stick. More recently the slightly softer sound of lamb's wool has been preferred – the hard felt beater tends to produce rather a smack. One always has two such beaters for playing rolls, since the timpani sticks usually demanded by composers for this purpose will do little more than stir the surface of the skin. These rollers, as they are often called, are usually double-ended, one end being smaller in diameter than the other, to allow for different tone colours. The double-ended beater is also useful for playing rolls on those occasions when a cheese-paring management leaves one doing something else with the other hand.

Tamtam and gongs

The best tamtams used in the first half of the twentieth century were all Chinese, some of them superlative instruments, the relics of the old Imperial Court. By mid-century most of them were worn out, either simply from use or because, as with the BBC Symphony's tamtam, a player had put a bell hammer through it. This is one of the great perils for percussion instruments. Nobody asks violinists to use metal rods on their strings, but few composers hesitate to ask us to use such things on our instruments. Elgar asks for a cymbal to be hit *fortissimo* with a metal rod.[29] Most of us have some sort of dustbin lid around, already cracked, which we don't mind risking, but Elgar would have got a better sound if he had simply left it as a normal pair-cymbal clash.[30] At least, earlier in the same work (figure 56), when he asked for side-drum sticks on timpani, the marking was *ppp*. Even at that level, his first timpanist, Charles Henderson, was unwilling to risk the little dents usually left in the timpani head by the small beads of a side-drum stick and used a pair of coins instead.[31]

Stravinsky asks for the tamtam to be scraped with a triangle beater in *Le Sacre du printemps*, and again the result may be an inferior sound on an old and perhaps already cracked instrument.[32] It is a common concept among musicians in general that while their instruments may be fragile and valuable and should be handled with kid gloves, percussion instruments are fair game and can be hit with anything and by anybody. It is up to all percussion players to disabuse them of this.[33] Meanwhile, we have to play the parts as best we can, cheating as much as possible, as violinists do when asked to play *col legno*.[34]

Most tamtams now come from Switzerland, where the firm of Paiste have succeeded in producing as good a tone as the old Chinese instruments. The proper beater is a heavily loaded mass of felt. The loading is important because the weight or mass of the stick affects the tone it produces and a light beater would only tickle the surface of a large tamtam. Playing the tamtam is more difficult than it looks because the sound builds up for a perceptible time after it has been struck. Unless preceded by a general pause, one can often play a semiquaver or two ahead of the beat for the maximum effect.

Several firms now make sets of tuned gongs in equal temperament for works such as Puccini's *Turandot* and Vaughan Williams's *Sinfonia Antartica*, and provided that managements are willing to hire them, it is no longer necessary to combine Burmese, Indonesian, and Malaysian scales on our concert platforms as we used to do. The main problems that arise are due to the vagueness of composers, partly confusing tamtams with gongs (the tamtam is the flat-faced instrument without a definite pitch; the gong often has a boss in the centre of the face and is tuned to a precise pitch) and partly failing to specify just what they want.

Tuned percussion

The xylophone we have already described; the only changes are an increased range and a glossier appearance, often with resonators apparently as long at the treble as at the bass in a gracefully curved arch. Each tubular resonator must match its air capacity to the pitch of the bar above it, but an internal plate soldered at the correct height for this purpose ensures that outward appearance is not marred by the requirements of inner efficiency. The marimba is a bigger and better xylophone, descending an octave or more lower, with wider and thinner bars so that the sound is more humming and less chippy; it is played with softer mallets. Both have the same problem nowadays that rosewood is an endangered species, and various substitutes, such as plastics, have been tried for the bars, some quite successfully. An instrument called a xylorimba, which is usually a xylophone with an extra bass octave, falls between two stools, for if the bars are thin enough to give a good marimba tone they are not chippy enough for a xylophone, and of course vice versa. It can be useful especially where space or cost is a consideration. All are laid out like a piano keyboard, but with the 'black' notes level with the 'white' to make it easier to move to and fro.

The vibraphone is in effect a marimba with metal bars.[35] A long rod runs through the top of each row of resonators, one for the 'white' notes and one for the 'black', with fixed to it a series of metal discs, one in the top of each resonator tube (ill. 44). With clockwork or electric motors turning the rods, the discs rotate to open and close the air columns contained in the tubes. This creates an amplitude throb which can be varied by controlling the speed of the motor. Clockwork has the disadvantage of running down at critical moments; electricity has the disadvantage of trailing wires and the search for sockets.[36]

44. Detail of a vibraphone, some 'black'-note bars removed to show the fans in the tops of the resonator tubes.

Parts written for all three instruments get more complex every year. Where it was enough to have one mallet in each hand, two became common and now three or more are usual and players are expected to produce chords as full as a pianist. They are also expected to sight-read almost anything. Back in 1950 there were only two or three players in London who could cope with anything put in front of them; everybody else expected to take it home and practise. Nowadays it is an exceptional player who needs advance notice.

The glockenspiel (American orchestral bells) has changed little. There was a brief period when alloy instruments became popular, but the greater brightness of steel was normally preferred.

Agricola's xylophone of 1528 was struck with little rods with round knobs, like very small side-drum sticks. The nineteenth-century beaters (we have no knowledge of what came between) were known in England as spoons, since they resembled a silhouette of a spoon seen from the side, a curved wooden beater with a narrow flat handle and a deeper, thicker, curved striking end. The general shape is not unlike a

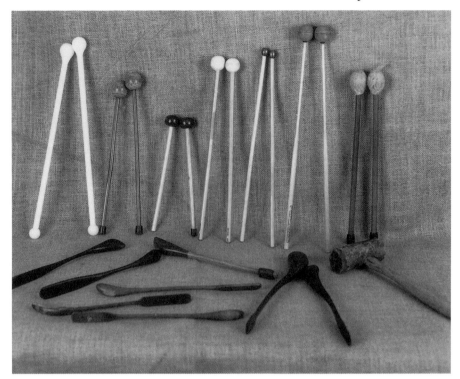

45. Beaters for tuned percussion: *left to right*: hard nylon for glockenspiel, two pairs of wood for xylophone, hard plastic and brass, both for glockenspiel, soft rubber and wool-covered, both for vibraphone; *front* 'spoons' for the old four-row xylophone and a bell hammer.

Hungarian *cimbalom* beater, though much more solid, and the two instruments were closely related in Hungary, the xylophone with sticks of wooden dowel for its notes being a cheap substitute for the *cimbalom* with its many wire strings.[37] Such beaters were certainly used in Britain into the twentieth century, but when the shape of the instrument changed from the older four-row layout to the modern quasi-piano keyboard, the beaters changed also to round wooden knobs on bamboo handles. With minor variation, and trials of numerous types of artificial materials, this or plastic is what is still used on the xylophone today (ill. 45).

The glockenspiel, when it was still made of light glass plates, was played with short beaters with a wooden disk on the end, sometimes D-shaped, with the curved face of the D covered with a strip of cloth glued on to protect the glass. When the bars became steel, round wooden knobs took over, followed by various artificial materials. Small brass knobs make a very bright and penetrating sound and are not hard enough to damage the steel bars.

The vibraphone, with its bars of aluminium alloy, must be played with much softer beaters, usually rubber or something similar covered with wool. The marimba is sometimes played with the same beaters or with sticks with soft rubber knobs. Players will always devise their own covering either for a special effect or because they prefer its sound to that of the standard beaters. Composers' demands for hard mallets on marimba and vibraphone should be resisted – expensive instruments are easily damaged.

Tubular bells (American chimes) have increased in range. At one stage, in Britain at least, a diatonic octave from E flat to e flat was all that was available because this was all that the military bands needed and they were the big customers. Nowadays orchestras are the main customers and bigger sets are available, fully chromatic so that they can be played in any key. They are still fairly limited in range, of necessity because for the best sound the tube must be struck at the edge of the cap on its upper end, and there is a limit to the height a player can reach. For works like *Tosca* and the *Symphonie fantastique* some orchestras resort to drainpipes, with a player perched precariously up a step ladder.

The tubular bell is not the ideal bell substitute. It is convenient and easily made, but it does not have the full tonal spectrum of a real bell. The Amsterdam Concertgebouw Orchestra has a set of rectangular steel plates which sound more realistic. Unfortunately it is impracticable to copy them because all that is known is that they were made from the armour plating of a British battlecruiser in the early years of the twentieth century.[38] Bronze mushrooms have been tried but the problem, as with anything resembling a bell in form, is that to produce any usefully low pitches a mass inconveniently large and heavy is needed. The Festspielhaus in Bayreuth experimented at one time with a wholly improbable substitute devised by Felix Mottl for *Parsifal*, a vast wooden frame with strings across it, plus five tamtams and a bass tuba. Cecil Forsyth described it better than anyone else.[39]

The smalls

Triangles have changed little over the years, though they are not as well made as they used to be and are more likely to harbour some traces of definite pitch. Most orchestral players have rigged up a gallows, fitting into the top of a cymbal stand, in which to hang the triangle in a short loop of nylon fishing line so that they can use two beaters for rapid rhythms.[40] The loop must be small so that the triangle does not twist or spin. A machine triangle is very useful for pit work and is described and illustrated (ill. 76) in Appendix 3.

The triangle is normally struck with a steel bar somewhat thinner than the instrument. Six-inch nails are popular; six-inch carriage bolts the same thickness (quarter-inch) are made of better steel and give a better sound, though one always carries some lighter steel beaters for different effects; knitting needles are useful. It is essential to have identical pairs of triangle beaters for playing fast or complex rhythms; beaters of different weight, thickness, or material inevitably produce different sounds.

Tambourines now more often have plastic heads than skin and may need to have the head rubbed with rosin for thumb rolls because polyester is more slippery than skin. At least one maker has produced a tambourine with a rigid plastic head with raised radial bars built in to catch the thumb.[41] The jingle ring, the tambourine without a head, is more often a feature of the pop group than of orchestral percussion.

The tenor drum seldom appears in the orchestra. In the military band it is played with beaters with solid felt heads, like small bass-drum beaters (the military and marching bass drum still often uses a solid felt beater or sometimes even a wooden club). In the orchestra, especially in such passages as Till Eulenspiegel's execution, heavy side-drum sticks are used, as they are in the German military band also.

Castanets are usually fixed on a handle, both for ease of playing and because it is quicker to pick them up and put them down than to detach the proper instruments from the thumbs. A skilled percussion section playing them properly on the thumbs can look very effective, especially if the concert is televised, and this does sometimes happen. For works like *Façade*, machine castanets, a pair of shells fixed to a board so that they can be played with sticks or with the fingers without having to pick them up, are almost essential. These are now commercially available, but most of us have made our own and these also are described in Appendix 3.

Whips are also often home-made, two slats of wood hinged at one end with a handle halfway down each slat so that they can be slapped together. The best hinges are a leather strap; metal hinges may slow down the action. The slapstick is a related instrument which can be held in one hand when the other hand is busy doing something else. The handle is integral with one of the slats and the other is hinged to it partway down. It was the use of this instrument in music-hall and circus acts that gave the comedy its name.

The whistles, hooters, and other effects demanded of us are innumerable. As we have said above, any noises too vulgar for the rest of the orchestra are given to the percussion. It sometimes needs some ingenuity to satisfy a composer, but most of us have drawers full of noise makers.

Steel drums

These are among the most recently invented musical instruments. Their origin is Trinidad in the West Indies, during and just after the 1939–45 War, when oil drums were easily available at the various American bases, though there is a considerable previous history of other bands and of brake drums and other scrap-metal objects which led up to them. Putting it excessively simply, the tops of oil drums, or more elegant simulacra of stainless steel, are hammered and dented to produce a number of discrete areas, each of which will produce a different pitch (ill. 46). The treble pans have a couple of dozen or more notes, the basses two to four, and the altos and tenors in proportion. Each pan is a gong chime on a single body and the beauty of their sound is due to the fact that while each marked-out area on the top of a pan produces a single pitch, there is some leakage from one area to its neighbours so that there is always a throb and an added resonance. There is a great deal of variation in the size of steel bands and in the number of parts and their nomenclature; the minimum is probably four-part, treble, alto, tenor divided between two pans, and bass divided between four, using standard rather than steel-band terminology. The number of pans in tenor and bass is greater because the areas for each note need to be wider and therefore fewer notes can be fitted on to the top of each pan. The steel band is beginning to come into the orchestra, and it is of course leading its own healthy life in its own culture.[42]

46. Steel drum, the second pan of a set, made in Camberwell by a local bus conductor, London, *c.* 1960.

Electronic percussion

This has taken two forms so far. One is imitation and the other is performing. There was a great deal of worry, in the early years of the synthesizer, that its use would put musicians out of work by allowing machines to do all the concerts, but this has not happened. The chief reason was monotony. The drum machine was very useful initially, but it proved to be too robotic; no musician is as regular as a metronome and even though many of us have practised incessantly in the endeavour to achieve such rhythmic accuracy, it is the fact that we have failed that makes music sound alive. Even when playing to a click track through earphones in the studio, the very slight vagaries of a human player have proved more attractive than a drum machine.

The other form of electronic percussion is the electronic kit. This has proved invaluable as a practice medium, for a drummer can set up a full kit and bash away as hard as possible without the family or the neighbours hearing a sound; only the player hears anything, but must of course be careful to keep the earphone volume low enough not to cause permanent damage to the hearing. The kit can also be fed to tape and to MIDI set ups and there is no reason why we should not have orchestral electronic simulacra as well as drum kits.

The future

Where do we go from here? One would guess in two directions: minimalist and maximalist. On the one hand we have the realization that the most effective percussion is often the least. On the other we have the desire for the most noise, the widest array on the back of the platform, and for the single drummer to be surrounded by the largest possible number of instruments. Possibly also we may achieve the fusion of the two: the large array played as quietly and subtly as possible.

Certainly, whatever may happen to the symphony orchestra, drummers are never going to be out of work, nor are composers and instrument makers going to stop inventing new sounds on new instruments and new ways of producing new sounds on old instruments.

Chapter 9

World Percussion

What we have described so far is, in the main, a very small portion and, save in our eyes, a not very enterprising part of mankind's use of percussion instruments. Nevertheless, a chapter such as this can be no more than the veriest sketch of the use of percussion in the rest of the world. Many of the books cited in the notes here will reveal a far greater variety both of the instruments themselves and of their use than we have space to describe. To make this easy we have deliberately chosen books that are well illustrated. Many also are the standard descriptive texts on the instruments and music of their respective areas.

'Primitive' is not a word that one is permitted to use today for anybody's music, but compared with that of other parts of the world it is the only appropriate word for our use of rhythm. Until the advent of jazz and ragtime, both of which derived from other cultures, our music was very squarely (and triangularly) written and the simplest syncopations could cause trouble. Even today most orchestras prefer to have the 5/4 movement of Tchaikovsky's Sixth Symphony beaten out in five rather than in the unequal two in a bar (2 + 3) which the music so clearly demands.

Few other musics are as simple as ours: New Guinea drumming, perhaps, where every man on the dancing ground has an hourglass-shaped drum, each beating his drum in time to his steps. Or perhaps the use of the dance shield in the Andaman Islands. This is a curved wooden shield which is placed on the ground, slightly bridged up in the centre so that the wide end stands clear of the ground to project the sound. The player holds the narrow end down with one foot like a seesaw, while stamping on the shield with the other foot.[1] Or perhaps the frame drums of the Arctic Circle, from the Greenland and Alaskan Eskimos round to Siberia.

The New Guinea drums (ill. 47), which are usually quite narrow, with head diameters of six inches or so (15 cm), sometimes even smaller, have bodies two or three feet long (60 to 90 cm) which contract to a narrow waist and then expand again, so that they function acoustically as stamping tubes. The hum of the air column inside the drums is the most significant element of the sound. This became apparent when Brian Cranstone played recordings of the Tifalmin people of the Sepik District highlands to the Ethnomusicology Panel of the Royal Anthropological Institute.[2] The drumheads are usually made of snakeskin with wax tuning pellets to help tune them to the internal air column and there are often pendant rattles of nut or sea shells.[3] There is a wide variety of shapes and patterns from different peoples on this huge island and its pendant archipelagos. While some

47. Drums from New Guinea.

types are well known and easily recognizable, nobody has as yet built up a general typology by which the generality, among them those illustrated here, could be assigned to any individual tribes or areas.[4] Elsewhere in Oceania skin drums are comparatively rare, though very ornate ones are known in parts of Polynesia, especially in the Marquesas Islands.[5]

The shaman's drum, used in many parts of the world, has a specific purpose: to induce trance and magical healing. The Siberian version is a frame drum made of a wooden hoop, covered with a skin on one side, and braced across the other with cross-bars of iron or twisted thongs from which iron bells and rattle-plates are suspended. The Lapp shaman's drum is differently made. A shallow wooden bowl is carved out, with enough of the back cut open for wide hand-holes that there is some doubt whether it is a frame drum or a shallow kettledrum. The head is painted with magical symbols and can be used for divination when held horizontally to see where, among the symbols, a pellet can settle.[6] The Eskimo's drum is similar in shape to the Siberian, though the frame is normally shallower and usually there are no cross braces nor iron jingles. Like the New Guinea drums, it is mainly used to accompany dancing and it is played by striking the frame as well as the drum with a beater made from sealskin.[7] Allegedly it is the only instrument known to the Eskimos of Greenland, though it seems almost incredible that they should have devised no other, no whistles, no bull-roarers, for example, even though both are easily made from the bones of the animals on which they live.[8]

The frame drum, of which our tambourine and the Eskimo and Siberian drums are examples, is one of the simplest forms of drum, a hoop of any material with a skin attached. The hoop can be made of withies or other light woods bent into a ring, or, like the tambourine, a strip of wood, with a skin attached in some way – the easiest is by folding the skin over the hoop and tucking it over the upper edge of the frame and under itself, or glueing it to the side. These techniques are used almost worldwide. Additional sounding elements of some sort are quite common, though pendant rattles, such as those on the Siberian drums, are comparatively rare. Central Asian frame drums often have a series of rings, overlapping like those of chain mail, fixed to the interior surface of the hoop.[9] In North Africa, the Near East and Southern Europe, and in our orchestral music, pairs of miniature cymbals or simpler metal discs are let into slots in the frame.

The use of a snare between the skin and the frame seems to be peculiar to North Africa; its European derivative in the Middle Ages had more usually a snare on the outer face of the skin, though how this was attached we not know. The North African examples (ill. 48) are usually knotted through small holes drilled in the shell and held in position by being gripped between the skin and the upper edge of the shell. With the Portuguese *adufe* and its Moroccan progenitor (ill. 49), the snare is usually internal, between the two heads of a square double-headed drum.[10] It is worth noting that of all the musical instruments in the world, that most widely played by women is the frame drum.[11] Such use is not exclusive; men also play it almost wherever it is found,

48. Frame drums: *bendir*, Libya (*left*) showing the internal snares, and *def*, Syria (*right*).

49. *Adufe*, Morocco (*left*) and Monsanto, Portugal (*right*).

but there are many areas in which women are permitted to play no other instrument, certainly no other drum.

A frame drum that has become very popular recently is the Irish *bodhrán*. It was partly due to my own initiative that it was recognized that this derived from a harvest instrument. In the Museum of Welsh Life in St Fagans there hang on the wall three semmets.[12] These are shallow trays, with a frame and a skin like that of a drum, though somewhat irregular in shape (ill. 50), which were used for winnowing grain, gently tossing it in the air so that the wind blows away the chaff, leaving the heavier grains behind. It seemed to me improbable that, if such objects were hanging in the barn when the end of the harvest was celebrated, as it is all over the world, they would not be used to accompany the dancing. Dr Roy Saer, who was then responsible for the musical instruments in that museum, kindly researched through the accession records and accounts of folk life and found that these semmets were indeed used in this way. I then asked Dr Micheál Ó Suilleabháin, from the University of Cork, whether this might have been the origin of the *bodhrán* and he also researched through similar sources and came to the conclusion that this was almost certainly correct.[13] The *bodhrán* today is widely available in music shops, commercially made for that market, but traditional instruments are still often made by a player from the frame of an old sieve covered with a goat skin. For good sound it is important that a drumskin be symmetrical in its radii. If the shell were irregular in shape, like the original semmets, the vibratory patterns would also be irregular and the sound likely to have a pronounced wobble; much the same result would attend a skin of grossly irregular thickness. This is why drums such as the modern folk-made *bodhrán* were often made on pre-existing frames that were known to be circular, such as a sieve, rather than

50. Semmet or winnowing tray from Crymych, Pembrokeshire, Wales.

twisting up a home-made frame, like those of the semmets, which might not be so successful. One maker when asked where he got his skins said that he had a shotgun – few farmers knew exactly how many goats they had![14]

One frame drum with a very strong sound, despite its quite small diameter, is the Nigerian *sákárà*. The reason for its strength is that the frame is of pottery (ill. 51). Striking a drum releases a finite amount of energy, and the more that is dissipated by shaking the frame, the less is available to come out in sound. Pottery is more rigid than wood and thus less of the energy is wasted in this way.[15]

Another pattern of pottery drum used over much of the southern frame drum area, from Morocco through to the Middle East is the goblet drum (ill. 52) known in some places as *darabukka*. Again the sound is powerful (modern instruments made of metal, with a plastic head, have a sharper ring but lack the carrying power of the traditional instruments) and the goblet shape, with its restricted neck where the bowl joins the stem, encourages a sympathetic resonance from the semi-enclosed air-body. The playing technique can be highly elaborate, especially in the Persian *dastgah* on the *zarb*, with complex rhythmic patterns and sonorities.[16] Players strike different parts of the head for differing tone qualities and in some areas use hand pressure to produce different pitches. This technique, and an increase in the complexity of the rhythms, is the more common the nearer one gets to India.

Indian music has the most complex rhythmic structure of all. The system of *tāla*, the repertoire of time units and patterns, is almost as elaborate as that of *raga*, the repertoire of scales and modes, to use as approximations the nearest equivalent terms from our own culture. Not only is there a wide range of possible numbers of beats in the time unit (in slow music calling the time unit a 'bar' or 'measure' can be

51. *Sákárà* pottery frame drums, Nigeria.

misleading) but within each structural 'beat' of the unit there can be many strokes on the drum.

The drums most widely used in this high-art classical music are the *tablā* and *bāyā*, a 'pair' of dissimilar kettledrums (ill. 53).[17] The *tablā*, played with the right hand, is a cylindrical wooden drum with a closed base. It is precisely tuned, normally to the *sa*, the 'tonic' of the *rāg*. The drumhead is made with an outer ring of layers of skin. A disc, made up from black wax and other compounds, covers almost the whole of the central area of the drumhead within the ring, leaving only a small annular area free. The head is tuned with wide rawhide thongs, passing through its strengthening ring, tensioned with cylindrical wooden blocks, like short segments of broomstick, between the thongs and the shell. The player hammers these down to raise the pitch, knocking them back up to lower it. The sound is short and sharp, not surprising when one considers the very small area of free skin. The *bāyā* is a deep bowl in shape. It is now usually made of metal, though pottery ones are still occasionally seen today, especially in village contexts. The skin has an off-centre tuning patch which is smaller than that of the *tablā* and the drum is not tuned, though the tension may be adjusted to overcome adverse climatic conditions with much smaller blocks under the tension thongs.[18] The player continually varies the pitch in performance by pressure with the heel of the left hand while playing with the fingertips, and the best players can cover a range of an octave or more, keeping strictly to the notes of the *rāg* being accompanied.[19] Less skilled players simply zoom up and down in pitch as seems appropriate.

Like all true high-art drums, the *tablā*, the various forms of the *darabukka*, and many frame drums are played with the fingers.[20] With sticks one has a very limited control over tone quality (as distinct from volume), whereas with the fingers an almost infinite variability and range of sonority is available. Drums in our culture are used almost exclusively for rhythmic purposes and even the timpani, although they must always be in tune with whatever is going on, have a very limited harmonic role and are even more limited melodically. The *tablā* on the other hand are the main accompanying instruments in North Indian classical music and their position is much like that of the piano in our music. We have sonatas for violin and piano and in North India similar recitals are given by *sitar* (a long-necked lute) and *tablā*.[21] Equally, the Indian equivalent of a *Lieder* recital would be given by a singer with *tambūrā* (a long-necked lute which provides an incessant drone) and *tablā*.

North Indian music was radically changed by Persian styles after the Moghul conquest in the thirteenth century, which was consolidated by the Emperor Akbar, who reigned from 1555 to 1605.[22] Southern India maintains an older tradition with an even greater range of *rāga*. Traditionally, the most important instruments there are the *vīnā* and the *mrdangam* or *pakhāvaj*, which are double-headed barrel drums.[23] One head is tuned, like that of the *tablā*, and the other is left untuned but is varied in pitch by hand-pressure in performance, like that of the *bāyā*. There is a legend that the *tablā* and *bāyā* were created by one of the Hindu gods simply by cutting a *mrdangam* in half. It seems more likely.

52. Goblet drums, *darabukka*: *(left to right)* Moroccan Berber, Israeli, Moroccan Arab, and pair of coupled dissimilar kettledrums, Fez, Morocco.

53. *Tablā* (*left*) and *bāyā* (*right*), i.e. as the audience sees them, with tuning hammer, North India.

however, that they were devised by adapting the Persian *naqqāra* or paired kettledrums, the origin of the medieval European nakers, to suit the playing techniques of the *mrdangam*. Similarly, the North Indian *sitar* has many of the features of the *vīnā*, the most important string instrument from before the Moghul invasion, built on to the much altered basis of the Persian *setār*, a three-course lute (*se-* three,*-tār* strings).

The ordinary paired kettledrums, the *nagārā* are also widely used in India (ill. 54). Instrumentally speaking there is little cultural division between India, Pakistan, Bangladesh, or any of the other countries and peoples making up the northern part of the Indian sub-continent, and therefore the terms 'India' and 'Indian' are used here without any national intent, but simply because it is impossible to differentiate musically between them. South Indian or Carnatic music and instruments, which show many differences from North 'Indian', are found in India proper and, with some considerable differences, in Sri Lanka. More common in Pakistan, and in those parts of India which were once ruled by a Muslim rajah, are the very large copper or iron *nagārā*, as large as, or larger than, our timpani. These were used for what is often called 'gate music', with shawms, the *shahnāī*, where we used trumpets, playing fanfares at fixed times and for entrances and exits, in exactly the same way as the trumpet and kettledrum ensembles of the European courts in the Renaissance and Baroque periods. They derived, as did the European, from the ensembles which can be seen in many Persian miniatures or paintings. Like European kettledrums, these instruments have a mainly rhythmic function and are therefore played with sticks. Tuning is achieved by manipulating the network of thongs and is fairly approximate – effect and ostentation are the main purpose of these instruments, as indeed they were in the European courts and still are in our cavalry regiments.

54. Three *nagara*, North India.

Rather different kettledrums are used in Burma. There they have two different circular chimes (ill. 55), one a circle of gongs fixed on a bamboo frame within which the player sits, the other a similar circular frame but supporting a ring of narrow kettledrums which, like the gongs, are each tuned to a different pitch.[24] Again the player uses his fingers on the drums, playing very rapid melodic or ostinato patterns with considerable virtuosity. There is little fundamental rhythmic variation, though much decoration. As was noted above, all Burmese music is in quadruple time, the units marked by the alternation of the 'ting' of a small pair of cymbals giving a bell-like sound and the 'tak' of a woodblock. There is a wide variation of tone quality with the drum chime, depending on where and how the player's fingers strike each drum.[25]

55. Bronze models of drum chime (*left*) and gong chime (*right*), Burma.

The Burmese use of the kettledrums may derive from Indian influence, but the use of goblet drums there must derive from contacts with Muslim traders coming across the sea from Oman and other active trading ports on the Persian Gulf. The gong-chime, and with it probably the circular arrangement of the drum-chime, surely comes from the South-East Asian and Indonesian gong-chime culture. Where this began is by no means certain, though naturally each country in that area claims primacy.[26]

The most highly-developed form today is the *gamelan* (roughly equivalent to 'orchestra') of Central Java (ill. 56). The nuclear melody is played by several instruments with bronze bars, the *sarons* and *demung* with quite thick bars fixed over a wooden trough and the *slenthem* with thinner bars, each over a tuned tubular resonator, today often made of painted tinplate instead of bamboo.[27] The two sizes of *saron* and the *demung* and *slenthem* are each an octave apart. The nuclear melody is decorated, like lacework, by the two *bonangs*, each of which is a set of a dozen or so bronze gong-kettles, each kettle looking somewhat like a priest's *biretta* with a protruding boss where the pompom would be. They are struck on the boss with wooden beaters wrapped in thick cord. The *bonangs* are also an octave apart, but since each has a range of two octaves there is an overlap. The player of each *bonang* strikes the kettles of both octaves, one with each hand, either simultaneously or alternately. The *genders*, which are higher-pitched versions of the *slenthem*, and which are also an octave apart, elaborate further as does the wooden-barred xylophone, the *gambang-kayu*.[28]

Rhythmic punctuation is provided by the *kethuk* and *kempyang* and the larger gong-kettles, the *kenong*, and the smaller hanging gongs, the *kempul*, though strictly the word 'gong' (a Javanese word which has come into English and most other European languages) is reserved for the great *gong ageng* and the smaller *gong suwukan*. These sound, as it were, the full stops (periods) and semicolons respectively of each sentence, with the *kenongs* and *kempuls* the commas.[29] Each name is onomatopoeic, *-tuk, -yang, -pul, -nong*, and *gong*. It takes some experience to realize the form of the slower or longer types of Javanese music because *gong* strokes to mark the end of each cycle can be several minutes apart.

56. *Gamelan* by Ud Soepoyo, Surakarta, Central Java, 1999. Bronze with ornately carved teak, decorated with gold leaf. This is the section in *Slendro* tuning, about one third of the whole. Commissioned by Margaret Ann Everist, Sioux City, Iowa for America's Shrine to Music Museum, University of South Dakota, Vermillion. *Back row, left to right:* two *kenongs,* two *saron demung* (the lowest pitched), *gong ageng,* five *kempuls, gong suwukan,* two drums *kendang gending* and *ketipul,* and *bonang panerus. Front row, left to right:* six *sarons,* three of them *saron barung,* the second from left *saron wayang,* and the two smallest *saron peking, slenthem, gender,* and *bonang barung.*

This whole orchestra, which can also include a fiddler and flautist on *rebab* and *suling* respectively as well as a solo singer and a chorus, is controlled by the drummer who sets the tempo and indicates changes of speed, music, and pulse by signals on his drums. He usually has three barrel-shaped drums, the *kendhang* and *ketipung* which are used together, and the *ciblon* to which the drummer changes for certain styles of music (mainly dance music and the *wayang*). Much of the music is played to accompany the *wayang* or shadow puppets. Everything is then controlled by the *dhalang,* the puppeteer, who moves the puppets and chants the narration. He gives rhythmic and other signals with strokes of beaters held in his feet on the wooden box in which the puppets are stored, and on a set of metal plates.[30]

The instruments are rather different in Bali, as is the manner in which they are played.[31] Even within Central Java there are marked differences in playing style and *gamelans* in Sunda and West Java are much simpler. On the South-East Asian mainland the gong chimes tend to form a part of a more varied orchestra. In Thailand, for example, a circle or a single row of gong kettles, arranged in a horseshoe with the two ends up in the air, is used with a xylophone, the *ranāt-thum,* and a metal-barred instrument of similar shape, the *ranāt-ēk.*[32] In the other islands such as the Philippines, small gong-chimes are used, among them the *kelantang,* a single row of seven gong kettles on a frame, with two larger hanging kettles and one hanging gong.

All these gongs and gong-kettles share the feature of a protruding boss in the centre. This is the common characteristic of almost all tuned gongs. While many flat-faced gongs may have a pitch, few are deliberately tuned and none as accurately as the bossed gongs. The best examples of these, certainly all the Central Javanese, are forged rather than cast. Each kettle is made from a cake of bronze which is heated in a forge and beaten out with hammers. The forging gradually shapes the disc-shaped cake into a shallow bowl and this is gradually deepened, with constant hammering and frequent reheatings, into the finished shape. The final tuning may be done by scraping and filing and polishing. The only instrument in the Javanese *gamelan* which is not polished is the great *gong ageng,* whose central boss is polished, with the rest of the surface left dark. The *gong ageng* is the soul of the *gamelan* and offerings are made to it whenever the *gamelan* performs.

The art of the gong smith was almost lost in Java in the early years of this century. The great smiths of Semarang, described and illustrated in such detail by Jacobson and Van Hasselt, were the last of their line.[33] Due to the influence and enthusiasm of Europeans and Americans, primarily Jaap Kunst before the Second World War and Mantle Hood after it, the craft was revived just before it died out and there is now a number of skilled craftsmen working once again.[34]

For those who cannot afford bronze, iron instruments are made at much less than half the cost, with a sound which, as many schools and other European and American institutions have found, while not as good as bronze, is quite tolerable.[35] The *gong* is of course always the most expensive instrument, even in an iron gamelan, and a traditional substitute in village and other small gamelans is the *gong kemodong*, two iron bars suspended over a pair of large pots as resonators. When they are struck simultaneously, the sound of the bars is surprisingly close to that of a true gong.

In the Philippines and some other areas the kettles are more often cast than forged and as a result they may have blow holes and other casting faults. Tuning these lighter instruments may be done by pushing the flat part of the face up or down with the fingers, and fine tuning by adding some wax or other compounds inside the boss to weight it.[36] Other gongs may be cast because of the high quality of their decoration. Those in Borneo, for example, with a wreath of dragons on the face, rampaging round the central boss, are far too elaborate to execute in any other way.[37]

A very different form of kettle is used in Burma among the Karen people (ill. 57). These go back into prehistoric times in the Dong-Song culture of Vietnam.[38] They are

57. Bronze drum, Karen People, Burma.

58. Pairs of small cymbals, China.

cast in several pieces: a circular skirt is made in two or more pieces, with the seams, where each piece is joined to the next, normally clearly visible, and a flat face, cast as a single disc decorated with rings and a central star, is fixed across the top of this skirt. There are often four or more bronze frogs standing at cardinal points on the edge of the face. Some of the more elaborate specimens have whole village scenes standing on the face of the drum, all cast in the same bronze. Franz Heger established a full typology of these instruments, based mostly on those in the Völkerkunde Museum in Vienna, and Bernet Kempers recently produced a very detailed study of them.[39] Fritz Kuttner's approach was rather different, an interesting and highly provocative text, suggesting advanced acoustical studies of the sort with which we are only now beginning to credit the ancient Chinese, as in Lothar von Falkenhausen's study, which is referred to below.[40] What is important from the musical point of view is that, although these instruments are often called kettle gongs, they are bronze drums rather than gongs. As Laurence Picken established, the membranophone merges almost imperceptibly into what we may call the diaphragmophone.[41] A membrane is a sheet of flexible and extensible material; a diaphragm may also be flexible (must be, in order to sound), but it is sufficiently rigid that it is not extensible. Nevertheless, it may vibrate in a manner very similar to that of a membrane, and it displays the same vibratory patterns that Chladni demonstrated with vibrating plates, that Kuttner associated very clearly with these bronze drums, and that Kirby showed applied also to drumheads.[42] It is not easy, in practice, to tell the difference between a very tightly tensioned membrane and a diaphragm.

Mantle Hood has suggested that bronze drums of this type may have been the progenitors of the Javanese gamelan.[43] It is also said that they were used in ancient China in much the way that we would use medals, to reward successful generals for a victorious campaign, and that they were thus a skeuomorph of a normal drum.[44]

Gongs are used in China, but these are very different from the Indonesian instruments. Most are flat-faced and they are then carefully made to be of indeterminate pitch. It is these from which our orchestral tamtams derive. Other patterns of gong are also used in China, among them one that rises sharply in pitch immediately after it is struck. Tuned gongs seem not to be characteristic of Chinese or Japanese music, save for very small instruments such as that mentioned above in connection with Roberto Gerhard's Symphony, and others of similar size, which are arranged on a frame as a small tinkling chime. Despite this, Puccini, in *Turandot* and *Madam Butterfly*, used tuned gongs to provide an 'oriental' atmosphere, and instruments are made for this purpose, by Paiste and other firms such as Ufip in Italy, tuned to our tempered scale. Other composers have taken advantage of their availability, using them simply as sounds rather than with any oriental implication, Vaughan Williams, for example, in his *Sinfonia Antartica*. While things are much better organized today, when that work was new, in the 1950s, performances had to be carefully coordinated with Covent Garden, for the Royal Opera possessed the only set of tuned gongs then in Britain. No performance of Vaughan Williams's Symphony was possible if the Garden was performing the Puccini operas.

Chinese cymbals differ in many respects from the European. There are three main varieties. One is very small, pairs of cup-shaped bells with a strong pitch. The second is cymbal-shaped, somewhat larger, fairly thick, with rounded domes. The latter are those noted earlier as resembling European medieval cymbals in appearance, and perhaps in sound. Both are illustrated in ill. 58. The third is much larger and thinner and these are instantly recognizable by their high, indented domes and by their

59. Chinese tomtoms, as used in jazz bands.

60. Pellet drums, *clockwise from front left:* Mexico; India; Tododaji Temple, Nara, (den-den demon drum); India, the head torn to show the interior; China; Taiwan; and Chinese bumblebee friction drum (*foreground*).

upturned rim – the outermost inch or so is bent upwards. The Chinese use them in pairs in bands, and especially for funerals. Used singly and suspended on a stand or post, they were very popular in our jazz bands under the name of Chinese crash. They have a very quick response and an almost equally fast decay, thus giving a bright splash of sound. One can be seen on the left arm of the trap tray in ill. 42.

Larger versions of the second type (at the back of ill. 61), with very wide high domes, are used in Tibet in the priestly rituals, often with the edges clattered together, rather than clashed with a single stroke. The instruments may also be played so that the cavities formed by the domes are partially occluded by the flat face of the opposing cymbal. By altering the extent of the occlusion, in much the same way as opening one's mouth to a greater or lesser extent while tapping the cheek, different sounds can be produced almost as though the cymbals are speaking. Also used in Tibetan rituals are much smaller cymbals, two or three inches (50–75 mm) in diameter and up to half an inch (12 mm) thick (in the foreground of ill. 61.). These have a very high, sweet sound.[45]

A variety of drums is used in China, ranging from large barrels, through pellet drums an inch or two in diameter, to tiny friction drums which sound like a bumblebee when whirled round their stick. Some are surprisingly high in pitch. The skin may look a foot or so in diameter, but the wooden body may be very thick, leaving only a very small area of skin free to vibrate. Some drums, especially those used as Chinese tomtoms in early jazz bands, with heads painted with a phoenix or dragon, contained a wire spring which rattled (ill. 59). When most Chinese drums are made, their heads are tensioned with ropes, as tightly as possible. A series of large-headed nails is driven through each head into the shell, and the fringe through which the ropes were threaded is cut off, leaving no trace of its presence.

The rattle drums (ill. 60) are sometimes toys, sometimes mendicants', and sometimes ritual instruments. Most are quite small and are fixed to the end of a stick, or are transfixed by the stick. Twirling the drum by rubbing the palms of the hands together with the stick between them makes two pellets, attached by cords to diametrically opposite points on the shell, strike the heads with a sharp rattling sound.

Very large drums are used in Japan, as many audiences in other countries will know, for a Japanese drum orchestra has taken part in several world tours with, as its central feature, an enormous barrel-shaped drum, several feet in diameter. There is sufficient interest in drums in Japan to support a special drum museum in Tokyo, and many different types are used for traditional, ritual and various folk musics.[46] Those used in the *Gagaku* court music and the *noh* plays are all rope-tensioned, but differently constructed from most other rope-tensioned drums. The heads are stitched on to iron rings which are much wider in diameter than the drum shell. Each skin is folded over its ring with a wide overlap and then stitched so that the circle of head within the stitch line is much smaller in diameter than the iron ring. The ropes pass over the rings and, for most of the drums, are then very tightly tensioned. The exception to this is the *ko-tsuzumi*, the hourglass drum of the *noh* plays, which is assembled anew for each performance, the two heads fitted to the shell, with added tuning patches carefully adjusted on the inner surface of each head, and then roped up. The ropes are quite loosely tied and the tension is continually adjusted while playing to produce varied effects.[47]

The *gagaku* or court music is one of the oldest musical traditions surviving today, for it has changed little over many centuries save getting far slower than the Chinese court music of the Tang dynasty of around the sixth century AD, from which it derived.[48] Some few of the instruments deriving from the days of contact between Japan and the Tang court survive in the Shôsôin Repository in Nara, including three drums and the remains of the heads for one of them, all dating from between the eighth and tenth centuries.[49] All three of these drums, while differing in detail, are similar to those still used in Japan in both the traditions discussed above. The surviving drumheads are identical in construction with those used today. There is to my knowledge no other museum in the world which has preserved musical instruments from antiquity in this way; these are not instruments which have been found archaeologically – this is material which has simply been in storage, much of it in perfect preservation, since the time that it was used, twelve to fourteen hundred years ago.

Pole-mounted drums are used ritually in Tibet, but these are rather smaller than those carried on ancient Chinese war chariots. The Tibetan ones are struck with a curved stick, shaped like a large question mark. Pellet drums are also used, but these are very different from the Chinese. They are made from a pair of human crania. The top of each skull is cut off just above the eyebrow ridges and these bone cups are fixed crown to crown to form a waisted drum. The drumheads are often said to be of human skin. The cords from which the pellets are suspended (the pellets may simply be knots in the cord or tape itself) are tied round the waist. The drum is held by its waist and sounded by twisting the wrist to and fro. The *damaru* (ill. 61) is used with a trumpet made from a human femur (thighbone) or tibia (shin bone) and a bell.[50] Also used are wooden pellet drums, some following much the shape of the skull drums and others in a rather simpler hourglass shape. These last are widely used in India, sometimes called monkey drums because they are used by animal trainers (ill. 60).

Another Chinese signal instrument is the *pan* or woodblock. This is much the shape of a brick with a long slot running below the upper surface, the thin wooden plate above the slot giving a sharp crack when struck. These rectangular woodblocks are also used in our music and were a standard feature of the jazz drum kit as one of the 'traps'. They must not be confused with another Chinese instrument, the *muyu* or temple block. Each is still used in our music, both as effects (two temple blocks of different sizes make a good tick-tock for instance) and simply as instruments. The temple blocks usually came in sets of four in a jazz kit, one reason why the back rail on a trap-tray (ill. 42) had four posts. In China they are ritual instruments, simplified versions of a fish's head; older instruments are in the shape of a fish with the slit in its back or belly. It is said that the reason for this imagery is that a fish has no eyelids and so is ever-wakeful and ever-ready to listen to prayer.

In passing, it is surprising just how many instruments of the early jazz bands derived from China, the tomtoms, crash cymbals, woodblock, and temple blocks among others. It is well known that the bands used whatever instruments were easily available and perhaps there were strong Chinese communities in New Orleans and Chicago, and their instruments cheaper or more accessible than the normal American. Research in this area of the social history of jazz is beyond the scope of this book, but it would be interesting to know how this came about.

The slit drum, a hollowed wooden block or log, is also widely used in Oceania, where it can reach very large sizes. New Guinea slit drums normally rest horizontally on the ground or on the floor of their own hut. The usual shape is a log of wood up to two or three feet in diameter and six or more feet long with a carved crocodile head projecting from one end and its tail from the other. The log is hollowed through the slit, which traverses most of the length of the drum, and the carvers normally leave a boss projecting into the cavity under the lip where it is struck.[51] Small, hand-held drums are also used but it is the large ones which are best known. On Malekula in the New Hebrides the large slit drums stand upright round the dancing ground, with smaller instruments lying at their feet (ill. 62).[52]

It was watching the construction of one of these drums that made Raymond Clausen realize that acoustically they were giant Helmholtz resonators, their pitch depending on the air body which they contained and more particularly on the area of the slit or opening. The people whom he was studying had determined to make a slit drum, lower in pitch than any other in honour of their chieftain. They chose a particularly large tree, hollowed it out, and made the slit as long as possible. To their horror, the pitch was higher than usual, for it is a characteristic of the Helmholtz resonator that, for a given air volume, the greater the area of open hole, the higher the pitch.[53]

61. Tibetan ritual instruments: (*left to right*) conch *dung-dkar*, skull drum *thod-dar*, large cymbals *sbug-chal* (*back*), bell *dril-bu*, larger skull drum, trumpet of human femur *rkang-gling* (*front right*), thunderbolt *rdo-rje* (*centre*), small cymbals *ting-shags* (*front centre*).

Slit drums in Fiji are somewhat different, for the normal *lali* resembles a trough, with an opening little narrower than the width of the hollow.[54] A special form, the *lali ne meke*, is often used by women to accompany singing and is a wooden bar (ill. 63) with a hollow on the underside to increase the resonance.[55]

Slit drums were also important in pre-Columbian Mexico as the *teponatzli*, and these were different again. They were hollowed out from the back, leaving the upper surface as two thin, rectangular tongues, integral with the body at each end, and with only very narrow slits separating them at each side and, at the centre, from each other. The hollow is then covered by fitting a wooden plate as a lid over the bottom. The slits are so narrow that the tongues are very strongly coupled to the air resonance of the box, in very much the same way as the tongue of a jews harp or trump is to the player's mouth, or the reeds of a mouthorgan or harmonium to their chambers.[56] Instruments of similar form are now widely used in our music, both as an attempt to fashion a precisely tuned 'log drum' to satisfy the demands of composers such as Berio and Stockhausen, and as something for children's percussion bands in such ensembles as Carl Orff's *Schulwerke*, for which boxes with a number of tongues cut in their upper surface are made. Skin drums were also used in ancient America, but comparatively few have survived the ages. One famous exception, a large, standing single-headed drum, is illustrated by Martí and in many other books.[57]

Much of our knowledge of pre-Columbian Central and South American instruments comes from illustrations in codices and carvings and from models in pottery. From these it is clear that frame drums and cylindrical drums of various sizes were frequently used. The frame drum is still used by North American Indians, but most drums today, in both North and South America, tend to be derivative of our side drums and bass drums. In South and Central America the pipe and tabor is still a flourishing combination.[58] This is a survival from sixteenth- and seventeenth-century Spanish and Portuguese imports and is now thoroughly indigenized, to the extent that the 'pipe' is often a panpipe or a reed instrument, or even a horn, rather than the normal three-hole tabor pipe, though these are also used.[59] One use of a large drum, today often a bass drum lying with one side on the ground, is peculiar to several of the North American tribes. A group of men sits round it, each beating on it and singing.[60] There are very few other examples of a single drum that is played simultaneously by a group of people.

Tortoise carapaces are used in several ways in the Americas. Some were struck as a form of drum.[61] Others were rubbed, similarly to the *livika* or *nunut*, a three-tongued rubbed wooden instrument known only from New Ireland.[62] Others were used as rattles.[63] Hand rattles of various sorts are widely used in both North and South America. Some are carved wood, often highly decorative and important totemistically among the Indians of the North-West Coast of British Columbia.[64] Gourd and other materials are seen in pre-Columbian codices and carvings, showing people with hand-rattles of this sort, similar to the maracas of Latin American dance music. Such rattles

62. Slit drums on the dancing ground, Malekula, New Hebrides.

63. Percussion bar, *lali ne meke*, the underside showing the resonance chamber, Fiji.

are still widely used today, to the extent that one might say that rattles of all kinds were more important in the Americas than drums (ill. 66). Many pre-Columbian pottery figurines show people either holding rattles or with rattles attached to their bodies, especially their legs, and to their costumes. This remains a commonplace today among dancers throughout the Americas.[65]

It is a commonplace also in Africa, where leg rattles made of seed-pods, spiders' egg cases, folded iron 'pods' and many other materials are stitched to leather bands or fixed on pieces of wood and tied to dancers' legs.[66] Ill. 64 shows a small selection, using all the materials just mentioned. Hand rattles of all sorts are also used, often in the same hand as a drum stick or a bow or other instrument, for auxiliary rattles are a feature of many types of African music and instruments, as are the buzzing membranes on xylophones.[67]

The xylophone has many forms in Africa. The simplest consists of a few wooden bars across the outstretched legs of a player seated on the ground.[68] Developmental sequences of instruments are somewhat out of fashion today, but it has often been suggested that one could chart a progress from these instruments through the series of slabs of wood across a pair of banana stems lying on the ground, to those with bars fixed over a wooden trough, and thence to those attached to a frame with an individual resonator for each bar. These, while normally played on the ground, can be carried around from place to place. The sequence leads further to those whose frame is so adapted that they can be played while on the move. The culmination is in the full orchestras of elaborate instruments of varying sizes with each bar lying above a resonator of gourd of exactly the size best to resonate its pitch.[69] The fact that all these types, from the simplest to the most complex, are found both in Africa and in South-East Asia is the strongest possible argument to counter those who have claimed that the xylophone was invented in one of those two areas and carried thence to the other.[70]

The xylophone orchestras are characteristic of the Tswa and Chopi peoples of Mozambique, and the xylophones of these areas are beautifully made of special woods and carefully chosen gourds.[71] The same peoples, however, when working in the mines of South Africa, would make perfectly adequate instruments from whatever materials might be available, such as sawn-up floor boards, with tin cans as resonators.[72] As with

64. A selection of African leg rattles. *Left to right:* seed pods, Zambia; forged iron, West Africa; spiders' egg cases, probably Zambia; old shoe-polish tins, Kenya; *middle* cast bronze, Yoruba, Nigeria, *front* folded iron *kacacakai*, Zaria, Nigeria.

65. *Timbila*, xylophone, Tswa People, Mozambique, pre-1870.

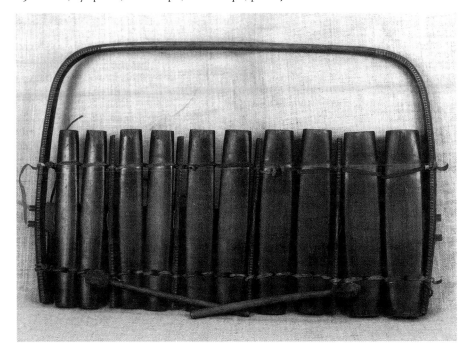

66. Rattles, Americas: maize seed in fish skin, Canada, and pair of maracas, Jamaica (*back*), Rosebud Sioux, USA (*middle left*), nut shell jingle, Brazil (*middle right*), folded bark, Eskimo, Newfoundland (*front centre*), and killer whale, Haida, British Columbia (*front right*).

most instruments all over the world, function is more important than beauty, though most musicians and most instrument makers will opt for both wherever possible. The *timbila* is built on a frame (ill. 65) and, while normally played with the frame resting on the ground, it can be played while standing or moving. This is true of many African xylophones. One of the signs of this is the presence of a rail, usually curved, on one side of the instrument which, when resting against the player's body, will prevent the bars from touching him and thus stifling the sound. There are probably more different types of xylophone in Central Africa than any other part of the world, and while all the African volumes of the *Musikgeschichte in Bildern* series referred to here illustrate a wide range in use, Olga Boone's *Les Xylophones du Congo Belge* has much detailed information on the range, the tunings, and the different methods of construction.[73] It is also in that area of Central Africa that one finds the names closest to marimba.

Most xylophones are played by a single player, but in East Africa, especially in Uganda and nearby areas, the common practice is to have three or more players on each.[74] The bars of this type are made and tuned, and carefully kept in safe storage, for the xylophone is made up for each occasion on which it is used. For performance, a pair of banana stems is cut and laid on the ground. The bars are placed across them, with thin sticks pushed into the banana stems between each bar to keep them apart.[75] The two principal players sit opposite each other playing interlocking parts on the same range of the instrument, with a third player at the treble end, and sometimes also a fourth at the bass end, playing *ostinati* on the two highest bars, and where relevant the two lowest.[76]

Other log xylophones, as these instruments are known, are smaller and are played by a single player, as usually are those which lie over a pit dug in the earth beneath them to act as a resonator. More portable are the trough xylophones, where the bars are fixed to the longer sides of a wooden box or trough. Neither the pit nor the trough make very efficient resonators, for they tend to amplify selectively only those bars whose pitch approximates to one of the resonance frequencies of the pit or trough, though as Jamie Linwood points out, they can be made more efficient by making them shallower at the treble end or by other devices to control their resonances.[77] The majority of xylophones are individually resonated (ill. 67), most commonly with resonators of gourd though sometimes of cowhorns or other materials. With very few exceptions the resonators have a hole in the side over which a membrane is fixed with wax or resin. The material of the membrane varies; Olga Boone mentions spiders' eggs, webs and nest material, and also something similar to cigarette paper; Linwood mentions animal peritoneum, presumably similar to goldbeater's skin.[78] The membrane buzzes and sings as a *mirliton* to sweeten the sound, with the result that the African xylophone, though ancestral to our own, has a very different tone quality. The technique of tuning the bars, briefly discussed above, was described in detail by Father Jones.[79] These techniques were firmly established and well recognized in Africa long before the forced transportation of Africans to the Americas, and their instruments remain more advanced tonally than our own.

An instrument not unlike the xylophone in its musical use, and often its name, is that which is variously known to us as *sanza*, *mbira*, or *kalimba*, though neither of the first two names is well received in Africa; the third name is most commonly found in Zimbabwe and South Africa.[80] A small selection is shown here in ill. 68. The instrument is most commonly a series of iron reeds or tongues, fixed to a wooden board, which in some areas is the upper surface of a box.[81] The board or box is held between the two hands and the reeds are plucked by the player's thumbs and sometimes forefingers. The arrangement of the reeds differs from all other

67. Xylophone, *balo*, Ghana, back view to show the gourd resonators with their spider's egg membrane mirlitons.

68. African *sanzas, mbiras,* and *kalimbas, (back row, left to right)* bamboo reeds, Cameroon or Nigeria; Uganda; unlocated with gourd resonator; with 'upper manual', Shona, Zimbabwe; unlocated, probably Congo; (*front row*) Shona, with gourd resonator; aluminium with iron back, Karawanjong, Uganda; unlocated West Africa; African Music Society alto 'kalimba' for export.

instruments, for instead of progressing evenly from bass to treble, the lowest-pitched reed is usually that in the centre, the pitch rising alternately left and right, the two highest notes being those at the outer edge on each side. This arrangement makes the playing technique, using just the thumbs with fixed hands, much easier than would a layout more akin to that of the xylophone. There are, of course, many variations; sometimes the longest and thus lowest reed is at one end and is plucked as an intermittent drone. The Zimbabwean *kalimba*, the most elaborate version of the instrument, has, as it were, an upper manual at one side of higher-pitched reeds. Almost all books on African music include illustrations of *sanzas*, the types differing according to their tribal provenance. Those that show most are François Borel's detailed description of those in the Ethnographic Museum in Neuchâtel and Jean-Sébastien Laurenty's typological survey of all those in the great museum in Tervuren on the outskirts of Brussels. One with some of the clearest illustrations of their construction is Jos Gansemans's book on Rwanda from the same source; the Tervuren museum has published some of the best and most detailed studies on African instruments, with photographs of several hundreds of each type of instrument as well as detailed drawings, measurements, and descriptions.[82]

The *sanza* shares much of its repertoire with the xylophone and has the great advantage of being more portable. Where the board is the top of a box, a hole in the underside may be covered by a membrane as a *mirliton* like that of the xylophone. The player may keep a finger over another hole, moving it to and fro to produce an amplitude vibrato. Alternatively, the buzz may be produced by small pieces of metal folded loosely round the stem of each reed. Another method is by hanging metal rings on a bracket fixed to the board or box, or nailing pieces of seashell or metal (today often bottle tops) loosely to the board. One way or another, the buzzers are universal on these instruments. Time was when the *sanza* was peculiar to Africa, but large versions of it, large enough to sit on, are found in the West Indies.[83] The reeds of the *sanza* are often made by hammering carpenters' nails or bits of thick wire; the favourite source for reeds for the Caribbean version used to be the springs of wind-up gramophones.

The xylophone and the *sanza* are found almost everywhere in Africa south of the Sahara. The slit drum has a rather more limited distribution, mainly in Central and West Africa.[84] Just as in Oceania, there is a wide variety of sizes and shapes, ranging from the hand-held to those two or three metres long, though the majority are under a metre. Some are simply wooden troughs, beaten on the lips of the trough, but others are shaped like a cut-out profile of a bell and others, especially in Congo (ill. 69), may have a squared-off dumb-bell-shaped slit.[85] This shape makes it easy to carve the two lips to different thicknesses, thus producing two different pitches, the thicker lower in pitch than the higher.

69. Slit drums, (*left*) with human head handle, Kwanga, Congo; (*centre*) carved as a grotesque face, Bali; (*right*) Congo; and (*front*) East Sepik, Papua New Guinea.

70. Hourglass 'talking'
drums, *kalangu,* Nigeria
(*left*) and *donno,* Ghana
(*right*).

Most African languages are tonal, so that a word will have several quite different
meanings, depending on whether one syllable is higher or lower than the next, or
both high-tone or both low-tone. In this way, it is possible to talk on an instrument,
imitating the pitch-pattern and the rhythm of words.[86] Considerable redundancy is
necessary because many words will share a pitch and rhythm pattern, but by building
up a context, often using descriptive phrases, meaning can be conveyed over great
distances. As it was explained to me by one of my Nigerian students, using an *ad
hominem* example: 'the man, the white man, the big tall white man, the big tall white
man with glasses, the big tall white man with glasses and a beard, the big tall white
man with glasses and a beard is coming', and so forth until a clear identification and
meaning is established.[87] This is, of course, the so-called African bush telegraph which
so puzzled and astonished early travellers. It was not widely understood outside Africa
until Father Carrington produced his book, one that was particularly needed by the
Church, for the texts of many hymns when translated initially into African languages
caused much irreverent mirth. The combination of text and melody, strait-jacketing a
literal translation on to the original European melody without the necessary regard for
pitch-pattern, produced many nonsenses.

Not only slit drums talk in this way. Any instrument capable of more than one pitch
can talk, including whistles and horns. One of the best-known types of 'talking drum'
is the hourglass-shaped *kalangu* and *donno* of Nigeria and Ghana. These (ill. 70) have two
heads which are linked by a multitude of tension cords running from head to head. With
the waist of the drum held between the upper arm and the body, squeezing the arm
inwards presses the cords into the waist of the drum, and so raises the pitch of the heads.
Considerable pitch variation is achieved and thus the drum can talk.

Drums in Africa are commonly used in groups. Multi-part music, in the European
Renaissance, was based on polyphony, a number of equally important melodic strands

woven together as we hear, for instance, in madrigals. African music is based on polyrhythmy, a number of equally important rhythmic patterns, similarly woven together. Just as a madrigal group may have a conductor, a drum group will have a master drummer, and in West Africa he often plays one of these hourglass drums. He will not only control the music and its pace, but he will also talk on his drum, commenting on the skill of the dancers, on the political news of the day, on the generosity or otherwise of the host or sponsor of the dance, and of course giving instructions to the other drummers and the dancers, while also keeping his own drum patterns going.

Pairs of drums, the goblet-shaped *ntumpan*, are similarly used in Ghana, one higher in pitch than the other, and so are drums which will produce more than one pitch by playing on different areas of the drum head. It was while working with a Ghanaian master drummer that Father Jones came to recognize what he termed the 'standard pattern' of African drum rhythms.[88] This pattern, usually played on the iron bell, is verbalized as kon-ko-lo-kon-kon-ko-lo, where kon and lo represent a crotchet and ko a quaver with, if an iron double bell is being used, one or both of the 'lo' on the lower-pitched bell.

kon ko lo   kon kon ko lo kon ko lo kon kon ko lo, etc.

Ill. 71 shows a single bell and double bells from Nigeria, Congo, and Ghana. In many drum orchestras one player maintains this or a similar figure as a constant *ostinato* to which all the other players can relate their own rhythmic patterns. Of the many *ostinati* used in Africa, Father Jones's standard pattern is by far the most common. The concept of the bell's role spread widely in the Americas, where it was often replaced by a hoe-blade or similar object, and by concussion sticks such as the claves. Double bells, incidentally, can also 'talk' and the Nigerian one illustrated here was made to shout the praises of the Emir of Kano.

71. Double and single iron bells: (*left to right*) double bell *kuge* with beater *kahon mariri*, Kano, Hausa Nigeria; single bell with beater, Congo; double bell, Ghana; and single bell *atoke*, with striker, Ghana.

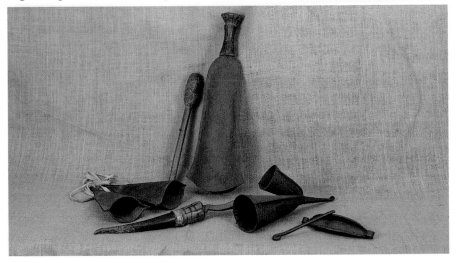

There is an enormous variety of African drums, far more than can be described in a single chapter of a book of this size. Several books have been devoted to this single subject, and of course all the books on Africa referred to illustrate many drums.[89] Every conceivable use of drums is found in Africa, from dance and other entertainment through signalling to ritual and the emblems of status. In Uganda, before the revolutions, the drums were the insignia of royalty, sometimes to the extent that the possessor of the drums became royal by that fact. The drums had their own herds of cattle, from which their heads were made and whose milk was offered to them daily, and whose butter was smeared on their heads.[90] Almost every conceivable shape of drum is found in Africa, as is almost every method for fastening the heads. Curt Sachs first designed his typology of head-fastening, which appears in his *History of Musical Instruments*, for his catalogue of the Malagasy collection in the Musée de l'Homme.[91] To these one can add glueing, using the natural glue of the head, or more commonly with wax or a similar substance, tying to pegs driven into the shell further down, and lapping in the European manner, which was probably seldom if ever seen in Africa in Sachs's day.

Equally, one can find in Africa almost every possible form of shell. As always, the simplest is the frame drum, though in parts of West Africa one finds a more elaborate and very heavily made rectangular frame which is played with one edge resting on the ground in front of the player. With one leg cocked over the drum, the player presses on the drumhead with the heel to raise the pitch.[92] Very similar drums, played with the same technique, are also found in the Caribbean.

Kettledrums are common and there is an enormous variety of shapes. The term kettledrum covers the bowl or cauldron pattern of our timpani, and also any shape of closed vessel with a skin across the open end, from gourds sliced across the equator to the great Uganda drums, which have parallel sides above a conical base and, unusually for a kettledrum, two heads.[93] The lower head serves as an anchor to the upper, the two linked with innumerable thongs of hide, enough that the wood of the shell is hidden behind them. It was mostly drums of this pattern that were the Royal drums, many as much as a metre in diameter and tall in proportion. The heads on these drums seem always to have the hair left on them, whereas the majority of African drums are hairless, like those of our orchestras.

Some kettledrums from Central Africa are in the shape of a human body, feet, legs, and the lower half of the torso, sliced across at the waist; others are the whole figure with the drum poised on the head, as loads of all sorts are commonly carried in Africa.[94] Both are often instruments of ritual and may be hung about with human bones and other accoutrements. Note that drums are classified by the shape of the drum itself. The fact that many of these anthropomorphic drums have legs does not make them footed drums. Because they have a closed shell, they remain kettledrums irrespective of how the kettle is supported or decorated.

In Ethiopian church music, kettledrums are used in chimes of half a dozen or more and can often be seen in the background of religious paintings. Much smaller drums, also closed vessels, are used by the Ibo in Nigeria in sets of up to a dozen in various ensembles.[95] On the Ivory Coast and in neighbouring areas players have a cluster of drums fixed together or a larger drum with smaller drums pendant upon it.[96] Drum chimes and orchestras are a widespread feature of African music.

Some drums sing to other drums. A larger drum may have a hole an inch or two wide in its side plugged by a small tube which has glued across one end a thin membrane to act as a kazoo and produce an added buzz.

Drums are not the only instruments struck as chimes in Africa. In Ethiopia bars of stone are suspended and struck to give bell-like sounds.[97] Single bars, usually wood or iron, are common in Christian churches in Muslim countries, but chimes are unusual. In West Africa there are other forms of stone chimes. In Togo sets of four or five flat stones are used, each giving a single pitch, but in Nigeria and other areas large boulders are struck, often giving off a whole series of pitches from different points on the same boulder.[98] Bernard Fagg first recorded the existence of rock gongs in 1956, and thereafter reports came from other anthropologists from many parts of the world until the phenomenon has now become widely recognized.[99] His wife has continued his research after his death and has now published over 130 rock gongs and rock-gong complexes worldwide.[100]

Another instrument used as a form of chime, again one whose use is not confined to Africa, is the mortar and pestle. Almost wherever grains or substances such as coffee are ground in a mortar (ill. 72), and wherever such activities are carried out by more

72. Mortar and pestle, Beduin, Israel.

73. *Tabl*, Morocco, with beater (*left*) and light stick (*right*).

than one person at a time, rhythms and counter-rhythms are produced. One person
will begin and another will start to pound between the strokes of the first; a third may
join in, fitting into the rhythm, and will be joined by as many others as there are in
the community. Nor is this sort of music confined to mortars, for bark cloth is beaten
in this way in Oceania and Indonesia, and blacksmiths worldwide hammer
antiphonally in rhythmic patterns far more interesting than those which Wagner gave
to the Nibelung. Almost anywhere else in the world than in their subterranean off-
stage caves, eighteen smiths would produce something much more enterprising![101]

Coffee and other grains are ground in this way throughout North Africa and the
Middle East. This is an area over which the conquests of Islam provided a unifying
culture from the early Middle Ages onwards, so that it is not surprising to see the
frame drums and pottery goblet drums which we have already described diffused
throughout the area. Nor is it surprising to see in Morocco drums beaten with a heavy
stick in one hand and a light stick in the other (ill. 73), with larger examples in
Algeria, almost exactly as they are played in Turkey.[102] Nor is it surprising to find them
in the Balkans, for this influence covered the arc from the Pyrenees round the whole
western, southern, and eastern shores of the Mediterranean and up through what is
now Eastern Europe to the gates of Vienna.[103] It was thus that the bass drum came into
Western Europe and with it the *alla turca* style of performance with beater and switch.

However, not all of Eastern Europe adopted this style. It is said that traditionally
no drums were used in Hungary, save in later military bands. For rhythmic
accompaniment a thumb might be rubbed on the table, much the way that we rub it
on a tambourine.[104] The only exception was the friction drum, an instrument used over
much of Europe and also in much of Africa.[105] This has a number of different forms
(ill. 74). One of the commonest is usually known by its Dutch name of *rommelpot* for
it features in many Dutch and Flemish paintings. A pot is covered with a skin in the

centre of which a stick stands in a pocket formed by tying the wet skin round the stick and then round the rim of the pot. Another variety has the stick in the interior of the drumshell, which is open at the bottom. Often the stick passes through the skin, with a peg through the upper end to prevent it being pulled back through the hole. The instrument is played by rubbing the hand up and down the stick. Instead of a stick, a cord or a hank of horsehair may be used, and this version became the orchestral lion roar demanded by Edgard Varèse in *Ionisation* and by other modern composers.

Henry Balfour, after describing and illustrating a wide range of friction drums from Europe, the Americas, Africa, and Asia, established a typology and suggested an origin.[106] The two simplest versions of a blacksmith's bellows are skin-covered vessels with tubing leading to the fire. On the one variety the blower propels the air out of the bellows by pushing the skin down with a stick fixed to its centre and then pulling up again on the stick to replenish the bellows with air. On the other, the bellows are pushed down by the feet and pulled up again by a rope. In either case, the sweating hands may slide on the stick or rope, thus producing a sound which was the voice of the magic which drew metal out of a stone, a sound which became that of the friction drum. It is an attractive theory which may well be true, though like all such theories it can never be proven.

One use common in southern Europe was for the so-called 'rough music' with which a community expressed its disapproval of certain modes of life-style. The presence of most of one's fellow villagers outside the house making the night hideous with friction drums, pots and pans, pieces of scrap-metal, hooters and other noise

74. Friction drums (*left to right*): Brazil; *simbomba*, Catalunya; 'Hippo drum', South Africa; '*rommelpot*', home-made ; lion roar, home-made.

75. Clappers, *matracas* for Holy Week, Catalunya (*left*), Easter clappers or bird-scarers, England (*right*), and a half pair of bones, England (*foreground*).

makers was often sufficient to persuade an offender to move to some other place, or at least to mend his or her ways. Friction drums were also used as noise makers on many more joyous occasions; Bálint Sárosi has recorded the use in a New Year first-footing song with a clapper bell and a pounding stick with rattling rings.[107]

Filippo Bonanni illustrated a friction drum in the late eighteenth century, associating it with the grape harvest.[108] His book shows many folk uses of percussion instruments in Europe and elsewhere, especially of course in Italy, and is the most important source we have from pre-modern times. He combines illustrations from antiquity with conventional musicians of his time and with ethnomusicology in a way which remained unparalleled until Tobias Norlind published his book on the history of instruments.[109]

Out of Bonanni's total of 152 plates, far more than half illustrate percussion instruments, a greater resource for us than any other book until we reach the modern encyclopaedias of percussion. Almost every instrument mentioned in this chapter appears in his pages.[110] Even among those plates which illustrate non-percussion instruments, a fair number such as the comb and paper and the bird whistles would wind up in our hands if any composer ever asked for them. Bonanni does need a careful eye, for his illustrations, many of which are copied from earlier sources or were made up from descriptions, often need some prior knowledge if they are to be recognized, and this is true even of the instruments of his own day. Nevertheless, it is an invaluable compendium of folk instruments, many of which, such as the ratchets and clappers used in Holy Week, from Palm Sunday to Easter Eve, are still with us today.[111]

The cog-ratchets are also used for other purposes: farmers use them to scare birds from the crops, football fans use them to encourage their teams, Air Raid Precaution Wardens carried them in Britain during the Second World War to warn against poison-gas attacks (fortunately never needed), police constables used to carry them to summon help, children use them as toys, and we use them in the orchestra (ill. 25). They are more often seen in theatre pits for pantomimes and slapstick comedy than on the orchestral platform. Whenever a comedian bent over, a rasp from the ratchet made him clap his hands to his bottom to see whether his trousers had split. But we have also seen them in Beethoven's Battle Symphony and they turn up in a few more recent scores.

The clappers take various forms but all consist basically of a board against which something, often a hinged hammer, can swing, as with the *triccaballacca*, still used in churches today.[112] They are spread widely across Europe, like the ratchets, and Ludvík Kunz illustrates a variety. Ill. 75 shows one that was bought on the Spanish side of the Pyrenees and another bought in Oxford.[113] The latter may have been a farmer's bird-scarer, or a boy's egg-clapper such as those that were used in the streets at Eastertide.[114]

Almost all the instruments described in this chapter can and do appear on our concert platforms and in our studios, as well as in their own domains. There is no limit to man's ingenuity in thinking of things to hit and of ways to hit them, and no limit to the demands of our composers. One possible exception is the rock gong – a boulder the size of a house is difficult to move. But now that we have satellite telephones, there is no reason why a musician in Nigeria should not take part in a concert where the rest of the orchestra is in the Royal Festival Hall or the Lincoln Centre, or even in both. This may be the way of the future, with music becoming truly international. Were it to happen, we can be sure that we shall be there.

Appendix 1

Playing Techniques

Side drum

The basic difference between playing technique on the side drum and that on all the other percussion instruments derives from the brevity of the side drum's sound. The only way to prolong it is through reiteration, and the sound is so short that repetition in the normal way, one stroke with each hand at the highest speed physically possible, would still sound as a rhythm and not as anything continuous. Who first thought of the idea of doubling the speed by taking advantage of the bounce of the stick and slapping it back to produce a second stroke, and when and where, we do not know, but since the word drum and other onomatopoeic terms seem to be coeval with the side drum's introduction in the mid-fifteenth century, this practice must have been built in from the beginning.

The technique is not easy to acquire, for a bounce alone is inadequate. Drop a ball and it will never return to the hand: the bounce is always weaker on each reiteration. What is needed is sufficient push within the bounce to make it as strong as the initial stroke, exactly as strong, neither more nor less. The technique is acquired by constant practice. One begins with two distinct strokes from each hand, starting with each stroke at a walking pace, da-da-ma-ma (the traditional syllabics), gradually accelerating until it changes from stroke-stroke to stroke-push and, after four or five years, a smooth and even roll is acquired. With it must come the ability to achieve any required loudness or softness (much more difficult than loudness), any necessary accentuation, and the ability to sustain the roll as long as necessary. The modern coiled wire snares make this easier than it used to be.

There are today two ways of holding the side-drum sticks, one the traditional and the other the matched grip. The traditional way is with the left hand at right-angles to the floor, the palm vertical, and the stick held in the fork between thumb and palm and steadied by the loosely folded ring finger. The right hand has the knuckles uppermost with the stick held between the ball of the thumb and the side of the forefinger. This grip arose because the drum was slung at the left side (hence the name side drum) suspended from a hook, hanging with the drumhead at a steep slope. If both hands were like the right hand (called the matched grip), the left elbow would stick up in the air at a very awkward angle. With the left stick held as described, the elbow drops comfortably to the player's side.

Since in the orchestra we always play with the drum on a stand, the head can lie horizontally and there is no need to treat the two hands differently. For the kit drummer, the matched grip has the advantage that it can be easier to reach the assembled instruments with either hand. However, it has the disadvantage that if one ever wishes to play on the march, and it is surprising how often one is asked to do so at outdoor events, the traditional grip is essential. Each player must choose on which to concentrate, but it is wise to practise both, for each has its own role and its own merits.

Timpani

Here again even repetition of strokes is the essence but it is achieved with a single stroke from each hand. The ideal speed varies with the tension of the drumhead and the dynamics: higher-tensioned heads require a faster roll than lower, and quieter rolls are slower than louder. Always it is the player's ear and experience that control the speed.[1]

The grip on the stick is very personal but it is the same with each hand. Many players keep the knuckles uppermost, holding the stick between the ball of the thumb and the side of the forefinger, as with the right-hand side-drum stick, but the tone is markedly better with the thumb uppermost, just behind the forefinger so that that finger acts as a bridge and helps to spring the stick off the drum. Even better is the grip that Lewis Pocock used, with the thumb opposite the middle finger and the three fingers, fore, middle, and ring, rocking below the thumb.[2] His wrists never moved at all, as they must in the previous two methods, only the fingers.

Whatever the grip, the secret of good tone is relaxation and the briefest possible contact between stick and skin. Ours (and the piano) are the only instruments where the act of creating the sound is the same as stifling it. If the stick remains on the drum (or the hammer on the string) any longer than a microsecond, it will act as a damper and kill the sound. This is why the piano has an escapement, a mechanism to flick the hammer away from the string; our wrists and fingers have to provide that escapement.

Cross-handing, one hand crossing over the other, is often unavoidable, but ingenuity can sometimes help. In Beethoven's Eighth Symphony, a third drum tuned to one of the Fs, placed with the high f drum between the two unison low F drums or vice versa, means a very easy handing. The very tricky ostinato in variation two of the second movement of E. J. Moeran's Sinfonietta is easily played if one hand plays the middle drum, the other hand crossing between the other two drums with some double beating. This makes the original version easy and the alternative simplified part even easier. Easier still if one puts the middle drum to one side so that the other hand does not have to fly over it.[3]

Cymbals

Just bang them together, many people think, but that is a recipe for disaster. Even the heaviest marching cymbals can be turned inside out and broken by an air lock. One is held steady until just before impact, and the other moves against it, upwards and

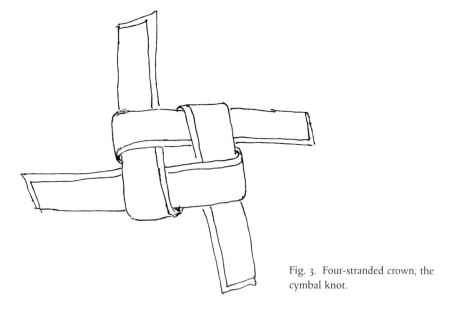

Fig. 3. Four-stranded crown, the cymbal knot.

towards, on a curving line. The middle phalange of the forefinger is against the leather pad, with the leather handle gripped between the ball of the thumb and the side of the forefinger and tensioned between the ring and little fingers and the base of the palm. Contact with the cymbal is then both secure and minimal. Relaxation of the wrists at the moment of impact improves the tone considerably.[4]

The cymbal strap is fixed with a four-stranded crown knot inside the dome, and the wise player checks both the knot (fig. 3) and the strength of the straps before every performance – a cymbal flying from the hand is dangerous as well as noisy.

Bass drum and tamtam

Never struck directly into the instrument save for very special effects, but always with a slight curve, usually at about four o'clock and halfway to the rim – never in the centre. The stability of the stand should always be checked – all the stories of a bass drum cascading through the brass and the woodwind, down from the heights of the platform, scattering players and instruments to left and to right, into the strings are true.

Rhythms

Because our sounds are short and because we are the rhythmic foundation of any ensemble, our rhythms must be precise. This takes practice. Hermann Scherchen has many good exercises in his book on conducting.[5] It helps with dotted rhythms to count the smaller note values, one, two, three on the longer note, and four on the shorter.[6] This avoids the common drift towards triplets. When playing in fives, a useful trick is to count six instead of one: 6, 2, 3, 4, 5, 6, 2, 3, 4, 5, etc., which avoids the old pitfalls of 1, 2, 3, 4, 5, -, 1, 2, 3, 4, 5, -, etc., or the triplet followed by a duplet or vice versa, both of which most of us have encountered (and had to allow for) among our colleagues.

Counting

Perhaps the most vital technique is silent. However brilliantly one may play, doing it at the wrong moment is unpopular. One should never be ashamed of using every trick one can think of to help count bars of rests. Sometimes, at rehearsal, one can mark an audible cue on the part, and hope that that player does not get lost! Even conductors get lost at times. One useful trick is to train one's fingers to mark bars automatically without one needing to think of it consciously. Then if one has lost count, if one is on the thumb it must at least be a one or a six, even if one has to guess whether eighty-one or ninety-one. Another is to trade gestures. One will often see a small motion of head or hand round the orchestra at letter A or figure 110. These rehearsal marks in older sets of parts are at logical points in the music, which can often be recognized as they pass. Modern editions, with a figure or letter every ten bars, are the bane of our lives, for they are seldom at these logical points. Ultimately, to learn to count accurately is even more important than to learn to play well – we have all got away with a fudged passage from time to time, but nobody ever got away with what we call a domino.

When we are playing, the one rule for all instruments is relaxation. A stiff wrist leads to poor tone, broken instruments, damaged or split heads. And when in doubt, play more quietly rather than more loudly. When we can't hear the orchestra, we're too loud.

Appendix 2

Lapping Drumheads

The modern plastic head comes ready-welded to its flesh hoop, and all the player need do is to put it on the drum and screw it up to tension. Natural skin is another matter.[1] It has to be selected, for unlike plastic no two animal skins are the same, then cut to size, soaked, lapped (American, tucked) on to the fleshhoop, and then carefully, over twelve or more hours, brought to tension as it dries.

The most difficult feature of lapping is keeping the tension equal at all points; it is very easy to pull harder at one point than another, and this will produce an uneven pitch. A head that is higher in pitch one side than the other can never produce a true sound.

Let us take the process of lapping a timpani head in sequence; the process on other drums is little different.

Choosing the head

The type of head will depend on the player's preference and intentions: calf or goat, clear or cloudy, thick (for early music on original or reproduction drums) or thin (for normal modern use). The general quality of the skin can be judged by its feel between the fingers; a skin that feels rough, dry, or hard will sound similarly, whereas a smooth and supple skin will respond accordingly. It should be as even in thickness as possible. This can be judged between finger and thumb, for one may safely ignore any variation finer than this will reveal. Feel all over, though, for there may be weak or hard spots. Most of us believe that the line of the backbone, usually easily visible as a line across the skin, should be diametric. If it is to one side of the centre line we fear that the head will vibrate asymmetrically and the tone will be poor. If there is a series of white dots across the head, like a string of beads, the animal once met a barbed wire fence; these may be points of weakness and the head is best rejected.[2]

Cutting to size

The head needs to be about four inches (ten centimetres) wider than the drum. This allows enough skin to lap round the fleshhoop and have a collar to come down over the side of the shell and not sit on top of the drum like a lid. An unusually small drum such as 19-inch or a side drum will require less but not as much less as one might think. A very narrow fleshhoop requires less, a thick one more; one needs enough for a one-inch collar plus one and a half times the circumference of the fleshhoop. The safest way to measure before cutting is to lay the fleshhoop on the skin and with a waterproof fine-line marker draw a circle round the hoop. Then with a two-inch (5 cm) spacer block draw another circle two inches wider than the hoop, making sure that the hoop has not moved from its position within the first circle. Cut off the surplus along the outer ring.

Soaking the head

The bath is the best place and the water must be cold. Hot water is more comfortable for the hands in winter but disastrous for the head, which can shrivel up into a nasty lump of skin. Half an hour should be enough, an hour at most.

Normal or reverse lap

This will depend on the type of counterhoop. With a plain iron counterhoop, such as one usually sees on hand-tuned drums, use the normal lap. For this one puts the skin face down, i.e. with the smoother side downwards. Every skin has one surface smoother than the other.[3]

With the L-shaped counterhoop that goes on top of and down one side of the fleshhoop, such as is normally used on pedal timpani, use the reverse lap, with the smooth side uppermost.

When lapping directly on to the counterhoop, as on many antique drums, also use the reverse lap.

Lapping the head

When doing this at home, as one usually will, lay down a pad of old towel, or some other protection to whatever surface one is working on; domestic harmony is just as important as musical.[4] Lay down the wet head (hence the need for the pad below it) whichever way up is appropriate according to the previous section. Many of us put a pile of two, three, or four upside-down soup plates under the centre of the skin to make sure that there will be a collar, the number of plates depending on the diameter of the skin and the depth of collar required; for a side drum use a saucer. Make sure the pile of plates is exactly central and make sure that the hoop is exactly centred to its ring (the first one that was drawn).

Now start to lap. This is most easily done with a proper lapping tool, a wooden handle, flattened on the under side, holding a blunt steel blade with an upturned end, but many people use the handle end of a dessert spoon or table spoon. Fold the edge of the skin inwards up over the hoop, round it, and then tuck it up between the skin and the hoop and up as far as the bent end of the tool will reach on the outer surface of the hoop (fig. 4). Put a spring clothes peg such as one uses on a washing line over

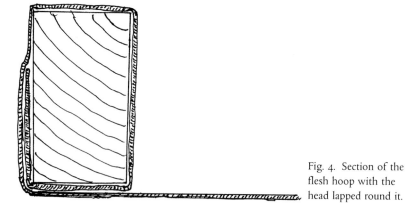

Fig. 4. Section of the
flesh hoop with the
head lapped round it.

that point; you will need a couple of dozen of these pegs. Do the same diametrically opposite. Then box the compass, doing it north, south, east, west, north-east, south-west, and so on. Make sure the tension stays even. Fill in the gaps, checking that there are no points where the skin is not properly tucked in, squinting down between hoop and skin.

Leave it for half an hour or so to begin to set.

Rub french chalk over the underside of the skin where it will rest on the rim of the drum.[5] Some people rub the rim of the drum shell with paraffin wax, or a candle, especially with pedal timpani, to avoid any creaks. It is worthwhile burnishing the rim to make sure there are no scratches or sharp edges that may harm the skin.

Put the head on the drum, making sure that the smooth side is uppermost. If the counterhoop is iron, put strips of paper on the edge of the head before putting the hoop on. This will avoid rust spots, which would weaken the head as well as look unsightly.

Make sure that the counterhoop is correctly located. On a surprising number of drums the brackets for the tuning screws are not spaced equally round the circumference.[6] This why one of the brackets on both hoop and drum often has a notch to show that these two should line up together. If there is no notch it is often useful to mark one bracket on each before taking the old head off.

Put in the tuning screws and turn them till they just bear on the counterhoop and that on the fleshhoop, making sure that it is not pulling down on one side more than the other. Every hour or so, take up a little slack, turning the screws north, south, east, west, etc., as before.

After twenty-four hours the drum should be fit to play.

Lapping on the counterhoop

This will always be a reverse lap. There is little difference from the above save that the brackets for the tuning screws have to pass through the head. A very sharp knife or scalpel will be needed. Bring the head up over the hoop, pulling a little too tight. Slit the head no more than absolutely necessary where it presses on the bracket. As the bracket passes through, the tension will relax slightly, which is why one pulled it too tight. Tuck in as usual. This is a terrifying process – there is no way to rectify any error.

Sometimes the brackets will unscrew from the hoop. If so, take them out, but keep each one beside its hole because hand-cut threads are not always interchangeable. Lap as normal and then with a red-hot iron burn through at each hole. The hot iron will raise a collar and prevent the head from splitting further. Alternatively, make a small X-shaped cut with the point of the scalpel. Be careful also to keep the tuning screws associated with their lugs on the drumshell, for again the screw thread may not be transferable to another bracket.

Reviving an old head

A head that is dry and stiff can often be revived by massaging it with good quality toilet soap. This is best done off the drum, but when time is short it can be done *in situ*.[7] Moisten the soap and the hands, rub the soap all over the head and rub it well in with the fingers. Have an old cloth handy to wipe off the dirt, for this will clean the head as well as revive it, and continue to rub soap in. When the head feels supple, stop and allow it to dry. When dry, wipe off any excess soap, but ideally it should all have been rubbed in.

This process was recommended by Lewis Pocock, Beecham's timpanist with the Royal Philharmonic after the separation from the Philharmonia, and has proved very successful.

Do not try lanolin. When I did so, it led to the ruin of two good heads and my best pair of timpani sticks.[8]

Appendix 3

The Need to be Inventive

Percussion players, more than most musicians, are at the mercy of the composers' whim. Whatever funny noise they may have in mind, or more often hovering at the edge of their mental ear, it is we who have to realize it. In recent years, with the growing use of multiphonics and such-like effects, our colleagues on other instruments have also been afflicted, but it is still we who bear the brunt of inventing a sound to fulfil their desires. To recall one famous example, when Benjamin Britten wanted the sound of footsteps in the desert sand for *The Prodigal Son*, it was no great difficulty for Jimmy Blades to produce a seed-filled tube and shoosh the seeds from one end to the other. But then Britten asked for the steps to differ. The solution was to make the tube conical, and hey presto! one foot was heavier than the other.[1]

Most of us can tell similar stories, especially any who have worked in film studios. I was once asked to imitate the sound of whales, for the film *Orca*. Whales do not talk percussively, but as always it was a percussionist's job to make them speak, just as I was part of the voice of the *Alien*. Our mental ears need always to be on the *qui vive* for ideas of how to make new sounds and how to produce the sounds for which the composer may have only the vaguest idea. Who first thought of dunking a gong into water while it was sounding? Who first used a fiddle bow on a cymbal or a gong? Who first used superballs on timpani or cymbals? I used a long, screw-threaded rod on a scrap Chinese crash cymbal to represent a lightning flash.[2] I used an Audubon Bird Call (a pewter rod twisted to and fro in a hole in a piece of wood) to represent the movements of a thievish spider.

We also often need to be mechanically adept. Managements are notoriously parsimonious on percussion. They would never expect a violinist to play the cello as well, but take an opera or ballet company on tour and one percussion player will be expected to cover what four did in London, and if he is unlucky the timpanist will be alone and have to cover his own part and all four percussion parts as well.

Double-ended sticks have been mentioned above. Usually this only means making a timpani beater head to fit the end of a side-drum stick, or adding a suitable knob to a timpani stick. Wire brushes on the end of side-drum sticks make one change practicable in *Façade* (in the 'Scotch Rhapsody', five bars before figure 4). A steel ring round the butt of a side-drum stick means that one can play the triangle with that in the 'Valse', instead of 'with the wood of the stick'; Walton preferred the resulting sound.[3]

The same task can be better performed by my machine triangle (ill. 76), which has two beaters whose proximal ends are tipped with cork so that one can play trills or

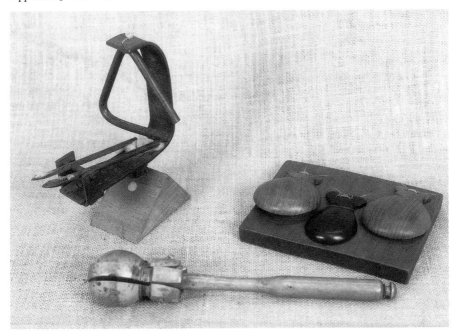

76. Machine triangle (*left*), machine castanets (*right*), both by Jeremy Montagu, orchestral castanets (*foreground*).

fast rhythms with whatever beaters one has in one's hand at the time, or with one's fingers. It is all easily made out of silver steel for the triangle, six-inch nails for the beaters, mild steel strip for the gallows and frame, and a bolt to fit into the top of a cymbal stand.

In *L'Histoire du soldat* one needs to have the bass drum flat. Screwing the legs from a floor tom-tom to the shell, which can then be adjustable in height and angle, is better than resting it on three chairs. A cymbal must be fixed to the shell of the bass drum, and this needs a special clamp, which Jimmy Blades made for me, so that it will be in the same plane as the drumhead, as cymbals were with the earliest models of bass-drum pedals.

In *Façade* machine castanets will be a help in several movements, though the ordinary orchestral castanets on a handle will also be needed, and a tambourine fixed on a post so that it can be played with drum sticks will be useful in addition to an ordinary one. Machine castanets are now commercially available, but it is not difficult to tie a pair of castanets tightly to a board with nylon fishing line, which is elastic enough to provide the necessary spring (ill. 76). Hollowing the board more under one shell than the other will provide the left-hand/right-hand contrast required in real castanet playing.

Equally important is being able to support within one's reach all the instruments required. Most of us have had to rig up contraptions of rods and stands. A small local garage is often sufficiently entertained at being asked to help a musician that they will go to considerable trouble to weld or braze iron rods together to produce the stand required. One made me a xylophone stand which would go into a heavy cymbal-stand base for a set up where there was no room for the instrument's four legs; one forked rod went through the 'black' note ladder and the other through the 'white' note ladder. Where they met, a vertical rod projected downwards to go into the stand.

It is often only with such devices that one can bring everything within reach. Minimal technical skills, such as the ability to cut a screw thread on a rod, can often be job-savers.

Appendix 4

Drummers

Since the Middle Ages drummers have been divided between kettledrummers and *hoi polloi*, the lowly who played tabors, side drums and everything else. Evidence is scanty, but one has the distinct impression that the nakerer was of higher status at the court than the taborer. Certainly he was always associated with trompes and trompours, just as later the kettledrummer was associated with trumpets and trumpeters.[1] Whether, though, his position could compare with lutenists, even more with harpers, is more difficult to assess. He may have been with the prince in the field, but the player of the softer instruments would have been with him in the privy chambers.[2] One suspects that as usual the drummer, whatever he played, may have been of somewhat lower caste than the string player.

Whether this remained true in the Renaissance and Early Baroque is less certain. As Edward Tarr says, in the introduction to his translation of Altenburg's treatise, 'His insistence on the rightness of the trumpeters' high social standing runs through the entire treatise', to which one should add that Altenburg himself stresses that kettledrummers are on an equal level with the trumpeters and that both are officers.[3] When one considers Mozart's status at the court of the Archbishop of Salzburg, and the general tendency to group musicians with lackeys and other servants, if the court trumpeters and kettedrummers really had the status of officers, they may have been better off than any other musicians.

Musicians have always had a somewhat ambivalent position. They may hobnob with royalty, as Mendelssohn did with Queen Victoria and Prince Albert, and was permitted to say (tactfully, of course) what he thought of their compositions and playing, but they would never be regarded as social equals. A young virtuoso like Mozart might even be dandled on a royal lap, but so would be a pet dog, and no doubt a dog that could perform entertaining tricks would be as highly regarded as a musician (and be cheaper to feed and house).

Members of high society could, without losing their status, be musicians. There are numerous references to court orchestras being maintained not just for the usual reasons of ostentation but so that the Prince could play in or direct the band. Although these were chamber orchestras it would seem improbable that there was the usual friendly interchange characteristic of our own chamber orchestras. It would have been more on a par with recent conductors such as Malcolm Sargent, to whom orchestral musicians never said much more than 'Yes, Sir Malcolm' and 'No, Sir Malcolm'. It is significant that some people, though coming from the same strata of society as the members of the orchestra, once doctored or knighted regarded themselves as being of quite another caste, not merely because as conductor or musical director they were in charge of the proceedings but as though they were higher beings. It would be interesting to know just how Altenburg's trumpeters treated the other musicians at the court!

On the whole, and certainly in England, orchestral musicians have been fairly low-caste. Even when, over Europe as a whole, after the social upheavals of the late eighteenth and early nineteenth centuries, they were no longer considered domestic servants, they never achieved the position of professional men, lawyers, doctors, and so on. With the establishment of the conservatories in Britain in the early years of the nineteenth century, those who were teaching there began to call themselves professors, but this only caused amusement in university circles. Music was a trade, not a profession in the eyes of professional men, and its professors were, at best, artisans.

So far as orchestras were concerned, it was always men. Not until our own time (has Vienna even yet?) have women been thought fit to work in the leading orchestras. In London, the BBC was the first to admit women, followed by the Philharmonia when that was founded in 1945. Provincial orchestras were more open-minded, partly because if London was taking all the best men, they were better off with the best women than with the second-rate men; this was certainly the policy of the London chamber orchestras. Even then, orchestras tended to be selective. Women as string players and woodwind were fine, even french horn at a pinch, but a woman trumpeter had a difficult time getting work, and as for a woman timpanist…. The Halle Orchestra in Manchester was an exception here, for Joyce Aldous was their timpanist for many years. This was despite the experience of the women's orchestras, which have existed, though seldom very well known, for at least a century, and even more the experience of the military bands of the women's branches of the services, where they had played bass drums and tubas on the march as happily as piccolos. Today that barrier has gone, and in theory at least women are at as much liberty to play percussion instruments as men. One does have to say 'in theory'. Despite all the claims of the Musicians' Union to equality of race and gender, one still sees far more men than women in orchestras, and the further back on the platform you look, the fewer the women.

Certainly in the first half of the twentieth century, and probably earlier, while string and woodwind players might come from any sections of society, percussion players were often ex-soldiers, trained in the army bands. Some brass came also through the Salvation Army and through the many works bands which were so important a feature of the nineteenth century, but it was only in the army that one could get proper training on drums unless, like James Blades, one taught oneself on the foundation of sketchy instruction from a friendly amateur musician.[4] Even when I became a student in 1948, percussion teaching at the conservatories was at nothing like the same level as for other instruments.

While this is no longer true, there is still a tendency towards a dichotomy between percussion and 'proper instruments', though the better the orchestra the less this tendency is found. Certainly there is a feeling in some circles that any fool can hit a drum. This is why in many amateur and student orchestras the conductor's girl friend (or boy friend) makes a hash of the timpani part. I played in many such orchestras in my student and beginner's days, either taking over the timpani when something more than usually tricky was on the programme or more often playing the side drum because it was realized that that instrument did require some proper training and skill. It is, in fact, why I became a percussion player in the first place. The horn section, my second study, was full so, as a first-study conducting student, 'Why don't you try percussion?' and I was pitched into First Orchestra with no training whatsoever.[5]

Still, we do have more fun than anyone else. We create more new sounds than most people, we are more likely to do things *ad lib.*, and if the worst comes to the worst, we can always drown the rest of the orchestra.

Notes

Introduction

1. I was the player concerned.
2. For the basis of classification of instruments see Erich M. von Hornbostel and Curt Sachs, 'Systematik der Musikinstrumente', *Zeitschrift für Ethnologie*, Jhrg. 1914, Heft 4 u. 5 (1914), 553–90, translated into English by Anthony Baines and Klaus Wachsmann in *Galpin Society Journal*, XIV (1961), 3–29. For the best brief general summaries of the manner in which percussion instruments function, see Laurence Picken's *Folk Musical Instruments of Turkey* (London: Oxford University Press, 1975), pp. 3–5 for idiophones and pp. 59–61 for membranophones.
3. E.g. Gerassimos Avgerinos, *Lexikon der Pauke* (Frankfurt am Main: Verlag das Musikinstrument, 1964), and *Handbuch der Schlag- und Effekt-instrumente* (same publisher, 1967) (Avgerinos was principal timpanist of the Berlin Philharmonic Orchestra); John Beck, ed., *Encyclopedia of Percussion* (New York: Garland, 1995); James Holland, *Percussion* (London: Macdonald and Jane's, 1978) (James Holland has been principal percussion with several of the major London orchestras; he is working on a new, larger book on similar lines); Karl Peinkofer and Fritz Tannigel, *Handbuch des Schlagzeugs* (Mainz: Schott, 1969) (the authors were orchestral musicans in Munich); Reginald Smith Brindle, *Contemporary Percussion* (London: Oxford University Press, 1970) (Smith Brindle is a composer, rather than a percussion player, and this is sometimes apparent in his text).

Chapter 1 Speculation and Antiquity

1. Alexander Buchner, *Musical Instruments Through the Ages* (London: Spring Books, n.d.), pls 6–7; *Colour Encyclopedia of Musical Instruments* (London: Hamlyn, 1980), pl. 9. Both these superbly illustrated surveys were originally published in other languages by Artia in Prague.
2. Leonard Williams, *The Dancing Chimpanzees* (London: Andre Deutsch, 1967).
3. Described, with a recording, by S. N. Bibikov, *The Oldest Musical Complex Made of Mammoth Bones* (Kiev: Academy of Science, Ukraine SSR, 1981), in Russian with French and English summaries.
4. Paul Collaer, *Südostasien*, Musikgeschichte in Bildern, I:3 (Leipzig: Deutscher Verlag für Musik, 1979), p. 10, and Abb. 1 and 2; Tran Van Khe, *La Musique Vietnamienne traditionelle* (Paris: Presses Universitaires de France, 1962), p. 10.
5. E.g. Graeme Lawson, 'Conservation versus restoration: Towards a handling and performance policy for excavated musical instruments....', Cajsa Lund, ed., *Second Conference of the ICTM Study Group on Music Archaeology, Stockholm, 1984* (Stockholm: Royal Swedish Academy of Music, 1986), vol. 1, 123–30.
6. There is a considerable number of books with titles in the vein of History of Music in

Pictures, and all are worth consulting. One of the best of them was compiled by Georg Kinsky in 1930 and was published simultaneously in German, French, English and Italian. The best in modern times is the series *Musikgeschichte in Bildern*, published by the Deutscher Verlag für Musik in Leipzig from 1961 until the financial crises following the reunification of Germany made further work impossible. Several volumes in that series are cited here under their authors' names, as is Kinsky's compilation, both in the notes and in the bibliography.

7.   Hans Hickmann, *Catalogue général des Antiquités Égyptiennes du Musée du Caire; Instruments de Musique* (Cairo: Imprimerie de l'Institut Français d'Archéologie Orientale, 1949), pp. 35–7 and pl. XXII; R. D. Anderson, *Catalogue of Egyptian Antiquities in the British Museum: III Musical Instruments* (London: British Museum Publications, 1976), pp. 26–8; Christiane Ziegler, *Musée du Louvre, Catalogue des instruments de musique égyptiennes* (Paris: Éditions de la Réunion des Musées Nationaux, 1979), pp. 68–9.

8.   Montagu, *The World of Medieval & Renaissance Musical Instruments* (Newton Abbot: David & Charles, 1976), ills 1 and 5; Tilman Seebass, *Musikdarstellung und Psalterillustration im früheren Mittelalter* (Bern: Francke Verlag, 1973), Tf. 37, 41, 93–9.

9.   R. D. Anderson (1976), p. 24, catalogue no. 6710.

10.   Max Wegner, *Griechenland*, Musikgeschichte in Bildern, II:4 (Leipzig: Deutscher Verlag für Musik, 1963), Abb. 27; James Blades, *Percussion Instruments and their History* (London: Faber, 1970), pl. 70.

11.   Hans Hickmann, *Ägypten*, Musikgeschichte in Bildern, II:1 (Leipzig: Deutscher Verlag für Musik, 1961), Abb. 30, 32, 46–7; Wegner (1963), Abb. 25, 62, 63; Günter Fleischhauer, *Etrurien und Rom*, Musikgeschichte in Bildern, II:5 (Leipzig: Deutscher Verlag für Musik, 1964), Abb. 8, 49, 68, 69.

12.   See the Egyptian catalogues cited above and Hickmann (1961).

13.   Hickmann (1949), 69354, pp. 109–10 and pls LXXV–LXXVIII; see also 69350 and 69353, pp. 107–8 and pls LXXI–LXXIV; Hickmann (1961), Abb. 42 and 72 show such a drum in use.

14.   Hickmann (1949), 69355, p. 110 and pl. LXXIX; Hickmann (1961), Abb. 70 shows such a drum in use.

15.   The shields of the *salii* are illustrated by Fleischhauer (1964), Abb. 21 and 22. The wooden dance shield from Tanzania in the Etnografiska Museum in Göteborg is no. 33.11.141a; 141b is its beater.

16.   Joan Rimmer, *Ancient Musical Instruments of Western Asia in the British Museum* (London: British Mseum, 1969), pl. VI a, b, and c.

17.   Subhi Anwar Rashid, *Mesopotamien*, Musikgeschichte in Bildern, II:2 (Leipzig: Deutscher Verlag für Musik, 1984), Abb. 49–55.

18.   Rashid, Abb. 58–9.

19.   Rashid, Abb. 60; Rimmer (1969), pl. V b.

20.   W. Perceval Yetts, *The George Eumorfopoulos Collection: Catalogue of the Chinese & Corean bronzes, sculptures, jades, jewellery and miscellaneous objects* (London: Ernest Benn, 1930), vol. 2, Bronzes: bells, drums, mirrors, etc. Drums in use in this way can be seen on pls I and II of Pen-Li Chuang, *Panpipes of Ancient China*, Institute of Ethnology, Academia Sinica, Monograph no. 4 (Nankang, Taipei, 1963).

21.   Chang Sa-hun, *Korean Musical Instruments* (Seoul: 1976), pp. 303–5 and 312–13, figs 74–5; Keith Howard, *Korean Musical Instruments* (Seoul: Se-Kwang, 1988), pp. 41–2, figs 13–14; Bang-Song Song, *Korean Music and Instruments* (Seoul: National Classical Music Institute, n.d.).

22.   Lothar von Falkenhausen, *Suspended Music: Chime-bells in the Culture of Bronze Age China* (Berkeley and Los Angeles: University of California Press, 1993).

23.   See also my review of Von Falkenhausen's book in *Galpin Society Journal*, LI (1998), 210–16.

24.   Fritz Kuttner, 'Prince Chu Tsai-Yü's Life and Work: a Re-Evaluation of His

Contribution to Equal Temperament Theory', *Ethnomusicology*, XIX:2 (May 1975), 163–206.

25. Rashid (1984), Abb. 129–33; Rimmer (1969), pls XVII–XX for bells and horses; Walter Kaufmann, *Altindien*, Musikgeschichte in Bildern, II:8 (Leipzig: Deutscher Verlag für Musik, 1981), Abb. 36 for elephants.

26. Rashid, pp. 98–101; also Rimmer (1969) pl. III; Joachim Braun, *Die Musikkultur Altisraels/Palästinas: Studien zu archäologischen, schriftlichen und vergleichenden Quellen* (Freiburg: Universitätsverlag and Göttingen: Vandenhoek & Ruprecht, 1999), Abb. III/5 1–13.

27. All the sources cited above on Egyptian material include numerous examples of *sistra*.

28. Exodus 28:34. See Montagu, *Musical Instruments of the Bible* (Lanham: Scarecrow Press, forthcoming).

29. I Corinthians 13:1. The Septuagint was the first Greek translation of the Old Testament, made around 200 BC in Alexandria.

30. Montagu, 'What is a Gong?', *MAN* (1965:5), 18–21; Jaap Kunst, 'A hypothesis about the origin of the gong', *Ethnos* (1947), 79–85 and 147.

31. Fivos Anoyanakis, *Greek Popular Musical Instruments* (Athens: National Bank of Greece,1979). This is a superbly illustrated book of over 400 pages. Italian banks also have an excellent record of such publications, though often smaller in size; it would be wonderful if those of other countries were to follow their example!

32. Utrecht: University Library 32; the lower illustration on f. 83, which refers to Psalm 150, the text of which is overleaf, is printed in many places, including pl. 1 in my *World of Medieval & Renaissance Musical Instruments* (1976), and Tilman Seebass (1973), pl. 96.

Chapter 2 The Middle Ages

1. For fuller information, see my *Musical Instruments of the Bible* (Lanham: Scarecrow Press, forthcoming).

2. Gwen & Jeremy Montagu, 'Beverley Minster reconsidered', *Early Music*, VI:3 (July, 1978), 401–15; Jeremy & Gwen Montagu, *Minstrels & Angels* (Berkeley: Fallen Leaf, 1998).

3. There are many possible ways of transcribing instrument names from other alphabets; on the whole, those of the *New Grove Dictionary of Musical Instruments*, ed. Stanley Sadie (London: Macmillan, 1984), are used here.

4. Jean Gimpel, *The Medieval Machine: The Industrial Revolution of the Middle Ages* (Aldershot: Wildwood House, 2nd edn, 1988).

5. Madrid: Escorial T.I.1. All the illustrations were published, in black and white, with detailed notes, by José Guerrero Lovillo, *Las Cántigas* (Madrid: Instituto Diego Velásquez, 1949). Some were published in colour by Matilde López Serrano, *Cántigas de Santa Maria de Alfonso X el Sabio, Rey de Castilla* (Madrid: Editorial Patrimonio Nacional, 1974).

6. Madrid: Escorial b.I.2. Published in full, including a facsimile, by Higinio Anglés, *La Música de las Cantigas de Santa María del Rey Alfonso el Sabio: Facsímil, Transcripción y Estudio Crítico* (Barcelona: Diputación Provincial de Barcelona: Biblioteca Central, 1943-64). Vol. I appeared last: *Facsímil del Códice j.b.2 de El Escorial.*

7. E.g. Tilman Seebass, *Musikdarstellung und Psalterillustration im früheren Mittelalter* (Bern: Francke, 1973), Tf. 58 (London: BL Add. MS 11695, f. 329) compared with his Tf. 35 (Escorial: *Cántigas* b.I.2, f. 286) or Montagu, *The World of Medieval & Renaissance Musical Instruments* (Newton Abbot: David & Charles, 1976), pl. 1 (Utrecht: UL 32, *The Utrecht Psalter*, f. 83) compared with pls 32 (*Cántigas* as Seebass) and 33 (London: BL Add. MS 49622, *The Gorleston Psalter*, f. 43v). Many of the Cántigas miniatures will be

found in each source, as well as elsewhere; all are in the facsimile volume of Anglés.

8.   B. 18, f. 1. Illustrated by Seebass (1973), Tf. 111.

9.   E.g. Seebass (1973), Tf. 93 (Stuttgart: Landes–B. Bibl. fol. 40, f. 163v – also pl. 5 in Montagu (1976)), 95 (St Gallen: Stifts–B. 22, f. 2), 98 (Paris: BN lat. 1, *The Bible of Charles the Bald*, f. 215v).

10. Some Beatus Apocalypse manuscripts with instruments are illustrated by Seebass (1973), Tf. 123 (Valladolid: UB, f. 199v and Madrid: BN B 31, f. 275v) and 124 (Seu d'Urgell: Catedral, f. 213v). For the instruments of Nebuchadrezzar's orchestra (Daniel 3:5, 7, 10, 15), see Montagu, *Musical Instruments of the Bible*.

11. Subhi Anwar Rashid, *Mesopotamien*, Musikgeschichte in Bildern, II:2 (Leipzig: Deutscher Verlag für Musik, 1984), Abb. 51–2 (Paris: Louvre, AO 4578), 53–5 (Philadelphia: Pennsylvania University Museum, CBS 16676, Urnammu Stele from Ur), and 56 (Ontario: Royal Ontario Museum 950.7.3, same source).

12. Jeremy & Gwen Montagu, *Minstrels & Angels* (1998), pls 116 and 117 (both York Minster choir screen) and many other sources.

13. See Laurence Picken, *Folk Musical Instruments of Turkey* (London: Oxford University Press, 1975), p. 4.

14. Legend has it that the cymbals used in the first performance of Debussy's *L'Après-midi d'un faune* were indeed antique, borrowed from one of the Paris museums. However, this was not the first French use of such cymbals – was such borrowing customary or was somebody already making such instruments?

15. When two notes a very small interval apart (less than a quarter-tone) are sounded simultaneously, a beating or vibration is heard at the speed per second of the number of Hertz (vibrations per second) that separate them. Players and tuners take advantage of this, for the slower the beat-rate the nearer the two pitches are to being in tune. As the difference approaches the quarter-tone, however, it becomes fast enough to be intensely disagreeable (howling like a wolf was a standard description) and at this sort of rate it becomes very difficult to perceive the pitch of either of the notes concerned.

16. Percival Price, *Bells and Man* (Oxford: Oxford University Press, 1983), pp. 84–5.

17. E.g. Seebass (1973), Tf. 41 (Milan: Ambrosiana C 128 inf, f. 45v) and 52 (Madrid: Archivo historico nacional 1240, f. 139).

18. André Lehr, *Het Middeleeuwse klokkenspel van Bethlehem* (Breda: Nederlandse Klokkenspel Vereniging, 1981). Three of the bells are illustrated by Price (1983), p. 96, and all by Lehr, *The Art of the Carillon in the Low Countries* (Tielt: Lannoo, 1991), pls 104 and 129.

19. Seebass (1973), Tf. 53 (Amiens: fonds escalopier 2, f. 116).

20. E.g. Price (1983), pp. 108, 111, 113.

21. Even using brass hammers on modern handbells (which, in a performance with Musica Reservata, we thought would be somewhat kinder to the bells than iron hammers) left little dents and chips, and this experience adds to the inherent improbability of the reality of such illustration.

22. J. Smits van Waesberghe, *Cymbala* (Rome: American Institute of Musicology, Studies and Documents, I, 1951), p. 14.

23. Hélène La Rue, 'The Problem of the Cymbala', *Galpin Society Journal*, XXXV (1982), 86–99 (p. 96); the reference to Gerson is to his vol. VII. I, p. 132.

24. No church bells sounded in Britain for almost the whole duration of World War II; their use was reserved as a warning of the German invasion which never came.

25. Julius von Schlosser, *Die Sammlung alter Musikinstrumente* (Vienna: Anton Schroll, 1920; facsimile, Hildesheim: Georg Olms, 1974), p. 94 and Taf. XLVI, C 270 and 271; for the history of the Catajo collection, see Alec Loretto, 'Catajo and Ganassi – an Italian castle and a flauto dolce', *FoMRHI Quarterly*, 91 (April 1998), Comm. 1570, 28–30.

26. Marin Mersenne, *Harmonie Universelle* (Paris: Sebastien Cramoisy, 1636), Livre Septiesme, p. 49; Michael Praetorius, *Syntagma Musicum II – De Organographia* (Wolfenbüttel: Elias Holwein, 1619), Sciagraphia XXII; Montagu (1976), pl. 83 (Paris:

BN MS fr. 9152, François Merlin and Jacques Cellier, *Recherche de Plusieurs Singularités,* c.1585, f. 167), pl. X (London: BL Add. MS 18851, 'The Isabella Breviary', c.1490, f. 184v), and pl. VII (Munich: Alte Pinakothek, The Master of Cologne, *The Virgin Surrounded by Angels,* c. 1415); Frank Harrison and Joan Rimmer, *European Musical Instruments* (London: Studio Vista, 1964), pl. 67d (Angers: Tapestry, c. 1375).

27. Christopher Page, 'Early 15th-century instruments in Jean de Gerson's "Tractatus de Canticis"', *Early Music,* VI:3 (July, 1978), 339–49 (p. 347).

28. Merlin and Cellier (c.1585), f. 185.

29. *Encyclopédie méthodique* (for which see below), pl. II, fig. 24.

30. Montagu (1976), pls 37 (Escorial: *Cántigas* b.I.2, f. 333) and 39 (Lincoln Cathedral); all the others are illustrated in Montagu, 'Was the Tabor Pipe Always as we Know it?', *Galpin Society Journal,* L (1997), 16–30.

31. G. & J. Montagu (1978) for Beverley; the medieval nave tabor is fig. 9 and the nineteenth-century north aisle tabor is fig. 8.

32. More details, with illustrations, will be found in Montagu, *Making Early Percussion* (London: Oxford University Press, 1976).

33. Some editions of the *Encyclopédie méthodique,* for example that (unspecified) which was the source for Picton Publishing's *The Manufacture of Musical Instruments* (Chippenham: 1975), show pl. II, fig. 26 with a snare, whereas that used by Minkoff Reprint for their facsimile (Geneva: 1972) does not; the accompanying pipe is quite different also, as is the *tambourin à cordes* (fig. 23).

34. E.g. in the Pitt Rivers Museum and the Bate Collection, both in Oxford. The latter was almost certainly made as a child's toy drum but was used as a tabor. So far as can be judged from wear patterns, the snare on the Bate Collection tabor appears to follow side-drum practice and to be on the lower head.

35. G. & J. Montagu (1978), fig. 10.

36. Constance Bullock-Davies, *Menestrellorum Multitudo* (Cardiff: University of Wales Press, 1978), an account of the feast when Edward, the first Prince of Wales, was knighted in 1306; Richard Rastall, 'The Minstrels of the English Royal Households, 25 Edward I – 1 Henry VIII: an Inventory', *Royal Musical Association Research Chronicle,* 4 (1964), 1–41, covering the period from 1301 onwards, and other similar sources.

37. Henry Holland Carter, *A Dictionary of Middle English Musical Terms* (Bloomington: Indiana University Press, 1961), p. 488.

38. Harrison and Rimmer (1964), pl. 65 (Staro Nagoricino: Church of St George).

39. Edmund A. Bowles, *La Pratique musicale au Moyen-Age / Musical Performance in the Late Middle Ages* (no place: Minkoff & Lattès, n.d.), pl. 30 (Vincent de Beauvoir, *Le Miroir historiale,* Chantilly, Musée Condé, MS fr. 136, f. 495).

40. *Cántigas* T.I.1, Guerrero (1949), lam. 181, *Cántiga* CLXV, and in colour López (1974), lam. 13.

41. Brigitte Bachmann-Geiser, *Die Volksmusikinstrumente der Schweiz,* Handbuch der europäischen Volksmusikinstrumente, I:4 (Leipzig: Deutscher Verlag für Musik, 1981), Taf. 41 (Bern Burgerbibliothek, MS hist. Helv. I. 3, *Amtliche Chronik,* p. 783, c.1478–83).

42. The timbre appears so often in medieval illustrations that it seems unnecessary to cite any examples; all the sources noted above show numerous examples, as do many others.

43. My wife points out that a regular five-pointed star is surprisingly easy to draw with a continuous line, making it simple to mark out the locations for the jingles in such a pattern.

44. Carter (1961), pp. 500–1.

45. Exodus 15:20–21.

46. E.g. Montagu (1976), pl. VI (London: BL MS Royal 19 D iii, f. 458).

47. E.g. James Blades, *Percussion Instruments and their History* (London: Faber, 1970), pls 108 (London: BL Add. MS 42130, f. 59) and 110 (London: BL Add. MS 27695, f. 13).

48. E.g. Harrison and Rimmer (1964), pl. 66 (Oxford: MS Bodl. 264 *Le Roman d'Alexandre,* f. 149v); also shown by Mary Remnant, *Musical Instruments of the West* (London: Batsford, 1978), pl. 142. An even larger pair is shown by Harrison and Rimmer, pl. 67a (Angers: Tapestry of the Apocalypse), clearly anticipating, in 1375 if the authors' attribution is correct, the use of timpani.

49. E.g. Montagu (1976), pl. 56 (Worcester: Cathedral, misericord South 9); also Blades (1970), pl. 109, and other sources.

50. Page (1978), p. 342 for the discussion, and pp. 346–7 for the text and its translation (to the meaning we suggest below!).

51. Catalogue II 218b; they were bought from Michael Morrow, who had found them in Dublin; no further provenance is known.

52. Bullock-Davies (1978) and Rastall (1964), as well as many other sources.

53. Carter (1961), pp. 317–18.

54. E.g. G. & J. Montagu (1978), pl. 44 right (Beverley: Minster triforium), and James Blades and Jeremy Montagu, *Early Percussion Instruments* (London: Oxford University Press, 1976), p. 5, left (Roslin: Rosslyn Chapel). See also the Turkish drums referred to above.

55. E.g. Seebass (1973), Tf. 41 (Milan: Ambrosiana C 128 inf. f. 45v and Piacenza: Capitolare 65, f. 262).

56. Edmund A. Bowles, *Musikleben im 15. Jahrhundert,* Musikgeschichte in Bildern III:8 (Leipzig: Deutscher Verlag für Musik, 1977), Abb. 69 (Bern: Burgerbibliothek, MS hist. helv. I. 16, Diebold Schilling, *Berner Chronik,* written for Rudolph von Spiesz, p. 204).

Chapter 3 The Renaissance

1. Illustrated by Georg Kinsky, *Musikgeschichte in Bildern* (also published in English, French, and Italian) (Leipzig: Breitkopf und Härtel, 1929/30), p. 41, fig. 2.

2. Heidelberg: Pal. germ. 848. Claude Riot illustrates a detail from f. 423 in *Chants et Instruments, Trouveurs et jongleurs au Moyen Age* (Paris: R.E.M.P.ART., 1995), p. 68. Reproductions from this manuscript of the German Meister- and Minnesingers appear quite widely.

3. Heidelberg: Pal. germ. 848, f. 13. The illustration of the Markgraf Otto IV of Brandenburg, with the two-handed drum in the lower field, accompanying two trumpeters and a bagpiper, is pl. 5 in Alfons Ott, *Tausend Jahre Musikleben: 800–1800* (Munich: Prestel Verlag, 1963). The drummer alone is on p. 100 of Riot (1995).

4. Edmund A. Bowles, *Musikleben im 15. Jahrhundert,* Musikgeschichte in Bildern, III:8 (Leipzig: Deutscher Verlag für Musik, 1977), Abb. 70 (Zürich: Zentralbibliothek, Ms. A. 120, f. 979: Heinrich Dittlinger, *Berner Chronik,* Bern, 1470).

5. Brigitte Bachmann-Geiser, *Die Volksmusikinstrumente der Schweiz,* Handbuch der europäischen Volksmusikinstrumente I:4 (Leipzig: Deutscher Verlag für Musik, 1981), Taf. 41 (Bern: Burgerbibliothek, MS hist. helv. I. 3, *Amtliche Chronik,* p. 783, c.1478–83).

6. Edmund A. Bowles, *Musikleben,* Abb. 69 (Bern: Burgerbibliothek, MS hist. helv. I. 16, Diebold Schilling, *Berner Chronik,* written for Rudolph von Spiesz, p. 204).

7. Sebastian Virdung, *Musica Getutscht* (Basel: Michael Furter, 1511), illustrated on f. D and described on that and the facing page.

8. *The Triumph of Maximilian I* (New York: Dover, 1964), text (translated by Stanley Applebaum), pp. 1–2; the woodcuts (one for the fifers and one for the drummers) are on plates 3 and 4.

9. Cologne: Wallraf-Richartz Museum; reproduced full-page and in colour by Marc Pincherle, *An Illustrated History of Music,* transl. Rollo Myers (London: Macmillan, 1967), p. 44, and less clearly in James Blades and Jeremy Montagu, *Early Percussion Instruments* (London: Oxford University Press, 1976), p. 8.

10. The Swiss drum is in the Historisches Museum, Basel, and is illustrated by James Blades, *Percussion Instruments and their History* (London: Faber, 1970), pl. 100, and in a number of other sources. Drake's drum is discussed by Cynthia Gaskell Brown, *The Battle's Sound* (Tiverton: Devon Books, 1996), pp. 12–20.

11. Antwerp: Musée Royal des Beaux-Arts, also illustrated in Blades (1970), pl. 101, though incorrectly called a tabor, and in Blades and Montagu (1976), p. 10.

12. Brown (1996), pp. 4–6.

13. Thoinot Arbeau, *Orchésographie* (Lengres: Iehan des Preyz, 1588), f. 7.

14. Arbeau, f. 8. Translations are those of the author; there are published English translations but because they are by dance scholars they tend to be unreliable, especially in technical details related to instruments.

15. Arbeau, f. 9.

16. Arbeau, ff. 9v–14. My son, permuting Arbeau's rhythms in an early encounter with a computer, while at school some thirty years ago, discovered that Arbeau had missed some.

17. William Byrd, *My Ladye Nevells Booke*, a manuscript in private possession, completed in 1591, first published (London: J. Curwen & Sons, 1926, reprint New York: Dover, 1969), p. 26, the fifth section of 'The battell'.

18. Andrew Ashbee, *Records of English Court Music* (Aldershot: Scolar Press, 1993), vol. VII, p. 151. These invaluable records were first published by Ashbee himself from his home in Snodland, commencing with vol. 1 in 1986.

19. Ashbee, vol. VII, p. 27.

20. Ashbee, vol. VII, p. 204.

21. Arbeau (1588), f. 21.

22. Arbeau, f. 22.

23. See p. 23 in the previous chapter.

24. Arbeau, f. 25.

25. Arbeau, f. 33v–7.

26. Arbeau, f. 30–2v.

27. Arbeau, f. 33v.

28. Arbeau, f. 94.

29. What is meant by 'plain, easily recognized' will vary from culture to culture. What that phrase would mean to an Indian or to an African would be mutually incomprehensible and both would be difficult for us to follow, whereas our triple and compound time would seem overly complex to Burmese traditional musicians with their invariable quadruple time. As one player observed to Dr John Okell, 'Of course we have triple time: one, two, three, –, one, two, three, –' (personal communication).

30. Stanley Sadie, ed., *The New Grove Dictionary of Musical Instruments*, (London: Macmillan, 1984), vol. 3, p. 118, *s.v.* Pipe and tabor, and on the front cover of many publications by the English Folk Dance and Song Society.

31. A catalogue is in preparation but it is as yet too early to give any bibliographical details. I am responsible for the description of the tabor and its beater.

32. The length of the stick is 391 mm (nearly 15½ inches); its width is 8 mm (about ⅓ inch) and its thickness varies from 9 mm at the handle end to 6 mm and then to 7.5 at the other end. The reproduction was kindly made for me by Dr Charles Foster, who is cataloguing the wind instruments found in the ship.

33. London: BL MS Royal 2A XVI, f. 98v, Psalm 80; Blades (1970), pl. 90, and Blades and Montagu (1976), p. 7. The king harping is on f. 63v, Psalm 51, Kinsky (1929/30), p. 98, fig. 2.

34. José Guerrero Lovillo, *Las Cantigas* (Madrid: Instituto Diego Velásquez, 1949), *Cántiga CLXV*, and Matilde López Serrano, *Cántigas de Santa Maria de Alfonso X el Sabio, Rey de Castilla* (Madrid: Editorial Patrimonio Nacional, 1974). Also illustrated by Edmund Bowles, 'Eastern influences on the use of trumpets and drums during the Middle Ages',

Anuario Musical, XXVI (Barcelona, 1972), 1–26 (pl. 1).

35. Père Benoît de Toul, *L'Origine de la tres illustre Maison de Lorraine* (Toul: Alexis Laurent, 1704), p. 425, citing the chronicle *M. S. de Lorraine*, with no further detail of that source: '*On n'avoit ni mi oncques vû des tabourins comme de gros chauderons qu'ils faisoient porter sur des chevaux*. Cette cronique veut parler de timbales.' The sentence in italics is quoted from Benoît by Georges Kastner, *Manuel général de musique militaire* (Paris: Didiot frères, 1848), p. 90, and thence by Curt Sachs, *Handbuch der Musikinstrumentenkunde* (Leipzig: Breitkopf und Härtel, 1930), pp. 85–6, and thence by Herbert Tobischek, *Die Pauke* (Tutzing: Hans Schneider, 1977), pp. 18–19, but none seems to have traced the original chronicle for further information.

36. Bowles (1972), p. 28.

37. Roy Thomson, letter of 4 November 1998. The Sealed Knot is a society which recreates English Civil War battles.

38. Journal de J. Aubrion, p. 314, cited by Victor Gay, *Glossaire archéologique du moyen âge et de la renaissance* (Paris: Librairie de la Société Bibliographique, 1887), *s.v.* Timbale.

39. Note, please, that the date given in the caption opposite p. 1 of the second printing of Blades and Montagu, *Early Percussion Instruments* (which appeared in 1977 with this additional plate), is wrong; it should be 1484/5, not thirteenth century. Also reproduced in Bowles (1972), pl. 4 and in Bowles (1977), Abb. 15.

40. *Maximilian I* (1964), pls 115 and 116.

41. Virdung (1511), illustrated on f. D and described on that and the facing page.

42. *State Papers Published Under the Authority of Her Majesty's Commission* (London: Commission for Publishing State Papers, 1849), *part V – continued*, vol. VIII, pp. 208ff., DXLVIII. I am most grateful to Dr Frances Palmer for drawing my attention to this source and for allowing me access to some pages of her unpublished doctoral thesis 'Musical Instruments at the Court of Henry VIII', University of Surrey, Guildford (1986).

43. Edmund Halle, *The Union of the Two Noble and Illustre Fameflies of Lancastre and Yorke* (London: Richard Grafton, 1548 and 1550), 'The tryumphaunte reigne of king Henry the viii', 31st year, f. 239v. Although this source is usually cited as 'Hall', his own spelling is invariably Halle. As one whose name commonly suffers the addition of an 'e', rather than its subtraction, I am strongly inclined to assume that he knew how he preferred to spell himself.

44. Ashbee, vol. VII, p. 80. The 'reward' is in James Gairdner and R. H. Brodie, eds, *Letters and Papers, Foreign and Domestic of the Reign of Henry VIII*, vol. XV (London: Her Majesty's Stationery Office, 1900), p. 307, no. 642.

45. Percival Kirby, *The Kettle-Drums* (London: Oxford University Press, 1930), p. 7; repeated by Blades (1970), p. 227, and by Tobischek (1977), p. 24.

46. *State Papers, part V – continued*, vol. IX, p. 138, DCCLXVII.

47. Kirby (1930), p. 7. Note that Kirby does not state whether Seymour had succeeded in retaining the services of these people. This reference is cited by the *Oxford English Dictionary* from *State Papers* IX, 501, as the first English use of 'kettledrum', on p. 1533 in the compact edition and p. 680 of the relevant volume of the full-size version.

48. *State Papers*, vol. IX, p. 201, DCCLXXXI.

49. *State Papers*, vol. IX, p. 253, DCCC, and, for the second part of that letter, Gairdner and Brodie (1900), Vol. XVII, p. 683–4.

50. Ashbee, vol. I (1986), pp. 1–2.

51. Ashbee, vol. I, p. 11; Edmund Bowles, *Musical Ensembles in Festival Books, 1500–1800* (Ann Arbor: University of Michigan Research Press, 1989), pp. 293–6 (but note that he is a year out; the coronation was in 1661, not 1660). There are many other relevant illustrations in this volume by Bowles.

52. Ashbee, vol. I, pp. 50–1, 12 November 1663, where Hans Bernihoski, who had already been noted as another kettledrummer, appears among the trumpets and John Mawgridge and five others, one of them a fife, are listed under the heading of Drummers.

53. Ashbee, vol. VII, pp. 383–98. One of the two inventories (London: BL, MS Harl. 1419) is also printed by Francis W. Galpin, *Old English Instruments of Music* (London: Methuen), pp. 292–300 in the first edition of 1910, 215–22 in the 1965 edition; for the Jewel House records, a letter from Dr Frances Palmer, 15 June 1998.

54. Albert Feuillerat, *Documents relating to the Revels at Court in the time of King Edward VI and Queen Mary (the Loseley Manuscripts)*; W. Bang, ed., Materialien zur Kunde des älteren Englischen Dramas, Bd XLIV (Louvain: A. Uystpruyst, 1914), p. 89, line 20ff. I am most grateful to Sydney Anglo who referred me to this source when I was trying to track down an unreferenced (and slightly inaccurate) mention of these drummers by Henry George Farmer in his *Handel's Ketttledrums* (London: Hinrichsen, 1960), p. 42, in 'Turkish Influence in Military Music'.

55. I owe the suggestion that the boy might have been an apprentice, in an essential part of his training, to Dr Edmund A. Bowles (personal communication, 19 July 2001).

56. Which again I owe to Sydney Anglo. I would also thank the Librarian of the Society of Antiquaries who very kindly permitted me to read this on a day when officially the library was closed.

57. *The diary of Henry Machyn, Citizen and Merchant-Taylor of London, from A. D. 1550 to A. D. 1563*, ed. John Gough Nichols, who added the words here in square brackets as footnotes (London: Camden Society, 1848), p. 76.

58. Machyn, p. 78.

59. She was queen in her own right, as Henry VIII's elder daughter (Edward VI, who died young, had been his only son), and it was this marriage that led to the attempted invasion by the Spanish Armada in 1588, when Philip tried to assert forcibly his right by marriage to the throne over that of Mary's younger half-sister, Elizabeth.

60. Machyn, p. 286.

61. Information kindly provided by Richard Mortimer, Keeper of the Muniments at Westminster Abbey, in a letter of 25 June 1998.

62. William Byrd (1964), 'The battell', particularly in the movement entitled 'The trumpetts' (pp. 24–5); the other movements seem more suggestive of side-drum patterns.

63. Kirby (1930), p. 8. Kirby also misspells Hentzner's name as Hentzer; Tobischek (1977), p. 26, quotes Kirby – being German he probably did not know that Elizabeth was still a child in 1548 and that her brother was then king; Blades (1970), p. 227, also quotes him but sensibly omits the date.

64. Paul Hentzner, *Itinerarium Germaniæ, Galliæ, Angliæ, Italiæ* (Norinbergæ, 1612), p. 137; Horace Walpole's translation, *A Journey into England by Paul Hentzner In the Year M.D.XC.VIII* (Twickenham: Strawberry Hill, 1757), p. 53.

65. My wife's translation.

66. Hentzner, pp. 156–7; Walpole's translation, p. 89.

67. *Hamlet*, Act I, scene iv, lines 10–12.

68. The fourth trumpet part was usually confined to tonic and dominant, as an alternative to the timpani.

69. Bowles (1989), pp. 41–2, fig. 18; Georg Kinsky (1929/30), p. 150, fig. 1.

70. Bowles (1989), pp. 363–72, fig. 166.

71. *Maximilian I* (1964), pl. 115.

72. Personal communication, 19 July 2001: 'This explanation was offered to me by the late timpanist of the Dresdner Staatskapelle (Peter Sondemann), who said that it had been passed down to him by his teacher, whose teacher had told him, etc., back through the generations.' I am most grateful to Dr Bowles for the story and for permission to quote it before its appearance in print in his forthcoming *The Timpani: A History in Pictures and Documents* (Hillsdale: Pendragon Press), whose 450 or so pictures will include all those timpani referred to in this and later chapters.

73. Uta Henning, *Musica Maximiliana* (Neu-Ulm: Ekkehart Stegmiller, 1987), p. 96; also Kinsky (1929/30), p. 75

74.   Journal de J. Aubrion, p. 314, cited by Victor Gay (1887), *s.v.* Timbale.

75.   Arbeau (1588), f. 6v

76.   See Appendix 2 for this process.

77.   Frank Harrison and Joan Rimmer, *European Musical Instruments* (London: Studio Vista, 1964), pl. 95. The complete set of woodcuts published by Trechsel as *Imagines Mortis* (Lyons, 1547), in which this was no. 5, 'Death goes forth', was published in enlarged facsimile by Frederick H. Evans as *The Dance of Death by Hans Holbein* (London, 1916).

78.   Caldwell Titcomb, 'Baroque Court and Military Trumpets and Kettledrums: Technique and Music', *Galpin Society Journal*, IX (1956), 56–81, p. 60, quoting Allain Manesson Mallet, *Les Travaux de Mars* (Amsterdam: Janson à Waesberghe, 1685).

79.   Catalogue no. S. 267–9; Julius von Schlosser, *Die Sammlung alter Musikinstrumente* (Vienna: Anton Schroll, 1920), p. 94 and Taf. XLVI.

80.   Bowles (1989), pp. 59–67, figs 26 and 26a.

81.   An instrument sometimes called the jew's harp or jew's trump, but which would be better referred to, following Frederick Crane's example, as the trump *tout court*. See Crane, ed., *Vierundzwanzigsteljahrschrift der Internationalen Maultrommelvirtuosen-genossenschaft*, 4 (1994), pp. 5–7. Jew's trump is the oldest English name, according to the *Oxford English Dictionary* (p. 1508 in the compact edition, p. 579 of the relevant volume in the original. It somehow seems typical of the general reaction to musical instruments that this first reference comes from the rates of Customs charges!). This reference dates from 1545 (the first reference to a jew's harp is fifty years later), whereas we have many surviving earlier trumps, some allegedly going back to Roman times, but no identifiable earlier name in English. Gallo-Roman examples will be found in *Le Carnyx et la Lyre* (Besançon-Orléans-Évreux: 1993), pp. 20–1, nos 3–7.

82.   Virdung (1511), f. Diij verso.

83.   Martin Agricola, *Musica instrumentalis deudsch* (Wittemberg: Georg Rhaw, 1529); reprint combined with the 1545 edition (Leipzig: Breitkopf und Härtel, 1896), pp. 118 and 279.

84.   Harrison and Rimmer (1964), pl. 95, where it is dated to 1523–5, Blades and Montagu (1976), p. 25, Kinsky (1929/30), p. 81, fig. 4. In Evans (1916) as 'The old woman', no. 46. In 'The old man', which immediately precedes it, the instrument is a psaltery.

85.   As 'Fossiles' in his satyrical *Le carnaval des animaux*.

86.   Walter Salmen, *Musikleben im 16. Jahrhundert*, Musikgeschichte in Bildern, III:9 (Leipzig: Deutscher Verlag für Musik, 1976), Abb. 28, by Christoph Weiditz, 1529. As Dr Bowles points out (personal communication), other instruments do appear in contemporary sources, but nevertheless there are far fewer than there are in medieval iconography and texts.

87.   Bologna: Pinacoteca Nazionale; reproduced in many books, including Pincherle (1960), p. 47.

88.   E.g. David Green, 'The Depiction of Musical Instruments in Italian Renaissance Painting', DPhil thesis, Oxford (1993).

89.   Blades (1970), pls 77 and 82.

Chapter 4 The Early Baroque

1.   See also my paper 'Organological Gruyère' given at the NEMA Conference on the Early Baroque at the York Early Music Festival, July 1999, which will appear in print in due course.

2.   Michael Praetorius, *Syntagma Musicum*, of which the second volume, *II – De Organographia* (Wolffenbüttel: Elias Holwein, 1619), covers musical instruments, and Marin Mersenne, *Harmonie Universelle* (Paris: Sebastien Cramoisy, 1636), of which the latter part, nearly half the whole, deals with instruments.

3.   But be warned: the scale is the Brunswick foot of 11.235 modern inches or 285.36 mm.

These very detailed figures are derived from Nicholas Bessaraboff, *Ancient European Musical Instruments* (Cambridge: Harvard University Press, for the Museum of Fine Arts, Boston, 1941), Appendix A, pp. 353–6. Note also that the scale is incorrectly drawn on some plates, with an occasional intrusive or missing half foot or other error.

4. These make the CNRS facsimile (1963), which was taken from his own copy with these notes and extra leaves, a much more useful text than the original edition. The third volume of this facsimile includes the instrument section. Note that this 'facsimile' is reduced in size, which makes his handwriting even harder to decipher.

5. James Talbot's manuscript (Oxford: Christ Church Music MS 1187) seems to have been compiled between 1683 and 1688; see Paul White, 'The Early Bassoon Reed in Relation to the Development of the Bassoon from 1636', DPhil thesis, Oxford (1993), pp. 99–100. The *Encyclopédie* seems to have appeared under various guises from 1751 onwards. The text on instruments most easily accessible today is a facsimile published as *Art du Faiseur d'Instruments de Musique et Lutherie* (Geneva: Minkoff Reprint, 1972), which derives from the edition of 1785.

6. Daniel Speer's *Grundrichter Unterricht der musikalische Kunst oder Vierfaches musikalisches Kleeblatt* (Ulm: Georg Wilhelm Kühnen) dates from 1697, in the earlier years of the next period, the High Baroque. Johann Ernst Altenburg's *Versuch einer Anleitung zur heroisch-musikalischen Trompeter- und Paukerkunst* (Halle: Joh. Christ. Hendel) was published in 1795, a century later, but looks back, certainly to the mid-eighteenth century and arguably to its beginning.

7. Praetorius (1619), p. 77, *s.v.* 'Tympanum Hieronymi'. All the translations from Praetorius, Speer, Mersenne, and Trichet are, like those from Arbeau and Virdung above, by the author.

8. With all chromatic notes the range would be a ninth, an octave and a tone, e.g. C to D, which seems improbable; with the one chromatic as on Agricola's xylophone, the range would be an octave and a seventh, e.g. C to B natural, which is even less probable.

9. Speer (1697), p. 220.

10. Pierre Trichet's *Traité des Instruments de Musique (vers 1640)*, ed. François Lesure (Neuilly-sur-Seine: Société de Musique d'Autrefois, 1957) seems to be almost unillustrated, but Lesure did not make this very clear; he reproduced two illustrations without saying whether there were others. Nor was it clear whether Trichet left some of his pages blank, save for a title, or whether Lesure had decided that these subjects were of no interest and not worth printing. Lesure published some supplementary material in *Galpin Society Journal*, XV (1962), 70–81, in the introduction to which he made it plain that at least some omissions were his choice. He referred there to five additional sections on percussion instruments, but presumably thought those not worthy of inclusion; he did not even tell us what instruments they covered. Two of these, the semantron, the iron or wooden bar which is used instead of a bell in churches in many Islamic areas, and bells themselves, appeared the following year in *Galpin Society Journal*, XVI (1963), 73–84. The other three are still Lesure's secret.

11. Jaap Kunst, *Music in Java* (The Hague: Martinus Nijhoff, 1949), p. 115 and Ill. 62, citing W. Lodewijckz, *D'Eerste Boeck*, which describes the first voyage from the Netherlands to the East Indies under Cornelis de Houtman, 1595–7.

12. According to Klaus Wachsmann , 'A Drum from Seventeenth Century Africa', *Galpin Society Journal*, XXIII (1970), 97–103 and pl. XV, the Ashmolean drum is 59 cm high and the upper end diameter is 25 cm; Praetorius's appears to be approximately 65 cm high (2 foot 3 inches in Brunswick feet) and 26 cm diameter (11 inches); they are otherwise identical.

13. But see Montagu, 'Ethnographical Material in Early Organological Texts', *MAN* (1965:107), 121–2.

14. Mersenne (1636), Livre Septiesme, p. 52. He has just discussed the side drum which he finds more interesting.

15. Trichet (1957), p. 177. There seems to have been a French tendency towards timpani of brass, where Germany and Britain preferred copper.

16. Cesare Bendinelli, *Tutta l'arte della Trombetta 1614* (Kassel: Bärenreiter, 1975); Girolamo Fantini da Spoleti, *Modo per Imparare a sonare di Tromba* (Frankfurt: Daniel Vuastch, 1638).

17. Allain Manesson Mallet, *Les travaux de Mars ou l'art de la guerre* (Amsterdam: Janson à Waesberghe, 1685), vol. 3, p. 98.

18. Altenburg (1795), p. 31.

19. Edward Tarr, *The Trumpet* (London: Batsford, 1988), p. 67.

20. Altenburg (1795), p. 91; quoted from Edward Tarr's translation, *Trumpeter's and Kettledrummer's Art* (Nashville: Brass Press, 1974), p. 91.

21. Claudio Monteverdi's *L'Orfeo: Favola in Musica* was first performed in Mantua in 1607. The score was published by Ricciardo Amadino in Venice in 1609 and has been reproduced in facsimile several times. One currently available is that by Studio per Edizioni Scelte, Florence, 1993. The 'Toccata', which opens the performance, is to be played by all the instruments together three times before the curtain rises, but the only instrument names on the five staves of the score are those of the trumpets, from top to bottom: Clarino, Quinta, Alto e basso, Vulgano (playing only g, the bottom space in alto clef), and Basso (playing only c, the space below the stave in tenor clef).

22. Altenburg (1795), p. 108.

23. Speer (1697), pp. 219–20.

24. No. XXXIV of *Polyhymnia caduceatrix et panegyrico*, 1619, ed. Willibald Gurlitt (Wolfenbüttel: Georg Kallmeyer, 1933).

25. The 'Tympanis' with a 'y' of Praetorius's note is an aberration due to church Latin; there is no letter 'y' in either classical Latin or Italian.

26. 'Darauf so bald eine Intrada zum Final'.

27. Speer (1697), p. 220.

28. SWV 472, no. 5. Published in *Neue Ausgabe Sämtliche Werke*, Bd 32, *Choralkonzerte und Choralsätze* (Kassel: Bärenreiter, 1971).

29. Percival Kirby, *The Kettle-Drums* (London: Oxford University Press, 1930), p. 10. Herbert Tobischek, *Die Pauke* (Tutzing: Hans Schneider, 1977), p. 43, incidentally, has misunderstood this reference and has tried to substitute a composer, Edward Johnson, for the playwright.

30. *Musica Britannica*, LI, ed. Michael Tilmouth (London: Stainer and Bell, 1986).

31. This could also be the first, it is certainly one of the first, appearances of the French oboe and bassoon in Britain. The exact date of their introduction is still uncertain, but it is thought to have been in the mid-1670s. See Paul White (1993), pp. 92ff., for some of the more recent discussion in this highly controversial area. Also Bruce Haynes, 'Lully and the rise of the oboe as seen in works of art', *Early Music* XVI:3 (August, 1988), 324–38 and, in greater detail, his *The Eloquent Oboe: A History of the Hautboy from 1640 to 1760* (Oxford: Oxford University Press, 2001).

32. Amsterdam: Rijksmuseum, no. 1135. Rembrandt's *The Night Watch* is no. 2016 in the same museum.

33. Alan Borg, 'Dating a Dutch Drum', *Country Life*, vol. CLVII no. 4052 (27 February 1975), p. 490. The photograph there shows the drum after restoration; that in James Blades and Jeremy Montagu, *Early Percussion Instruments* (London: Oxford University Press, 1976), p. 11, shows it as we found it; details of size are entabulated below and descriptions of its construction are in Montagu, *Making Early Percussion Instruments* (London: Oxford University Press, 1976), pp. 3ff. More photographs, showing many details, were deposited with the Armouries and are, of course, in my files. The measurements were taken in inches. The catalogue number of the drum is XVIII. 120 and it is now on display in the War Gallery of the Royal Armouries Museum in Leeds (information kindly provided by Chris Gravett, Curator of Arms and Armour, 18 June 1998).

34. A scarf joint is a tapered overlap, each side of the overlap reducing evenly so that the thickness remains constant with no lumps or bulges. A glued scarf joint on a modern side drum is about an inch long; on this drum, as was normal in the period, it was over six inches.

35. We were not then permitted to remove the head from that end, so the width and depth of the snare bed could not be measured; the width has been measured here from the ridges on the head against a scale in a photograph. A photograph of the snare bed is plate 13 in Cynthia Gaskell Brown, *The Battle's Sound* (Tiverton: Devon Books, 1996).

36. Brown (1996), p. 12 and pl. 15 (the photograph is mine, not as attributed).

37. I am most grateful to the Bursar of the College, in whose office the drum resides, for permission to examine, measure, and photograph the drum, and to Dr Maurice Byrne for having introduced me to it.

38. Mersenne (1636), Livre Septiesme, Des instrumens de percussion, Proposition XXVI, p. 51; for the material of Drake's drum, Brown (1996), p. 13.

39. Mersenne, p. 52 for donkeys, p. 55 for wolves. Maximilian's timpani were said by Aubrion in 1492 to have heads of asses' skins. (Journal de J. Aubrion, p. 314, cited by Victor Gay, *Glossaire archéologique du moyen âge et de la renaissance* (Paris: Librairie de la Société Bibliographique, 1887), *s.v.* Timbale.).

40. Trichet (1957), p. 176. Dr Ephraim Segerman kindly provided the 2 mm figure (email, 10 August 1999), citing M. Namreges, 'A String Diameter on Mersenne's Bass Viol', *FoMRHI Quarterly*, 23 (April 1981), Comm. 343, 77–8.

41. Mallet (1685), vol. 3, p. 12.

42. André Philidor, *Partition de Plusieurs Marches et batteries de tambour tant françoises qu'Etrangères avec les airs de fifre et de hautbois a 3 et 4 parties, L'an 1705* (Paris: Minkoff France, 1994), facsimile of Versailles: Bibliothèque municipale, MS musical 168. This includes numerous *batteries* with the shawm parts which they accompany, and also marches for trumpets, shawms, and timpani. Georges Kastner, *Manuel général de musique militaire à l'usage des armées françaises* (Paris: Didiot Frères, 1848), reprints some of them in his Batteries et Sonneries, pp. 2–8, newly numbered pages which come at the end of the book, following p. 391.

43. Maurice Byrne, '*The English March* and Early Drum Notation', *Galpin Society Journal*, L (1997), 43–80.

44. Byrne, (1997), fig. 15, p. 72, and fig. 16, p. 75.

45. Beethoven, *Wellingtons' Sieg oder die Schlacht bei Vittoria*, op. 91, perhaps better known as The Battle Symphony, on which more below.

46. Andrew Ashbee, *Records of English Court Music*, vol. VIII (Aldershot: Scolar Press, 1995), p. 118.

47. Ashbee, vol. III (Snodland: author, 1988), p. 88.

48. Mersenne (1636), p. 53

49. G[eneviève] Thibault, Jean Jenkins and Josiane Bran-Ricci, *Eighteenth Century Musical Instruments: France and Britain* (London: Victoria and Albert Museum, 1973), p. 182, no. 119. It was then in the collection of Mme la Comtesse de Chambure (Geneviève Thibault), and may now be preserved in the Musée de la Musique in Paris, like much of her collection, perhaps as E. 980.2.503, one of the 730 instruments bought from her family on 3 June 1980. See Florence Gétreau, *Aux origines du musée de la Musique: Les Collections Instrumentales du Conservatoire de Paris, 1793–1993* (Paris, Klincksieck and Réunion des musées nationaux, 1996), 737. This is one of 110 pages towards the end of the book, the first complete chronological list of all the museum's acquisitions ever to be published. It is also the first list of the museum's holdings since Gustave Chouquet's catalogue of 1884 and its three supplements by Léon Pillaut, the last of which appeared in 1903 – Chouquet's and Pillaut's catalogue has recently been reprinted, but any quotation, however trivial and presumably including even citation of the title page, is banned by a notice under Swiss law.

50. Maurice Guis, Thierry Lefrançois and Rémi Venture, *Le Galoubet-tambourin* (Aix-en-Provence: Édisud, 1993).
51. Biscaya, or more often Viscaya, is the name of one of the Basque provinces.
52. Trichet (1957), p. 177. French is less precise than English in this respect, using *cuivre* to mean either brass or copper, and thus this may not contradict Mersenne. *Leton* (*laiton* in modern French) is the same as English latten or sheet brass, a term used for the thick plates of brass that were used on medieval and later tombs and memorials.
53. Mersenne (1636), Livre Troisiesme des Instrumens à chordes, Proposition XXVII, p. 175.
54. André Lehr, *The Art of the Carillon in the Low Countries* (Tielt: Lannoo, 1991).
55. See Giuseppe Paradossi, *Modo Facile di Suonare il Sistro nomato il Timpano*, Bologna, 1695; *Collezione di Trattati e Musiche Antiche Edite in Fac-Simile* (Milan: Bollettino Bibliografico Musicale, 1933), and Albi Rosenthal, 'Two Unknown 17th Century Music Editions by Bolognese Composers', *Collectanea Historiae Musicae*, II (Florence: 1957), 373–8. I owe the reference to the latter to Professor James Tyler (letter, 14 May 1981), as well as his comments on the music in the tutor.
56. Franca Falletti, Renato Meucci, and Gabriele Rossi Rognoni, *La musica e i suoi strumenti: La Collezione Granducale del Conservatorio Cherubini* (Florence: Giunti and Firenze Musei, 2001), 226–7.
57. Mersenne (1636), Livre Septiesme, pp. 50–1; Trichet (1957), pp. 182–4.
58. Heinrich Scheibler, 'The Aura', *Allgemeine musikalische Zeitung*, 30 (24 July 1816); translated by Leonard Fox, ed., *The Jew's Harp: A Comprehensive Anthology* (Lewisburg: Bucknell University Press, 1988), pp. 87ff.
59. *Vierundzwanzigsteljahrschrift der Internationalen Maultrommelvirtuosengenossenschaft* which, despite its name, is edited by Professor Frederick Crane in Mount Pleasant, Iowa.
60. Idioglottal: the feather cut in but remaining attached to the rest of the body; heteroglottal: a feather fixed into a frame made of some different material.
61. Mersenne (1636), pp. 47–8.
62. Second movement, bars 78ff. At the back of the orchestra the work is often known as Liszt's Triangle Concerto.
63. Mersenne (1636), pp. 48–9.
64. Trichet (1957), p. 182.

Chapter 5 The High Baroque

1. The Talbot Manuscript, Oxford: Christ Church Music MS 1187. Christ Church is one of the colleges of Oxford University but is always referred to simply as Christ Church: never as Christ Church College.
2. See Paul White, 'The Early Bassoon Reed in Relation to the Development of the Bassoon from 1636', DPhil thesis, Oxford (1993), pp. 94ff. and especially pp. 99–100.
3. From Anthony Baines, 'James Talbot's Manuscript', *Galpin Society Journal*, I (1948), 9–26, covering the wind instruments, onwards through many other volumes of the *Journal*. A complete edition of the manuscript is in active preparation under the auspices of the Galpin Society.
4. Talbot MS, file no. 15. I must express my gratitude to the librarians at Christ Church for their help in navigating through so unwieldy a bundle of papers.
5. Talbot MS, file no. 11.
6. Talbot MS, file no. 14, p. 35. In file D, Talbot acknowledges Finger as his source for this information.
7. Talbot MS, file no. 14, pp. 11–13.
8. Daniel Speer, *Grundrichter Unterricht der musikalische Kunst oder Vierfaches musikalisches Kleeblatt* (Ulm: Georg Wilhelm Kühnen, 1697).
9. Speer, pp. 188–260. The section on *Heerpaucken* is on pp. 219–21.

10. Joseph Friedrich Bernhard Caspar Majer, *Museum Musicum Theoretico Practicum, das ist Neu-eröffneter Theoretisch- und Practischer Music-Saal* (Schwäbisch Halle: Georg Michael Majer, 1732), pp. 73–4.

11. Much of this description is drawn from Christopher de Hamel, *Scribes and Illuminators*, one of the Medieval Craftsmen series published by the British Museum in 1992. I am grateful to Roy Thomson, Chief Executive of the Leather Conservation Centre in Northampton, for this and other references and for patiently answering many ignorant questions on leathers and skins.

12. Sue Thomas, 'Leathermaking in the Middle Ages', 1–8, and L. A. Clarkson, 'Developments in Tanning Methods During the Post-Medieval Period (1500–1850)', 11–21, both in R. Thomson and J. A. Beswick, eds, *Leather Manufacture Through the Ages*, Proceedings of the 27th East Midlands Industrial Archaeology Conference, October, 1983).

13. Speer (1697), p. 219.

14. James Blades, personal communication.

15. Such crooks were already known by 1619, for one is illustrated by Praetorius as a *Krumbbügel* on his plate VIII, no. 13, and another is shown inserted between the mouthpiece and the body of his *Jäger Trommet*, no. 11 on the same plate.

16. James Blades, *Percussion Instruments and their History* (London: Faber, 1970), p. 253.

17. Lully, *Œuvres complètes* (Paris: Revue Musicale, 1931ff).

18. Herbert Schneider, *Chronologisch-thematisches Verzeichnis Sämtliche Werke von Jean-Baptiste Lully (LWV)* (Tutzing: Hans Schneider, 1981).

19. The Louvre was then the royal palace in Paris, as distinct from suburban Versailles, rather than the museum that it is today, and this was the picture gallery of the palace, a hall large enough to present such a performance and accommodate an audience.

20. For the *trompettes marines* see Cecil Adkins and Alis Dickinson, *A Trumpet by any other Name: a History of the Trumpet Marine* (Buren: Frits Knuf, 1991), p. 50, quoting a report in the *Mercure Gallant* of 1667, perhaps referring to a later performance.

21. A transcription of the score for these two dances, taken from this complete edition, is in Adkins and Dickinson, p. 119. On p. 121 they include a similar use from Alessandro Scarlatti's *Mitridate Eupatore* of 1707.

22. At least we can say that all three of these works are earlier than *Thésée* of 1675 which is usually cited as the first appearance.

23. *Jean-Baptiste Lully, The Collected Works*, series IV, *Sacred Works*, vol. 5 (New York: The Broude Trust, 1996).

24. André Philidor, *Partition de Plusieurs Marches et batteries de tambour tant françoises qu'Etrangères avec les airs de fifre et de hautbois a 3 et 4 parties, L'an 1705* (Paris: Minkoff France, 1994), facsimile of Versailles: Bibliothèque municipale, MS musical 168. Also Caldwell Titcomb, 'Baroque Court and Military Trumpets and Kettledrums: Technique and Music', *Galpin Society Journal*, IX (1956), 56–81, examples 2–6. Blades (1970), pp. 237–40, reproduces the *Marche a 2* in much reduced facsimile of the original version. Titcomb gives the date as 1683 but the facsimile clearly says 1685. This march was also published by McGinnis and Marx, New York in 1965, edited by Josef Marx, as *march for two pairs of kettledrums, andré and jacques philidor*.

25. Suggested by Edmund Bowles (personal communication).

26. Philidor (1705), 129–43.

27. Julie Anne Sadie, ed., *Companion to Baroque Music* (London: J. M. Dent, 1990), p. 136, *s.v.* Philidor, and pp. 94–5. See also E. H. Fellowes, 'The Philidor Manuscripts: Paris, Versailles, Tenbury', *Music & Letters*, XII (1931), 116–29. Fellowes identifies the manuscript with the marches as Versailles City Library MS 1163; Titcomb and Minkoff both as MS 168.

28. Examples are the 1690 and 1691 odes *Arise my Muse* and *Welcome Glorious Morn*; examples of similar odes which do have kettledrum parts (Purcell's term for the

timpani, as was normal in England) include the 1694 ode *Come ye Sons of Art Away.*

29. Andrew Ashbee, *Records of English Court Music*, vol. II (Snodland: the author, 1987), p. 34: 1690, December 8, A list of his Majesty's servants above stairs who are to attend his Majesty in his voyage to Holland and who are paid in the Treasury Chamber; later lists give the precise dates.

30. Peter Holman, *Four and Twenty Fiddlers* (Oxford: Clarendon, 1993), p. 431.

31. Holman (1993), p. 430. Holman also mentions Peter Downey's plausible reconstruction of these parts: Peter Downey, 'What Samuel Pepys heard on 3 February 1661: English trumpet style under the later Stuart monarchs', *Early Music*, XVIII:3 (August, 1990), 417–28 (p. 426), and Andrew Pinnock's and Bruce Wood's denial of their probability: Andrew Pinnock and Bruce Wood, 'A counterblast on English trumpets', *Early Music*, XIX:3 (August, 1991), 436–42 (p. 442).

32. *A Collection of Ayres, Compos'd for the Theatre, and upon Other Occasions.* By the late Mr. Henry Purcell. Printed by J. Heptinstall for Frances Purcell, London, 1697.

33. Dates are taken from Franklin B. Zimmermann, *Henry Purcell, 1659–1695* (London: Macmillan, 1963).

34. In Hellmut Schultz, ed., *Deutsche Bläsermusik vom Barock bis zur Klassik, Das Erbe Deutscher Musik*, Bd. 14 (Kassel: Nagel, 1961), pp. 19–20.

35. Jiří Sehnal, ed., *Denkmäler der Tonkunst in Österreich*, Bd 151 (Graz: Akademische Druck- u. Verlagsanstalt, 1997): Heinrich Ignaz Franz Biber, *Instrumentalwerke Handschriftlicher Überlieferung*, pp. 45–52 and 53–68 respectively.

36. Johann Ernst Altenberg, *Versuch einer Anleitung zur heroisch-musikalischen Trompeter- und Paukerkunst* (Halle: Joh. Christ. Hendel, 1795), pp. 133–42.

37. In Paul Nettl, ed., *Denkmäler der Tonkunst in Österreich*, Bd 56 (Vienna: Universal, 1921), pp. 19–21.

38. Guido Adler, ed., *Denkmäler der Tonkunst in Österreich*, Bd 49 (Vienna: Artaria, 1918), pp. 1–47.

39. *Instruments de Musique XVIème et XVIIème Siècles* (Brussels: Musée Instrumental, 1969), p. 84, nos 96 and 97.

40. Victor-Charles Mahillon, *Catalogue descriptif & analytique du Musée Instrumental du Conservatoire Royal de Musique de Bruxelles*, vol. II (Gand: Ad. Hoste, 1896), p. 199, nos 900 and 901.

41. Julius von Schlosser, *Die Sammlung alter Musikinstrumente* (Vienna: Anton Schroll, 1920), p. 94 and Taf. XLVI, C 266, from the Catajo Collection.

42. Helmut Hoyler, *Die Musikinstrumentensammlung des Kölnischen Stadtmuseums* (Cologne: 1993), p. 284, no. 364; catalogue no. KSM 1983/351 a+b.

43. Letter 12 August 1998 from the Director of the Museum, Dr Werner Schäfke, to whom, and especially to the Conservator, Frau Habel-Schablitzky, I am most grateful.

44. Sotheby & Co., *Catalogue of Highly Important Musical Instruments* (London: 21 November 1974), lot 58. Illustrated in the catalogue (facing p. 20).

45. In the caption to their photograph on plate 80 in my *World of Medieval & Renaissance Musical Instruments.*

46. This last is probably no. 21 on p. 21 of Zdzisław Szulc's catalogue, *Muzeum Wielkopolskie Katalog Instrumentów Muzycznych* (Poznań: 1949).

47. These and the following drums in Prague were described in more detail in Montagu, 'The Society's First Foreign Tour', *Galpin Society Journal*, XXI (1968), 4–23 (pp. 11–13).

48. Persistent rumours suggest that much of this collection has vanished in recent years. It may be hoped that these drums survive, perhaps still where we saw them, in the stores in the Bertramka Villa, where Mozart lived while writing *Don Giovanni.*

49. John Henry van der Meer, *Verzeichnis der Europäischen Musikinstrumente im Germanischen Nationalmuseum Nürnberg, Band I, Hörner und Trompeten, Membranophone, Idiophone* (Wilhelmshaven: Heinrichshofen, 1979), pp. 103–4, Abb. 153–6.

50. I am particularly grateful to Frau Habel-Schablitzky for having measured the funnels so

carefully on the drums in Cologne. As will be apparent from the lack of other such measurements above, I failed to do so during the Galpin Society's Foreign Tour. I had not at that date realized their importance and the scarcity of any information about them.

51. One of the few *lacunae* in Van Der Meer's catalogue is that these variations are not noted there, but this may have been due to reluctance to disturb an undamaged head.

52. Catalogue no. 65695 and 65696.

53. Letter from Cynthia Hoover, Curator of Musical Instruments, 11 July 1973.

54. A further letter from Robert Sheldon, 10 August 1973.

55. Johann Christoph Weigel, *Musicalisches Theatrum* (Nuremberg: Weigel, c.1715–25), Blatt 15.

56. Harry Taylor told me of once finding a funnel in a drum which he was asked to provide with a new head for a school in Guildford.

57. Henry George Farmer, *Handel's Kettledrums* (London: Hinrichsen, 1960). This is a revised edition of a book first published in 1950 and it seems that all or most of its contents were first published in various military periodicals, but no bibliographical history is provided. The present reference is to 'The Great Kettledrums of the Artillery', pp. 85–96, the article to which the title of the book refers. Farmer's illustration is unfortunately a modern drawing based on an unspecified contemporary source.

58. As noted above, the brass parts in the original performance were tripled and it has been suggested that, of the timpani, there were two pairs of normal drums and one pair of double drums, plus the side drums. I have once performed the work in this way, using my own unique pair of double drums and two pairs of normal cavalry drums, and the sound was most impressive. The double drums and one pair of the cavalry drums are shown in ill. 21.

59. Farmer (1960), p. 96.

60. Charles Burney, *An Account of the Musical Performances in Westminster Abbey and the Pantheon, May 26th, 27th, 29th; and June the 3rd, and 5th, 1784. In Commemoration of Handel* (London: Printed for the benefit of the Musical Fund, 1785), 'Commemoration of Handel', pp. 7–8.

61. Blades (1970), p. 255.

62. They are the only drums I remember seeing which have proportionately different diameters for the air hole in the base, 10 and 15 mm.

63. Illustrated in Blades (1970), plate 117. It appears not to be in the printed *Catalogue of the Collection of Musical Instruments* by G. I. Blagodatov (Leningrad: Muzyka, 1972, in Russian) and although we were told by the curator, Vladimir Kosheleff, that it was a reconstruction of an eighteenth century Russian folk instrument, it is indubitably a genuine double drum of the mid-eighteenth century or earlier (Blades captions it as c.1650 which is probably rather too early). Unfortunately its companion has not been found. There is also a number of normal eighteenth-century kettledrums in that museum.

64. Edmund A. Bowles, 'The double, double, double beat of the thundering drum: the timpani in early music', *Early Music*, XIX:3 (August 1991), 419–35 (p. 422).

65. Sotheby & Co. (1974), lot 58. A pair of beaters, plus a third beater, were lot 59.

66. Bowles (1991), p. 421 illustrates a late seventeenth-century craftsman doing this; he also illustrates (p. 423) the engraving by Weigel cited above.

67. Even without any great experience in such matters, one can detect and quantify very slight differences of, for example, paper thickness between finger and thumb.

68. L. A. Clarkson (1983), p. 18.

69. Roy Thomson, 'The Nineteenth Century Revolution in the Leather Industries', 24–33, in Thomson and Beswick (1983), pp. 30–2. I am grateful to Mr Thomson for providing me with these references.

70. Georges Kastner, as we shall see in chapter 7, describes the sticks in use in the late

1830s, and attributes their invention to M. Schneitzhoeffer, timpanist at the Paris Opéra, 1815–23.

71. Blades (1970), pl. 113; Edmund Bowles, *Musical Ensembles in Festival Books, 1500–1800* (Ann Arbor: University of Michigan Research Press, 1989), fig. 18; also figs 237 and 238.

72. Speer (1697), p. 220.

73. Altenburg (1795), p. 128.

74. Bowles (1991), p. 424, quotes Johann Philipp Eisel, *Musicus autodidaktos* (Erfurt: Johann Michael Funck, 1738), pp. 67ff., to this effect.

75. Bowles (1991), p. 426.

76. Dr Bowles, in a lengthy and extraordinarily helpful response to an early draft of this book, wrote that his opinion was based not on his performance activities but more 'as a musicologist looking at historical evidence of performance practices', an area in which he has certainly greater knowledge than I, as will be apparent in his forthcoming *The Timpani: A History in Pictures and Documents*.

77. Speer (1697), p. 220.

78. Wolfgang Schmieder, *Thematisch-systematisches Verzeichnis der musikalischen Werke von Johann Sebastian Bach; Bach-Werke-Verzeichnis* (Leipzig: Breitkopf und Härtel, 1950), BWV 214 and 248 respectively.

79. Altenburg (1795), p. 129

80. *Einfache Zungen, Doppel- oder gerissene Zungen, Tragende Zungen, Doppel-Kreuzschläge, Wirbel, Doppel-Wirbel* respectively.

81. These syllabics, familiar from nursery rhymes and imitation, as well as genuine, madrigals, have a strong historical background and appear in almost every wind instrument tutor of those periods.

82. Altenburg (1795), p. 132, is very firm about the officer status of trumpeters and kettledrummers and their right to wear ostrich feathers in their hat in token of this status, which raised them above the level of side-drummers and fifers.

83. The flam is a grace note played immediately before the main note, as noted above when its use was demanded by Arbeau on the fifth stroke of his basic march rhythm.

84. Bowles (1991), prints this in more modern notation, p. 427, ex. 2.

85. Eighth notes into sixteenths. The timpani part in the set of orchestral parts in the old Novello edition provided both Handel and Mozart in the same part. Bowles (1991), p. 430, prints the final bars of the Mozart version of each of the three choruses in which Handel used timpani, but this illustrates only the cadential elaboration.

86. Despite which I normally play the former, more exciting version!

87. At least two eighteenth-century editions of Corelli's Opus 5 Violin Sonatas were published with the graces as Corelli was said to have played them, by Estienne Roger (Amsterdam: 1710) and John Walsh (London: 1711). Studio per Edizione Scelte (Florence: 1979) produced a facsimile of the former in the back of their facsimile of the first edition (Rome: 1700). Telemann published his *Methodische Sonaten* in Hamburg in 1728 and 1732, which taught the same style. These are printed as Band 1, ed. Max Seiffert, of the *Georg Philipp Telemann Musikalische Werke* (Kassel: Bärenreiter, 1955). There are other similar publications, though none for timpani.

88. The standard reference for most aspects of French style is François Couperin's *L'art de toucher le clavecin* (Paris: 1717).

89. Speer (1697), p. 221. I am indebted to Kai Tönjes for the elucidation of this passage. His translation into English of the whole of the third leaf of Speer's clover is extremely useful and is now being prepared for publication. I am grateful to him for permitting this use of his text in advance of his own publication.

90. Tobias Norlind illustrates several in his *Systematik der Saiteninstrumente I: Geschichte der Zither* (Stockholm: Musikhistorisches Museum, 1936), cols 73–4.

91. Bálint Sárosi, personal communication c.1967. See also Bálint Sárosi, *Die*

Volksmusikinstrumente Ungarns, Handbuch der europäischen Volksmusikinstrumente, I:1
(Leipzig: Deutscher Verlag für Musik, 1967), pp. 26–8 for drums and pp. 61–2 for the
Trommelbaßgeige, the *gardon*.
92. Norlind (1936), cols 165–6 and 167–8.
93. *Œuvres complètes*, A. Durand et fils, Paris, from 1900 onwards. The series editor was
Camille Saint-Saëns and volume editors included Vincent d'Indy, Paul Dukas, Claude
Debussy, Reynaldo Hahn, and other leading composers of the period, none of whom
was an historical musicologist.
94. This may be unfair – perhaps the reason is that no publisher feels that there would be
any market for such scores with adequate economic return.
95. Schmieder (1950), BWV 53, pp. 71–2.
96. I have not attempted to find autograph or contemporary manuscript sources.
97. Alan Phillips, *The Story of Big Ben* (London: Her Majesty's Stationery Office, 1959).
98. Alfred Dürr, 'Zur Echtheit des Kantate "Meine Seele rühmt und preist"', *Bach Jahrbuch*,
Jhrg. 43 (1956), 155.
99. Karl Hasse, 'Die Instrumentation J. S. Bachs', *Bach Jahrbuch*, Jhrg. 26 (1929), 90–141 (p.
127).
100. The Hallische Händel edition of the oratorio (Kassel: Bärenreiter, 1962) has 'Carillon in
F' but this is clearly a nonsense, for the music in which it appears is in the key of C
major and the carillon part is written with one flat in its key signature. If it were in F, it
would sound a tone lower than the other instruments and would be in the wrong key,
whereas if it were in G, everything would fall into place, and this must have been what
Handel intended.
101. Winton Dean, *Handel's Dramatic Oratorios and Masques* (London: Oxford University Press,
1959), p. 275.
102. Reprinted by Percy M. Young in the *Saul* volume of the *Kritische Bericht* of the Hallische
Händel-Ausgabe (Kassel: Bärenreiter, 1964), p. 55, no. 21.
103. Cambridge: Fitzwilliam Museum MS 6 I 15.
104. Again a manuscript part inserted into London: BL MS RM20 f 10, folio 16.
105. Winton Dean (1959), pp. 177 (revival of *Acis*, *Trionfo*, and *L'Allegro*), 322 (*Il Penseroso*),
and 275 (*Saul*).
106. 'A short Account of the various sorts of Organs used for Church Service' by W. L. of
Leicester, *The Gentleman's Magazine* (1772), 562–5: '[Bernard Smith] made sometimes in
the great organ what has been called a Block Flute. The pipes of this stop are at the
pitch of a fifteenth [two octaves higher than written], but larger bodied. Their tone is
clear, sweet, & piercing, resembling that of the steel bars used for the Carillon in the
oratorio of Saul'. Quoted from Percy M. Young (1964), p. 55, no. 20.
107. For a struck bar, free at both ends, the thicker the bar, other things being equal, the
higher will be the pitch.
108. André Lehr, *The Art of the Carillon in the Low Countries* (Tielt: Lannoo, 1991).
109. I am grateful to Peter Ward-Jones, Anthony Hicks, and Donald Burrows for their help
and useful discussion on this instrument. I would emphasise that these very
hypothetical speculations are mine and that they share no part of the blame for them!
110. Probably what we would now call a *flûte d'amour* since it was in the key of B flat, the
same key as the two surviving instruments of that size by Stanesby jr, a maker who is
known to have worked for Handel, one of which is in Modena in the Museo Civico
and the other in Oxford in the Bate Collection.
111. Mette Müller, 'Klokken er et musikinstrument', *Arv og Eje*, Viborg (1985), p. 142. I am
grateful to her for drawing my attention to this instrument and for her kindness in
sending me a copy of her article.
112. H. W. Hitchcock, *The Works of Marc-Antoine Charpentier: Catalogue Raisonné* (Paris:
Picard, 1982), p. 366, no. 495.
113. Shirley Thompson, *The Autograph Manuscripts of Marc-Antoine Charpentier: Clues to*

Performance, PhD thesis, University of Hull, 1997. I am very grateful to Dr Graham
Sadler for providing this reference and to Dr Thompson for permission to quote it.

114. Lehr (1991), fig. 178, perhaps the earliest illustration of a bell foundry, and 199, a
mortar by François Hemony, one of the greatest bell-founders, with the inscription
'The bells sound over the dead, mortars over the sick. François Hemony made me in
1661' (Lehr's translation of the Latin inscription). This is only eleven or twelve years
before Charpentier wrote for mortars.

115. For one episode in the television series *Jesus of Nazareth* with music by Maurice Jarre.
The kleptomaniac spider was for a Peter Sellers film and the whale was called *Orca*, but
I cannot remember for what film a composer and I visited every likely supplier in
Soho's Chinatown. Perhaps we were following in the footsteps of Charpentier's
drummer, for his mortars also had to be tuned to specific pitches.

Chapter 6 The Classical Period

1. Bach used horns and timpani in five cantatas, nos 79 (in 1735), 91 (second version
1732/5), 100 (1735), and 195 (1737 or 1741) last movement only, all in the key of G, and
in cantata 143 in B flat. Whether this cluster of dating is significant we do not know,
but it is worth noting.

2. The only effective method of dating such developments is by the music that was
written for the instruments. Mozart's first symphony with trumpets in E flat (no. 39, K.
543) dates from 1788; Haydn's from 1793 (no. 99); Beethoven's from 1804 (no. 3, the
Eroica), though he had used E flat trumpets in a Minuet, no. 4 of WoO. 7 in 1795 (for
which my thanks to Jonathan Del Mar, letter of 28 October 1998), and in the finale of
the *Geschöpfe des Prometheus* ballet in 1800, which uses the same theme as the finale of
the Eroica. With more perseverance one might find earlier examples by other
composers, but it would be by only a very few years.

3. Some examples are Haydn symphonies, nos 54, 88, 92 Oxford, 94 Surprise, 100
Military, all in G major, as well as some slow movements in that key in works in C or
D such as Symphony 93.

4. Because so few surviving timpani are dated, it is often necessary to glean information
about the instruments from the music as here, for music is written only for instruments
that are available.

5. Haydn Symphonies 98 and 102, both in B flat, and the *Sinfonia Concertante*, also in that
key, and Beethoven Symphony no. 4 in B flat, op. 60.

6. Letter, 30 October 1998. Note that he firmly denies that my resulting hypothesis could
be correct.

7. When *Peter Schmoll* was first produced in 1801 there were only two drums; the third was
added, as were two clarinets and a third trombone, when the overture was revised as a
separate concert work. For Georg Vogler's *Samori*, see Edmund A. Bowles, 'Nineteenth-
Century Innovations in the Use and Construction of the Timpani', *Journal of the
American Musical Instrument Society*, V–VI (1979–80), 74–143 (p. 80). Dr Bowles, who
first told me of this use in *Samori*, kindly sent me a copy of the timpani part,
transcribed from Munich: Staatsbibliothek MS Mus. pr. 2° 1043.

8. David Charlton, 'Salieri's Timpani', *Musical Times*, CXII, no. 1544 (October 1971),
961–2, citing a manuscript score in London: BL Add. MS 16119. I am most grateful to
Dr Charlton for drawing this article to my attention and for encouraging me to cite it,
and also to draw heavily, in the next chapter, on his researches into the Paris Opéra
and its repertoire.

9. Edmund A. Bowles, (1979–80), 76–7.

10. Jimmy Blades suggested an elegant solution to the problem of Beethoven 8, which we
shall discuss below: tune a third drum to either octave, placing the unison drums to
right and left of the singleton. The passage then lies easily under the hands.

11. Bowles (1979–80), note 2, cites François Fétis, 'Nouvelles Timbales', *Revue et gazette musicale de Paris*, 3 (1836), p. 370, for this.

12. One is illustrated in the exhibition catalogue edited by Wilfried Seipel, *Für Aug' und Ohr; Musik in Kunst- und Wunderkammern*, Schloß Ambras, 1999 (Vienna: Kunsthistorisches Museum, 1999), no. 41, pp. 136 and 139.

13. Charlton (1971), p. 961.

14. The opening of Act 2, Florestan's aria.

15. Op. 123, completed in 1823.

16. It is essential not to lose count of the bars rest while doing this!

17. By 'controlled double strokes' here and elsewhere I mean what a side drummer might call an open roll, playing two notes with each hand in such a way that they are correct for rhythm and tempo and do not degenerate into a close or indeterminate roll.

18. Nancy Benvenga, *Timpani and the Timpanist's Art*, Skrifter från musikvetenskapliga institutionen, Göteborg, 3 (Gothenburg, 1979), p. 38. It is as well to be aware that this was a Swedish doctoral thesis where the custom is to publish the thesis as a book before the examination rather than after it, so that there is a significant number of statements throughout the book which she would have wished to be able to correct.

19. This matter is discussed more fully in Appendix 1.

20. A notorious example is at figure 13 in the first movement of the New World Symphony where eight bars of minims, each with its own *tr*, are followed by four bars rest and then twelve bars of minims, each with three slashes through the stem. Are these the same or not, and if not how do they differ?

21. Edmund A. Bowles, *The Timpani: A History in Pictures and Documents* (Hillsdale: Pendragon, forthcoming).

22. Interesting that all three of these examples were for London. Were timpanists more enterprising there than in Vienna? Or did they need some extra excitements to keep them awake?

23. Some people might suggest that the timpani belongs in the *ripieno* but much of what it plays has a solo character.

24. The 6th edition of the Köchel Catalogue of 1964 moves K. 188 to K. 240b and K. 187 is relegated to Anhang C 17.12.

25. Georges Kastner, *Manuel général de musique militaire à l'usage des armées françaises* (Paris: Didiot Frères, 1848), pp. 1–55, separately paginated after the appendix ending on p. 391.

26. His antics, many of which did convey instructions to the band, have spawned a myriad of little girls, twirling batons to no effect other than the decorative and competitive.

27. Laurence Picken, *Folk Musical Instruments of Turkey* (London: Oxford University Press, 1975), pp. 66–115, pls 11–13.

28. Gerassimos Avgerinos, *Handbuch der Schlag- und Effekt-instrumente* (Frankfurt am Main: Verlag Das Musikinstrument, 1967), p. 149, Abb. 163; Karl Peinkofer and Fritz Tannigel, *Handbuch des Schlagzeugs* (Mainz: Schott, 1981), p. 28. A switch made of craft-shop basketry cane is a good substitute today.

29. Julius von Schlosser, *Die Sammlung alter Musikinstrumente* (Vienna: Anton Schroll, 1920), C 270 and C 271, p. 94 and Taf. XLVI.

30. Some of the British uniforms can be seen in Hugh Barty-King, *The Drum* (London: The Royal Tournament, 1988); note, though, that not all the illustrations are contemporary with their subject. More, though mainly nineteenth century, are illustrated in Jack Cassin-Scott and John Fabb, *Military Bands and their Uniforms* (Poole: Blandford Press, 1978); captions naming instruments should be treated with considerable care. Every regimental and military museum in every country displays either such uniforms themselves or paintings showing examples of them, for all the armies of Europe followed these fashions.

31. James Blades, *Percussion Instruments and their History* (London: Faber, 1970), pl. 129. Also published by Henry George Farmer (*Military Music*, published without any colophon

32. listing publisher, place, or date), p. 41, and doubtless elsewhere, for Farmer often repeated the same illustrations. Also as the endpapers of Cassin-Scott and Fabb (1978).

32. Kastner (1848), pp. 163ff. gives the figures for the French establishments at different dates.

33. Illustrated in Arthur W. J. G. Ord-Hume, *Barrel Organ* (London: George Allen & Unwin, 1978), fig. 69, and in more detail in Alexander Buchner, *Mechanical Musical Instruments* (London: Batchworth, n.d.), pls 131–2.

34. *Bermerkungen für die Aufführung* by Beethoven, dated Vienna, December 1815, the preface to the full score published by Breitkopf und Härtel, Serie 2, no. 1, with the plate mark B 10, in the Beethoven *Gesammtausgabe*. Translations are mine.

35. There is no exact equivalent for *Kapellmeister* in English so it is quite often used without translation. As is clear from the literal meaning of chapel-master, it derived from posts such as Bach held at Leipzig. It grew to mean director of music in general, without any ecclesiastical connotation, but here it seems to mean sub-conductors or perhaps friends of Beethoven's who were experienced conductors and music directors and whom he had persuaded to come along and help out.

36. Examples can be seen in Brigitte Bachmann-Geiser, *Die Volksmusikinstrumente der Schweiz*, Handbuch der europäischen Volksmusikinstrumente I:4 (Leipzig: Deutscher Verlag für Musik, 1981), Taf. 14c; Bálint Sárosi, *Die Volksmusikinstrumente Ungarns*, Handbuch der europäischen Volksmusikinstrumente, I:1 (Leipzig: Deutsche Verlag für Musik, 1967), pp. 22–3; and Ludvík Kunz, *Die Volksmusikinstrumente der Tschechoslowakei*, Teil 1, Handbuch der europäischen Volksmusikinstrumente I:2 (Leipzig: Deutscher Verlag für Musik, 1974), pp. 38–9 and Taf. 1a and 1b.

37. R. M. Longyear, 'Ferdinand Kauer's Percussion Enterprises', *Galpin Society Journal*, XXVII (1974), 2–8.

38. Longyear, ex. 1.

39. Longyear, ex. 3.

40. Longyear, ex. 4.

41. Longyear, p. 7.

Chapter 7 The Romantic Period

1. *Sistro* has been used in Italian for several instruments in inventories and catalogues over the centuries, often for xylophone and similarly shaped instruments, occasionally for tambourine and commonly for triangle.

2. Alberto Zedda, ed., *La Gazza Ladra* (Pesaro: Fondazione Rossini Pesaro, 1979), pp. xl–xli, and, for the date, p. xxxvi. Castil-Blaze was the publisher as well as the editor.

3. Author's translation.

4. Berlioz says that this is the first such use of the bass drum in Paris; Hector Berlioz, *Traité d'Instrumentation et d'Orchestration* (Paris: Henry Lemoine, nouvelle édition, c.1855. The first edition was 1834), p. 275.

5. Curt Sachs, *Real-Lexikon der Musikinstrumente* (New York: Dover, 1964), p. 5a.

6. David Charlton, 'New Sounds for Old: Tam-Tam, Tuba Curva, Buccin', *Soundings*, 3 (1973), 39–47, and also in his doctoral thesis, 'Orchestration and Orchestral Practice in Paris, 1789 to 1810', Cambridge (1973), a mine of information in this area, from which he has very kindly permitted me to quote.

7. Berlioz, *Traité*, p. 280.

8. Georges Kastner, *Traité général d'instrumentation*, 2ᵉ Edition *entièrement revue par l'Auteur et augmentée d'un* Supplément (Paris: C. Philipp, c.1844; the first edition was 1836).

9. Kastner, *Méthode complète et raisonnée de Timbales* (Paris: Schlesinger, 1845).

10. Berlioz, *Traité*, pp. 253–4.

11. According to Edmund A. Bowles, 'Nineteenth-Century Innovations in the Use and Construction of the Timpani', *Journal of the American Musical Instrument Society*, V–VI

(1979–80), 74–143 (p. 85), he had originally written the part for 32 drums with 20 players, but realized that no orchestra would ever allow that.

12.   As I was once, under Sir Thomas Beecham in the Royal Albert Hall with a blaze of brass coming from each quarter of the gallery, a small but professional chorus so that they sang every note exactly on the beat, and all of us rolling for dear life.

13.   Berlioz, *Traité*, p. 267.

14.   In the notes to his edition of the *Fantastic Symphony*, Norton Critical Score (New York: W. W. Norton, 1971), p. 201.

15.   Edmund A. Bowles, 'The double, double, double beat of the thundering drum: the timpani in early music', *Early Music*, XIX:3 (August 1991), 419–35 (p. 425).

16.   Bowles (1991), 433, footnotes 39 and 40.

17.   Percival Kirby, *The Kettle-Drums* (London: Oxford University Press, 1930), pp. 39–42.

18.   I once nailed the disc of leather to the end and got badly caught when the head of the nail produced a very unpleasant clank on the tube.

19.   Such bell trees are still popular as a percussion effect, more commonly in the studios, perhaps, than on the concert platform, and usually played *glissando* with a metal rod, rather than struck individually with a hammer.

20.   Kastner, *Traité*, Supplement, p. 56.

21.   Berlioz, *Traité*, p. 275.

22.   *Traité*, p. 275. Here, and elsewhere, author's translation.

23.   *Traité*, p. 310.

24.   Kastner, *Traité*, Supplement, p. 49, referring to p. 58 of the main text.

25.   Kastner, *Traité*, p. 59; Supplement, p. 49. As we shall see below, it was the publisher who took fright at the idea.

26.   Kastner, *Traité*, p. 59.

27.   Antonín Reicha, *Traité de Haute Composition Musicale* (Paris: A. Laurenc, 1835), pp. 331–51.

28.   Kastner, *Traité*, Supplement, p. 50, referring to p. 59 of the main text. Author's translation.

29.   Nancy Benvenga, *Timpani and the Timpanist's Art*, Skrifter från musikvetenskapliga institutionen, Göteborg, 3 (Gothenburg, 1979), p. 52, note 28.

30.   Kastner, Supplement, p. 51.

31.   I remember playing many three- and four-drum works on two pedal timpani when on tour with the Festival Ballet for lack of space in some pits. It can usually be done, but it gets strenuous for works tuned to G, c, and f; the continual jumps of a fourth are not good for the heads.

32.   Edmund Bowles (1979–80), p. 88.

33.   Even then the two middle drums suffer, for the lower one still has to cover G to c and the upper B to e flat.

34.   Catalogue no. 2204 in Irmgard Otto, *Musik Instrument Museum Berlin: Ausstellungsverzeichnis* (Berlin, 1965). It was perhaps a little unfair to judge tone quality in a museum gallery rather than a concert hall, but it did make me wonder about all the things one reads about the importance of the acoustical effect of the shells.

35.   Derision did not stop Sir Thomas Beecham from doing just that.

36.   Bowles (1979–80), p. 108; Nancy Benvenga (1979), p. 5; Herbert Tobischek, *Die Pauke* (Tutzing: Hans Schneider, 1977), pp. 147–9.

37.   British patent no. 7505.

38.   James Blades, *Percussion Instruments and their History* (London: Faber, 1970), pl. 193. The harmonicon is similar to a xylophone, but with bars of stone drawn from Skiddaw (Blades, pp. 82–4).

39.   The drums illustrated were made, or anyway stamped, by Köhler of London; an almost identical system by the Parisian maker Gautrot has also been seen, and he was probably the inventor, and perhaps the maker. See the Gautrot Aîné & Cie, *Catalogue des Instruments de Musique* (Paris: 1867), reprinted as *Larigot (Bulletin de l'Association des*

Collectionneurs d'Instruments à Vent) N° X Spécial, April 1999, pp. 88–9.

40. Gabriele Rossi Rognone, *La musica alla corte del Granduchi: Music at the Grand-ducal Court* (Firenze: Giunti, 2001), 84–5.

41. Franca Falletti, Renato Meucci, Gabriele Rossi Rognone, *La musica e i suoi strumenti: La Collezione Granducale del Conservatorio Cherubini* (Firenze: Giunti and Firenze Musei, 2001), 224–5.

42. Bowles (1979–80), fig. 3; Tobischek (1977), 162–5.

43. Kastner, *Traité*, p. 60, footnote. Since this is in the main text, presumably it appeared in the original edition of 1836.

44. Quoted in Edmund A. Bowles, 'Mendelssohn, Schumann, and Ernst Pfundt: A Pivotal Relationship between Two Composers and a Timpanist', *Journal of the American Musical Instrument Society*, XXIV (1998), 5–26, pp. 14–15.

45. Edmund Bowles's excellent article in *JAMIS*, V–VI (1979–80), has been an invaluable source for much of this section. A simplified version of that article is his 'The Kettledrum' in John H. Beck, ed., *Encyclopedia of Percussion* (New York: Garland, 1995), 201–26. His forthcoming book from Pendragon, *The Timpani: History in Pictures and Documents*, goes into even greater detail with even more illustrations.

46. Illustrated by Blades (1970), pl. 136 after they had been restored, and here as they were before the restoration.

47. We are now drawing ahead of ourselves into the period of the next chapter. Nevertheless, it seems sensible to cover the mechanization of the timpani, however briefly, in a single context.

48. Edmund A. Bowles (1995), p. 215.

49. Bowles (1979–80), (1995), and forthcoming; Tobischek (1977); Benvenga (1979).

50. Modern taste would blench at using any bass drum in Handel's music, let alone something this size.

51. Kastner, *Traité*, Supplement, pp. 51–2.

52. Blades (1970), pp. 307–8, pl. 147 and fig. 41.

53. Bálint Sárosi, *Die Volksmusikinstrumente Ungarns*, Handbuch der europäischen Volksmusikinstrumente, I:1 (Leipzig: Deutscher Verlag für Musik, 1967), pp. 12–13.

54. Vida Chenoweth, *The Marimbas of Guatemala* (Lexington: University of Kentucky Press, 1964).

55. These points are easily found by sprinkling a fine powder (chalk, talcum powder, fine sand) on the bar and striking it repeatedly while watching the powder collect in a little heap at the nodes.

56. Many of these details are drawn from Father A. M. Jones, 'Experiment with a xylophone key', *African Music*, 3:2 (1963), and others from Jamie Linwood, 'The Manufacture of Tuned Percussion Instruments in Indonesia and Africa – a Selective Study', PhD thesis, London Guildhall University (1995), which also goes into considerable detail on the techniques used in Africa and on the methods of tuning free-free bars.

57. We can be certain that he did not mean the mouthorgan, as used in the recording with words by Ogden Nash (spoken by Noël Coward) with pianists Leonid Hambro and Jascha Zeyde, and André Kostelanetz and his orchestra on a ten-inch Philips LP, NBR 6001 (No2602 R), and, according to the Internet, Odyssey Y 32359.

58. This is the instrument for which Mozart wrote his *Adagio and Rondo*, K. 617 in 1791. For the date and place of the invention, see Stanley Sadie, ed., *The New Grove Dictionary of Musical Instruments* (London: Macmillian, 1984), *s.v.* Musical Glasses (by Alec Hyatt King), vol. 2, pp. 725–6.

59. Certainly the one time I played it, on an extra large bass drum in a recording at the Abbey Road Studios with the Royal Philharmonic Orchestra, Sir Malcolm Sargent specified exactly where he wanted each stroke to come. The bells commence at figure 16 in the Russian Collected Edition score and the cannon nine bars after 17.

60. Edwin Ripin, *The Instrument Catalogs of Leopoldo Franciolini* (Hackensack: Joseph Boonin, 1974).

61. Musée Instrumental du Conservatoire Royal de Musique de Bruxelles (and the same in Flemish), 1 rue Villa Hermosa, B-1000 Brussels. Mahillon's original catalogue, in five volumes (1880–1922), is still available in a facsimile reprint from Les amis de la musique (Brussels, 1978).

62. Lesley Lindsay Mason Collection, Museum of Fine Arts, 465 Huntingdon Avenue, Boston, MA 02115, for the European instruments in which see Nicholas Bessaraboff's monumental catalogue, *Ancient European Musical Instruments* (Cambridge: Harvard University Press, for the Museum of Fine Arts, Boston, 1941). Galpin also sold them a considerable number of non-European instruments, no catalogue of which has been published. Some appear in A. C. Moule, 'Chinese Musical Instruments', *Journal of the North-China Branch of the Royal Asiatic Society*, XXXIX (1908), 1–160 and pls I–XIII, which has been reprinted several times in recent years (e.g. Liechtenstein: Kraus Reprint, 1967).

63. The Metropolitan Museum of Art, Fifth Avenue at 82nd Street, New York 10028. The original six-volume *Catalogue of the Crosby Brown Collection of Musical Instruments* (1901–7) is long out of print, but several sectional catalogues and specialist publications are available.

64. Brian W. Harvey and Carla J. Shapreau, *Violin Fraud* (Oxford: Clarendon, 1997) is worth consulting in this area. The first edition, by Harvey alone, covered English law; this second edition covers American conditions also.

65. Cynthia Gaskell Brown, *The Battle's Sound* (Tiverton: Devon Books, 1996), pp. 4–5.

66. All such work, whether 'plausible' or 'modern', should be marked in some place where it will not be visible to the casual visitor but will be clearly seen, without the use of such devices as ultra-violet light, on detailed inspection.

Chapter 8 The Twentieth Century

1. In a footnote in the score at its first entry, *fff* at figure 129 in the Finale, Mahler says that 'the sound should be short and strong but dull, <u>not</u> [his underline] metallic (like an axe-blow)'. The hammer is always referred to as such but to avoid a metallic sound what is normally used is a large carpenter's mallet. James Holland, *Percussion* (London: Macdonald and Jane's, 1978), p. 96, makes the sensible point that with the growing tendency towards concrete floors in concert halls one may need to strike a rostrum instead of the floor, and Gerassimos Avgerinos, *Handbuch der Schlag- und Effekt-instrumente* (Frankfurt am Main: Verlag das Musikinstrument, 1967), p. 79, recommends striking a plank.

2. Perhaps it is worth noting that although all references, including the score, say that only two timpanists are required, one of them needs three hands at figure 138. Even if the piccolo drum for the high b natural is put where both players can reach it, one of the two timpanists would have to hold two sticks in one hand, as on a xylophone. Alternatively, the tamtam or bass drum player reaches over and plays the high Bs as well as their own notes.

3. My translation. The published English translation of the original French list of instruments in the edition in the New Music Orchestra Series, San Francisco (1934), and quoted with the whole score in Morris Goldenberg, *Modern School for Snare Drum* (New York: Chappell, 1955), pp. 163–84, needs to be treated with care.

4. Specifically cornet, not trumpet, and specifically tenor/bass trombone with the 'plug' in the back-bow to lower the fundamental pitch from the tenor B flat to the bass F.

5. James Holland (1978) reprints the final bars as they stand in the part on his pages 202–4; Goldenberg (1955), pp. 122–32, prints the whole percussion part, some as it is in the original part but more, including the finale, transcribed, though less usefully than

the Blades version referred to below. He also reprints the complete percussion parts of many other works, including the Bartók *Sonata*, Rimsky-Korsakov's *Capriccio espagnol*, and Borodin's *Polovtsian Dances*.

6. Holland, pp. 250–61.

7. The new edition (London: Chester Music, 1987), edited by John Carewe and with the whole of Ramuz's text, not just those parts which coincide with the music, has a wholly re-edited and consistent percussion part by James Blades, based on his own performances under Stravinsky's direction. The score also reprints as an appendix for comparison the original published percussion part of 1924.

8. Holland, p. 219.

9. Philharmonia miniature score no. 400 (Vienna: Universal Edition, 1956). The old-fashioned pedal cymbal makes a more suitable sound than the modern high-hat; for these see below in the description of the development of the drum kit.

10. I was the percussion player for that production.

11. The Dadaists, led by composers such Alois Hába, wrote in microtones and bemused the public in other ways. *Musique concrète*, much of which depended on *sons trouvés*, miscellaneous sounds recorded and manipulated, only became possible with the invention of the wire recorder, and the availability of that and subsequently the tape recorder, which happened in the early 1950s.

12. Examples of many works of this sort can be found in books on contemporary music, and especially in Reginald Smith Brindle's *Contemporary Percussion* (London: Oxford University Press, 1970) and in James Holland's forthcoming book on a similar subject.

13. Jeremy Montagu, 'On the Reconstruction of Mediaeval Instruments of Percussion', *Galpin Society Journal*, XXIII (1970), 104–14; 'Capriol's Revenge, a conversation between James Blades and Jeremy Montagu wherein the pupil instructs the master', *Early Music*, I:2 (April 1973), 84–92; James Blades and Jeremy Montagu, *Early Percussion Instruments from the Middle Ages to the Baroque* (London: Oxford University Press, 1976); Jeremy Montagu, *Making Early Percussion Instruments* (London: Oxford University Press, 1976). My reconstructions of the instruments are illustrated in the first, second, and last of those titles and may be heard on many recordings with Musica Reservata and other ensembles.

14. Steven Schick's 'Multiple Percussion', 257–63, and John Beck's 'Percussion Ensembles', 269–73, both in John Beck, ed., *Encyclopedia of Percussion* (New York: Garland, 1995), are useful introductions to this area.

15. Georges Kastner, *Manuel général de musique militaire à l'usage des armées françaises* (Paris: Didiot Frères, 1848); Constant Pierre, *La facture instrumentale à l'exposition universelle de 1889* (Paris: Librairie de l'Art Indépendant, 1890); Pierre, *Les facteurs d'instruments de musique* (Paris: Sagot, 1892); Johann Joachim Quantz, *Versuch einer Anweisung die Flöte Traversiere zu spielen* (Berlin: Johann Friedrich Boß, 1752).

16. I became a music student in 1948 and a member of the Musicians' Union in January 1950.

17. Lloyd S. McCausland, 'The Plastic Drumhead: Its History and Development', in Beck (1995), 277–80.

18. Personal communication.

19. Laurence Picken, *Folk Musical Instruments of Turkey* (London: Oxford University Press, 1975), fig. 9 on p. 79 and pl. 12.

20. Edward Elgar, Enigma Variations, Variation 13. The score still says with side-drum sticks, allegedly because it was printed in German as well as English and the Germans had no coin of similar weight and size.

21. Information on these instruments has appeared in the musical press in both Britain and America, but the acoustical information here, like the photograph, has kindly been provided by Mr de Mowbray himself (letter, 14 November 1999).

22. In 1957 the timpanist of the Warsaw Philharmonic was using, with some success, the

plastic foam which is employed for furniture padding.

23. Gerassimos Avgerinos, *Lexikon der Pauke* (Frankfurt am Main: Das Musikinstrument, 1964), p. 33, *s.v.* Flanell; he cites no reference for this date.

24. Percival Kirby, *The Kettle-Drums* (London: Oxford University Press, 1930), plate opposite p. 28, and description on pp. 28–31. Henri Pape was the first, initially in the mid-1820s, to use felt for piano hammers and dampers, which he is said to have obtained by cutting up old felt hats.

25. The balsa core must be drilled across the grain for the shaft – drilling it down the grain encourages it to break up segmentally. A cork-borer is the best tool for this, for a twist drill wanders in wood so soft.

26. There is nothing rudimentary about rudimental drumming. The rudiments are the basic techniques such as flams, ruffs, paradiddles, and so forth, but their combination and use in rudimental drumming require extremely high levels of technique, far higher than are usually required for normal orchestral work.

27. One can check the pitch of sticks either by hitting each in turn while tossing it gently into the air or while holding it lightly at a nodal point, two-ninths of its length from the end, in each case to ensure that it can vibrate freely. If the pitches of the two sticks are very different from each other, one tries another pair or rematches the pairs from one's own stock of sticks.

28. I have heard Jimmy Blades do this many times, leaving younger players open-mouthed. Whether anyone can still do it today, I do not know.

29. Enigma Variations, fig. 82.

30. Maggie Cotton, *Percussion Work Book* (Birmingham: author, 1993). This extremely useful book, by the principal percussion of the City of Birmingham Symphony Orchestra, lists every work in that orchestra's repertoire, alphabetically under the composer's name, with a list of the instruments and the number of players required, frequently with useful advice for getting round any problems, as here where she recommends fooling the conductor by painting a side-drum stick silver.

31. With the change to the new coinage, most British timpanists carefully reserved a few half-crowns, the traditional 'beater', or some old pennies with this work in mind.

32. From figure 103, continuing to just after figure 152.

33. A violinist leaving the platform once tapped on my timpani with the back of his bow. I reached my timpani stick to his violin, and he won't ever do that again.

34. *Col legno*, 'with the wood'. With modern wire strings this can chip the varnish off the bow; in earlier times, when players used gut strings, this would have done less harm, but even then valuable bows could get damaged.

35. Not keys. Unlike those of the organ, from which harpsichords and pianos derive the name, they do not open anything.

36. A further disadvantage is that some electric guitarists and vibe players die every year because cables get trodden on and insulation broken, resulting in short circuits and other problems.

37. Bálint Sárosi, *Die Volksmusikinstrumente Ungarns*, Handbuch der europäischen Volksmusikinstrumente, I:1 (Leipzig: Deutscher Verlag für Musik, 1967), pp. 12–15.

38. Verbal information from one of the resident percussion players when I first saw the plates in 1957. A Sheffield steel-master had hoped to take over the Royal Philharmonic Orchestra after Sir Thomas Beecham's death; attempts to interest him in the duplication of these plates came to naught.

39. Cecil Forsyth, *Orchestration* (London: Macmillan and Stainer and Bell, 2nd edn 1935), pp. 54–5, *s.v.* Bells. Quoted in my *The World of Romantic & Modern Musical Instruments* (Newton Abbot: David & Charles, 1981), pp. 118–19.

40. This is the most treacherous of all percussion instruments, especially in *pianissimo*, when it is all too easy to stop the beater just before it reaches the triangle, and most players would agree that suspension on a gallows is very suitable.

41.   An example, with the name *Sound* and made in Israel by Halilit, was given to me
      c.1990 by Pamela Jones, then principal percussion in the Jerusalem Symphony
      Orchestra.
42.   In the early 1960s R. F. G. van Bueren wrote a suite, *The Four Winds*, for chorus,
      orchestra, and five-part steel band, which I conducted. Many other composers have
      written works since then. Two useful texts on the steel bands are Peter Seeger, *Steel
      Drums: How to Play Them and Make Them* (New York: Oak, 1964), and Jeffrey Thomas,
      'Steel Band/Pan' in Beck (1995), 297–331.

Chapter 9 World Percussion

1.   Paul Collaer, *Südostasien*, Musikgeschichte in Bildern, I:3 (Leipzig: Deutscher Verlag für
      Musik, 1979), Abb. 73 and 74: two well-known photographs, taken by E. H. Man
      before 1880, which appear in many books on ethnomusicology.
2.   Cranstone, B. A. L., 'The British Museum Ethnographical Expedition to New Guinea,
      1963–4: a Preliminary Report', *British Museum Quarterly*, vol. XXIX, no. 3/4 (1965),
      109–18. The recordings and photographs and films were made by Mr D. J. Lee; he and
      Cranstone were the only personnel.
3.   Hans Fischer, *Schallgeräte in Ozeanien: Bau- und Spieltechnik – Verbreitung und Funktion*
      (Baden-Baden: P. H. Heitz, 1958). Translated by Philip Holzknecht and ed. Don Niles
      as *Sound-Producing Instruments in Oceania* (Boroko: Institute of Papua New Guinea
      Studies, revised edition, 1986; the revisions are important and the first edition of 1983
      should be avoided).
4.   Paul Collaer, *Ozeanien*, Musikgeschichte in Bildern, I:1 (Leipzig: Deutscher Verlag für
      Musik, 1964), Abb. 20, 21, 78–81, 92–104 show a few of the many types.
5.   Collaer (1964), Abb. 82–9.
6.   There are several relevant articles on both Lapp and Siberian shamans' drums by Ernst
      Emsheimer in his *Studia ethnomusicologica eurasiatica*, Musikhistoriska Museets Skrifter 1
      (Stockholm, 1964), and *Studia Ethnomusicologica Eurasiatica II* (Stockholm: Kungl.
      Musikaliska Akademien, 1991).
7.   Paul Collaer, *Amerika*, Musikgeschichte in Bildern, I:2 (Leipzig: Deutscher Verlag für
      Musik, 1967), Abb. 7 for Alaskan Eskimo and Abb. 8 and 10 for Greenland. An English
      version was published as *Music of the Americas* (London: Curzon Press, 1973) with the
      same plate numbers.
8.   Personal communication many years ago from Poul Rovsing Olsen in Copenhagen.
9.   K. Vertkov, G. Blagodatov, and E. Yazovitskaya, *Atlas of Musical Instruments of the Peoples
      Inhabiting the USSR* (Moscow: State Music Publishers, 1975, the second edition with
      English summaries), 392 from Azerbaijan, 428–9 from Armenia, 497 from Georgia, 577
      from Turkmenia, 611 from Uzbekistan, 656 from Tajikistan; also Jean During, *La
      Musique Iranienne* (Paris: Recherche sur les Civilisations, 1984), pl. 4 and p. 93.
10.   For Portugal, see Ernesto Veiga de Oliveira, *Instrumentos Musicais Populares Portugueses*
      (Lisbon: Fundação Calouste Gulbenkian, 1966), pp. 76–8, pls 54–73. For Morocco, see
      Salah Cherki, *Musique Marocaine* (Mohammedia: Fedala, 1981). For a visible internal
      snare, see Paul Collaer and Jürgen Elsner, *Nordafrika*, Musikgeschichte in Bildern, I:8
      (Leipzig: Deutscher Verlag für Musik, 1983), p. 114 and Abb. 144.
11.   A useful survey of such practices, including material on ritual use, is Veronica
      Doubleday, 'The Frame Drum in the Middle East: Women, Musical Instruments and
      Power', *Ethnomusicology*, 43:1 (1999), 101–34.
12.   Nos 98.331 from the Gower Peninsular, 04.282 from North Wales, and 67.7/1 from
      Crymych, all mid-nineteenth century. These are described in detail in the descriptive
      report on the musical instruments in the Museum which I compiled in 1990.
13.   Micheál Ó Suilleabháin, 'The Bodhran', *Treoir*, vol. 6, no. 2, pp. 4–7, and no. 5, pp.
      6–10 (March and April 1974). This all arose during a conference of the United

Kingdom branch of the International Council for Traditional Music (now the British Forum for Ethnomusicology) which we organized at St Fagans.

14. Personal communication from David Z. Crookes, quoting an unnamed maker.

15. Laurence Picken, *Folk Musical Instruments of Turkey* (London: Oxford University Press, 1975), p. 61. This book is the most important of the past half-century as a study of the typology of instruments of all sorts, not only those of Turkey.

16. Ella Zonis, *Persian Music* (Cambridge: Harvard University Press, 1973), pp. 172–5. While melodic patterns are discussed in great detail, there is little on rhythmic patterns (see pp. 126–37) and no examples of drumming. Further information will be found in Jean During (1984), pl. 2 and pp. 87–91.

17. Alain Daniélou, *Südasien*, Musikgeschichte in Bildern, I:4 (Leipzig: Deutscher Verlag für Musik, 1978), Abb. 5.

18. I use short pieces of ⅜ inch wooden dowel, and I have seen a wooden pencil broken into segments for this purpose when nothing else was to hand.

19. There is no real English equivalent of the word '*rāg*'; it means something between mode and scale, with elements of both, and mood as well as mode. *Rāgs* can vary between simple ones like *bhairavi*, approximately the white notes of the piano from E to E, through others which have one series of notes in ascent and a different series in descent, to others which have a zigzag pattern instead of straight ascent and descent. A fuller, and more accurate, description can be found in N. A. Jairazbhoy, *The Rāgs of North Indian Music* (London: Faber, 1971).

20. In normal speech the one name, *tablā*, covers both drums, which are always used together in Indian classical music.

21. Daniélou (1978), Abb. 16. Compact discs of North Indian classical music are widely available, and there are many of *sitar* and *tablā* and even some of *tablā* alone on which these techniques can be heard.

22. Jairazbhoy (1971), pp. 16–20.

23. Daniélou (1978), Abb. 4 and 6 for the *mrdangam* and *pakhāvaj* respectively, and Abb. 13 and 14 for the South Indian *vīnā*.

24. Collaer, *Südostasien* (1979), Abb. 72.

25. My small knowledge of Burmese music (there is little recent information available in print) derives from the talks given by Dr John Okell to the Ethnomusicology Panel of the Royal Anthropological Institute and from copies of his field recordings which he was generous enough to give me.

26. Heinrich Simbriger, *Gong und Gongspiele*, Internationales Archiv für Ethnographie (Leiden: E. J. Brill, 1939).

27. It is conventional today in English, now that the *gamelan* is so widely played in Europe and America, to add an 's' to words for their plural form, though the correct Javanese plural is formed by duplication, for instance *saron-saron*.

28. I used the word 'lacework' above. A better, though perhaps less familiar, comparison for this decoration upon decoration would be with the Mandelbrot sets which are generated by computers.

29. Not a very good analogy but perhaps helpful.

30. Jaap Kunst, *Music in Java* (The Hague: Martinus Nijhoff, 1949ff.); Neil Sorrell, *A Guide to the Gamelan* (London: Faber, 1990); Montagu, *The Javanese Gamelan Kyai Madu Laras* (Oxford: The Bate Collection of Historical Instruments, 1985ff.). There are many other introductions to the *gamelan*.

31. Colin McPhee, *Music in Bali* (New Haven: Yale University Press, 1966).

32. Since *xulon* is Greek for wood, xylophone should be used only for the wooden-barred instruments, though one does use 'xylophone family' to cover all the instruments of this pattern irrespective of their material. For Thailand, see David Morton, *The Traditional Music of Thailand* (Berkeley: University of California Press, 1976); Dhanit Yupho, *Thai Musical Instruments* (Bangkok, 1960); and Collaer, *Südostasien* (1979), Abb. 42–4, 53, and p. 58.

33. Edw. Jacobson and J. H. van Hasselt, *De Gong-Fabricatie te Semarang* (Leiden: E. J. Brill, 1907).
34. Neil Sorrell (1990), pp. 44–54, and Jamie Murray Linwood, 'The Manufacture of Tuned Percussion Instruments in Indonesia and Africa – a Selective Study', PhD thesis, London Guildhall University (1995).
35. The iron instruments are cheap enough that it usually costs more to send them to Europe or America than it does to buy them.
36. I was shown this technique of tuning by pressure on the face in the Department of Ethnomusicology at UCLA in 1970.
37. Collaer, *Südostasien* (1979), Abb. 140.
38. Collaer, Abb. 3 and 71.
39. Franz Heger, *Alte Metalltrommeln aus Südost-Asien* (Leipzig: Hiersemann, 1902); Alfred Janata, *Musikinstrumente der Völker* (Vienna: Museum für Völkerkunde, 1975); A. J. Bernet Kempers, *The Kettledrums of Southeast Asia*, Modern Quaternary Research in Southeast Asia, 10 (Rotterdam: A. A. Balkema, 1988).
40. Fritz Kuttner, *The Archaeology of Music in Ancient China* (New York: Paragon House, 1990).
41. Picken (1975), p. 60, last paragraph. I should add that 'diaphragmophone' is my coinage and that Dr Picken should not be blamed for it.
42. Ernst Chladni, *Entdeckungen über die Theorie des Klanges* (Leipzig: Weidmann, 1787); Kuttner (1990), pp. 138ff. and figs 7.24 to 7.29; Percival Kirby, *The Kettle-Drums* (London: Oxford University Press, 1930), pp. 40–2.
43. Mantle Hood, *The Evolution of Javanese Gamelan Book I – Music of the Roaring Sea* (Wilhelmshaven: Heinrichshofen, 1980).
44. W. Perceval Yetts, *The George Eumorfopoulos Collection: Catalogue of the Chinese & Corean bronzes, sculptures, jades, jewellery and miscellaneous objects*, vol. 2, Bronzes: bells, drums, mirrors, etc. (London: Ernest Benn, 1930).
45. Mireille Helffer, *Mchod-rol: Les instruments de la musique tibétaine* (Paris: CNRS, 1994), pp. 160–90.
46. The Drum Museum is at 2-1-1 Nishiasakusa, Taito-ku, Tokyo.
47. William Malm, *Japanese Music and Musical Instruments* (Rutland: Charles E. Tuttle, 1959), pp. 91–3 and 122–7.
48. L. E. R. Picken, 'Tunes Apt for Tang Lyrics from the Shō Part-Books of Tōgaku', *Essays in Ethnomusicology – A Birthday offering for Lee Hye-ku*, Korean Musicological Society (1969), and many volumes of *Tang Court Music* (Cambridge: Cambridge University Press), transcribed by Laurence Picken and his colleagues from the *Gagaku* repertoire.
49. Kenzô Hayashi et al., *Musical Instruments in the Shôsôin* (Tokyo: Nihon Keizai Shimbun Sha, 1967), pp. vi, xiv, xxii–xxiii, and pl. 26, 176–80.
50. Helffer (1994), pp. 121–59 for the pole drum and 232–50 for the *damaru*.
51. Collaer, *Ozeanien* (1964), Abb. 68–74; the internal boss can be seen in Abb. 70.
52. Raymond Clausen provided much information, and the illustration used here, on the music of Malekula in the days when he, Nazir Jairazbhoy, and I were running the Ethnomusicology Panel of the Royal Anthropological Institute, but tragically he never published any of it before his untimely death. His papers and working notes were generously deposited by his wife in the Pitt Rivers Museum, Oxford. See also Collaer (1964), Abb. 65–7.
53. Raymond Clausen, personal communication. For Helmholtz resonators see Hermann Helmholtz, *On the Sensations of Tone*, translated by Alexander J. Ellis (London, 2nd edition 1885; facsimile New York: Dover, 1954), pp. 43–4 and Appendix II, pp. 372–4. This factor of the area of open hole is of considerable importance in controlling the pitch of many other instruments, both wind and strings, and I have been grateful to Dr Clausen for this observation ever since he made it.
54. Collaer (1964), Abb. 77.

55. I was incorrect in my 'What is a Gong' article (*MAN*, 1965:5), 18–21, in suggesting that this was a form of slit drum. Andrew Tracey of the African Music Society pointed out in conversation that the *lali ne meke* was a form of xylophone bar and that the hollow would not only increase the resonance but would lower the pitch of the bar. Collaer (1964) uses the same photograph of the instrument in use (Abb. 76) as I did in my article.

56. Samuel Martí *Alt-Amerika*, Musikgeschichte in Bildern, II:7 (Leipzig: Deutscher Verlag für Musik, 1970), Abb. 31 and 89–91.

57. Martí, Abb. 32.

58. Collaer, *Amerika* (1967), Abb. 49, 58, 59, 66.

59. Collaer, p. 122, Abb. 34, 35, 69, 70.

60. Collaer, Abb. 49; Alan P. Merriam, *Ethnomusicology of the Flathead Indians* (New York: Wenner-Gren Foundation for Anthropological Research, 1967), pp. 49–50, pls I, II; Thomas Vennum Jr, *The Ojibwa Dance Drum: its history and construction*, Smithsonian Folklife Studies, 2 (Washington, 1982).

61. Martí (1970), Abb. 85.

62. Collaer, *Ozeanien* (1964), Abb. 57, 58.

63. Collaer, *Amerika* (1967), Abb. 4.

64. Collaer (1967), Abb. 12–15.

65. Collaer (1967), Abb. 35, 51.

66. Jos Gansemans, *Les Instruments de Musique du Rwanda* (Tervuren: Musée Royal de l'Afrique Centrale, 1988), pl. 4; Gerhard Kubik, *Westafrika*, Musikgeschichte in Bildern, I:11 (Leipzig: Deutscher Verlag für Musik, 1989), Abb. 43, 44; Gerhard Kubik, *Ostafrika*, Musikgeschichte in Bildern, I:10 (Leipzig: Deutscher Verlag für Musik, 1982), Abb. 66, 76, 77, 98, 109, 110; Jos Gansemans and Barbara Schmidt-Wrenger, *Zentralafrika*, Musikgeschichte in Bildern, I:9 (Leipzig: Deutscher Verlag für Musik, 1986), Abb. 25, 56, 57, 115, 132, 133, 135, 141; Percival R. Kirby, *Musical Instruments of the Native Races of South Africa* (London: Oxford University Press, 1934), pls 1–3, are just a few of the many books and illustrations which show leg rattles in Africa.

67. Gansemans (1988), pls 9, 57–60 and front cover.

68. Gerhard Kubik, *Westafrika* (1989), Abb. 32.

69. Xylophone makers often plant gourds in succession so that there will always be a full range of sizes available when they are called upon for an instrument.

70. A. M. Jones, *Africa and Indonesia: The Evidence of the Xylophone and other Musical and Cultural Factors* (Leiden: E. J. Brill, 1964), for east to west; M. D. W. Jeffreys, 'Review Article: Africa and Indonesia', *African Music* 4:1 (1966/1967), 66–73, for west to east.

71. Hugh Tracey, *Chopi Musicians* (Oxford: International African Institute, 1970), especially pp. 118–42.

72. Hugh Tracey, *African Dances of the Witwatersrand Gold Mines* (Johannesburg: African Music Society, 1952), plates on pp. 116–40.

73. O. Boone, *Les Xylophones du Congo Belge* (Tervuren: Musée du Congo Belge, 1936). The Museum is now the Musée Royal de l'Afrique Centrale.

74. Kubik, *Ostafrika* (1982), pp. 19–21 and Abb. 24, 25 and 28.

75. Margaret Trowell and K. P. Wachsmann, *Tribal Crafts of Uganda* (London: Oxford University Press, 1953), pp. 314–20.

76. There is a common tendency to refer to the bars of a xylophone as keys, analogously to those of a keyboard instrument, but unlike the keys of the organ, from which the term was transferred to the clavichord and thence to the harpsichord and piano, the bars do not open anything, and this usage should be avoided.

77. Linwood (1995), p. 223.

78. Boone (1936), pp. 90ff.; Linwood (1995), p. 205.

79. A. M. Jones, 'Experiment with a xylophone key', *African Music*, 3:2 (1963), 6–10. Both construction and tuning, with much attention to the whole acoustical process, are treated in even greater detail in Jamie Linwood's doctoral thesis.

80. The term 'thumb-piano' is so inaccurate, for there is no resemblance to a piano, that it should never be used.

81. It was Hugh Tracey who, in conversation, rightly maintained that these iron tongues, as they are usually termed (these instruments are often called lamellaphones), are really reeds, similar to those of the trump and the mouthorgan, and especially those of the musical box.

82. François Borel, *Les Sanza* (Neuchâtel: Musée d'Ethnographie, 1986); J. S. Laurenty, *Les Sanza du Congo* (Tervuren: Musée Royal de l'Afrique Centrale, 1962); Jos Gansemans (1988), pp. 50–70 and pls 20–1.

83. Jos Gansemans, *Volksmuziekinstrumenten, Getuigen en Resultaat van een Interetnische Samenleving: een Organologische Studie met Betrekking tot Aruba, Bonaire en Curaçao* (Tervuren: Musée Royal de l'Afrique Centrale, 1989).

84. Kubik, *Westafrika* (1989), Abb. 6, 35–7, 87; Jean-Sébastien Laurenty, *Les tambours à fente de l'Afrique Centrale* (Tervuren: Musée Royal de l'Afrique Centrale, 1968).

85. Laurenty (1968), nos 28–70; the bell-shaped are nos 145–215; Gansemans and Schmidt-Wrenger (1986) show many types on Abb. 168–73, 204–8, 215–17 and 227.

86. J. A. Carrington, *Talking Drums of Africa* (London: Carey Kingsgate Press, 1949; reprinted New York: Negro Universities Press, 1969).

87. Personal communication from Azubikye Ifionu (whose first name is low, low, high, middle tone, as I remember when another drummer called him to take a turn).

88. Kubik, *Westafrika* (1989), pp. 152 and 153 are of special interest here because the photographs show an Ashanti drummer recording the *atumpan* in the early years of this century for R. S. Rattray (Abb. 150) – both the original photograph and the recording are in the archives of the Pitt Rivers Museum, Oxford – and master-drummer Desmond Tay playing the same music for Father Jones on the machine which Jones devised for recording drum patterns. Full details of his work are in A. M. Jones, *Studies in African Music* (Oxford: Oxford University Press, 1959); the second volume consists entirely of transcriptions.

89. A classic in this field is Heinz Wieschhoff, *Die Afrikanischen Trommeln* (Stuttgart: Strecker und Schröder, 1933), and a very recent example is Andreas Meyer, *Afrikanische Trommeln: West- und Zentralafrika* (Berlin: Museum für Völkerkunde, 1997); as always, the Tervuren catalogue is very thorough for that area, in this case Olga Boone, *Les Tambours du Congo Belge et du Ruanda-Urundi* (Tervuren: Musée du Congo Belge, 1951).

90. Curt Sachs, *The History of Musical Instruments* (New York: W. W. Norton, and London: Dent, 1940), p. 35.

91. Sachs (1940), pp. 460–2; Curt Sachs, *Les Instruments de Musique de Madagascar* (Paris: Institut d'Ethnologie, 1938), pp. 26–36.

92. Meyer (1997), Abb. 176–9.

93. Trowell and Wachsmann (1953), pp. 369ff. and pl. 88.

94. Marie-Thérèse Brincard, ed., *Sounding Forms: African Musical Instruments* (New York: The American Federation of Arts, 1989), pp. 102–5.

95. Chinyere Nwachukwu, 'Taxonomy of Musical Instruments of Mbaise, Nigeria', MA thesis, Queen's University of Belfast (1981), and Meki Nzewi, 'Master Musicians and the Music of Ese, Ukom, and Mgba Ensembles in Ngwa, Igbo Society', PhD thesis, Queen's University of Belfast (1973).

96. Francis Bebey, *African Music* (London: George Harrap, 1975), p. 93.

97. Michael Powne, *Ethiopian Music* (London: Oxford University Press, 1966), pp. 22–3 and pl. 3.

98. For Togo, Bebey (1975), pp. 91–2; for Burkino Faso, Kubik (1989), Abb. 171.

99. Bernard Fagg, 'The discovery of multiple rock gongs in Nigeria', *MAN* (1956), 17–18. Subsequent reports in *MAN* often linked rock gongs with slides and other fertility symbols.

100. M. C. Fagg, *Rock Music* (Oxford: Pitt Rivers Museum, 1997).

101. The anvils first appear in *Das Rheingold* 32 bars before the end of Scene 2.
102. Paul Collaer and Jürgen Elsner (1983), Abb. 120; Laurence Picken (1975), pl. 11.
103. Yury Arbatsky, *Beating the Tupan in the Central Balkans* (Chicago: Newberry Library, 1953).
104. Bálint Sárosi, *Die Volksmusikinstrumente Ungarns*, Handbuch der europäischen Volksmusikinstrumente, I:1 (Leipzig: Deutscher Verlag für Musik, 1967), p. 25, and personal communication in conversation.
105. Sárosi, p. 27, and illustrated also in most of the African books already cited.
106. Henry Balfour, 'The Friction Drum', *Journal of the Royal Anthropological Institute*, 37 (1907), 67–92 and pls XII–XIV.
107. Sárosi (1967), music example on p. 28.
108. Filippo Bonanni, *Gabinetto Armonico* (Rome, 1723), pl. LXXXIII.
109. Tobias Norlind, *Musikinstrumentens historia i ord och bild* (Stockholm: Nordisk Rotogravyr, 1941).
110. All the better that Dover have made available an inexpensive reprint of all the plates, albeit much reduced in size and without Bonanni's original captions, as Frank Harrison and Joan Rimmer, *The Showcase of Musical Instruments* (New York: Dover, 1964).
111. Bonanni (1723) and Harrison and Rimmer (1964), pls 112, 113, 114, 117, 118.
112. Bonanni etc., pls 117, 123.
113. Ludvík Kunz, *Die Volksmusikinstrumente der Tschechoslowakei* Teil 1, Handbuch der europäischen Volksmusikinstrumente, I:2 (Leipzig: Deutscher Verlag für Musik, 1974), pp. 19–21.
114. Bonanni etc., pl. 128.

Appendix 1 Playing Technique

1. What sound like distinct strokes to the player merge, if properly played, into a continuous sound to the audience.
2. Described in detail by Pocock's pupil Andrew Shivas, *The Art of Tympanist and Drummer* (London: Dennis Dobson, 1957).
3. I owe both these tips to my master Jimmy Blades, an ever-ready help when in trouble.
4. This I learned from Harry Eastwood when one day we were both playing cymbals at different points, and he got twice the volume for half the effort; 'You just do it like this,' he said, and relaxing the wrists and arms was what he did.
5. Hermann Scherchen, *Handbook of Conducting* (London: Oxford University Press, 1933; reprinted Oxford, 1989).
6. It is also a very easy way to deal with dotted rhythms when teaching music to beginners – make them count the smallest units rather than try to divide the larger.

Apendix 2 Lapping Drum Heads

1. Calf is the preferred skin for normal use, but goat also has its advantages; the process described here is the same for each.
2. This implies that one has personal access to the supplier, which is always advisable, even to the extent of travelling a hundred or more miles; if access is impossible insist, when ordering, on the right to reject any skins that are thought inadequate on arrival.
3. Warning: this is often more easily judged before the skin is soaked so check then and mark it unobtrusively on the edge so that when the head is wet you still know which side is which.
4. One can use newspaper but if the ink is unstable it may transfer to the skin and if it does, it is there for ever.
5. Unscented talcum powder such as baby powder will do; the smell of a scented powder is apt to linger.

6. Engineers tend to look at our drums and hoot with laughter at any idea that the shells are truly circular. Tone and tuning would be much better if they were.

7. Strictly, whenever one takes a head off the drum it should be removed from its fleshhoop and relapped, but this is often a counsel of perfection. The reason for doing this is that the rim of the shell beds into the head, and once removed it will never go back exactly into place.

8. I owe the knowledge of how to lap heads to Harry Taylor, author of *The Art and Science of the Timpani* (London: John Baker, 1964), who, on a Royal Philharmonic tour of Germany, was shocked to hear that I did not know how to do this. He described the whole process so clearly over a litre of beer that I have lapped all my own heads ever since.

Appendix 3 The Need to be Inventive

1. James Blades, *Drum Roll* (London: Faber, 1977), p. 251.

2. Jimmy Blades's idea. The cymbal was already very battered before the run of that play and even worse after it.

3. Anecdotal from James Blades.

Appendix 4 Drummers

1. Henry Holland Carter, *A Dictionary of Middle English Musical Terms* (Bloomington: Indiana University Press, 1961; facsimile New York: Kraus Reprint Corp., 1968), pp. 317–18, *s.v.* Naker, Nakerer.

2. Constance Bullock-Davies, *Menestrellorum Multitudo* (Cardiff: University of Wales Press, 1978), pp. 142–4, *s.v.* Nakarier, and pp. 21–2, describing the attendance of Hugh de Naunton, Harper, and elsewhere.

3. Edward H. Tarr, *Trumpeter's and Kettledrummer's Art* (Nashville: Brass Press, 1974), p. v; Johann Ernst Altenburg, *Versuch einer Anleitung zur heroisch-musikalischen Trompeter- und Paukerkunst* (Halle: Joh. Christ. Hendel, 1795; facsimile Leipzig: Deutscher Verlag für Musik, 1972), p. 33, item IV, translated by Tarr on his p. 34.

4. James Blades, *Drum Roll* (London: Faber, 1977), pp. 11–12.

5. I had six weeks to learn to produce a side-drum roll for the first acoustic test in the partly-constructed Royal Festival Hall. The programme included the National Anthem (making me the first person to play in that hall under a conductor) and Rimsky-Korsakov's *Capriccio espagnol*. My roll kept drying up, trying to play *pianissimo* during the violin cadenza.

Bibliography

This bibliography lists only the works referred to within this book. Thus, while reasonably wide-ranging, especially in the musics of other cultures, it does not pretend to be comprehensive. However, almost every book and article listed here will be found to contain references and bibliographies of its own, and these will, in their turn, lead to other sources.

Particularly valuable further resources are specialist bibliographies such as Jaap Kunst, *Ethnomusicology*, 3rd edn (The Hague: Martinus Nijhoff, 1959) with Supplement (1960), still invaluable despite its cut-off date of almost half a century ago. While only the *New Grove Dictionary of Musical Instruments* is cited here, all the manifestations of the *New Grove*, both the new updated version of the main *New Grove Dictionary of Music and Musicians* (2001) and the various spin-off volumes and compilations, have comprehensive and up-to-date bibliographies.

A colleague with a particular bent for bibliographic research is Edmund Bowles, and his forthcoming work *The Timpani*, cited below, will contain the most complete bibliography ever published on that instrument.

So far as possible, facsimiles and reprints of older texts have been listed, to aid reference to originals, rather than to translations which, especially in regard to percussion instruments, are so often unreliable.

One deliberate duplication here is the citation of museum catalogues, both alphabetically under their author's name, where one is known, and in a special section alphabetically under 'Museum' and therein under the present English name of the town. This, again, does not pretend to be comprehensive but it does include some of the more important examples. Regrettably, few museums treat percussion instruments seriously.

One deliberate policy has been the inclusion of well-illustrated works, pre-eminently the volumes of the *Musikgeschichte in Bildern* series (the History of Music in Pictures) and its companion series, the *Handbuch der europäischen Volksmusikinstrumente*, both published by the Deutscher Verlag für Musik in Leipzig. The demise of those series as a consequence of the reunification of Germany, with a very different approach to subsidized research-based publication, is one of the tragedies of our subject. When using books with limited numbers of illustrations, such as the present volume, one can find descriptions tantalizing and vague (however precise they may have seemed to the author), terminology frequently inaccurate, especially in translation, whereas pictures show what was there, so that all books of such-like title are prime sources for further information.

Adkins, Cecil, and Alis Dickinson, *A Trumpet by any other Name: A History of the Trumpet Marine* (Buren: Frits Knuf, 1991).
Agricola, Martin, *Musica instrumentalis deudsch* (Wittemberg: Georg Rhaw, 1529; reprint combined with the 1545 edition, the illustrations in facsimile, Leipzig: Breitkopf und Härtel, 1896); translation William E. Hettrick, (Cambridge: Cambridge University Press, 1994).
Altenburg, Johann Ernst, *Versuch einer Anleitung zur heroisch-musikalischen Trompeter- und Paukerkunst* (Halle: Joh. Christ. Hendel, 1795; facsimile Leipzig: Deutscher Verlag für

Musik, 1972); translated by Edward H. Tarr as *Trumpeter's and Kettledrummer's Art* (Nashville: Brass Press, 1974).

Anderson, R. D., *Catalogue of Egyptian Antiquities in the British Museum: III Musical Instruments* (London: British Museum Publications, 1976).

Anglés, Higinio, *La Música de las Cantigas de Santa María del Rey Alfonso el Sabio: Facsímil, Transcripción y Estudio Crítico* (Barcelona: Diputación Provincial de Barcelona: Biblioteca Central, 1943–64).

Anoyanakis, Fivos, *Greek Popular Musical Instruments* (Athens: National Bank of Greece, 1979).

Arbatsky, Yury, *Beating the Tupan in the Central Balkans* (Chicago: Newberry Library, 1953).

Arbeau, Thoinot, *Orchésographie* (Lengres: Iehan des Preyz, 1588; facsimile of the 1596 reprint Geneva: Minkoff Reprint, 1972).

Ashbee, Andrew, *Records of English Court Music*, vols I–IX (some volumes initially Snodland: author; now all Aldershot: Scolar Press, 1986ff.).

Avgerinos, Gerassimos, *Handbuch der Schlag- und Effekt-instrumente* (Frankfurt am Main: Verlag Das Musikinstrument, 1967).

Avgerinos, Gerassimos, *Lexikon der Pauke* (Frankfurt am Main: Verlag Das Musikinstrument, 1964).

Bachmann-Geiser, Brigitte, *Die Volksmusikinstrumente der Schweiz*, Handbuch der europäischen Volksmusikinstrumente I:4 (Leipzig: Deutscher Verlag für Musik, 1981).

Baines, Anthony, 'James Talbot's Manuscript', *Galpin Society Journal*, I (1948), 19–26.

Baines, Anthony, and Klaus Wachsmann, 'Erich M. von Hornbostel and Curt Sachs: Classification of Musical Instruments: Translated from the original German', *Galpin Society Journal*, XIV (1961), 3–29.

Balfour, Henry, 'The Friction Drum', *Journal of the Royal Anthropological Institute*, 37 (1907), 67–92 and pls XII–XIV.

Barty-King, Hugh, *The Drum* (London: The Royal Tournament, 1988).

Bebey, Francis, *African Music* (London: George Harrap, 1975).

Beck, John H., ed., *Encyclopedia of Percussion* (New York: Garland Publishing, 1995).

Beck, John, 'Percussion Ensembles', in John H. Beck, ed., *Encyclopedia of Percussion* (New York: Garland Publishing, 1995), 269–73.

Bendinelli, Cesare, 'Volume di tutta l'arte della Trombetta' (Verona: Accademia Filarmonica, MS 238; facsimile as *Tutta l'Arte della Trombetta 1614*, Kassel: Bärenreiter, 1975).

Benvenga, Nancy, *Timpani and the Timpanist's Art*, Skrifter från musikvetenskapliga institutionen, Göteborg, 3 (Gothenburg: 1979).

Berlioz, Hector, *Traité d'Instrumentation et d'Orchestration* (Paris: Henry Lemoine, nouvelle édition, 1855; facsimile Farnborough: Gregg International Publishers, 1970).

Bessaraboff, Nicholas, *Ancient European Musical Instruments* (Cambridge: Harvard University Press, for the Museum of Fine Arts, Boston, 1941).

Bibikov, S. N., *The Oldest Musical Complex Made of Mammoth Bones* (Kiev: Academy of Science, Ukraine SSR, 1981, in Russian).

Blades, James, *Drum Roll* (London: Faber, 1977).

Blades, James, *Percussion Instruments and their History* (London: Faber, 1970).

Blades, James, and Jeremy Montagu, 'Capriol's Revenge, a conversation between James Blades and Jeremy Montagu wherein the pupil instructs the master', *Early Music*, I:2 (April 1973), 84–92.

Blades, James, and Jeremy Montagu, *Early Percussion Instruments from the Middle Ages to the Baroque* (London: Oxford University Press, 1976).

Blagodatov, G. I., *Catalogue of the Collection of Musical Instruments* (Leningrad: Muzyka, 1972, in Russian).

Bonanni, Filippo, *Gabinetto Armonico* (Rome: 1723; all the engravings reprinted, with new captions by Frank Harrison and Joan Rimmer and much reduced in format, as *The Showcase of Musical Instruments*, New York: Dover, 1964).

Boone, Olga, *Les Tambours du Congo Belge et du Ruanda-Urundi* (Tervuren: Musée du Congo Belge, 1951).

Boone, O., *Les Xylophones du Congo Belge* (Tervuren: Musée du Congo Belge, 1936).

Borel, François, *Collections d'Instruments de Musique: Les Sanza* (Neuchâtel: Musée d'Ethnographie, 1986).

Borg, Alan, 'Dating a Dutch Drum', *Country Life*, vol. CLVII, no. 4052 (27 February 1975), 490.

Bowles, Edmund A., 'The double, double, double beat of the thundering drum: the timpani in early music', *Early Music*, XIX:3 (August 1991), 419–35.

Bowles, Edmund A., 'Eastern influences on the use of trumpets and drums during the Middle Ages', *Anuario Musical*, XXVI (Barcelona, 1972), 1–26.

Bowles, Edmund A., 'The Kettledrum', in John H. Beck, ed., *Encyclopedia of Percussion* (New York: Garland Publishing, 1995), 201–26.

Bowles, Edmund A., 'Mendelssohn, Schumann, and Ernst Pfundt: A Pivotal Relationship between Two Composers and a Timpanist', *Journal of the American Musical Instrument Society*, XXIV (1998), 5–26.

Bowles, Edmund A., *Musical Ensembles in Festival Books, 1500–1800* (Ann Arbor: University of Michigan Research Press, 1989).

Bowles, Edmund A., *Musikleben im 15. Jahrhundert*, Musikgeschichte in Bildern, III:8 (Leipzig: Deutscher Verlag für Musik, 1977).

Bowles, Edmund A., 'Nineteenth-Century Innovations in the Use and Construction of the Timpani', *Journal of the American Musical Instrument Society*, V–VI (1979–80), 74–143.

Bowles, Edmund A., *La Pratique musicale au Moyen-Age / Musical Performance in the Late Middle Ages* (no place stated: Minkoff & Lattès, n.d.).

Bowles, Edmund A., *The Timpani: A History in Pictures and Documents* (Hillsdale: Pendragon Press, forthcoming).

Braun, Joachim, *Die Musikkultur Altisraels/Palästinas: Studien zu archäologischen, schriftlichen und vergleichenden Quellen* (Freiburg: Universitätsverlag and Göttingen: Vandenhoek & Ruprecht, 1999).

Brincard, Marie-Thérèse, ed., *Sounding Forms: African Musical Instruments* (New York: The American Federation of Arts, 1989).

Brown, Cynthia Gaskell, *The Battle's Sound* (Tiverton: Devon Books, 1996).

Buchner, Alexander, *Colour Encyclopedia of Musical Instruments* (London: Hamlyn, 1980).

Buchner, Alexander, *Mechanical Musical Instruments* (London: Batchworth, n.d. but *c.*1960; in several other languages from other publishers).

Buchner, Alexander, *Musical Instruments Through the Ages* (London: Spring Books, n.d. but *c.*1956).

Bullock-Davies, Constance, *Menestrellorum Multitudo* (Cardiff: University of Wales Press, 1978).

Burney, Charles, *An Account of the Musical Performances in Westminster Abbey and the Pantheon, May 26th, 27th, 29th; and June the 3rd, and 5th, 1784. In Commemoration of Handel* (London: Printed for the benefit of the Musical Fund, 1785; facsimile New York: Da Capo, 1979).

Byrne, Maurice, '*The English March* and Early Drum Notation', *Galpin Society Journal*, L (1997), 43–80.

Le Carnyx et la Lyre (Besançon-Orléans-Évreux, 1993).

Carrington, J. A., *Talking Drums of Africa* (London: Carey Kingsgate Press, 1949; reprinted New York: Negro Universities Press, 1969).

Carter, Henry Holland, *A Dictionary of Middle English Musical Terms* (Bloomington: Indiana University Press, 1961; reprinted New York: Kraus Reprint Corporation, 1968).

Cassin-Scott, Jack and John Fabb, *Military Bands and their Uniforms* (Poole: Blandford Press, 1978).

Chang Sa-hun, *Korean Musical Instruments* (Seoul, 1976).

Charlton, David, 'New Sounds for Old: Tam-Tam, Tuba Curva, Buccin', *Soundings*, 3 (1973), 39–47.

Charlton, David, 'Orchestration and Orchestral Practice in Paris, 1789 to 1810', PhD thesis, Cambridge (1973).

Charlton, David, 'Salieri's Timpani', *Musical Times*, CXII, no. 1544 (October 1971), 961–2.

Chenoweth, Vida, *The Marimbas of Guatemala* (Lexington: University of Kentucky Press, 1964).

Cherki, Salah, *Musique Marocaine* (Mohammedia: Fedala, 1981).

Chladni, Ernst Florens Friedrich, *Entdeckungen über die Theorie des Klanges* (Leipzig: Weidmann, 1787).

Chuang, Pen-Li, *Panpipes of Ancient China*, Institute of Ethnology Academia Sinica, Monograph no. 4 (Taipei: Nankang, 1963).

Clarkson, L. A. , 'Developments in Tanning Methods during the Post-Medieval Periods (1500–1850)', in R. Thomson and J. A. Beswick, eds., *Leather Manufacture Through the Ages*, Proceedings of the 27th East Midlands Industrial Archaeology Conference (1983), 11–23.

Collaer, Paul, *Amerika*, Musikgeschichte in Bildern, I:2 (Leipzig: Deutscher Verlag für Musik, 1967).

Collaer, Paul, *Music of the Americas* (London: Curzon Press, 1973).

Collaer, Paul, *Ozeanien*, Musikgeschichte in Bildern, I:1 (Leipzig: Deutscher Verlag für Musik, 1964).

Collaer, Paul, *Südostasien*, Musikgeschichte in Bildern, I:3 (Leipzig: Deutscher Verlag für Musik, 1979).

Collaer, Paul, and Jürgen Elsner, *Nordafrika*, Musikgeschichte in Bildern, I:8 (Leipzig: Deutscher Verlag für Musik, 1983).

Cotton, Maggie, *Percussion Work Book* (Birmingham: author, 1993).

Crane, Frederick, ed., *Vierundzwanzigsteljahrschrift der Internationalen Maultrommelvirtuosen-genossenschaft*, 4 (1994).

Cranstone, B. A. L., 'The British Museum Ethnographical Expedition to New Guinea, 1963–4: a Preliminary Report', *British Museum Quarterly*, XXIX, no. 3/4 (1965).

Daniélou, Alain, *Südasien*, Musikgeschichte in Bildern, I:4 (Leipzig: Deutscher Verlag für Musik, 1978).

Dean, Winton, *Handel's Dramatic Oratorios and Masques* (London: Oxford University Press, 1959).

De Hamel, Christopher, *Scribes and Illuminators* (London: British Museum, 1992).

Diderot, Denis, and Jean Lerond d'Alembert, *Encyclopédie Méthodique* (Paris: 1785; facsimile of part: *Art du Faiseur d'Instruments de Musique et Lutherie,* Geneva: Minkoff, 1972).

Doubleday, Veronica, 'The Frame Drum in the Middle East: Women, Musical Instruments and Power', *Ethnomusicology*, 43:1 (1999), 101–34.

Downey, Peter, 'What Samuel Pepys heard on 3 February 1661: English trumpet style under the later Stuart monarchs', *Early Music*, XVIII:3 (August 1990), 417–28.

During, Jean, *La Musique Iranienne* (Paris: Recherche sur les Civilisations, 1984).

Dürr, Alfred, 'Zur Echtheit des Kantate "Meine Seele rühmt und preist"', *Bach Jahrbuch*, Jhrg. 43 (1956), 155.

Emsheimer, Ernst, *Studia ethnomusicologica eurasiatica*, Musikhistoriska Museets Skrifter 1 (Stockholm, 1964).

Emsheimer, Ernst, *Studia Ethnomusicologica Eurasiatica II*, Kungl. Musikaliska Akademien (Stockholm, 1991).

Fagg, Bernard, 'The discovery of multiple rock gongs in Nigeria', *MAN* (1956), 17–18.

Fagg, M. C., *Rock Music* (Oxford: Pitt Rivers Museum, 1997).

Falkenhausen, Lothar von, *Suspended Music: Chime-bells in the Culture of Bronze Age China* (Berkeley: University of California Press, 1993).

Falletti, Franca, Renato Meucci, and Gabriele Rossi Rognoni, *La musica e i suoi strumenti: La Collezione Granducale del Conservatorio Cherubini* (Florence: Giunti and Firenze Musei, 2001).

Fantini da Spoleti, Girolamo, *Modo per Imparare a sonare di Tromba tanto di Guerra Quanto Musicalmente in Organo, con tromba Sordina, col Cimbalo, e ogn'altro istrumento* (Frankfurt: Daniel Vuastch, 1638; facsimile Nashville: Brass Press, 1972).

Farmer, Henry George, *Handel's Kettledrums* (London: Hinrichsen, 1960).

Farmer, Henry George, *Military Music* (no colophon listing publisher, place, or date).

Fellowes, E. H., 'The Philidor Manuscripts: Paris, Versailles, Tenbury', *Music & Letters*, XII (1931), 116–29.

Feuillerat, Albert, *Documents relating to the Revels at Court in the time of King Edward VI and Queen Mary (the Loseley Manuscripts)*; W. Bang, ed., Materialien zur Kunde des älteren Englischen Dramas, Bd XLIV (Louvain: A. Uystpruyst, 1914).

Fischer, Hans, *Schallgeräte in Ozeanien: Bau- und Spieltechnik – Verbreitung und Funktion* (Baden-Baden: P. H. Heitz, 1958). Translated by Philip Holzknecht and edited by Don Niles as *Sound-Producing Instruments in Oceania* (Boroko: Institute of Papua New Guinea Studies, revised edition, 1986).

Fleischhauer, Günter, *Etrurien und Rom*, Musikgeschichte in Bildern, II:5 (Leipzig: Deutscher Verlag für Musik, 1964).

Forsyth, Cecil, *Orchestration* (London: Macmillan & Stainer and Bell, 1914ff., 2nd edn, 1935).

Fox, Leonard, ed., *The Jew's Harp: A Comprehensive Anthology* (Lewisburg: Bucknell University Press, 1988).

Gairdner, James, and R. H. Brodie, eds, *Letters and Papers, Foreign and Domestic of the Reign of Henry VIII*, vols XV and XVII (London: Her Majesty's Stationery Office, 1900).

Galpin, Francis W., *Old English Instruments of Music* (London: Methuen, 1910ff.).

Gansemans, Jos, *Les Instruments de Musique du Rwanda* (Tervuren: Musée Royal de l'Afrique Centrale, 1988).

Gansemans, Jos, *Volksmuziekinstrumenten, Getuigen en Resultaat van een Interetnische Samenleving: een Organologische Studie met Betrekking tot Aruba, Bonaire en Curaçao* (Tervuren: Musée Royal de l'Afrique Centrale, 1989).

Gansemans, Jos, and Barbara Schmidt-Wrenger, *Zentralafrika*, Musikgeschichte in Bildern, I:9 (Leipzig: Deutscher Verlag für Musik, 1986).

Gautrot Aîné & Cie, *Catalogue des Instruments de Musique* (Paris: 1867); reprinted as *Larigot (Bulletin de l'Association des Collectionneurs d'Instruments à Vent) N° X Spécial*, April 1999.

Gay, Victor, *Glossaire Archéologique du Moyen Age et de la Renaissance* (Paris: Librairie de la Société Bibliographique, 1887).

Gerson, Jean de, *Canticordum du Pelerin*, VII/I, 132.

Gétreau, Florence, *Aux origines du musée de la Musique: Les Collections Instrumentales du Conservatoire de Paris, 1793–1993* (Paris, Klincksieck and Réunion des musées nationaux, 1996).

Gimpel, Jean, *The Medieval Machine: The Industrial Revolution of the Middle Ages* (Aldershot: Wildwood House, 2nd edn, 1988).

Goldenberg, Morris, *Modern School for Snare Drum* (New York: Chappell, 1955).

Green, David M, 'The Depiction of Musical Instruments in Italian Renaissance Painting', DPhil thesis, Oxford (1993).

Grove, see Sadie, Stanley.

Guerrero Lovillo, José, *Las Cantigas* (Madrid: Instituto Diego Velásquez, 1949).

Guis, Maurice, Thierry Lefrançois and Rémi Venture, *Le Galoubet-tambourin* (Aix-en-Provence: Édisud, 1993).

Halle, Edward, *The Union of the Two Noble and Illustre Fameles of Lancastre and Yorke* (London: Richard Grafton, 1548 and 1550; facsimile Menston (now Aldershot): Scolar Press, 1970).

Harrison, Frank, and Joan Rimmer, *European Musical Instruments* (London: Studio Vista, 1964).

Harrison, Frank, and Joan Rimmer, *The Showcase of Musical Instruments* (New York: Dover, 1964).

Harvey, Brian W., and Carla J. Shapreau, *Violin Fraud* (Oxford: Clarendon, 1997).

Hasse, Karl, 'Die Instrumentation J. S. Bachs', *Bach Jahrbuch*, Jhrg. 26 (1929), 90–141.

Hayashi, Kenzô, et al., *Musical Instruments in the Shôsôin* (Tokyo: Nihon Keizai Shimbun Sha, 1967).

Haynes, Bruce, *The Eloquent Oboe: A History of the Hautboy from 1640 to 1760* (Oxford: Oxford University Press, 2001).

Haynes, Bruce, 'Lully and the rise of the oboe as seen in works of art', *Early Music*, XVI:3 (August, 1988), 324–38.

Heger, Franz, *Alte Metalltrommeln aus Südost-Asien* (Leipzig: Hiersemann, 1902).

Helffer, Mireille, *Mchod-rol: Les instruments de la musique tibétaine* (Paris: Centre National de la Recherche Scientifique, 1994).

Helmholtz, Hermann, *On the Sensations of Tone*, translated by Alexander J. Ellis (London: 2nd edition, 1885; facsimile New York: Dover, 1954).

Henning, Uta, *Musica Maximiliana* (Neu-Ulm: Ekkehart Stegmiller, 1987).

Hentzner, Paul, *Itinerarium Germaniæ, Galliæ, Angliæ, Italiæ* (Norinbergæ: 1612); the English section translated and edited by Horace Walpole with Latin and English on facing pages as *A Journey into England by Paul Hentzner In the Year M.D.XC.VIII* (Twickenham: Strawberry Hill, 1757).

Hickmann, Hans, *Ägypten*, Musikgeschichte in Bildern, II:1 (Leipzig: Deutscher Verlag für Musik, 1961).

Hickmann, Hans, *Catalogue général des Antiquités Égyptiennes du Musée du Caire: Instruments de Musique* (Cairo: Imprimerie de l'Institut Français d'Archéologie Orientale, 1949).

Hitchcock, H. W., *The Works of Marc-Antoine Charpentier: Catalogue Raisonné* (Paris: Picard, 1982).

Holland, James, *Percussion* (London: Macdonald and Jane's, 1978).

Holland, James, a book forthcoming on contemporary percussion.

Holman, Peter, *Four and Twenty Fiddlers* (Oxford: Clarendon, 1993).

Hood, Mantle, *The Evolution of Javanese Gamelan Book I – Music of the Roaring Sea* (Wilhelmshaven: Heinrichshofen, 1980).

Hornbostel, Erich M. von, and Curt Sachs, 'Systematik der Musikinstrumente. Ein Versuch', *Zeitschrift für Ethnologie*, Jhrg. 1914, Heft 4 u. 5 (1914), 553–90.

Howard, Keith, *Korean Musical Instruments* (Seoul: Se-Kwang, 1988).

Hoyler, Helmut, *Die Musikinstrumentensammlung des Kölnischen Stadtmuseums* (Cologne: 1993).

Jacobson, Edw., and J. H. van Hasselt, *De Gong-Fabricatie te Semarang* (Leiden: Rijks Ethnographisch Museum, 1907).

Jairazbhoy, N. A., *The Rāgs of North Indian Music* (London: Faber, 1971).

Janata, Alfred, *Musikinstrumente der Völker* (Vienna: Museum für Völkerkunde, 1975).

Jeffreys, M. D. W., 'Review Article: Africa and Indonesia', *African Music*, 4:1 (1966/1967), 66–73.

Jones, A. M., *Africa and Indonesia: The Evidence of the Xylophone and other Musical and Cultural Factors* (Leiden: E. J. Brill, 1964).

Jones, A. M., *Studies in African Music* (Oxford: Oxford University Press, 1959).

Jones, A. M., 'Experiment with a xylophone key', *African Music*, 3:2 (1963), 6–10.

Kastner, Georges, *Manuel Général de Musique Militaire à l'Usage des Armées Françaises* (Paris: Didiot Frères, 1848).

Kastner, Georges, *Méthode complète et raisonnée de Timbales* (Paris: Schlesinger, 1845).

Kastner, Georges, *Traité général d'instrumentation*, 2ᵉ Edition *entièrement revue par l'Auteur et augmentée d'un* Supplément (Paris: C. Philipp, c.1844; the first edition was 1836).

Kaufmann, Walter, *Altindien*, Musikgeschichte in Bildern, II:8 (Leipzig: Deutscher Verlag für Musik, 1981).

Kemp, Will, *Kemps Nine Daies Wonder* (London: E. A. for Nicholas Ling, 1600).

Kempers, A. J. Bernet, *The Kettledrums of Southeast Asia*, Modern Quaternary Research in Southeast Asia, 10 (Rotterdam: A. A. Balkema, 1988).

Kinsky, Georg, *Musikgeschichte in Bildern* (Leipzig: Breitkopf und Härtel, 1929/30; also published in English, Italian, and French).

Kirby, Percival, *The Kettle-Drums* (London: Oxford University Press, 1930).

Kirby, Percival R., *Musical Instruments of the Native Races of South Africa* (London: Oxford University Press, 1934).

Kubik, Gerhard, *Ostafrika*, Musikgeschichte in Bildern, I:10 (Leipzig: Deutscher Verlag für Musik, 1982).

Kubik, Gerhard, *Westafrika*, Musikgeschichte in Bildern, I:11 (Leipzig: Deutscher Verlag für Musik, 1989).

Kunst, Jaap, 'A hypothesis about the origin of the gong', *Ethnos* (1947), 79–85 and 147.

Kunst, Jaap, *Music in Java* (The Hague: Martinus Nijhoff, 1949ff.).

Kunz, Ludvík, *Die Volksmusikinstrumente der Tschechoslowakei*, Teil 1, Handbuch der europäischen Volksmusikinstrumente, I:2 (Leipzig: Deutscher Verlag für Musik, 1974).

Kuttner, Fritz, *The Archaeology of Music in Ancient China* (New York: Paragon House, 1990).

Kuttner, Fritz, 'Prince Chu Tsai-Yü's Life and Work: a Re-Evaluation of His Contribution to Equal Temperament Theory', *Ethnomusicology*, XIX:2 (1975), 163–206.

La Rue, Hélène, 'The Problem of the Cymbala', *Galpin Society Journal*, XXXV, (1982), 86–99.

Laurenty, J. S., *Les Sanza du Congo* (Tervuren: Musée Royal de l'Afrique Centrale, 1962).

Laurenty, Jean-Sébastien, *Les tambours à fente de l'Afrique Centrale* (Tervuren: Musée Royal de l'Afrique Centrale, 1968).

Lawson, Graeme, 'Conservation versus restoration: Towards a handling and performance policy for excavated musical instruments…', Cajsa Lund, ed., *Second Conference of the ICTM Study Group on Music Archaeology, Stockholm, 1984* (Stockholm: Royal Swedish Academy of Music, 1986), vol. 1, 123–30.

Lehr, André, *The Art of the Carillon in the Low Countries* (Tielt: Lannoo, 1991).

Lehr, André, *Het Middeleeuwse klokkenspel van Bethlehem* (Breda: Nederlandse Klokkenspel Vereniging, 1981).

Lesure, François, 'Pierre Trichet's *Traité des Instruments de Musique*: Supplement', *Galpin Society Journal*, XV (1962), 70–81.

Lesure, François, 'Pierre Trichet's *Traité des Instruments de Musique*: Supplement (continued)', *Galpin Society Journal*, XVI (1963), 73–84.

Linwood, Jamie Murray, 'The Manufacture of Tuned Percussion Instruments in Indonesia and Africa – a Selective Study', PhD thesis, London Guildhall University (1995).

Lodewijckz, W., *D'Eerste Boeck, De Eerste Schipvaart der Nederlanders naar Oost-Indië onder Cornelis de Houtman*, 1595–7; ed. G. P. Rouffaer and J. W. IJzerman (The Hague, 1915).

Longyear, R. M., 'Ferdinand Kauer's Percussion Enterprises', *Galpin Society Journal*, XXVII (1974), 2–8.

López Serrano, Matilde, *Cántigas de Santa Maria de Alfonso X el Sabio, Rey de Castilla* (Madrid: Editorial Patrimonio Nacional, 1974).

Loretto, Alec, 'Catajo and Ganassi – an Italian castle and a flauto dolce', *FoMRHI Quarterly*, 91, Comm. 1570 (April 1998), 28–30.

McCausland, Lloyd S., 'The Plastic Drumhead: Its History and Development' in John H. Beck, ed., *Encyclopedia of Percussion* (New York: Garland Publishing, 1995).

Mahillon, Victor-Charles, *Catalogue descriptif & analytique du Musée Instrumental du Conservatoire Royal de Musique de Bruxelles* (Gand: C. Annoot-Braeckman, vol. 1, 1880; Gand: Ad. Hoste, vols 2–4, 1896, 1900, and 1912; Brussels: Th. Lombaerts, vol. 5, 1922; facsimile of all five, Brussels: Les Amis de la Musique, 1978).

Majer, Joseph Friedrich Bernhard Caspar, *Museum Musicum Theoretico Practicum, das ist Neueröffneter Theoretisch- und Practischer Music-Saal* (Schwäbisch Halle: Georg Michael Majer, 1732; facsimile, Kassel: Bärenreiter, 1954).

Mallet, Allain Manesson, *Les Travaux de Mars ou l'Art de la Guerre* (Amsterdam: Janson à Waesberghe, 1685).

Malm, William, *Japanese Music and Musical Instruments* (Rutland: Charles E. Tuttle, 1959).

Martí, Samuel, *Alt-Amerika*, Musikgeschichte in Bildern, II:7 (Leipzig: Deutscher Verlag für Musik, 1970).

Maximilian I, The Triumph of (New York: Dover, 1964).

Meer, John Henry van der, *Verzeichnis der Europäischen Musikinstrumente im Germanischen Nationalmuseum Nürnberg: Band I, Hörner und Trompeten, Membranophone, Idiophone* (Wilhelmshaven: Heinrichshofen, 1979).

Merlin, François, and Jacques Cellier, 'Recherches de Plusieurs Singularités' (Paris:

Bibliothèque National, MS français 9152, c.1585).

Merriam, Alan P., *Ethnomusicology of the Flathead Indians* (New York: Wenner-Gren Foundation for Anthropological Research, 1967).

Mersenne, Marin, *Harmonie Universelle* (Paris: Sebastien Cramoisy, 1636); reduced-size facsimile of Mersenne's own copy with interleaved and marginal autograph material (Paris: Centre National de la Recherche Scientifique, 1963).

Meyer, Andreas, *Afrikanische Trommeln: West- und Zentralafrika* (Berlin: Museum für Völkerkunde, 1997).

Montagu, Gwen & Jeremy, 'Beverley Minster reconsidered', *Early Music*, VI:3 (July 1978), 401–15.

Montagu, Jeremy, 'Ethnographical Material in Early Organological Texts', *MAN* (1965:107), 121–2.

Montagu, Jeremy, *The Javanese Gamelan Kyai Madu Laras* (Oxford: The Bate Collection of Historical Instruments, 1985ff.).

Montagu, Jeremy, *Making Early Percussion Instruments* (London: Oxford University Press, 1976).

Montagu, Jeremy, *Musical Instruments of the Bible* (Lanham: Scarecrow Press, forthcoming).

Montagu, Jeremy, 'On the Reconstruction of Mediaeval Instruments of Percussion', *Galpin Society Journal*, XXIII (1970), 104–14.

Montagu, Jeremy, 'The Society's First Foreign Tour', *Galpin Society Journal*, XXI (1968), 4–23.

Montagu, Jeremy, 'Was the Tabor Pipe Always as we Know it?', *Galpin Society Journal*, L (1997), 16–30.

Montagu, Jeremy, 'What is a Gong?', *MAN* (1965:5), 18–21.

Montagu, Jeremy, *The World of Baroque & Classical Musical Instruments* (Newton Abbot: David & Charles, 1979).

Montagu, Jeremy, *The World of Medieval & Renaissance Musical Instruments* (Newton Abbot: David & Charles, 1976).

Montagu, Jeremy, *The World of Romantic & Modern Musical Instruments* (Newton Abbot: David & Charles, 1981).

Montagu, Jeremy & Gwen, *Minstrels & Angels* (Berkeley: Fallen Leaf, 1998).

Morton, David, *The Traditional Music of Thailand* (Berkeley: University of California Press, 1976).

Moule, A. C., 'Chinese Musical Instruments', *Journal of the North-China Branch of the Royal Asiatic Society*, XXXIX (1908), 1–160 and pls I–XIII, reprinted several times in recent years (e.g. Liechtenstein: Kraus Reprint, 1967).

Müller, Mette, 'Klokken er et musikinstrument', *Arv og Eje* (Viborg: 1985), 141–56.

Museum Catalogues:

Berlin:

Meyer, Andreas, *Afrikanische Trommeln: West- und Zentralafrika* (Berlin: Museum für Völkerkunde, 1997).

Otto, Irmgard, *Musik Instrument Museum Berlin: Ausstelungverzeichnis* (Berlin: Musik-Instrumenten Museum, 1965).

Besançon:

Le Carnyx et la Lyre (Besançon-Orléans-Évreux: 1993).

Boston:

Bessaraboff, Nicholas, *Ancient European Musical Instruments* (Cambridge: Harvard University Press, for the Museum of Fine Arts, Boston, 1941).

Brussels:

Instruments de Musique XVIème et XVIIème Siècles, Musée Instrumental de Bruxelles en l'Hôtel de Sully à Paris (1969).

Mahillon, Victor-Charles, *Catalogue descriptif & analytique du Musée Instrumental du Conservatoire Royal de Musique de Bruxelles* (Gand: C. Annoot-Braeckman, vol. 1, 1880; Gand: Ad. Hoste, vols 2–4, 1896, 1900, and 1912; Brussels: Th. Lombaerts, vol. 5, 1922; facsimile of all five, Brussels: Les Amis de la Musique, 1978).

See also Tervuren

Cairo:

Hickmann, Hans, *Catalogue général des Antiquités Égyptiennes du Musée du Caire: Instruments de Musique* (Cairo: Imprimerie de l'Institut Français d'Archéologie Orientale, 1949).

Cologne:

Hoyler, Helmut, *Die Musikinstrumentensammlung des Kölnischen Stadtmuseums* (Cologne, 1993).

Florence:

Falletti, Franca, Renato Meucci, and Gabriele Rossi Rognoni, *La musica e i suoi strumenti: La Collezione Granducale del Conservatorio Cherubini* (Florence: Giunti and Firenze Musei, 2001).

Rognone, Gabriele Rossi, *La musica alla corte del Granduchi: Music at the Grand-ducal Court* (Firenze: Giunti, 2001).

London:

Anderson, R. D., *Catalogue of Egyptian Antiquities in the British Museum: III Musical Instruments* (London: British Museum Publications, 1976).

Rimmer, Joan, *Ancient Musical Instruments of Western Asia in the British Museum* (London: British Museum, 1969).

Yetts, W. Perceval, *The George Eumorfopoulos Collection: Catalogue of the Chinese & Corean bronzes, sculptures, jades, jewellery and miscellaneous objects*, vol. 2, Bronzes: bells, drums, mirrors, etc. (London: Ernest Benn, 1930).

London and Paris:

Thibault, G[eneviève] (Mme de Chambure), Jean Jenkins, Josiane Bran-Ricci, *Eighteenth Century Musical Instruments: France and Britain* (London: Victoria & Albert Museum, 1973).

Nara:

Hayashi, Kenzô, et al., *Musical Instruments in the Shôsôin* (Tokyo: Nihon Keizai Shimbun Sha, 1967).

Neuchâtel:

Borel, François, *Collections d'Instruments de Musique: Les Sanza* (Neuchâtel: Musée d'Ethnographie, 1986).

Nuremberg:

Meer, John Henry van der, *Verzeichnis der Europäischen Musikinstrumente im Germanischen Nationalmuseum Nürnberg: Band I, Hörner und Trompeten, Membranophone, Idiophone* (Wilhelmshaven: Heinrichshofen, 1979).

Oxford:

Montagu, Jeremy, *The Javanese Gamelan Kyai Madu Laras* (Oxford: The Bate Collection of Historical Instruments, 1985ff.).

Paris:

Gétreau, Florence, *Aux origines du musée de la Musique: Les Collections Instrumentales du Conservatoire de Paris, 1793–1993* (Paris: Klincksieck and Réunion des musées nationaux, 1996).

Sachs, Curt, *Les Instruments de Musique de Madagascar* (Paris: Institut d'Ethnologie, 1938).

Ziegler, Christiane, *Musée du Louvre: Catalogue des instruments de musique égyptiennes* (Paris: Éditions de la Réunion des Musées Nationaux, 1979).

Poznań:

Szulc, Zdzisław, *Muzeum Wielkopolskie Katalog Instrumentów Muzycznych* (Poznań: 1949).

St Petersburg:

Blagodatov, G. I., *Catalogue of the Collection of Musical Instruments* (Leningrad: Muzyka, 1972).

Tervuren:

Boone, Olga, *Les Tambours du Congo Belge et du Ruanda-Urundi* (Tervuren: Musée du Congo Belge, 1951).

Boone, O., *Les Xylophones du Congo Belge* (Tervuren: Musée du Congo Belge, 1936).

Gansemans, Jos, *Les Instruments de Musique du Rwanda* (Tervuren: Musée Royal de l'Afrique Centrale, 1988).

Gansemans, Jos, *Volksmuziekinstrumenten, Getuigen en Resultaat van een Interetnische Samenleving: een Organologische Studie met Betrekking tot Aruba, Bonaire en Curaçao* (Tervuren: Musée Royal de l'Afrique Centrale, 1989).

Laurenty, J. S., *Les Sanza du Congo* (Tervuren: Musée Royal de l'Afrique Centrale, 1962).

Laurenty, Jean-Sébastien, *Les tambours à fente de l'Afrique Centrale* (Tervuren: Musée Royal de l'Afrique Centrale, 1968).

Vienna:

Heger, Franz, *Alte Metalltrommeln aus Südost-Asien* (Leipzig: Hiersemann, 1902).

Janata, Alfred, *Musikinstrumente der Völker* (Vienna: Museum für Völkerkunde, 1975).

Schlosser, Julius von, *Die Sammlung alter Musikinstrumente* (Vienna: Anton Schroll, 1920; facsimile Hildesheim: Georg Olms, 1974).

Seipel, Wilfried, *Für Aug' und Ohr: Musik in Kunst- und Wunderkammern*, Schloß Ambras, 1999 (Vienna: Kunsthistorisches Museum, 1999).

Norlind, Tobias, *Musikinstrumentens historia i ord och bild* (Stockholm: Nordisk Rotogravyr, 1941).

Norlind, Tobias, *Systematik der Saiteninstrumente I: Geschichte der Zither* (Stockholm: Musikhistorisches Museum, 1936).

Nwachukwu, Chinyere T., 'Taxonomy of Musical Instruments of Mbaise, Nigeria', MA thesis, Queen's University of Belfast (1981).

Nzewi, Meki E., 'Master Musicians and the Music of Ese, Ukom, and Mgba Ensembles in Ngwa, Igbo Society', PhD thesis, Queen's University of Belfast (1973).

Ord-Hume, Arthur W. J. G., *Barrel Organ* (London: George Allen & Unwin, 1978).

Ó Suilleabháin, Micheál, 'The Bodhran', *Treoir*, vol. 6, nos 2 and 5 (1974), 4–7 and 6–10.

Ott, Alfons, *Tausend Jahre Musikleben: 800–1800* (Munich: Prestel Verlag, 1963).

Otto, Irmgard, *Musik Instrument Museum Berlin: Ausstelungverzeichnis* (Berlin: Musik-Instrumenten Museum, 1965).

Page, Christopher, 'Early 15th-century instruments in Jean de Gerson's "Tractatus de Canticis"', *Early Music*, VI:3 (July 1978), 339–49; reprinted in Page, *Music and Instruments of the Middle Ages* (Aldershot: Variorum, 1997).

Paradossi, Giuseppe, *Modo Facile di Suonare il Sistro nomato il Timpano* (Bologna: 1695; *Collezione di Trattati e Musiche Antiche Edite in Fac-Simile*, Milan: Bollettino Bibliografico Musicale, 1933).

Peinkofer, Karl, and Fritz Tannigel, *Handbuch des Schlagzeugs* (Mainz: Schott, 1981; an English translation of the first, and substantially less complete, edition of 1969 was published by Schott in 1976 as *Handbook of Percussion Instruments*).

Phillips, Alan, *The Story of Big Ben* (London: Her Majesty's Stationery Office, 1959).

Picken, Laurence E. R., *Folk Musical Instruments of Turkey* (London: Oxford University Press, 1975).

Picken, L. E. R., 'Tunes Apt for T'ang Lyrics from the Shō Part-Books of Tōgaku', *Essays in Ethnomusicology – A Birthday offering for Lee Hye-ku* (Korean Musicological Society, November 1969), 401–19.

Pierre, Constant, *La Facture Instrumentale à l'Exposition Universelle de 1889* (Paris: Librairie de l'Art Indépendant, 1890).

Pierre, Constant, *Les Facteurs d'Instruments de Musique* (Paris: Sagot, 1892).

Pincherle, Marc, *An Illustrated History of Music*, translated by Rollo Myers (London: Macmillan, 1967).

Pinnock, Andrew, and Bruce Wood, 'A counterblast on English trumpets', *Early Music*, XIX:3 (August 1991), 436–42.

Powne, Michael, *Ethiopian Music* (London: Oxford University Press, 1966).

Praetorius, Michael, *Syntagma Musicum II – De Organographia* (Wolffenbüttel: Elias Holwein, 1619; facsimile Kassel: Bärenreiter, 1958).

Price, Percival, *Bells and Man* (Oxford: Oxford University Press, 1983).

Quantz, Johann Joachim, *Versuch einer Anweisung die Flöte Traversiere zu spielen* (Berlin: Johann Friedrich Boß, 1752).

Rashid, Subhi Anwar, *Mesopotamien*, Musikgeschichte in Bildern, II:2 (Leipzig: Deutscher Verlag für Musik, 1984).

Rastall, Richard, 'The Minstrels of the English Royal Households, 25 Edward I – 1 Henry
    VIII: an Inventory', *Royal Musical Association Research Chronicle*, 4 (1964), 1–41.
Rejcha, Antonín, *Traité de Haute Composition Musicale* (Paris: A. Laurenc, 1835).
Remnant, Mary, *Musical Instruments of the West* (London: Batsford, 1978).
Rimmer, Joan, *Ancient Musical Instruments of Western Asia in the British Museum* (London: British
    Museum, 1969).
Rimsky-Korsakov, Nikolay, *Principles of Orchestration* (St Petersburg: Edition Russe de
    Musique, 1922; reprinted New York: Dover, 1964)
Riot, Claude, *Chants et Instruments, Trouveurs et jongleurs au Moyen Age* (Paris: R.E.M.P.ART.,
    1995).
Ripin, Edwin M., *The Instrument Catalogs of Leopoldo Franciolini*, Music, Indexes and
    Bibliographies, 9 (Hackensack: Joseph Boonin, 1974).
Rognone, Gabriele Rossi, *La musica alla corte del Granduchi: Music at the Grand-ducal Court*
    (Firenze: Giunti, 2001).
Rosenthal, Albi, 'Two Unknown 17th Century Music Editions by Bolognese Composers',
    Collectanea Historiae Musicae, II (Florence: 1957), 373–8.
Sachs, Curt, *Handbuch der Musikinstrumentenkunde* (Leipzig: Breitkopf und Härtel, 1930).
Sachs, Curt, *The History of Musical Instruments* (New York: W. W. Norton, 1940).
Sachs, Curt, *Les Instruments de Musique de Madagascar* (Paris: Institut d'Ethnologie, 1938).
Sachs, Curt, *Real-Lexikon der Musikinstrumente zugleich ein Polyglossar für das gesamte
    Instrumentengebiet* (Berlin: Julius Bard, 1913; reprinted with Sachs's additional notes for a
    second edition, New York: Dover, 1964).
Sadie, Julie Anne, ed., *Companion to Baroque Music* (London: J. M. Dent, 1990, and Oxford:
    Oxford University Press, 1998).
Sadie, Stanley, ed., *The New Grove Dictionary of Musical Instruments* (London: Macmillan, 1984).
Salmen, Walter, *Musikleben im 16. Jahrhundert*, Musikgeschichte in Bildern, III:9 (Leipzig:
    Deutscher Verlag für Musik, 1976).
Sárosi, Bálint, *Die Volksmusikinstrumente Ungarns,* Handbuch der europäischen
    Volksmusikinstrumente, I:1 (Leipzig: Deutscher Verlag für Musik, 1967).
Scheibler, Heinrich, 'The Aura', *Allgemeine musikalische Zeitung*, 30 (24 July 1816); translated by
    Leonard Fox, ed., *The Jew's Harp: A Comprehensive Anthology* (Lewisburg: Bucknell
    University Press, 1988), 87–96.
Scherchen, Hermann, *Handbook of Conducting* (London: Oxford University Press, 1933;
    reprinted Oxford, 1989).
Schick, Steven, 'Multiple Percussion', in John H. Beck, ed., *Encyclopedia of Percussion* (New
    York: Garland Publishing, 1995).
Schlosser, Julius von, *Die Sammlung alter Musikinstrumente* (Vienna: Anton Schroll, 1920;
    facsimile Hildesheim: Georg Olms, 1974).
Schmieder, Wolfgang, *Thematisch-systematisches Verzeichnis der musikalischen Werke von Johann
    Sebastian Bach: Bach-Werke-Verzeichnis* (Leipzig: Breitkopf und Härtel, 1950 and 1990).
Schneider, Herbert, *Chronologisch-thematisches Verzeichnis Sämtliche Werke von Jean-Baptiste Lully
    (LWV)* (Tutzing: Hans Schneider, 1981).
Seebass, Tilman, *Musikdarstellung und Psalterillustration im früheren Mittelalter* (Bern: Francke,
    1973).
Seeger, Peter, *Steel Drums: How to Play Them and Make Them* (New York: Oak, 1964).
Seipel, Wilfried, *Für Aug' und Ohr: Musik in Kunst- und Wunderkammern*, Schloß Ambras, 1999
    (Vienna: Kunsthistorisches Museum, 1999).
Shivas, Andrew A., *The Art of Tympanist and Drummer* (London: Dennis Dobson, 1957).
Simbriger, Heinrich, *Gong und Gongspiele*, Internationales Archiv für Ethnographie (Leiden: E.
    J. Brill, 1939).
Smith Brindle, Reginald, *Contemporary Percussion* (London: Oxford University Press, 1970).
Song Bang-Song, *Korean Music and Instruments* (Seoul: National Classical Music Institute, n.d.).
Sorrell, Neil, *A Guide to the Gamelan* (London: Faber, 1990).

Sotheby & Co, *Catalogue of Highly Important Musical Instruments, Thursday, 21st November, 1974* (London: Sotheby, 1974).

Speer, Daniel, *Grundrichter Unterricht der musikalische Kunst oder Vierfaches musikalisches Kleeblatt* (Ulm: Georg Wilhelm Kühnen, 1697; facsimile Leipzig: Peters, 1974; English translation of the instrument section, Kai Tönjes, 1998, as yet unpublished).

State Papers Published Under the Authority of Her Majesty's Commission (London: Commission for Publishing State Papers, 1849). Much is reprinted in modern spelling in Gairdner and Brodie (1900).

Szulc, Zdzisław, *Muzeum Wielkopolskie Katalog Instrumentów Muzycznych* (Poznań: 1949).

Talbot, James, Manuscript (Oxford: Christ Church Music MS 1187).

Tarr, Edward, *The Trumpet* (London: Batsford, 1988).

Tarr, Edward H., *Trumpeter's and Kettledrummer's Art* (Nashville: Brass Press, 1974).

Taylor, Henry W., *The Art and Science of the Timpani* (London: John Baker, 1964).

Thibault, G[eneviève] (Mme de Chambure), Jean Jenkins, Josiane Bran-Ricci, *Eighteenth Century Musical Instruments: France and Britain* (London: Victoria & Albert Museum, 1973).

Thomas, Jeffrey, 'Steel Band/Pan', in John H. Beck, ed., *Encyclopedia of Percussion* (New York: Garland Publishing, 1995).

Thomas, Sue, 'Leathermaking in the Middle Ages', in R. Thomson and J. A. Beswick, eds, *Leather Manufacture Through the Ages*, Proceedings of the 27th East Midlands Industrial Archaeology Conference, 1983, 1–10.

Thomson, Roy, 'The Nineteenth Century Revolution in the Leather Industries', in R. Thomson and J. A. Beswick, eds, *Leather Manufacture Through the Ages*, Proceedings of the 27th East Midlands Industrial Archaeology Conference, 1983, 24–35.

Titcomb, Caldwell, 'Baroque Court and Military Trumpets and Kettledrums: Technique and Music', *Galpin Society Journal*, IX (1956), 56–81.

Tobischek, Herbert, *Die Pauke* (Tutzing: Hans Schneider, 1977).

Tracey, Hugh, *African Dances of the Witwatersrand Gold Mines* (Johannesburg: African Music Society, 1952).

Tracey, Hugh, *Chopi Musicians* (Oxford: International African Institute, 1970).

Tran Van Khe, *La Musique Vietnamienne traditionelle* (Paris: Presses Universitaires de France, 1962).

Trichet, Pierre, *Traité des Instruments de Musique (vers 1640)*, ed. François Lesure (Neuilly-sur-Seine: Société de Musique d'Autrefois, 1957). Two supplements appeared in *Galpin Society Journal*, XV (1962), 70–81, and *Galpin Society Journal*, XVI (1963), 73–84.

Trowell, Margaret, and K. P. Wachsmann, *Tribal Crafts of Uganda* (London: Oxford University Press, 1953).

Veiga de Oliveira, Ernesto, *Instrumentos Musicais Populares Portugueses* (Lisbon: Fundação Calouste Gulbenkian, 1966).

Vennum, Thomas, Jr, *The Ojibwa Dance Drum: Its history and construction*, Smithsonian Folklife Studies, 2 (Washington: 1982).

Vertkov, K., G. Blagodatov, and E. Yazovitskaya, *Atlas of Musical Instruments of the Peoples Inhabiting the USSR* (Moscow: State Music Publishers, 2nd edn, 1975).

Virdung, Sebastian, *Musica Getutscht* (Basel: Michael Furter, 1511; facsimile Kassel: Bärenreiter, 1970), translated by Beth Bullard (Cambridge: Cambridge University Press, 1993).

Wachsmann, K. P., 'A Drum from Seventeenth Century Africa', *Galpin Society Journal*, XXIII (1970), 97–103 and pl. XV.

Waesberghe, J. Smits van, *Cymbala*, American Institute of Musicology, *Studies and Documents*, I (Rome, 1951).

Wegner, Max, *Griechenland*, Musikgeschichte in Bildern, II:4 (Leipzig: Deutscher Verlag für Musik, 1963).

Weigel, Johann Christoph, *Musicalisches Theatrum* (Nürnberg: Weigel, c.1715–25; facsimile Kassel: Bärenreiter, 1961).

White, Paul, 'The Early Bassoon Reed in Relation to the Development of the Bassoon from 1636', DPhil thesis, Oxford (1993).

Wieschhoff, Heinz, *Die Afrikanischen Trommeln* (Stuttgart: Strecker und Schröder, 1933).

Williams, Leonard, *The Dancing Chimpanzees* (London: Andre Deutsch, 1967).

Yetts, W. Perceval, *The George Eumorfopoulos Collection: Catalogue of the Chinese & Corean bronzes, sculptures, jades, jewellery and miscellaneous objects*, vol. 2, Bronzes: bells, drums, mirrors, etc. (London: Ernest Benn, 1930).

Young, Percy M., *Saul, Kritische Bericht* of the Hallische Händel-Ausgabe (Kassel: Bärenreiter, 1964).

Yupho, Dhanit, *Thai Musical Instruments* (Bangkok: 1960).

Ziegler, Christiane, *Musée du Louvre, Catalogue des instruments de musique égyptiennes* (Paris: Éditions de la Réunion des Musées Nationaux, 1979).

Zimmermann, Franklin B., *Henry Purcell, 1659–1695* (London: Macmillan, 1963).

Zonis, Ella, *Persian Music* (Cambridge: Harvard University Press, 1973).

Index